GDAŃSK

GDAŃSK
National Identity in the Polish–German Borderlands

Carl Tighe

PLUTO PRESS
London • Concord, Mass

First published 1990 by Pluto Press
345 Archway Road, London N6 5AA
and 141 Old Bedford Road, Concord
MA 01742, USA

British Library Cataloguing in Publication Data
Tighe, Carl
  Gdańsk.
  1. Poland. Gdańsk Political events, history
  I. Title
  943.82

  ISBN 0-7453-0346-3

Library of Congress Cataloging in Publication Data
Tighe, Carl, 1950-
  Gdańsk : national identity in the Polish–German borderlands / Carl
  Tighe.
    p.   cm.
  Includes bibliographical references.
  ISBN 0-7453-0346-3.
  ISBN 0-7453-0474-5(pbk.)
  1. Gdańsk (Poland)—History.   I. Title.
DK4670.T54 1990
943.8'2—dc20   90-33209
                                                        CIP

Typeset by Stanford Desktop Publishing, Milton Keynes
Printed in Great Britain by Billing and Sons Ltd, Worcester

Contents

Acknowledgements

I wish to acknowledge the financial assistance of the Welsh Arts Council and the Twenty Seven Foundation. A shorter version of this book was circulated as a Polish *samizdat* manuscript in the winter of 1986. Sections of this book have appeared in *Planet, The Journal of European Studies* and *The Monthly Review*. I would like to thank the following for their help: Ola Iwanowska, Chris Kirby, Mrs M. Mihajda, Dr Z. Kubacki, Dr K. Sroka, Dr Z. Zgorzelski, Kazimierz Lelewicz, Margaret Watt, Roger Pratt, Liz King-Utz, J.J. Coles, Oliver Reynolds, Ela Perepeczko, Danuta Depa, Gisele Kirby, Charlotte Kollath, Wynn and Karen Thomas, Dr J. Turner, Dr J. Worthen, Connie Rumpf, Neil Jones, Trevor Greenley, Brian and Linda Wasileski, Krysia Bławat, Halina and Tadek Orłowscy, Łucja Szatoba, Bill Brand, Kasia Mroczkowska-Brand, Adam Gosiewski, Lydia Turner, Olga Hubicka, Krystyna Przybysz, Maryla Rosółkowska, Ela Słota, Marta Sawicka, Krystyna Warhoł, Ela Zemła, Tim Saunders, Tony Bianchi, Jacqui Dempster, Mike Bor, Shirley Bor, Elaine and Andy Squire, Madeleine and Luke Rose, Sue Parlby, Tamara Deutscher, Andrew Russell, David Emmerson, Antony Polonsky, Lydia Kairska, Josephine Way, Jurek Gomułka, Lynn Whitney, Jack Stauder, Timo Hulkko, Delyth Evans and Nigel Jenkins, Professor W.C.Brice, and the late Brian Way.

My very special thanks to: Ilse Kohl, Sharon Wood, Mary Niesłuchowska, Jacqui David, Frances Hudson, Mariola Żychowska, Pat O'Rourke and Mick O'Rourke – their kindness and generosity sustained me throughout the project.

Foreword

One of the major themes of this book is the impact of industrialisation and capitalism on the formation of national identities and national struggle in East-Central Europe. The book was written in the belief that this was an important but neglected aspect of European history. A great deal has happened in East-Central Europe while this book was awaiting publication: the face of the East bloc has changed, and suddenly the subject of this book is a matter of urgent concern. The main arguments – that German nationalism helped create Polish nationalism; that both were part of the complex reaction to the advancing of industrialisation and capitalist organisation; that Germany's drive to the east is about to be resumed by economic rather than military means; that Poland's geopolitical reality is still that of third-comer to industrial organisation; that Poland's reaction to the penetration of German capital will probably result in increasing pressure on the national identity – have been confirmed by recent events.

The strikes of 1988–9 led to round-table talks between the Polish government and Solidarność and then to 'almost democratic' elections in which the Communist Party suffered massive humiliation. 'People Power' swept across East-Central Europe. East Germany held on as long as it could, but finally the Berlin Wall was breached. Almost at once West German leaders of the CSU Party argued that the end of Hitler should not mean the end of the Reich. Chancellor Kohl made it clear that he considered the Polish–German border treaty of 1970 no longer valid, and that Poland would have to renegotiate (perhaps unsuccessfully) its western border with the new united Germany. Kohl visited Silesia where Polish Germans greeted him with banners that read: 'Helmut, remember you are also *our* Chancellor.'

In East Germany too, support for the right-wing Republican Party grew at an incredible rate during the run-up to the 1990 elections – demonstrators carried banners showing maps of Germany with its 1939 borders – and it seemed that Kohl was going to get support from them for his worryingly negative attitude towards Poland. East German chauvinism also found vent in

vii

attacks on blacks and Vietnamese.

Talk of German unification understandably makes the Poles very nervous. The Communist Party left them with awesome economic problems: inflation was running at 1,000 per cent per month; 75,000 government-owned workshops and 'production units' had closed, putting more than 150,000 people out of work. The number of unemployed was expected to reach 1 million by the end of 1990 and to total nearly 4 million by 1991. In Gdańsk the privatisation of the shipyards, which needed an estimated US $50 million of foreign investment to make them viable, would result in the loss of over 3,500 jobs.

The ability to think politically seems to have been dangerously impaired as a result of 45 years of 'Communism'. Economic hardship as sudden and as massive as this could hardly be absorbed with ease, and with no left wing to offer any resistance there was a predictable rise in right-wing opinion – not only in the understandable and naïve belief that the free market would solve all of Poland's problems, but also a ubiquitous admiration of Britain's Mrs Thatcher. The right-wing, nationalist, anti-Semitic KPN (Confederation for an Independent Poland) became more active. On 1 May 1990, 16 registered right-wing, Catholic, nationalist, 'traditionalist' political parties held a Conference in Warsaw. As well as selling copies of *The Protocols of the Elders of Zion*, they attacked Adam Michnik for his support of Communism and for his Jewish origins, called Solidarność a neo-Communist organisation, called for the restoration of Poland's eastern territories, called for anti-abortion legislation and warned against the forces of Jewry and Freemasonry that were attempting to ruin Poland. Ironically, at the same time in another part of Warsaw, at a May Day rally, the same things were being said by former Communists now members of the Social Democratic Party. It is now said that Poles are so dissatisfied with the democratic politics and free-market economics that membership of the reformed official trades unions is higher than that of Solidarność.

There is talk that Poland will be the new Taiwan or Korea – a place where a disciplined and skilled industrial workforce can be found at very low wage cost. The human price and the inevitable national reaction to such a prospect has hardly been understood. The Polish parties of the right and centre, Solidarność, and the reformed 'official' unions of OPZZ, have all voiced their concern at the speed of Western economic penetration, and all have protested at the sale of Polish industrial wealth and property to the West – particularly to Germany – while the Poles still endure high prices and low wages. It is perhaps for this reason that the right-wing parties advocate close economic and military links with the USSR.

It has become clear that the problems that set the Second World War in motion (and before that the First World War) are still lurking, and have been present just under the surface all this time.

The themes of this book have been brought sharply into focus by the events of early 1990. To a great extent Europe is about to be restored to the state of play that existed before 1939. On the one hand the East–West divide has crumbled and the peoples of East-Central Europe have the opportunity to think and act for themselves. On the other, now that the superpowers have retreated a little and political life has been restored to Europe – both East and West – the processes of advancing industrialisation and the idea of national identity that were found in the logic of capitalism that was so crudely, hideously, extended and distorted by the Nazis, are to be resumed. Germany, even from within the EEC, has again found a cheap labour market and a place to sell its products on its eastern borders.

We are witnessing a very complex set of events – not only the collapse of the Stalinist empire, but the resumption of that European economy interrupted by the Second World War and the descent of the Iron Curtain. Germany, it seems, is about to become what it always claimed it would be: a European super-power. Poland is a poor nation on the eastern border of an incredibly powerful Germany, a Germany about to become stronger still through unification. Germany is still the world focus for economic and financial entry to Eastern Europe. And just as Poland is part of Germany's natural economic hinterland, so Poland will almost certainly be unable to sell its industrial goods in the West. As Rosa Luxemburg predicted, Poland will find its natural economic hinterland in the Baltic states, Bialorussia, Ukraine, Bulgaria and Romania. Almost certainly there will be a growth of national feeling as 'Western capital', German and Polish, penetrates local and domestic markets.

In all this the city of Gdańsk – the stalking horse of this book – has an abiding and unique significance. Whatever happens, Gdańsk remains a focal point for these tensions, a crucial site of exchange between two rates of economic growth, a meeting place between East and West, industry and agriculture, Poles and Germans, the old Europe and the new, the old Europe within the new.

Carl Tighe
June 1990

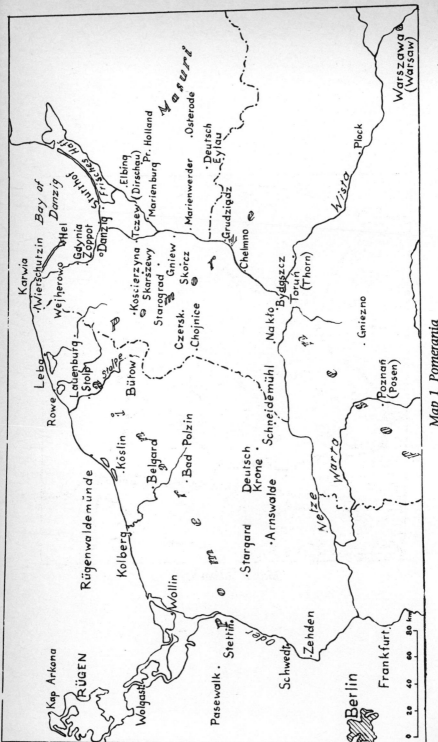

Map 1 Pomerania

Map 2 Kaszubia

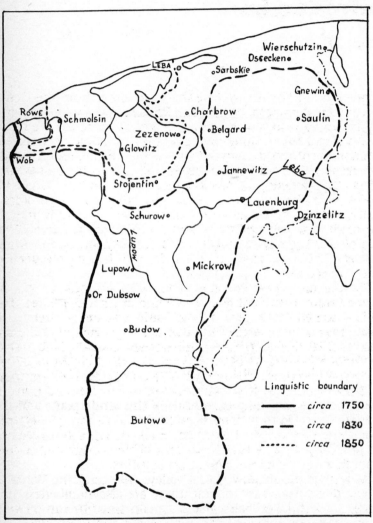

Map 3 Polish–German speech boundaries (after Professor Gayre)

Introduction

Pomerania. In English we take the word either from the German place-name Pommern, or the Latin Pomerani, the name of a group of Slav tribes who settled there. The Polish name for the place is Pomorze, meaning Along or Beside the Sea. Pomerania currently forms most of the coastline of the People's Republic of Poland. It is a rectangular area approximately 150 miles wide and 90 miles deep – approximately 24,103 square miles, an area larger than Wales, but smaller than Ireland. It is bounded on all sides by water. To the north lies the Baltic, to the east runs the river Vistula, to the west the river Odra, to the south the rivers Warta and Notec. The city of Bydgoszcz (Bromberg), situated in the gap between the rivers Notec and Vistula, guards the only dry route into Pomerania.

For the most part Pomerania lies within a belt of low hills formed from a terminal glacial moraine of the last ice age. These hills – sometimes known as the Baltic Stadium – stretch right along the southern edge of the Baltic. The geography of the province is that of a gently undulating sandy coastal plane 300–650 feet above sea level. The hill Wiezyca rises to a height of 1,079 feet above sea level, but it is unique. The dunes and hills are topped and interspersed with woods of birch, oak, beech and pine. The Baltic beaches are really extensions of this sandy plane and there it is still possible to pick up sizeable chunks of top quality amber from pine sap deposited when the area was last submerged some 60 million years ago. Ninety per cent of the world's amber comes from Pomerania and the adjoining coastlines.

As well as the shallow glacial valleys that carry the Warta and Notec rivers from east to west, there are also numberless small, deep, brackish lakes – also glacial – maintained by run-off waters from the sandy soil. Pomerania is a damp and foggy place, especially in winter. Water barriers define modern Pomerania very neatly, and over the centuries those same water barriers have served to prevent the peoples of Pomerania from ever being totally overrun by invaders. Over the centuries Germans, Poles, Celts, Goths and Balts have all settled in the area, but there are other places on the north European plane that are more easily accessible and open to conquest.

In historical and geographical terms, Pomerania extends westwards, beyond the river Odra. German scholars refer to the area west of the Odra – which they call the Oder – as Vorpommern (Near-Pomerania). But now, for all practical purposes, Pomerania stops at the Polish–East German border; beyond that point Pomerania exists only in a geographical sense and leads an existence derived from past rather than current political realities. Brandenburg Pomerania, to give it its full title, is cut off linguistically and politically from the bulk of Polish Pomerania, and when Poles speak of Pomerania they refer only to that part currently under their control.

Eastern Pomerania and the city of Gdańsk have at various times been part of Danzig-West Prussia and Royal Prussia. This region has been called Pomerlia, Pomerela and Pomerelia – little Pomerania. As early as the seventeenth century mapmakers had begun to define Pomerelia as lying along the north bank of the river Notec, and the west bank of the Vistula, an area of Slav occupation that was later to become known as the Polish Corridor. The Corridor in its turn contained Kaszubia, homeland of the last stubborn remnant of the once fiercely independent Slav Pomeranians. Occasionally the Slav history of the area, the lingering Slav-Kaszubian presence on the edge of the German orbit, is acknowledged by German historians who sometimes refer to Pomerelia as Slavinia.

For the waves of German and Scandinavian settlers arriving from the west, Pomerania was never a particularly attractive place. Having crossed the Odra the Germans found themselves hugging the Pomeranian shoreline to avoid the lakes and untamed forests. Most German settlers moving eastwards seem to have taken ship somewhere around Kołobrzeg (Kolberg) not to return to land again until they had reached East Prussia, when Pomerania was far behind them. Saxon and Danish settlement in the Middle Ages was almost entirely restricted to a narrow coastal strip in the north west. While the Slavs clung tenaciously to the south-eastern remainder, there was a strip of mixed German–Polish settlement in between. Even if these people did not live in total harmony, as long as politicians did not exploit their differences, they lived in a state of tolerant indifference to each other. It was never a question of inundation, of the Slav population being swamped by wave after huge wave of German settlers. In fact it seems that the number of Scandinavian or German settlers was really always quite small and that German power in Pomerania operated not through overwhelming settlement, but through social, political and linguistic influence: the power of certain kinds of social organisation to generate greater wealth and material comfort, the certainty of a 'superior' social organisation or national identity. Over the centuries the German settlers, and then their Germanised neighbours, drew Pomeranian Poles into their social and linguistic orbit, into their political organisation and ambition. Slowly, but never completely, the Pomeranian Slavs were Germanised.

Successive waves of settlers in Pomerania either gave up and went elsewhere or settled down with those who were there before them, their colonisation incomplete. Though access to the sea was always desirable for the Polish state, the Poles generally found it easier and more rewarding to push eastwards towards the Black Sea. Not only was the silent, damp hostility of Pomerania daunting, but the relatively sparse, less well organised peoples to the east of Poland were more easily subdued. Yet, with the exception of the Poles who expelled the German population by force after they had incorporated Pomerania in 1945, thus reversing a major trend in Polish history by establishing a lengthy Polish coastline, no invader has succeeded in making Pomerania entirely their own. Always some residue of previous settlement, some lingering resistance, persisted.

In 1980 the Polish writer Tadeusz Kur drew up a chart to show the number of years the Germans and Poles had controlled Gdańsk (Danzig), the principal city of eastern Pomerania. Like most Poles of his generation he was concerned to show that Poland's seizure of what was by 1945 a predominantly German city was not simply 'the spoils of war', a part of the post-war dismemberment of the German Reich, but had foundation and legitimation in history. His list of years of possession was intended to be a guide to the strengths of German and Polish claims on the place:

Poland	960–1308
Teutonic Knights	1308–1466
Poland	1466–1793
Prussia	1793–1806
Free City	1806–1815
Prussia	1815–1919
Free City	1919–1939

Totals: Poland 675 years: Germany 275 years: Free City 29 years. The dates divide the history of the city very accurately, but the ascription of the periods is typical of the way the history of the area has been written by rival Polish and German factions.[1]

It is by no means certain that the city should be attributed to Poland in the first period simply because the state of Poland did not as yet exist. A loose collection of tribes under the leadership of the Polanie tribe was well formed by this stage and would eventually develop into the Polish state, but throughout this period Gdańsk and Pomerania were guarded by fiercely independent Pomeranian princes who from time to time made what they saw as temporary short-term alliances with the Polanie. Although by 1138 the Poles probably had greater control over Pomerania and Gdańsk than ever before, the Polanie state was broken up at the death of King Bolesław III and divided among his sons; for all practical purposes the Polanie state ceased to exist. In the following years Polish kings made strenuous efforts to reunite the Polanie state and to recover Pomerania and the port of Gdańsk, but by this time the Scandinavian and German invasions were well under way and it became increasingly difficult to maintain any influence in the area. From 1038 the Pomeranian princes ruled themselves and even after the Poles re-established some control at the battle of Nakło in 1122, Gdańsk and most of Pomerania seem to have remained very largely outside the direct influence of the Polish state. Władysław Łokietek's efforts to control the city ended in an anti-Polish rising in 1308 followed by a Danish invasion and the seizure of the city by the Teutonic Knights.

The period allocated to the Teutonic Knights is not entirely satisfactory either. Although the Grand Master of the Order and the majority of the Knights were always German, a substantial minority of the Knights were from Britain, the Low Countries, Ireland and France. For the most part they were out for the glory of the Teutonic Order's crusading zeal and for individual loot rather than for any idea of state or nationality. They lived before the formation of the German state, and before the modern concept of 'nationality'. And even then, to describe Gdańsk as German in those years is to disguise a lurking Pomeranian pride, a frustrated will to independence and self-government: the inhabitants – by this time mixed German, Polish and Pomeranian – tried to shake off the Knights in 1410 and again in 1454. Nor were they happier with the years of Polish fiefdom that followed: they rose against the Poles in 1526 and again in 1577.

It is not possible to simply tot up the years of rule by one power or another as if it were the cost of some shopping expedition. The whole business is far more complex. The nature of the rule and the nature of the rulers defy this kind of activity. It would probably make fewer people happy to say that while Gdańsk and Pomerania remained within the orbit of the Polish state for long periods, the area was under continual pressure to become a German province; that while the Poles held sway there from time to time this was never for as long or as thoroughly as the Poles would have liked. On the other hand Germanisation proceeded almost unchecked, but never with complete or overwhelming success. Until the Treaty of Versailles gave the Polish state reason to think otherwise by enshrining principles of national self-determination in the allocation of borders and peoples, the Polish state had for the most part accepted tribute and suzerainty from Gdańsk in lieu of direct rule.

Whoever controlled the place, the fact remains that its water barriers preserved its poverty and remoteness, and helped to keep the place economically and politically backward. Where this did not make the inhabitants downright reactionary, the proximity of both the German and Polish states tended to polarise national identities as they formed. This gave the area a centrifugal force that made neither Germany nor Poland happy, since within its mixed population it produced loyal Germans living next door to stubbornly Polish Poles. The area produced people typical of insecure marcher territories – people who felt threatened by the proximity of others, who took their identity to extremes, who wished to impose that identity on their neighbours. But in Pomerania there was also a very large category of people for whom nationality and language were facts of life rather than causes for dispute, who saw no particular advantage in changing their language or nationality, in being other than what they and their neighbours were, and who simply wished to be left alone to get on with the difficult business of wresting a living from the reluctant Pomeranian soil.

The impact of industrialisation was to accentuate the differences between Eastern and Western Europe, to draw a line between those areas that were socially and economically advanced and those that lagged behind. For the most part it was in the interest of the advanced industrial societies of Western Europe to keep the grain basket of the East in a backward condition. The Prussians, whose territories were to straddle the underdeveloped East and the increasingly capitalist, industrialised West, were relative latecomers to both capitalism and industry. They found that in order to take full advantage of industrial development they needed the finance generated from overseas empires. Lacking overseas possessions in the style of the British, French, Belgian and Dutch, the

Germans made a bid for what was left of Africa but failed spectacularly to make up the lost years of colonial experience needed to turn these possessions to their advantage. Hoping to generate capital and markets as well as military superiority nearer home the Prussians set about turning their eastern marches into a near equivalent of empire: their middle classes became a lieutenant class for the Junker politicians, and the Junkers themselves skilfully diverted economic unrest away from their own declining function into the colonisation of the east and the suppression of the Poles.

Prussian efforts to colonise the east had an undeniable and increasingly obvious racist element, which after 1870 transferred unchanged into a new united German Reich. The insensitive policy of Germanisation, however, backed by increasing German industrial might, provoked strong Polish antagonism where before only a willingness to share in technological advance and mutual benefit from within the Prussian state had existed. In general German efforts to extend their markets into eastern and south-eastern Europe provoked a hostile nationalist reaction which culminated in the assassination of Archduke Ferdinand at Sarajevo in 1914. That event saw the start of a war with Germany's western and eastern neighbours – a war which had been provoked because German industrialisation was tied directly to the rise of German national ambition and national identity, and to the frustrated will to empire that grew out of the late changeover to capitalist modes of political and economic organisation. Defeat in this war fed directly into the growth of nationalist and racist policies developed by the Nazis between the wars and was again visited upon the inhabitants of the Polish–German borderlands.

It was to rectify failed connections, to wipe out the shame of defeat by imposing national, industrial and racial superiority in the east that Germany went to war in 1939. Just before the invasion of Poland, and again before the invasion of Russia, Hitler had the German armies issued with maps that showed they were on a crusade to recover once-German lands. Initial victories allowed the Nazis, the spearhead of the racist, national, industrial ideology, to implement a brutal solution to the questions of race and identity that had by now become a paranoid German obsession of monstrous proportions.

Soviet victory in 1945 allowed the Poles to cut off the long arm of East Prussia, reverse German dreams of empire, push the Germans back across the Odra for the first time since the dawn of recorded Polish history, and colonise (or re-colonise) Gdańsk and

Pomerania in the hope that they had finally squashed the German *Drang nach Osten* (Drive to the East).

No matter how rival 'historical claims' are framed, Polish Gdańsk now stands where German Danzig once stood; where once there was German Stettin there is now Polish Szczecin; where once there was Bromberg there is now Bydgoszcz; Kolberg has been replaced by Kołobrzeg; the river Odra was once the Oder; the Notec was once the Netze; the river Warta was once the Warthe; Gdynia was once Gdingen and also Gottenhaven. The river name Vistula is used by neither Germans nor Poles since it is the English name probably derived from either Saxon usage or from the Latin name for a river that very few Romans ever saw. The Poles call the river the Wisła. The Germans call it the Weichsel.

But this overmeasure of names is only the beginning. To favour one rather than the other is usually to indicate an attitude on the part of the user and to beg a whole series of questions to which there are no simple answers. Poles find the use of German names puzzling, anachronistic and threatening: the user is thought to be making the point that in spite of more than 40 years of occupation and Poland's 'historical claim' to these lands, these places are after all German. Germans, on the other hand, find the use of unfamiliar and 'unpronounceable' Polish names inexplicable and faintly ridiculous since these places are known to them only by 'older', 'real', German names: the user is thought to be endorsing the Polish seizure of Pomerania in 1945 and to be denying German rights to their former *Heimat* or homelands in the east.

It is a tricky business to know exactly how to refer to places at different times, but in general it is important to know who is using the name and exactly what that name refers to in terms of particular historical formations. For example it would be inaccurate to refer to the 'city of Gdańsk' in the nineteenth century simply because the place was under German control and was known throughout the world as Danzig (or Dantzik, Dantzike or Dantzig). The Poles were the only ones to call it Gdańsk, and even then many Poles referred to it as Danzig. It would, however, be correct to refer to the city as Gdańsk after March 1945.

The history of Pomerania and Gdańsk is a curious blend of direct German colonisation and lingering Slav identity. Understandably the Poles fear that one day vengeful Germans will return to repossess the homes and farms they once held. Since the decisions of Yalta and Potsdam gave Poland huge tracts of eastern Germany – including the German city of Danzig – the Polish government's Instytut Zachodny (the Institute of the West) has produced a barrage of propaganda to convince the world of its

unassailable historical claim to these lands. Only in the 1980s
under the premiership of General Jaruzelski were Polish scholars
allowed to shake off the official nationalist line and produce more
accurate, realistic and sensitive research work.

These issues – the impact of capitalist organisation in the
changeover to an urban and industrial society on the second- and
third-comers to the industrial revolution – are an invisible thread
that runs though German-Polish relations. By 'pulling' the single
thread of Gdańsk and its past a great deal is revealed about the
very fabric of European history, about the passions that once ani-
mated the German people, the nationalist policies their leaders
developed in the name of the German people, the nationalist reaction it provoked among their eastern neighbours and the
continuing effect that the nightmare of German racial policy has
had on the thinking of current Polish leaders. There are 15 million
German residents in West Germany who once had homes in
Eastern Europe; there are more than 7 million Poles who now
occupy homes and farms that once belonged to Germans; the
West German government is still buying out the remaining 1
million Germans from Poland – 200,000 of them in 1988;
Chancellor Kohl has addressed the Union of Exiled Silesians – the
first Chancellor to do so for over 20 years – and warned the Poles
that one day a reunited Germany may come looking for its lost
lands; the East Germans and Russians contemplated (and perhaps
even canvassed) a new partition of Poland during the lifetime of
Solidarność, and in 1989–90 one of the first acts of the new 'democratic' Republican Party of both East and West Germany was to
demand the restoration of the 1939 German borders.

As the Soviet Union struggles to come to terms with the suppressed nationalist ambition of its republics released by *perestroika*
and *glasnost*, and the Polish government struggles to cope with
the country's economic problems, it has become increasingly
important to trace this fugitive and lethal course of events within
the wider framework of East–West relations, to chart precisely the
history of the city of Gdańsk. In one sense the continuities are
clear: in the same way that Polish and German lords maintained
serfdom in Pomerania long after it had disappeared elsewhere in
Europe in order to prolong the benefits of cheap labour in the
grain trade to Western Europe, so Polish state capitalism has taken
up a similarly exploitative stance in wresting profits from its
workers in ever harsher circumstances so that it might compete in
international markets for shipbuilding and heavy industry.
Poland, and in particular the city of Gdańsk, can tell us a great
deal about the nature of the continuing time lag between the East

and West European economies, about the pressures the spread of industry and capitalist organisation has put on particular communities. Solidarność is very much a part of the continuing reaction to this history and this process.

Arguably peace has been maintained in Europe not because the Second World War solved the problems of east-central Europe but because the real ability to wage war has been taken from the European powers and shifted to the superpowers. They have, each in their own way, sat on the problems of nationalism and national identity. As the USA comes under increasing pressure to withdraw its troops and missiles from Western Europe, and with the success of *perestroika* and the example of the Soviet withdrawal from Afghanistan, there will be an alteration in the nature of the Soviet military presence in Eastern Europe. The idea of a nuclear-free *Mitteleuropa* has been canvassed more and more openly by thinkers of both East and West. But inevitably the removal of Soviet and American forces will lead to a revival of the long-suppressed nationalisms of both Eastern and Western Europe, as *perestroika* has done in the southern USSR. In the winter of 1980 the Polish dissident Jacek Kuroń, in an article that aroused considerable interest and alarm, stressed that the growth and existence of Solidarność as a reaction to the deteriorating economic situation would almost certainly strengthen nationalist feeling and nationalist conflicts within the Soviet Union, and would aid centrifugal forces throughout the East bloc.[2] In Polish terms his fears were confirmed by the growth of the ultra right-wing, anti-semitic, nationalist group KPN (Confederation for an Independent Poland) led by Leszek Moczulski, but elsewhere by ethnic strife in the Soviet Union, Romania, and the growth of the Republican Party in East Germany. It appears that Solidarność has cleared space for what it took to be democratic social and political processes only to realise that those processes were also open to their own lurking and long-suppressed right wing, who gathered strength as reforms progressed.

It is one of the saddest ironies of European history that the Poles – perhaps the most sensitive barometer of German political and territorial ambition – always felt that the removal of American forces from West Germany suggested by the *Bundeswehr* generals in December 1988 would encourage a reciprocal gesture from the Soviets. A proposal for the withdrawal of Soviet troops from East Germany such as that announced by Gorbachev in 1988 would, the Poles felt, lead to the destruction of the Berlin Wall and the possibility of a reunited Germany, thus leaving them again at the mercy of still simmering German eastern ambitions.

To open a book of Polish–German history is to open a Pandora's box full of complicated, many-limbed insects – all with several unfamiliar names, each with unlikely ambitions, obscure origins and unlovely habits. They are creatures of nightmare, but their monuments are real enough: mass graves, concentration camps, displaced persons, ruined, shattered lives by the million; the still-visible ash and bone that lines Polish rivers and fertilised the fields is all that remains of Nazi victims; an estimated 50 million people died in the Second World War, 37 million of them in Eastern Europe, 6 million of them Polish. On the German side over half a million died after the war had finished, in the expulsions from Poland. The war in the East was fought with almost unbelievable savagery precisely because it was a war not only for the survival of particular ideas and ideologies, but also over who and what people were in terms of racial and national identity – matters in which for the most part they had no choice at all.

There is a need for a wide perspective on the history of the city of Gdańsk. The impact of Western capitalism on the eastern borderlands of Central Europe created rival national identities. It was economic change – the Western need to change the nature of its societies in order to industrialise and at the same time keep the European East as a socially and politically undeveloped grain basket – that created the enduring basis of nationality conflict across the Polish–German borderlands. It was there across the cities of Danzig, Posen, Breslau, Oppeln, Stettin and the rest that the multilingual, multicultural, agricultural identities of the eighteenth century were repeatedly racked and stretched to create the monolingual, monocultural, national and nationalist, industrial identities of the twentieth century.

Gdańsk or Danzig – whatever we call it – the place itself is strategically important: it has always been a major site of exchange between East and West, between Germans and Poles, between the eighteenth and twentieth centuries, between different eras of economic development, between different religions and ideologies. In more ways than one it is the place where East meets West. It is the border where, as Günter Grass put it, Germany played out its 'Operatic Dreams' of national identity, with consequences for the whole world.

Part I
8000 BC–1918

1
Early History: Gyddanyzc to Danczik

Because it lay well outside the area of the Roman Empire recorded history came late to Pomerania. Greek and Roman scholars wrote down the tales of returning travellers and merchants, but few, it seems, ventured as far as Pomerania, and those who did left no written records. Consequently it is very difficult to assess any national claim to be the first, original or authochthonous population of the territory.

It seems likely that settlement of Pomerania began with neolithic peoples around 8000 BC – as soon as the ice sheets had withdrawn to the north – and occupation has been continuous ever since. These first inhabitants were part of a group of peoples sharing a Baltic culture. Their pots, flints, bone tools, battle axes and collections of animal tooth jewellery were consistent across a wide range of territory stretching from East Prussia and Lithuania, westwards to Pomerania and the river Odra. By the end of the fifth century BC it seems likely that this culture had spread across Poland to occupy most of the lower Vistula basin.

The incised pots and lids of these early peoples have been found at Grabowo, Suchacz and Stargard, and the brooches, axes, hoes and distinctive spiral pins of their Bronze Age descendants have been found all over Pomerania. Excavations at Rzucewo between 1923 and 1936 revealed a settlement that had been continuously inhabited for various periods of over a hundred years and which was a major centre of neolithic life.[1] Some German scholars claim these people as early Germans and call their culture Haffküsten-kultur, the culture of the Frisches Haff and the Kurisches Haff. Some Polish scholars claim them as Proto-Slavs and call their culture Young Proto-Slav. Others – perhaps recognising that this culture is probably a direct ancestor to neither German nor Polish states – favour naming it simply Rzucewo Culture.[2]

Around the end of the sixth century BC, when the early inhabitants of Pomerania had established quite a substantial settlement at Wielka Wieś, Goths began to arrive and settle along the Pomeranian coast, on the Vistula delta and along the lower Vistula valley. It is possible that the Goths founded a colony at

3

Oksywie (Oxthöft), and took over the settlement at Wielka Wieś. Gdańsk and Gdynia may have been founded by earlier peoples, but there is a possibility that their names commemorate Gothic settlement. The early Baltic culture waned, and by about AD 100 the Balts had retreated east of the Vistula. Nevertheless Baltic settlement in Pomerania had been long enough and dense enough to pass on river and place names to the incoming peoples and several of these have survived into modern times: Saulin (Strzebielin), Labehn, Powalken, Straduhn (Strudnica), Karwen (Karwia), Karwen (Kawcze), Rutzau (Rzucewo), Labuhn (Labuń Wielky), River Persente (Parsęta).[3]

We have no written records, and the archaeological record is uncertain, but it is unlikely that there were Slav peoples in Pomerania at this time. The classical scholars were avid recorders of life beyond their borders through travellers' tales and military memoirs. Pliny's *Natural History* (*c.* AD 53–67) recounts that Nero sent a trader from Carnuntum on the Danube to the Baltic coast to buy amber. The merchant travelled over 600 miles – considerably further than the most distant of the Baltic amber deposits – and returned with enough amber to encrust Nero's arms and armour, his carriage and even the nets in his arena in a constantly changing display. Unfortunately the merchant did not record any descriptions of the people he met – Slav, German, Celt or Balt.

Tacitus too, with first-hand experience of life along the Roman frontier, wrote his *Germania* in AD 98 and listed all he knew and all he had heard from the wandering tribes of the frontier about the peoples who lived along the Baltic shores. He was able to distinguish various German and Celtic tribes, to accuse the mysterious Venedi tribe of having fallen into disgusting habits, and even placed a Finnic people roughly where Estonia is now: beyond them, he said, was 'the stuff of fables'. However he, like Pliny, failed to record Slav peoples in Czechoslovakia, in Eastern Germany, in Poland or along the Pomeranian shores. In this connection it is interesting that the Alexandrian Ptolemy (*c.* AD 100–178) wrote in the Introduction to his *Geography* that he knew of the town of Calisia (Kalisz) as part of the amber route from the Baltic, yet did not connect the town, the route or the trade with the Slavs.

By about AD 200–400 there were well-developed settlements at Oksywie, Białęcino, Słuchowo, Półchleb and Choszczno. Although the Romans did not know of any Slavs in Pomerania they nevertheless had trade links with whoever lived there. The Amber Trail from the beaches around Kołobrzeg, through Poland, Czechoslovakia and Germany into the Roman Empire had been

well established long before 400 BC and one of the largest Roman
coin hoards outside the Empire, found in the Pomeranian town of
Lubowo, was probably amassed from the amber trade.[4]

When the Goths migrated out of their settlements along the
Vistula between 150 BC and AD 230 they established control of territory in the Ukraine and it is now thought that this was the area
that contained the bulk of the Slav peoples. The Slavs at this time
are believed to have been an agrarian, subject people along the
north-eastern slopes of the Carpathian mountain range, south of
the rivers Pripet and Sejm, along the headwaters of the Siret, Prut,
Dniester and Bug rivers. Though he did not know who they were,
Herodotus probably had the Slavs in mind when in 515 BC he
mentioned the 'Scythian farmers' who lived two days' march
north of the Dniepr river. Ptolemy also located the Slavs
(Soubenoi) on the Dniepr and north of the Black Sea.[5]

Linguistic evidence suggests very strongly that the Slavs spent
their early years in contact with various Iranian peoples –
Cimmerian, Scythian and Sarmartian. Polish scholars have identified three modern Polish words taken from ancient Irani religious
worship and thought to date from this contact: Bóg, Raj and święty
– God, Paradise and holy.[6] This accords with other linguistic evidence. Because all the Slav languages share common words for
certain trees, plants and wildlife it is thought that the various Slav
languages cannot have begun to split away from their common
ancestor until quite late. They had their origin in an area where
the birch, ash, elm, maple and hornbeam all grew, and where
wolves, otters, bears, beavers, salmon, eel and hares could all be
found. The plants the Slavs knew in their early years did not grow
east of the Caspian Sea, nor did they grow in north-eastern Europe.

They expanded to colonise areas that the nomadic Huns had
conquered but chosen not to settle.[7] The Slavs went from strength
to strength: they moved across the headwaters of the Vistula, then
around AD 550 across the headwaters of the Odra. By the end of
the seventh century AD the Slavs had penetrated the Elbe-Saale
region, were settled along the Mulde, Spree, Havel and Odra rivers,
and had probably penetrated Mecklenberg and Pomerania.

It is highly likely that by the time the early Slav tribes arrived in
Pomerania the place was thinly populated by a racial mixture com-
prising the Bronze Age peoples descended from the original Iron
Age settlers, overlaid with Balts, Goths, and perhaps even a few
Scythians and Celts. At some time around AD 650 Theophilactus
Simokattes met three wandering Slavs on Roman territory; they
claimed to come from the Baltic. This is the first record of Slavs in
the area.

It is possible that there were very large Slav settlements in Pomerania by the eighth century AD. Certainly by the tenth century they were well established in centres at Gdańsk, Starogard, Sławno, Biołogard, Kołobrzeg, Wolin, Stargard, Pyrzyce and Cedynia. However, the first written confirmation that the Slavs had occupied territory between the Carpathian mountains and the Baltic came in the year AD 965, when Ibrahim-Ibn-Jakub wrote in Arabic of his journey from Tortosa to the court of the Polanie King 'Mesko'. He described the Polanie tribe as living north of Karako (Kraków) and Boima (Bohemia), west of the Bulgars and east of the lands of King Nakon, who lived along the German borders. With this reference the embryonic Poles in the shape of the Polanie tribe enter recorded history.[8]

At the height of their westward expansion the Slav tribes occupied lands far to the west of the current Polish border on the river Odra. They penetrated areas occupied and settled by German tribes – who were themselves comparatively recent arrivals from Scandinavia. The Slavs are thought to have settled around the mouth of the river Elbe, within a few miles of modern Bremen, Hildesheim, Fulda and Regensberg; they are known to have reached and settled in Würzburg, had scattered dwellings west of Hamburg, Magdeburg, Erfurt, Hallstadt and Linz. Their presence in these places may have been small, but east of the Elbe they dominated all previous tribal groupings.

As usual with these early peoples they took their names from or gave their names to the areas in which they settled. The evidence of their settlement still survives in place names. The Lubuszanie are commemorated in the town names Lubsko, Lubusz, Lubasz, Lubianka and Słubice; the Sprewianie by the river Spree and the town of Spremberg; the Połabianie settled along the Elbe, which in Polish is called the Łaba; the Warnowie founded the town of Warna – now called Waren; the Ranowie settled the island of Rana (Rügen). The Pyrzyczanie almost certainly founded the settlement of Pyrzyce (Pyritz); the Wołiniarnie probably founded Wołogoszcz and Wolin (Wollin); the Słowincy left the town of Sławno (Schlawe); the Łebanie gave their name to Łebno, Lębork, Lake Łebsko and the river Łeba; the Wielunczanie left behind the town of Wielen and the surname Wieluhn or Weluhn, which can still be found in and around Gdańsk.[9]

The Slavs of Pomerania probably differed very little from other Slav tribes. Almost certainly they celebrated their continued existence by worshipping ancestors and a wide variety of fertility gods. Pomeranian society was well developed and the various communities had potters, comb-makers, amber-workers, bead-makers, goldsmiths and blacksmiths. They traded in honey, furs and wax, they learned copper smelting and the use of money from neighbouring Celtic tribes to the south, but still used barter. Their diet consisted of beer, mead, barley, millet, wild fruit, bread, milk, cheese, eggs, beef, pork, game and groats. The English Saint Boniface (martyred at Dokkum and buried in Fulda, 754), who worked mainly in Thuringia and Hess, but also among the Slavs who had filtered across the Elbe basin from the east, found them to be a gentle and virtuous farming people, a complete contrast to the Germanic Franks and Bavarians.

By the tenth century there was a salt mine west of Kołobrzeg and substantial Slav settlements, trading centres and sites of religious worship at Chełmno, Gdańsk, Łeba, Ujscie, Kołobrzeg, Szczecin, Starogard, Pyrzyce, Wolin and Sławno. From Hamburg to Szczecin the place names remind us that this now German stretch of coastline was once settled by Slavs. The town names ending in 'itz' are descended from the Slav word endings 'ice', 'ec' and 'icki'. Town names ending in 'ow' also commemorate Slav settlement by preserving a Slav genitive plural ending. It is still possible to see Slav meanings in some cases: Ribnitz from ryby, fish; Grabow, from grab, literally 'of the hornbeams'. Further south Leipzig derives its name from Lipsk, the place of the lindens.

This was the high point of the Slav westward expansion though, and it was short lived. Scandinavian Viking migration into the same area continued and there was increasing competition for space in northern Germany. By the start of the tenth century the Vikings had established a settlement on the island of Wollin. The Slav province of Branibor slowly but surely began the transformation that would see it become the German province of Brandenburg. Within a very short time the Slav province of Pomorze would also come under pressure to metamorphose itself into the German province of Pommern.

The appearance of Slav tribes east of the Elbe, within the territories of the old Roman Empire, had not gone unnoticed among the Germans. The Duchy of Bavaria was alarmed by the influx of Slavs and approached the Holy Roman Emperor Charlemagne. In AD 771 the Emperor and the Bavarians concluded a peace treaty and together determined to put an end to Slav incursions by establishing a series of protectorates along their eastern borders. In 805 Charlemagne laid out his *Limes Sorabicus* – the Sorbian Wall, named after the Lusatian Sorbs. This border ran from Regensberg to Bamburg, north through Erfurt, along the river Elbe to Kiel and so to the Baltic. Only in the south, where there was no continuous water barrier, was the border ineffective. The *Limes Sorabicus* was not designed to halt all movement across the north European plane though: the Scandinavians continued to move eastwards, across the Elbe into Slav territory.

The empire of Charlemagne was Christian. The Slavs, however, still held to their tribal religions, and this gave the German drive to the east something of a crusading aspect. For many of the migrating Germans – particularly those from Scandinavia – Christianity was a mere convenience and in private they clung to old gods which were not so different from those favoured by the Slavs. The transition from tribal gods to state God may have been something the Germans were willing to entertain because of the obvious material rewards of larger and more powerful tribal groupings and alliances. The Slavs had no such prospect before them as long as they clung to their gods. With no sense of a shared or common identity, with an undeveloped sense of local government and central authority, the Slavs were easy prey to the hierarchic German tribes whose social structure was geared to migration and war.

In AD 912 Otto of Saxony was crowned as Holy Roman Emperor Otto I. His coronation put quite a different aspect on Saxon and Bavarian marauding in the east. Whereas before the drive to the east had been characterised simply as an attempt to convert the heathen Slavs to Christianity, the German–Polish borderlands were now to become the site of a struggle by proxy between the German emperors and the Papacy for the domination of Europe through the extension of their respective influences. It was a contest that was to last in various forms for over 400 years.

By the middle of the tenth century the Saxons had overrun the Veleti, Sorbs and Wends, Obodrzyce, Lutici and finally the Lubuszanie. The Lubuszanie had been part of the Polanie tribal group under King Mieszko I (*c.*960–992, Ibrahim-Ibn-Jakub's King 'Mesko') and it was probably their fate that alerted the Polanie to the German threat. With the loss of his Lubusz territories Mieszko realised that if the Franks, Bavarians and Saxons were allowed to cross the Odra unchallenged there would be little he could do to reverse their advance. For the Germans by far the easiest route into central Poland was through Pomerania, where the Pomeranian tribes were thinly scattered, poorly organised and intent on feuding with each other. Up to this point Pomerania had not been a part of the Polanie scheme of things, but the threat of invasion was a good opportunity for Mieszko to 'unite' the Pomeranians under his leadership. It was almost inevitable that the expanding Polanie state should come into conflict with the expanding German states in the area of Pomerania.

Mieszko first tried to pre-empt a Saxon invasion of Pomerania by forming an alliance with the Pomeranian princes. The princes, however, were not interested. Mieszko was forced to turn south to the neighbouring Czechs for an ally against the Germans. It must have been apparent that as long as the Polanie remained outside the Christian faith they would be legitimate targets for the marauding German princes. Only by converting to Christianity and offering his lands to the Pope, to receive them again in 'usufruct' as was the custom of those times, could Mieszko rob the Germans of their just cause, gain a powerful ally, and through the new religion impose a uniformity of identity and purpose on the various Slav tribes under his control. To this end in 966 Mieszko married the Christian princess Dobrava, daughter of the Czech King Boleslav the Fierce, and a little later had himself baptised at the town of Ratyzbona (Regensburg).

Mieszko's manoeuvres failed to impress the Germans. They decided that the quarrelsome heathen lords of Pomerania would give them easy lodgement east of the Odra and had soon gathered sufficient force to menace western Pomerania. In 972 Mieszko took his army north and gave battle against the Saxon Margrave Hodon at Cedynia (Zehden). The Polanie were successful and threw the Saxons back across the Odra. The fact that the battle had taken place inside Pomeranian territory was a powerful persuasion to the princes to form an alliance with the victorious Polanie, though some now wished to make an alliance with the vanquished Saxons in order to get the Polanie out of Pomerania.

In spite of this victory Mieszko's grip on western Pomerania was tenuous. In order to maintain his hold and ensure peaceful coexistence with the neighbouring Germans he had to pay some form of tribute to the German Emperor Otto II in 984. Even this did not work, however, and in 991 Mieszko was forced to place his lands – including Pomerania – under special Papal protection. According to the *Dagome Iudex*, one of the oldest documents relating to Poland and currently lodged in the Vatican Library, Mieszko controlled the whole of Pomerania at his death in 992.

The Pomeranian princes 'enlisted' to Mieszko's cause were fiercely independent and resented the Saxons and Polanie in equal measure. As far as they were concerned Pomerania was no more the property of Mieszko than it was that of Margrave Hodon. Equally though, they were unprepared to band together to resist the invaders. In spite of the fact that Pomerania guarded the Polanie's northern borders, it was a place that held little real interest for the Polanie. They secured no lasting ties with the area and it was never fully integrated into the Polanie state. The Polanie alliance with the surly, prickly, backward Pomeranians never progressed beyond an unreliable agreement against the Saxons. Pomerania's lakes and forests, its damp, sullen, inhospitable aspect, and poor farmland held scant attraction for Mieszko or for the Piast kings who came after him. Had the area not become a point of honour the Polish kings might well have preferred to expand their territory to the south and east where the land was richer and the population more easily subdued. At this stage in the history of the Polish state access to the sea was not an issue.

The Pope, in an effort to forestall German missionary activity in the area, sent Bishop Wojciech Slavnikov – better known in the West as Adalbert, the exiled Bishop of Prague (955–997) – as an envoy to the Polanie. Adalbert stayed for a while among the Polanie and then at the suggestion of Bolesław Chrobry the Brave (992–1025) moved on to the Baltic to work among the heathen Pomeranians and take ship for east Prussia. In *The Life of Adalbert of Prague*, written in 999 and currently lodged in the Vatican Library, we learn that Adalbert took ship for Prussia at the port of 'Gyddanyzc' – a substantial settlement with 'urbs'. This is the first recorded reference to the settlement that was to become Danzig and later Gdańsk.

A jealous priest or priestess clubbed the zealous Adalbert to death with an axe in 997. Bolesław bought his remains from the Prussians for a sack of gold and buried what was left of his missionary bishop in front of the altar at Gniezno cathedral. The great cast bronze doors of the cathedral display scenes from his life, and although the doors were made *c.*1175 by Flemish craftsmen, the Prussians depicted there seem accurate enough; with short hair, long moustaches, swords and kilts they cannot have changed very much from the time of Adalbert's death. Pope Sylvester II made Adalbert into a saint, and his tomb drew Emperor Otto III of Germany to pray in the year 1000. As a result of this journey Otto recognised Bolesław's sovereignty and established a bishopric at Kolberg (Kołobrzeg) and an archbishopric at Gniezno, so that the process of bringing the Pomeranians to Christ – and from thence into Otto's empire – might continue. Adalbert's brother Radim was appointed the first archbishop of Gniezno.[10]

Other Czech and German missionaries moved among the Pomeranians, the Vistulanians and the various Silesian tribes, but their work of conversion was undertaken with an insensitivity born of competition. The result, in 1035–7, was a massive revolt against the Church and a widespread return to pagan practices. Archaeologists were later to find evidence of extensive fire damage to Gyddanyzc in the ruins of Gdańsk and it is possible that the whole settlement was destroyed in the uprising. Though some historians tend to see these events as directed against the Church and the nobles, the revolt was also a gesture of pagan religious belief and a measure of tribal independence from the Polanie.

It is probably a mistake to think of the Polanie state in terms of the dense social and legal network that makes up a modern state. Polanie arrangements were a shifting pattern of convenience for the various tribal groupings under their leadership; semi-autonomous tribes would band together in alliance either through treaty or coercion and would remain so only as long as they considered it advantageous, or so long as the recognised leader could bring sufficient pressure to bear on them.

Archaeological evidence gathered during the ten years of reconstruction that followed the Second World War showed that Gyddanyzc at this time was made up of a series of closely linked hamlets and fortified areas. The centre of this complex development lay on a fortified island at the confluence of the Motława and Vistula rivers. The island was well protected and had extensive marshlands and a lake immediately to its south. To the west and south of the island there were wooden quays, and entrance was over a wooden bridge or by ferry. On the eastern side of the island there was evidence of a royal palace. On the two low sandy hills to the west of the town were the fortified villages of Biskupia Górka and Grodzisko (Bischofsberg and Hagelsberg). It is estimated that the population at the time of Adalbert's visit must have been around 1,000. There were roads leading out to the north towards Oliwa (Oliva), Sopot (Zoppot), Wejeherowo and Oksywie, south along the 'Amber Trail' to Skórcz and Pruszcz (Praust), and west into Kaszubia. A road also led eastwards out over the sand hills and marshlands to the Vistula delta.[11]

The Polanie state began to disintegrate almost as soon as King Mieszko died. Around the year 1030 the Polanie entered a period of anarchy and confusion. The Pomeranian princes regarded Mieszko's successors with scant respect, perhaps even with open disdain, and from the death of Bolesław I Chrobry the Brave (992–1025), the local Pomeranian princes seem to have ruled themselves: King Kazimierz I Odnowiciel the Restorer (1038–58) failed to restore Pomerania to the Polanie in 1039 and again in 1054. Bolesław II Szczodry the Bold (1058–79), was boldly outfaced by the Pomeranians in the last year of his reign. However, things were by no means straightforward even within the rule of the princes. In 1107 Duke Światobor died after splitting Pomerania between his three sons: eastern Pomerania including Gyddanyzc was awarded to Bogusław I.

Bolesław III Krzywousty the Twistymouth (1102–38), decided that he too would try to win back Pomerania, but his efforts coincided with the invasion of Polanie territories by the German Emperor Henry V. Probably the Pomeranians felt that while Bolesław was occupied with the Germans, he would not pay them too much attention and they began a series of raids into Greater Poland. Bolesław beat the Pomeranians at the battle of Nakło in 1113, and after a struggle of over 13 years subdued the Pomeranian centres at Szczecin, Kamień, Wolin, Białogard and Kołobrzeg. The Pomeranians were forced to recognise Bolesław as their ruler, but still the Polanie did not try to insist on any very close management of the area, and unlike other Polanie territory, rule in Pomerania was indirect and only accomplished through the agency of local princes.

Almost all Polish kings since Mieszko had acknowledged the power of the German Emperor by paying tribute, in return for which they received their crown and their title. Indeed, the Polish word *książe* meant prince, and their word for king derived from contact with the Emperor Charlemagne: Charles – Karl – Karol – *król*. In 1135 Bolesław III decided that in order to keep his troublesome northern lands and prevent the Germans from stirring up the Pomeranian princes he would resume his suspended payment of tribute to Emperor Lothar III. Lothar's decision to let Bolesław keep Pomerania had as much to do with Henry V's failed invasion as it did with the welcome influx of tribute from the Polanie. For the Germans Pomerania was much more trouble than it was worth – for the moment.

Bolesław took his Christianising mission very seriously, and his efforts were given added urgency by the fact that the Danish Vikings were beginning to conduct their own campaign against the heathen Pomeranians. Bolesław appealed to the Vikings' rivals, the Margraves of Brandenburg, and at enormous personal expense enlisted the help of Bishop Otto of Bamberg. Bishop Otto had been waging a vigorous war on the heathen Sorbs and Wends of Lusatia. In 1124 he travelled at Bolesław's request to Szczecin. There he noted several pagan temples and, entering one, found that it was dedicated to the god Triglaw (Three Heads). He cut off the three heads of a statue of the god and sent them to Pope Callistus II. In 1128 Bishop Otto returned to Pomerania and destroyed several temples and sites of worship including a major shrine at Wolgast and a temple at Wolin. Whereas he had previously been happy to set up churches and shrines to the memory of Saint Adalbert, now, and unknown to Bolesław, Bishop Otto was in the pay of the German King Lothar of Supplinburg. Bishop

Otto created a new Bishopric at Wolin under the See of Bamberg to replace the one at Kołobrzeg – that is, he located the control of religious organisation in western Pomerania very firmly within a German orbit.[12]

At his death in 1138 Bolesław shared out Polanie territory between his four sons. From this time on the Polanie powers were too divided to resist Danish incursions and the Pomeranian princes were left to fight a war for which they were hopelessly inadequate. In 1181 one of the Pomeranian princes elected to pay homage to Frederick Barbarossa, and with this western Pomerania was finally detached from Polanie control. In 1252 the Pomeranian district of Lubusz passed to Frederick Barbarossa and the Margraves of Brandenburg who were then poised to push on towards Gyddanyzc.

Throughout the period the Pomeranian princes around Gyddanyzc behaved as an independent power. In 1186 Prince Sambor I founded the Cistercian Abbey at Oliwa, granted it the right to collect tithes and exemption from customs duties and taxes. He also financed the construction of a stone church at the abbey, parts of which can still be seen embedded in the walls of the Oliwa cathedral. In 1236 a charter was granted to 'Civitas Danczik', not by the Polish king, but by Swiętopełk II (1220–66). He also sent to Kraków for the Dominicans to come to Danczik and build a stone church dedicated to Saint Nicholas – the church of Swięty Mikołaj still stands on Place Dominikanski, a reminder of this powerful, spirited and independent Pomeranian ruler. Swiętopełk was succeeded by his son Prince Mściwój II, but in 1294 he died childless after agreeing that his land would pass to the Polish state. Less than a year later his successor Przemysł II was assassinated at Rogózno, possibly on the orders of the Margraves of Brandenburg, but perhaps on the order of the Poles who were anxious to re-establish control over the lands promised them by Mściwój.

In 1261 and again in 1263 the city elders sought and received charters under Lübeck law, signifying that the city had become a part of the growing Hanseatic League. While it is clear that this did not imply German control of the city it is also clear that the charters were sought without permission from Poland. It is significant that although Gyddanyzc, the older form of the city name, had now given way to both Germanic Danczik and Polish Gdanie and Gydanie, which were used more or less simultaneously, the charters were granted to Danczik. The fact was that with or without permission from the Poles the 'urbs' of the city were expanding, and they were doing so under the increasing influence of German settlers and traders.

The reason for this growth was simple. Danczik was ideally placed to supply a vast area of Eastern Europe with the lenten and Friday fare of salt herring so important to the Catholic diet. As Eastern Europe converted to Christianity so demand grew. But no city could grow fat or become rich on a diet of herring alone. Danczik was the centre of growing trade between East and West – particularly the export of grain from the growing feudal estates of Poland. The Baltic was the effective medium in which this exchange took place. The Hanseatic League was determined to create a monopoly of trade with Western Europe by closing the Baltic to outside merchants. Over the years Danczik and Hamburg were to grow rich on this monopoly trade. By 1308 the provinces of Danczik and eastern Pomerania were linked by treaty to an increasingly profitable Polish economic hinterland, but for the most part were quite independent of direct Polanie control.

By the time the vigorous and ambitious Władysław I Łokietek the Elbow High (1306–33), became both Duke of Pomerania and King of Poland, Danczik's trade position was improving rapidly, a fact which made a German or Danish military move against the city – to the detriment of the Poles – ever more likely. The Margraves of Brandenburg, having swallowed up south-western Pomerania, were busy colonising it with imported settlers. They had pressed eastwards to gain territory along the Odra and the lower Warta to drive a Germanic wedge between western Pomerania and Poland. To the north of the Brandenburgers lay the Danes, whose Neumark possessions stretched to the Baltic. Surveying his forces and the enormous task of reuniting the lands that Bolesław had broken up, Władysław had to admit that the situation was almost hopeless. The Brandenburgers and the Danes were well organised and land-hungry. They had a determination and socio-military organisation that the Poles simply could not match. Władysław began to look around for possible allies. On the north-eastern banks of the Vistula stood the territory of the Teutonic Knights. They were Władysław's liegemen and allies, and it was to this powerful crusading military order that Władysław turned for help. It was a decision that was pregnant with consequence.

The presence of the Teutonic Knights in Prussia stemmed from the division of Polanie territory by Bolesław III in 1138. Bolesław's grandson, Konrad I of Mazowie, found that his territory's ability to wage war against the heathens on his northern border was limited. He grew tired of chasing the Borussians and Warmians through the trackless forests, was unable to lure them to give battle en masse and lacked the resources and manpower necessary to launch his own invasion of Prussia.[13] In 1226 Konrad had pleaded that the Borussians were about to invade his territory and promised to grant the Teutonic Order the province of Chełmno if they would help. By 1230 the Knights had secured the blessing of Pope Gregory IX and set about their work. By 1300 their realm had grown beyond the tiny area Konrad had allotted them and had become a state in its own right – a state that nursed enormous territorial ambition.

The Knights were by no means all German. While in general they may have been thugs and outcasts, the crusade against the heathen – a licence to loot and murder sanctioned by Papal dispensation – had attracted more than a gloss of Europe's aristocracy and the footloose, adventuring strata of their lieutenant classes. Chaucer's Knight had fought in Prussia, and Henry Derby, later known as the English King Henry IV, campaigned there in 1390 and 1392 and took part in the siege of Wilno.[14] It was assumed by most of that class that a spell in Prussia was a necessary part of the training for leadership. The methods employed by the Teutonic Knights were crude but effective: they converted the Borussians to Christianity in their thousands or they put them to the sword in like number. Frequently they did both. A contemporary observer noted that there was a ratio of 4,000 dead for every 8 converted. Having killed off the bulk of the population they restocked the area with settlers creating an area of Germanic population far to the east of the other German states and the bulk of the German peoples. There is no doubt that under the guise of a religious order intent upon Christianising the heathen, the Knights created a ruthless militaristic state.[15]

By 1300 the Teutonic Knights had established a network of strong brick-built forts across their territory. They had massacred the Nadruvi and subdued the Barti, Notangi and Warmi, so that less than 170,000 Balts and Borussians survived in the whole territory. The Knights established 54 towns, 890 villages and 19,000 farms – all stocked with German settlers. It is hardly surprising that the Baltic Borussian language had died out entirely by the seventeenth century. The surprise is that it survived so long. The state set up by the Knights derived its authority directly from the Church and from specific crusades sanctioned by the Pope. It acknowledged no earthly authority other than the Pope, but when it suited them – in affairs between the Knights and the Polish state - the Knights set the authority of the Pope aside and did just as they pleased.

In 1308 the Danes, by manipulating the discontented and resentful Danczik burghers, who were led by the Pomeranian

Święca family, managed to create an anti-Polish uprising in Danczik. While the Polish Duke Przemysław tried to put down the rising, the Danes seized their moment and attacked the city from their Neumark territories. Władysław could do little to resist the move and despatched his envoy Judge Bogusza to the Teutonic Knights to request their assistance in clearing the Danes out. What Judge Bogusza and Władysław could not know was that the Knights had long been plotting to squeeze the Poles and Pomeranians out of the Baltic altogether by making a grab for all the land that lay between Prussia and the Mark of Brandenburg. The Knights found that the pretext of going to war to help the Poles regain and protect Danczik from the Danes would allow them access to the territory at much reduced cost.

The details are not clear, but it seems that the Danes had made a deal in which they sold the Knights their 'rights' in the city. When the Teutonic forces appeared at the city gates on 13 November 1308 the Danish defenders simply melted away. Just as Judge Bogusza and the Poles were congratulating themselves on their success the Knights revealed their real intentions. Knowing that the Święca family had been hostile towards the Poles and suspecting that they would prove equally intractable under Teutonic rule, the Order took 16 members of the family and beheaded them. Later commentators say that this was the signal for a general massacre of the Slav population of 10,000. Certainly there is archaeological evidence in the layer of charred timbers in the area of Osiek (German Hachilwerk), the original area of Slav settlement, which dates from about this time. It is true the settlement lay in the shadow of the Pomeranian Princes' castle, but it is possible that the place burned down by accident during the Knights' take-over, or even that instead of a massacre the Knights contented themselves with putting the Slav settlement to the torch as a warning. Though the Knights were a bloody crew, they had little to gain by massacring the population of this prosperous port, and one of their first acts on taking over the city was to grant the inhabitants of Osiek (who were presumably still alive) the right to rebuild their homes – a policy which is hardly consistent with genocide. Perhaps just to be on the safe side, the Knights also set about constructing a castle of their own on the edge of the Slav settlement.

The Święca family's bid to rid Danczik of Poles had hopelessly misfired, and now the Grand Master of the Teutonic Order hastened from Venice to inspect his new possession. Władysław did not let matters rest. He took his grievance to the Pope, who wrote to the Order asking for an explanation. The Knights replied that there had indeed been an incident in the city and that the Poles and Pomeranians had been harbouring renegades and bandits. When the Knights had demanded the surrender of these anti-social elements, they said, the locals had been so overcome with remorse that they themselves had slain all the bandits, burned down their homes and taken themselves off, the Knights knew not where. It was a reply worthy of any modern politician. In 1320 the Pope sent a special investigator to look into the dispute, but even after a report that the Knights were clearly in the wrong, they refused to surrender the city to the Poles.

The plotting of the Pomeranian Princes had lost the Poles their only contact with the sea, and as a result developments in Poland were to be screened off from Western European observation for the next century or more. The loss of access to the sea was eventually to become an issue that, entwined with the issue of German settlement of 'Polish' lands and the question of national identity, would fester deep within the later German and Polish states. Even at this stage it was clear that Poland had great difficulty in persuading the Pomeranians that they should become Polish in any full measure, in fact great difficulty in holding onto the place at all. It is also clear that it was this very independence, this centrifugal force, that made the place such easy prey for the Danes, Margraves and Knights. There was a current of opinion that said the Poles should accept the Knights' seizure of Danczik: as early as 1314 the Archbishop of Gniezno excommunicated the Princes of Głogów for daring to give up their 'ancient claim' to the 'Polish' lands of Pomerania.

The Teutonic Knights were not content merely to possess Danczik. The whole logic of their society had become that of restless conquest and settlement. In 1327 they began raiding south into the nearby Polish provinces of Kujawia and Mazowia. In 1331 Polish soldiers fought a pitched battle with the rearguard of such a raid at Płowce. The following year the Knights annexed Kujawia outright and King Kazimierz III Wielky the Great (1333–70), was forced to sign a truce with them.

The Poles still pursued their case against the Knights. Kazimierz went again to the Papal court and Pope Gregory ordered the Knights to leave Danczik. However, by this time the German Emperor had confirmed the Knights' purchase of Danish 'rights'. The Knights ignored the Pope's instructions and eventually Pope Gregory reversed his decision. In 1339 Kazimierz obtained a Papal Inquiry in both Warsaw and Rome and was granted another decree against the Knights. This time the Order questioned the right of the court to interfere in their affairs.

In 1343 Kazimierz married his daughter Elżbieta to the

Pomeranian Prince Bogusław of Słupsk and Sławno in the hope that this would be the foundation and rallying point for a military alliance. The Pomeranians, however, saw no advantage in siding with the Poles. Kazimierz had no option but to conclude an 'Eternal Peace' with the Teutonic Knights. Kazimierz confirmed the Knights in their possession of Chełmno and, in exchange for Kujawia and Dobrzyn, surrendered his rights in Danczik and Pomerania. While the Knights paid Kazimierz tribute, they were free to continue their work of settling Pomerania, converting the place into a province of German language and culture: the possibility of a thoroughly Polish Pomerania receded entirely until the resurgence of Polish fortunes in 1918.

Although it is convenient to refer to the German and Polish states at this time, they were far from the monocultural, monolingual societies the writings of later nationalist historians might lead us to suppose. Indeed, if we were to assume that these states acted as nation-states, their behaviour would make little sense. The Poles, for example, strove to reunite the lands once controlled by the Piast dynasty and to contest the growing power of the German empire and the Danish state, but this was not a simple anti-German reaction to a 'Germanic threat'; the Polish state was at the same time busily engaged in absorbing huge numbers of German settlers into Polish society. From the fourteenth century onwards it was not unusual to find towns in Poland that were entirely German-speaking. Large areas of land around Szczecin, the Vistula delta, the upper reaches of the Dunajec and virtually the whole of Silesia were to be solidly settled by Germans. Around Kraków, Toruń, in western Pomerania, and throughout Wielkopolska, there were dozens of towns where the population was eventually more than 50 per cent German: the Polish cities of Tczew, Gniew, Elbląg, Toruń, Szczecin and Kluczbork – to name but a few from a great host – owe, if not their foundation, then at least their development in the medieval period to German settlers. Polish monarchs encouraged the Germans to settle because they helped to bring the Polish plains under the plough, and brought with them technical expertise, finance and new farming methods and thus helped to generate capital.[16]

German settlers and Jewish immigrants – both of whom king Kazimierz invited in great numbers – helped to fill the gaps in Polish social organisation. In traditional Polish society there was very little by way of a middle class. Poles were either the nobility _ the *szlachta* – or they were peasants. Until Poland developed its own money-making middle class, and its own towns and manufacturing classes, this great gulf would remain. It was necessary for the Poles to import those skills and structures they lacked if they were to evolve a complex many-layered, social organisation. In areas like Pomerania and Silesia, where the Germans came to massively outnumber the Poles, there was little pressure on the newcomers to become assimilated Poles. Indeed, there was enormous pressure on the Poles to Germanise themselves. The Polish state, just like the Danes, the Germans and the Teutonic Knights, absorbed those people they could make use of – regardless of language. The struggles were not so much between Germans and Poles, but between competing multilingual societies. In general Polish rulers do not seem to have thought in terms of national identity, but rather in terms of their territory as a personal income-generating possession. Inevitably, as capitalist organisation of markets spread across Europe and the accompanying idea of the nation-state developed, this was to change. The question of allegiance to a largely unified, uniform state, to a language and to a particular and much simplified national identity, was to become paramount.

The Teutonic Knights were slow to grant Danczik its trading and city rights. It is probable that while they were involved in litigation with the Poles in Rome they saw no reason to hurry. But under the Knights there was an impressive series of building projects, and much of the current city layout was established. The Knights built a number of streets running away at right angles from the River Motława (Motlau), extended the area of settlement into what is now the Główne Miasto (town centre), set up a new town north of the Stare Miasto (old town), and to the south started building in what was to become the Przedmieście and Spichrzów Island areas. Around 1343 the Knights began to build city walls on the landward side of the city; when these were finished in 1410 they would have 16 gates with drawbridges across a moat and over 20 towers. The Knights also began the construction of the enormous brick Gothic St Mary's Church, St John's Church, Artus Court, the original Town Hall, the Church of St Brigid's, St Elizabeth hospital, the Crane Gate, St Mary's Gate, Church of the Holy Trinity, and the Church of St Catherine. They improved the port and quay facilities. Sawmills, blacksmithing shops, cooperages, tanneries, granaries and warehouses all sprang up. On the small island not far from their castle there appeared the six-storey high Great Mill. Drainage schemes initiated by the Knights dried out much of the surrounding fen, so that the lake that had once protected the southern approaches to the city now disappeared. As trees were felled for the massive building programme the nearby

forests receded, leaving more land for development: the New
Garden and Long Garden suburbs began to appear. To the north
of the city the tiny hamlet of Langfuhr announced itself. In 1371
the river Vistula flooded its banks, and when the waters withdrew
the inhabitants found the river some distance to the east of its old
bed. The additional space allowed the expansion of the shipyards.

The Teutonic Knights have a grim reputation, but it would nevertheless be wrong to think of Danczik under their rule as some
kind of Sparta of the North. The Knights spent a great deal of the
money raised through high taxes on military hardware and on
their campaigns, but this money also found its way into the
churches and the pockets of the merchants who dealt for the
Knights. As well as embarking on the programme of building the
knights also encouraged artwork of various kinds. Danczik never
spawned its own school of painters, and the artists who lived in
the city were never as widely known or as prolific as those of contemporary French and Italian schools, but the fine and vivid
works of Hans Memling (c.1433–94), who is best known for his
painting The Last Judgement, are well worth study. The surviving
paintings from Danczik locate the city very firmly within West
European artistic traditions. The Lamentation by the Master of the
Altar of Saint Elizabeth, dated around 1400, is distinguished for
the facial expressions it conveys; The Martyrdom of Saint Catherine
by an unknown workshop painter, dating from around 1435,
is another interesting example of the city's artwork, and, with its
well-observed Polish and black figures, reflects not only an
element of anti-Polish propaganda, but also direct contact
with, and observation of, Africans.[17]

By the start of the fifteenth century, the population of the city
had leapt from about 1,000 in AD 997, and a probable 10,000 in
1308, to over 20,000 people. About three quarters of these people
lived in the Główne Miasto and Osiek districts. It is thought that
sometime between the tenth and fifteenth centuries the first
Jewish settlers arrived to live in the outlying districts of
Hoppenbruch and what was eventually to become Altschotland.
By the fifteenth century the majority of the inhabitants of the city
were almost certainly of German origin or were Germanised Slavs.

Throughout the fourteenth century Danczik was a prosperous
place. The shoals of herring that inhabited the Danish Sound
brought in an almost guaranteed income from the Catholic hinterland, and the outflow of grain to Western Europe was rising
steadily. The peasant farmers of Pomerania lived in a style that,
compared with the increasingly arduous obligations of serfdom
that were being developed in Poland, was comparatively free. The

Teutonic Knights dared not instigate a regime as harsh as that imposed on the growing number of Polish serfs simply because they would have frightened away the settlers they were so keen to attract. Pomerania under the Knights had to be attractive enough both to bring and hold the settlers, but this did not mean that relations between the Knights and the citizens were always cordial. There were popular uprisings against the Knights in 1361 and in 1378. Two Polish historians have written:

> The Knights' methods of rule had aroused indignation and opposition among the local inhabitants in Prussia and Pomerania, in the towns as well as in the villages, and gave rise to a longing for unity with Poland. For such large towns as Toruń and Gdańsk ties with Poland meant much more advantageous prospects for economic development.[18]

In part this must be so. The large German populations of the major cities may well have seen advantages in closer trade links with Poland, but even so, they must also have seen the lower level of social and economic development among the Poles – particularly in the matter of serfdom. Even for the Slav population of Pomerania Poland was an alien place which had not controlled Pomerania directly since about 1138. For these people, discontent with irksome trade restrictions and heavy taxation was one thing, but a union with Poland was neither good business sense nor good political sense. A 'longing for unity with Poland' tells us more about the authors of the remark, and about the later nationalist attempts to colonise history retrospectively in the name of the nation-state than it does about the opinions of fourteenth- and fifteenth-century Danczikers.

In the 1390s there was increased trade with Western Europe – particularly with Britain. As British cloth manufacturers began to seek alternative markets to the Low Countries British wool became one of the major imports to Danczik. The merchants of Bristol, Coventry, London and, above all, Hull, were so successful in their Danczik trade that they earned a series of complaints from other Hanseatic towns which, with the decreasing size of the herring shoals in the Denmark Sound, were just beginning to feel an alteration in their circumstances. As early as 1391 the British had established a privileged trading position in Danczik.

By 1410 the Polish state – now part of a close dynastic union with Lithuania – had reconstituted itself with all the territories it had possessed before its division by Bolesław. The only area it had been unable to recover was Pomerania and the port of Danczik. The Knights continued their forays into Lithuanian territory, and this, coupled with ancient Polish grievances against the Knights, hardened the Polish–Lithuanian state into a firm resolve to settle accounts. On 15 July 1410 the Polish and Lithuanian army – which included Czechs, Hungarians, Ruthenians, Russians and even Tartars – met and defeated the Teutonic Order in battle at Grunwald (Tannenberg). When the Poles broke into the baggage train they found thousands of pairs of iron shackles for the prisoners the Knights had expected to take for ransom. By the end of the battle 11,000 Knights were dead and a further 14,000 had been taken prisoner; the Grand Master of the Order, Ulrich von Jungingen, was slain, and Władysław II Jagiełło, Grand Duke of Lithuania and King of Poland, was presented with the personal standard of the Prussian Bishop of Pomerania. The citizens of Danczik were quick to sense the new power on their doorstep, and immediately elected to pay tribute to the Poles. The Knights had lost the battle, but they had no intention of relinquishing their hold on the city or of letting the local burghers outmanoeuvre them. As soon as the Knights had identified the civic leaders responsible for the decision – a local councillor and the two mayors, Leczków and Hecht – they had them assassinated.

Even though Polish historians make much of the victory at Grunwald, there was very little by way of immediate practical result. The Poles and Lithuanians found that their gentry were too depleted, their finances too slim, and their armies too diverse, dispersed and tired to follow up the victory with any further campaigning. Rather than wage a protracted war they stood little chance of winning for a territory that would undoubtedly prove hostile and difficult to hold, the Polish–Lithuanian state signed a Peace Treaty with the Knights in 1411. Under the treaty the Poles received the Pomeranian Duchy of Słupsk, but the Knights retained Pomerania, the Vistula delta and the port of Danczik. The growth of the Polish grain trade made it necessary that Poland should have access to the sea either through its own port or through a vassal state, but the Treaty of 1411 left the Knights sitting astride the grain route. It was, as Norman Davies has remarked, 'a very tame treaty for such a famous battle'.

2
Renaissance to Partition: Danczik to Dantzig

After their defeat at Grunwald the Knights were forced to impose ever harsher discipline, and an increasingly arduous tax burden on their subjects. Teutonic attitudes did little to endear the Knights to the townsfolk, and when in 1440 the Union of Prussian Gentry and Towns was formed – and promptly made illegal by the Knights – it had the immediate support of most of the city's middle and merchant class. On 6 June 1454 the Union felt strong enough to renounce formally all allegiance and loyalty to the Knights. At almost the same time the Poles announced their decision to incorporate Danczik. These actions signalled the start of the Thirteen Years War. Danczik was to share the brunt of the economic burden rather than the military struggle against the Knights. The citizens did little actual fighting but preferred instead to hire foreign mercenaries. Their economic contribution was explicitly recognised by King Kazimierz IV Jagiellonczyk when he granted the city the Great Privilege in 1457.

The Great Privilege was one of a series of charters bestowed on the city in the years 1454–77 which gave the Danczikers the right to decide for themselves which foreign merchants would be allowed to trade and settle in the city. They also allowed the city, as a special mark of Polish favour, to place a crown over its traditional emblem of two crosses. Perhaps the most important right recognised in these charters was that of opening and closing the port on their own initiative. Inevitably, Polish scholars, keen to maximise Polish control of the place, stress that royal approval was required to open or close the port, while German scholars point out that the charters say it needed the consent of the Polish king or one of the town councillors. It was probably just as well that these rights were granted since, if they had not, the city would very likely have taken them for itself – and the Poles were in no position to contest the matter. The Teutonic Knights were still far from vanquished, and the Poles would at this stage have been sorely tried had Danczik decided that it wanted nothing to do with either rival power. The charters did no more than acknowledge the status quo.

The Peace Treaty of Toruń in 1466 awarded Pomerania, Chełmno, Warmia and Żuławy to Poland, and restricted the Knights to East Prussia so that they were obliged to move their headquarters from Malbork to Königsburg. The Peace of Toruń brought material benefits to Danczik. The city's defensive walls were extended, the Crane Gate on the Motława was constructed, the timber market was formalised, and there began to appear dwelling houses four and five storeys high in the city centre. St Mary's church had side naves and a tower added to it, and the beautiful and austere Holy Trinity Church was founded, along with the Court of St George, the churches of St Bartholemew and St Joseph, and the tower of the main Town Hall – a list which in total comprises virtually all of the architectural features the modern tourist to the city would recognise.

With the peace treaty of 1466 came an increase in Poland's contacts with Scandinavia, Holland, Denmark, Italy, Spain, Britain and the Middle East. By this time the herring shoals of the Danish Sound had completely disappeared and it was necessary for the Danczik fishing fleet to go much further to satisfy the Polish market; under licence from the Danes the Danczikers broke the British and Norwegian near-monopoly on Atlantic fishing and sailed to Iceland in search of salt-cod, hake and salmon. The collapse of the Knights' power in Danczik also meant that Western countries could now see the possibility of profitable enterprise in the city.

Trade with Britain and Holland became particularly important. The British began trading in the Baltic as soon as the Knights were pushed back beyond the Vistula, but their main efforts came after 1533 beginning with the construction of their own trading establishment – Das Englisches House, The English House – in the city centre. Around 1557–8 British and Scottish cloth merchants, some of the city's most successful clients, who had been busy setting up a small cloth manufactory, obtained a guarantee of freedom of worship, exemption from taxation and the right to make independent trading policy without hindrance from the city authorities. The Merchants of Bristol and the Company of the Merchant Adventurers of York sent out ships laden with woollen goods and cloth. On their return the ships bringing timber, grain, malt, beer, silver, amber, knives, swords, Hungarian copper, Wieliczka salt, furs and glass, would call at Grimsby, Hull and Sandwich. It was trade with Poland through the fourteenth, fifteenth and sixteenth centuries that introduced the words 'horde', 'sable' and 'spruce' into the English language.[1]

British ignorance about the Baltic up to this point was to some extent excusable. At the tail end of the war against the Teutonic Knights the Hanseatic League had virtually sealed off the Baltic to set up a monopoly trading scheme that excluded the British. By 1470 very few British ships were to be found in the Baltic simply because they could not find trade at reasonable rates and also because the British preferred their traditional markets in the Low Countries. The outbreak of the Seven Years War between Denmark and Sweden in 1563 had damaged Baltic trade patterns. The closure of the Danish Sound meant that the British cloth trade suffered severely, and in the bitterly cold winter of 1565–6 over 200 grain ships were forced to wait in Danczik harbour for both war and weather to break. The melting of the ice in Danczik harbour signalled a fall in the price of bread throughout Western Europe.

The end of the Seven Years War saw the Dutch better placed than the British to take up Baltic trade. Under the 1544 Treaty of Speyer the Dutch had free passage through the Danish Sound. Of the 3,000 ships that passed through in the years 1560–9, over 75 per cent were Dutch. The effect of this was to shift the European centre of economic gravity by making Antwerpen and Amsterdam ports of transshipment for Polish grain. Most of the grain went on to Italy and Spain, but in the years 1562–9 over 23 per cent of the grain consumed in Holland came from Poland – the bulk of it via Danczik. The British war with Spain closed off access to the Low Countries and forced the British to make greater efforts in the Baltic. From the 1560s to the 1590s the British 'factors' or agents of British merchants operated in increasing numbers to open up Prussian, Polish and Russian markets. One young York cloth factor, Henry Wympnye, was to die in Poland in 1597 while about his master's business. The British also attacked Dutch grain ships bound for Spain and this forced the Poles to send an Ambassador via Danczik to the court of Elizabeth I in 1596 to plead with the British not to interfere with their trade – Elizabeth dismissed the Polish envoy as an 'heraldum', an upstart windbag.

The East European grain basket, through the institution of serfdom, was to provide a margin of surplus for the growing populations of the West, and was to stimulate the Western woollen and shipbuilding industries. It has been estimated that grain exports through Danczik more than doubled every 30 years: 1491/2 13,260 tons; 1537 20,500 tons; 1563 155,000 tons; 1618 340,500 tons. By 1563 more than 10 per cent of Poland's entire grain output passed through Danczik. Some idea of the wealth generated by this trade may be grasped when it is realised that by the end of the fifteenth century the population of Danczik stood at about 35,000 – more than a third larger than either Poznań or Kraków. Compared to this Warsaw was a mere village. Although the whole of Western Europe benefited from the trade it was the Dutch who dominated. In 1618 only 90 British merchantmen plied the Baltic, as compared to the 1,794 Dutch ships. In 1642 alone, 2,052 Dutch ships called at Danczik.[2] The Dutch were so effective as middlemen, traders and sailors that by 1624 the British Privy Council forbade importers of Baltic goods the use of any but British ships. Yet such was the demand for grain that in the end they were forced to make an exception of ships carrying grain from Danczik, and by 1675 the British had installed James Sanderson as British Consul in 'Dantzig'.[3]

At first the bulk of the grain marketed at Danczik's Green Bridge came from the newer, middle-sized estates of Poland and Pomerania founded after the despatch of the Knights. These estates were almost always located along the major navigable waterways – the rivers Odra, Netze, Warthe and Vistula – so the estate owners, tenants and free peasants of several villages would often band together to find an agent or broker to ship their surplus grain to port. The magnates of the great estates seem to have been rather slower to understand there was money to be made from grain, but as they realised how small their costs were compared to their massive potential production, so they too began to send their grain to the Green Bridge. Before very long the larger estates had begun to force their smaller competitors out of business and to absorb their land. However, in order to maintain profits, both the larger estates and the surviving medium estates found they needed to keep costs as low as possible, and this encouraged the use of unpaid estate labour.

It was not until 1525 that the Order of Teutonic Knights was secularised: the Grand Master of the Order, Albrecht von Hohenzollern, converted to Lutheranism, became Duke of Prussia and swore an oath of allegiance to Poland. But such a move still did not make the Poles happy. Albrecht had been reluctant to secularise the lands of the Order and the Danczik patrician Moritz Ferber, Bishop of Ermland, who was also a member of the Polish Senate and had the ear of the Polish Crown, was sure that Albrecht had only promoted the new sect of Lutheranism in order to support Danczik's separatist feelings at the expense of both Catholicism and Poland. However, while the Poles might have been able to limit the spread of Lutheranism within their own territories, there was little they could do about it in the lands still controlled by the Duke of Prussia, especially since Albrecht, in moving towards the new creed, had massive backing from the mainly German populations of Danczik and the other Pomeranian and Prussian ports. At a time when Western Europe was busy shedding the last vestiges of the feudal system to create the more productive, profitable and efficient market economy, the removal of the threat of the Teutonic Knights allowed the Poles to reintroduce serfdom to the Polish and German landowners of Pomerania. During the fifteenth century the privileges granted to settlers and smallholders by the Teutonic Knights were slowly eroded and then finally abolished altogether.

With Western Europe's increased demand for grain, the Polish nobles considered it essential to tie the peasants to the land. Serfdom was introduced initially by increasing the feudal obligations of the local peasantry, and by buying out smallholders but allowing them to remain on their farms in return for labour in lieu of rent. It was no longer possible for a Pomeranian peasant or smallholder to buy, sell, bequeath or inherit land without the squire's permission. The right to marry outside the village without the consent of the local squire, and the right to appoint or elect local dignitaries also disappeared. The gentry closed its grip on the peasantry by establishing a hold on the administration of justice, claiming the right to make appointments to the local bench. Under the Knights serfdom inherited from the rule of the Pomeranian princes had virtually disappeared. Its reappearance allowed the Poles to create an economy based on virtual slavery, an economy that was labour intensive, incredibly cheap and therefore resistant to all mechanical innovation. The serfdom of Kaszubia in particular was to become one of the most backward of all Europe. There the lords maintained an iron grip on an illiterate, divided peasantry whose lot was doubtless made worse by being linguistically and ethnically isolated from the predominantly German class of owners, and who were geographically isolated from the body of Polish speakers by distance and by intervening German settlement.

Even with the advantage of serfdom the grain trade was hazardous. The southernmost landlords, deep in Poland and the Ukraine, their grain sold a year in advance, would begin to organise rafts for the transport of their merchandise down river in late August and early September; raftsmen would begin the journey as soon as the harvest was completed in September and October. If the journey was still in progress when the rivers froze then the raftsmen would have to winter-over en-route. The bulk of the grain would arrive in Danczik after the spring thaw. Once the grain was sold, the journey to London or Amsterdam might take another two to three weeks, to Spain or Italy a further three to four months, depending on the winds and weather.

It was increasingly clear that Danczik's wealth was derived from a backward, exploitative and unstable relationship with the small-holders, free peasants and serfs. In Pomerania it was a situation of almost unbridled despotism, a system that was maintained there in particular because of the tensions that existed between the various linguistic and ethnic groups. It was a situation in which the peasants and serfs were left with no natural leaders, where the agents and chandlers who profited from the grain trade had no desire for change, and the gentry had no reason to wish for improvement. In inland Pomerania, where local internal markets were supplied with grain and produce, and where no foreign markets were possible because of the low yield and difficulties of transportation, these feudal estates were virtually self-contained; the landed gentry saw serfdom as the only way of making any profit at all out of the grain trade. In areas closer to the main waterways, or within easy carting distance of the main towns – Danczik, Elbing, Stettin – the estates tended to be slightly more relaxed but still backward in every way. Ironically, it was the wealth to be made from the grain trade that made the reintroduc-tion of serfdom possible: the continued effort to undercut rivals maintained the system, but it was the West European demand for cheap grain that kept Poland, and indeed the whole of Eastern Europe, as a backward region whose agricultural produce was to support the technological and social advances of the West without sharing in those advances at first hand.

By no stretch of the imagination could Danczik be described as 'Polish' in these years. Very little trace of the Polish language in the city can be found: all official documents are in German and Latin. The Pomeranians, though Slavs, had resisted the Poles as much as they had resisted the Teutonic Knights, and the citizens of Danczik, though they were German in language and outlook, were still inclined to put a high price on their independence. The increased Polish influence in the city after the defeat of the Teutonic Knights was more than balanced out by the influx of 'Germanic' settlers from Germany, Holland, Sweden, Denmark and England. Even settlers from Italy and Scotland soon became absorbed into the Germanic rather than into the Polish scheme of things. That such a mixture of peoples should all become loyal Danczikers is a puzzle to later observers whose sensibilities have been formed within the idea of the nation-state. The history of Danczik had been to absorb foreigners and make money through trade with as much ease as possible rather than to confine trade by

erecting linguistic barriers. Language was a problem to be overcome, not enshrined. Trade was all. At this stage the community
of languages, with its attendant crises of identity, meant far less
than it does today. Language was important for social and business reasons, but it did not define or delimit a person.

In Dantzig, as with most other towns in what was to become
the Polish–German borderlands, it was not language or race alone
that stood to divide people, but the question of religion. The
advent of Lutheranism, combined with the existing language
differences, produced a sharp social divide between the German
burghers and the rest. It was this factor that prevented the
Polonisation of the Pomeranian gentry and landowning class. At
first, Calvin and Zwingli, the Swiss reformers who were in competition with the Lutherans, made some headway simply because,
unlike the Lutherans who used German, the Calvinists wrote and
preached in Latin – a language common to the Polish nobility. In
general though, while the Reformation was eventually to create
the Polish Socinian movement, neither Lutheranism nor
Calvinism found fertile ground in Eastern Europe. In Poland in
particular, there was already a widespread and virulent anti-
clerical feeling among the nobility – who disliked the Church's
exemption from taxation and were jealous of its power and wealth
– and this undercut the critical basis of much of the Reformist
stance. In Poland the elective monarchy was balanced by the
power of the independent landed nobility who saw themselves in
competition with the Church and the Crown for control of the
peasantry. Urban development in Poland was still poor, and the
urban classes tended to be German settlers who would probably
have supported the monarchy against a nobility they saw as domi-
nating both the provincial and national diets through their hold
on the grain trade.

Humanism had still made very little impact upon the eastern
Baltic area by the 1520s. The monasteries of the Franciscan and
the Augustinian orders of the area had long held to a simple and
radical lifestyle not unlike the ideals and principles of the early
Celtic monastic tradition. When the new Lutheran preachers
arrived in the area it was to these monastic houses that they
turned, and it was these monasteries that later provided preachers
and which became in themselves centres of publication. The
Lutherans, by using the German language, gained a hold in territories that were heavily Germanised – the Baltic ports in particular
– and they gained a growing following after about 1534, when
most of Pomerania seems to have accepted religious reforms, but
even more so after about 1550. At Belbuck in Pomerania the

Premonstratian House produced its own teacher, Johannes Bugenhagen, who went on to become a leading evangelist; as early as 1525 the Lutherans produced preachers like the Pomeranian evangelist Andreas Knopken, who led the reformers in Lithuania.

From the Baltic ports German traders, missionaries and corn agents carried evangelical reformism into Poland through the network of Germanic trade and settlement in a dim echo of the growth of the Hanseatic League, the Teutonic Knights and earlier waves of German settlement. As the reforms progressed the princes and dukes of Mecklenberg and Pomerania used the new creed to foster the independence of town councils, who were themselves greatly in favour of the reforms, knowing that the more self-directing the towns became the more the Poles would be discomforted and unable to find easy lodgement. Later it would become necessary for the princes to rein in the town councils and the Lutherans, but for the moment reform was a useful instrument of policy. The Polish nobility gradually came to be identified with the refusal to reform, and for their part, saw the new religions as an attempt to convert them to a system of worship that would undermine their social standing and property. Where the Polish nobility did convert, it was primarily to the Latin speaking Calvinist cause. It was only a matter of time before Lutheran emphasis on the German language emphasised diverging lifestyles and the rapid development of different cultural allegiances. Very soon Catholic and Calvinist Poles alike saw Lutheranism as German cultural colonisation thinly disguised in anti-clerical reformist garb.

Zygmunt I Stary the Old (1506–48), favoured the Latin humanists and the power of Rome; he did not take to the new evangelism and he attempted to put down the Lutherans in Dantzig. As a Catholic Pole he feared that the Lutheran reforms would interfere with the orderly government of the city, and worse, that the city might renounce its allegiance to Poland. In 1526 he tried to enforce a ruling that all Lutherans were heretics, but in response Dantzig rose up against him. Pomerania lacked powerful local Polish lords to enforce such an edict and the new religion progressed unchecked. Some later writers claim that the 1526 uprising – the result of a Polish attempt to interfere with the city's guaranteed freedom of worship – was simply a protest at the lifestyle of the Dantzig burghers and an affirmation of the spirit of Reformation.[4] By this time, however, Lutheranism was well established among the predominantly German burghers. Protest was directed at the Catholic gentry in and around Dantzig only in so far as these people were seen as agents of an intolerant Polish state in a city whose German-speaking citizenry had already embraced reform. The Dantzigers were to resist Calvinism – which began to make an appearance in the city after about 1548 – as strongly as they resisted Catholicism.

Lutheranism in Dantzig, far from being a form of social protest that could not find expression within the Catholic Church, was increasingly a means of identity, reaction and opposition to Polish efforts at control. Steadfast resistance to outside interference meant that an unusually tolerant atmosphere prevailed in the city. Dantzig's remarkable Gymnazium – where Poles and Germans, Catholics and Lutherans, all studied – owed its existence to the educative zeal of tolerant Lutherans. The Lutheran Dantzigers, sandwiched between the Catholics and the Calvinists, between the Poles and the ambition of the Prussian Hohenzollerns, had ample opportunity for friction of all kinds: the Prussians were anxious to woo them from their loyalty to the Polish state, the Poles were keen to renounce their charters and promises. In general the Dantzigers seem to have pursued their chosen faith with remarkable catholicity, tolerance and lack of bigotry.

Capitalist enterprise was born out of the opposition to feudal society. The independent city states of Italy and the ports and towns of the Hanseatic League were vital in this process, since it was in them that the straightjacket of feudalism could be thrown off and the pursuit of profitable enterprise undertaken with most ease. Liberating departures from Catholicism were confirmed in these cities by the growth of banking and insurance; the great German banking house of Fugger reached out from its base in Augsburg to establish its office in Warsaw and its contacts in Dantzig. In the first 20 years of the sixteenth century the Fuggers established considerable financial interests and control in the Baltic area. The Fukkier wine shop (Fukkier, a corruption of Fugger) can still be found on Warsaw's Old Town Square, a reminder of times when Dantzig and Warsaw were linked to Antwerpen, Lisbon, Venice and London in the gradual changeover to capitalist business organisation. Cities like Dantzig made money by making cash work through banks and investments to make more money and provide investment capital for the expansion of shipping, housing and industry. They helped to create lucrative homogeneous internal markets, and even Martin Luther himself did not dare tell the Dantzigers to give up the practice of usury.[5]

In 1577 the delicate balance of Dantzig's loyalty to its religion and to the state of Poland was tried a second time. When the

Hungarian István Báthory was elected king of Poland he had decided to press ahead with his plans for the propagation of the Catholic faith. As part of a complicated manoeuvre to get the Pope to finance a war against the Turks he went to war with Russia. The Dantzig burghers were unhappy about this. They had not voted in favour of Báthory at the elections, but had preferred Maximillian II. They were annoyed by Báthory's crusading Catholicism, and were convinced that his wars would upset trade on the Baltic. Báthory lay siege to Dantzig for over six months before the citizens paid him off with 200,000 złoty. At the end of the siege Báthory carefully reassured the Dantzigers by confirming the city's religious and civil liberties. Again the city remained loyal to Poland. And why should it not do so? Poland paid for that loyalty with the gift of the virtual monopoly of the Polish grain trade. The grain more than paid for the loyalty. Though later observers were to wonder how a city so German in its culture and religion could be so hostile to Prussia and the Teutonic Knights, and so loyal to Poland at the same time, in general the arrangements suited both Poland and Dantzig well.

In art and civic architecture – as in the grain trade – the Dutch dominated throughout this period: Antonis van Obbergen designed the Great Arsenal (1605) and the new Town Hall (1586–95); Abraham van Den Blocke designed the sculptures on the city's main Upland Gate (c.1588), designed the southern face of the new Artushof (1616–17), and also the superbly Italianate Golden Gate (1609) that both closed and framed the Long Market. Andreas Schlüter, Bartolomäus Ranisch, Tilman van Gameren, Itzaak van den Blocke, Hans Vredemann de Vries, Paul van Dorne, Hermann Hahn (c.1570–1623), Frederick Hendrickson Vroom, Andreas Stech (1635–97), Cornelius von dem Bosch, Johan Kramer, Jan Wijbe, Daniel Schultz (1615–83), Anton Möller (1563–1611), Wilhelm van der Meer – all of either German or Dutch origin – brought the Renaissance Gothic style in both art and architecture to its height in the city.

Most of the Dantzig burghers did not own great estates and so put their profits back into their businesses or into the construction of ever more magnificent houses for themselves. The houses were built five or six storeys high on a very narrow frontage. They had impressive stone entrance balconies with carved gargoyles, water spouts and balustrades. The ground floor consisted mainly of a reception area in the form of a hallway with portraits, decorated friezes, carvings and a gallery for musicians. The entrance hall could also serve as a dance floor. Upstairs there were arcades, wood tile floors and decorated ceilings. Connecting each floor was an ornate carved staircase created by a master craftsman.

The city's finances were also assisted by revenues from the construction of the Polish navy in the Dantzig shipyards, though initially the burghers had been against the idea lest the Poles should use their fleet to control the sea lanes and blockade the city.

As usual, the exact nature of the relationship between Dantzig and the Polish state has been something of a sticking point for rival scholars. Polish historians tend to believe that the city's formal dependence on Poland made it *ipso facto* a part of the Polish state. German scholars, on the other hand, incline to think that the formal link did not represent the actual situation at all, and that for all practical purposes the city governed itself and conducted its own external and internal affairs as it saw fit, while paying the taxes and tribute necessary to its independence to the Polish monarchy. The city had certainly taken the lead in the war against the Teutonic Knights, but if this was seen as evidence of anti-German feeling, then it should also be pointed out that twice the city had risen up to defy Polish attempts to interfere with religious freedoms. The city conducted its official business with Poland in German or Latin, and while under the nominal control of Poland, sent its ambassadors and agents to England, France and Scandinavia on reciprocal arrangements. The city conducted its own correspondence with Henry VIII and Elizabeth I, and with the Russian, Prussian and French monarchs. It would be fair to say that the citizens were Dantzigers first and foremost – the rest was mere convenience.

The Polish grain trade dominated the life of the city. Although the Poles grew the grain, that was almost their only part in the process; everything else to do with the grain trade was in 'foreign' hands. Kicke, Schultze, Kinke, Wichman, and the 500 other Dantzig agents who toured the countryside to act as middlemen between the estate owners and the merchants, were German. The companies they worked for were often British or Dutch. By 1650 the British and Dutch grain merchants had given up their seasonal migration to the city and had set up permanent agencies there: 50 Dutch agencies and 20 British – mostly Scots – were resident in the city by the middle of the seventeenth century, and many of the Dutch had even begun to settle families in residence and to take up Dantzig citizenship: Arndt Pilrom, Helmut von Tweenhuysen, Gilles Thibault, Hans Ghybrechtsen de Veer, Pieter Pels – these are among the names of the Dutch residents who worked for Amsterdam head offices.

The grain trade was regulated by the Dantzig burghers who often owned the land on which the great grain warehouses stood, or who hired out the labouring gangs used to shift the grain from raft to barge, from barge to warehouse, from warehouse to ship. The Dantzigers also administered the port, issued licences and permits to trade and collected the various taxes and tariffs. These powerful citizens were almost exclusively of German or Dutch origin. In 1675, for example, we know that the four burgomeisters, who would in turn be the next four city presidents, were Krumhausen, van Bummeln, van Bodecker and von der Lind. Three clearly of Dutch or Flemish extraction and one almost certainly German. There were no Poles on the city council, on the local councils, on the judges' bench, or on the magistrates' bench. Similarly, there were no Poles among the resident Dantzig merchants, and only a handful of Polish landowners had houses in the city. Among the huge lists of artists and architects who are known to have worked in the city, only one distinctly Polish name appears. Jan Strakowski, who worked with his brother Jerzy, designed the much-neglected Żuławy Gate, and also built the city Arsenal from a design by Antonis van Obbergen.

We know that Poles figured as accountants at the grain warehouses and, even though their professional slang was mainly German, we know that Poles figured among the raftsmen who brought the grain to the Green Bridge. We know that Poles were also predominant among the captains and crews who took the grain out of port – ordinances prohibiting fires on ships moored near the granaries were usually issued in Polish – but in general the Poles were absent from the upper reaches of public and commercial life in Dantzig during this period. Mateusz Deisch, an engraver, artist and mapmaker who lived and worked in the city around the 1760s, left a series of portraits decorated with snatches of songs, ballads and street cries. He shows the Dantzig Poles as street-traders and vendors, tinkers, chimney sweeps, fortune-tellers, beggars and street entertainers. Poles seem to have made very little impression on the city. Given the city's independent cast of mind, the difficulty of penetrating such a well-organised commercial set-up, the growing difference of religion, the steady stream of mainly Protestant foreigners sympathetic to German culture and language who settled in Dantzig and the Polish state's interest in expansion towards the Black Sea, the weak Polish position in the city is hardly surprising.[6]

Ironically, the local gentry found that while the grain trade flourished on their terms they could afford to show an interest in Poland and things Polish. As the overreach of the Reformation slowly gave way to a reaction and there was a discernible move towards the traditional values of the Catholic Church, this trend became more emphatic. As part of this swing to Catholicism, in 1678–81 Bartholomäus Ranisch and Andreas Schlüter, under the patronage of King Jan Sobieski III, built the Dantzig Royal Chapel, from a design by Tilman van Gameren, to accommodate the city's Catholics who had been displaced by the Lutherans from the huge St Mary's Church which stood just next door. Printers in Dantzig took advantage of the fashion for things Polish to produce specially prepared Polish grammar and vocabulary books for the gentry – over 90 such publications were sold in the second half of the seventeenth century, and in 1678 a special Polish school was set up by Jan Łanganowski. The gentry may have been interested in Poland for social and religious reasons, but the burghers were interested for business reasons alone, and they set up a regular mail service between Warsaw and Dantzig in the 1560s. While remaining loyal to the Polish state, the burghers, merchants and agents remained solidly and resolutely German in their language and outlook. In this respect it is significant that the city's badge – a crown above two crosses – appears constantly as a design motif in the architecture of the period, but the Polish eagle appears very infrequently, and only once – supported between two angels above the entrance to the Renaissance Town Hall – in a place of civic importance.

The overwhelmingly German and Lutheran feeling of the city was doubtless reinforced by the various waves of settlers. Anabaptists arrived from Münster; Scots arrived after the trade agreements and religious guarantees of 1557–8 and gave their name to the Neuschotland and Altschotland suburbs established by the Jews. After the Scots came the Dutch Mennonites, who, under threat of persecution at home, accepted sanctuary and guarantees of religious freedom to settle on the isolated, swampy alluvial plane of the Vistula delta and on the flood plane to the south-east of Elbing. The town of Prussische Holland (now Pasłęk) commemorates their settlement. They built dykes and drained the fens, controlled the flood patterns, altered the channels of the delta and recovered from the river's mucky claw the silt-rich land that lay beneath. The Poles called these free peasants *Olędrzy* or *Holendry*, a corruption of the word Hollander which in time passed into colloquial use as the name for any foreigner settling in Poland. The arrival of the Dutch, Scots and Germans more than balanced out any creeping Polonisation of the Dantzig gentry, but nevertheless the trend remained. As the seventeenth century progressed and the grain trade ran into difficulties, the remaining

Polish gentry and the recently Polonised gentry saw the growing social and political attractions of Warsaw and were lured away to permanent residence there, leaving Dantzig more than 90 per cent German and Protestant.

The rise of Swedish military power was an absolute disaster for the Poles and the Dantzigers. They invaded Poland and besieged Dantzig in 1626–7, and the knock-on effects were felt throughout the Vistula hinterland. Suddenly, after 100 years of the grain trade, Poland was cut off from British, Dutch, Italian, Spanish and Middle Eastern markets for its produce. The Swedes plundered Poland ruthlessly. They stole livestock, destroyed mills and farms, wrecked valuable equipment and pressed the local peasantry as slave labour. After a fierce naval encounter off Oliwa a truce was signed. Following the 1635 Peace Treaty signed at Sztumska Wieś, Dantzig was returned to Polish control, but only on condition that the Swedes recieved 3.5 per cent of the Vistula trade revenues. The money the Swedes received from this arrangement over the next 20 years was probably just sufficient to pay for a second invasion of Poland under the leadership of King Charles X Gustavus.

The Peace Treaty of Oliwa, signed in 1660, ended more than five years of hostilities during which Dantzig and Pomerania suffered very badly. In 1655 alone the city lost 9,000 inhabitants to plague and siege. In 1650 the population of the city had been around 77,000, but by 1660 it had been reduced to about 44,500. In the surrounding countryside more than half the peasants and smaller farmers had disappeared. When the French, Dutch and British ships anchored in Dantzig sound in the 1660s they were prepared to pay record prices for Polish grain, but they could find none to buy. The contacts, habits and skills required by the grain trade had been broken and scattered by the Swedes. The British despaired of Polish ability to repair the damage. In 1630 they had already begun large-scale work to drain the fens and levels of Bedfordshire – to extend their rye, barley and oat production, and to produce their own wheat. This work was then extended to the lowlands and fens of Lincolnshire, Cambridgeshire, Essex, Suffolk and Norfolk. By 1685 no less than 108 British merchants ships were regularly trading in the Baltic and importing goods from Dantzig, but they were no longer after grain. Instead, they brought back iron, hemp and flax, potash, pitch, canvas, oak planking, linen, hog bristles and glass. The Baltic grain trade never recovered.

Dantzig suffered further setbacks. In 1709 the plague carried off over 24,000 citizens, reducing the population to about 48,000. They were still making valiant efforts to recover from this when disputed monarchial elections in Warsaw drove King Stanisław Leszczyński to take refuge in Dantzig. Leszczyński had been the city's favoured candidate in the elections. It was not simply that they paid for their monopoly of the Polish grain trade by supporting the Polish candidate, but a question of good business sense. In contrast to Frederick Augustus II, the good natured buffoon who was the Saxon candidate, Leszczyński was an enlightened, cultured and intelligent reformer. The Dantzigers hoped that he would restore the city to its former glory and eminence by reforming the backward Polish agricultural system, by abolishing serfdom and fostering greater enterprise. Frederick Augustus relied upon Russian influence, and Dantzigers feared that he was something of a German–Russian Trojan horse – that if elected he would prove incapable of resisting Prussian and Russian territorial ambitions. History was to prove them right.

Leszczyński was trapped in Dantzig for nearly five months while the combined Russian and Saxon armies laid siege. Eventually he fled to Prussia disguised as a peasant, and left behind him a city with 2,000 damaged and destroyed buildings, with the surrounding countryside flooded and ravaged just as thoroughly as it had been by the Swedes. Leszczyński's resignation from the monarchy meant that all reform was postponed for decades, and that under the Saxon monarch the Russians and Prussians could do much as they pleased. His weak leadership allowed the Polish gentry and military caste – the *szlachta* – to drift further and further into a vigorous, almost mindless self-interest bordering on the anarchic. The manipulation of Poland's elected monarchy by predatory neighbours showed that while on the one hand this unique institution represented a fine flowering of democratic invention, on the other, the lack of discipline in its application and workings left the country's ability to maintain its independence very questionable.

In 1772, by dint of tireless effort and interminable intrigue, Frederick William I of Prussia gained control of the east bank of the river Vistula, the Westerplatte peninsula and a huge slice of Pomerania up to the gates of Dantzig. Internal dissent and rampant self-interest among the Polish nobility in Warsaw, coupled with poor leadership from their elected monarch, left the Poles easy prey to the Russians, Prussians and Austrians. While the Prussians did not gain control of the city, the fact that they now held the whole of the lower Vistula meant that they were able to levy taxes on all Polish grain entering Dantzig – at this stage about 140,000 tons per year. Also the Prussians were poised to seize the city when they were ready. The Poles realised too late the practical inadequacies of their magnificent experiment in monarchial democracy and organised chaos. Their elegant Sarmartian lifestyle was based upon an agricultural and political system that could not withstand assault from outside and which was already paralysed from within. Foreign influence at court had aggravated the right of parliamentary veto to the point where it had become a kind of nervous twitch among the nobility.

As the Poles realised the rapacious character of their neighbours, they tried to organise some resistance and to reform what was left of their state. They tried to promote insurrection in the lost lands by promising an end to serfdom, but the Prussians had already taken the wind from their sails by making the same offer to all those who supported them. It was too late. On 23 January 1793 the Russians and Prussians partitioned Poland a second time. Prussia took Dantzig. Anna Schopenhauer, mother of the Dantzig-born philosopher, wrote in her diary: 'This morning disaster fell upon my poor town like a vampire ...' The local militia manned the barricades, but they were no match for the Prussian army.

On 24 October 1795 a third partition wiped Poland from the maps of Europe for over 100 years. Under the Prussians, the margin of tolerance the city had developed in the matter of its mixed population of Poles and Germans, and its relation to the idea of Poland, were to undergo a radical and unpleasant reappraisal.

3
Prussian Danzig

As industrialisation advanced eastwards across Europe, so social and political pressures within the logic of capitalist organisation helped to simplify and solidify national identities as part of the new economic and political order. Poland, Silesia, Brandenburg and Prussia were all slowly drawn into the West European economic orbit. Yet the fact of West European industrial growth also had the opposite effect too: these places were not drawn into the new scheme of things in exactly the same way or on exactly the same conditions as France, Britain, Belgium and Holland – the original members of the industrial club. Industrialisation served to divide Europe into east and west, roughly along the line of the river Elbe. West of the river lay a quite distinct series of societies, differentiated from each other by the varying pressures and responses to industrialisation, geography and language. To the east of the Elbe the western demand for grain and timber had helped create and then kept in place a series of societies based upon the feudal manorial order of lords and serfs. Western Europe's first colonial possessions were in the immense grain basket of the Prussian and Polish latifundia.

The Polish and Prussian land owners – Junker and *szlachta* alike – had responded to the western demand for grain by exploiting the two commodities they had at hand: labour and land. In exchange for exports of grain they received money with which they purchased manufactured goods and luxury items. The result was that the eastern lords saw no reason to modernise their society, no reason to foster the growth of industry. At a time when Western Europe was enjoying the first benefits of industrial society, trade with the west was actually stultifying social progress and the development of industry in Poland and Prussia, and particularly in backward Pomerania.

After the first partition of Poland in 1772 Danzig remained independent but tied to what remained of the Polish state by trade and treaty. Unlike most of the other Prussian monarchs, who were genially indifferent to Poland and things Polish, Frederick William II had a deep contempt for the Polish nobility. While he expressed no great desire to conquer Poland, he had ambitions to build a land bridge of Prussian-controlled territory from Brandenburg to East Prussia, and to regulate the grain trade through Danzig and along the Vistula in order to raise revenues to expand and equip the Prussian army. Frederick did not care to see that these ambitions could only be satisfied at Poland's expense and that they threatened Poland's existence.

By 1793 it is estimated that West Prussia – the area that now contained Danzig and Pomerania – had a total population of around 647,000. Of these, 371,000 were thought to be Protestant, 271,000 Catholic and 5,000 Jews. While the Jews were both Polish and German speakers, not all the Catholics were Polish, yet nearly all the Protestants were German.[1] Though Danzig was by this time 90 per cent Protestant and almost entirely German in character and culture, the city still feared the worst from Prussian rule. Even those Danzigers who felt relief at being removed from the lax and distant hand of Catholic Warsaw were soon to see this as cold comfort when they began to experience Prussian rule. Within 20 years the Prussians had ruined what remained of Danzig's grain trade and the population of the city had plummeted to what it had been at the end of the fourteenth century.[2]

Prussia's new territories were no great source of satisfaction on any level. The Prussians were horrified to learn that in Pomerania and Danzig the surviving Polish nobility were reluctant to work for the new authorities and much preferred to lease out their estates to tenant farmers while they lived off the income in Warsaw. Such an attitude merely confirmed Frederick's worst prejudices against the Poles. Though he established a military academy at Chełmno in 1776 specifically for the sons of the Polish nobility, this was not consistent with his general line of thought. Under Frederick Pomerania experienced intensive Germanisation.

Frederick, a man of limited imagination who thought himself to be the very model of a modern enlightened despot and who had travelled in Poland in his younger years, believed that the Polish nobles and gentry were fools and madmen, deluded Catholic warmongers who lived in a perpetual fog of political weakness and drunken anarchy. The Polish peasants were at best, he thought, poor, lazy and dirty, exceptionally ignorant, negligent of social obligation and therefore of little use to either the military or industry in any civilised and modern state. The very idea of Poland was an insult to everything Frederick thought Prussia stood for, and the only hope he held out for the Poles was that partition and Germanisation would turn them into useful members of society. He made the Poles on his territory pay double the level of taxes paid by Germans, encouraged the Poles to sell up and move out and refused to rent out Royal Estates to Poles, declaring that he would rather see Danzig merchants working Pomeranian soil. It is hard to know who was the more aggrieved by this insult. Frederick insisted that Polish nobles must either live on their estates in Prussia or sell up their holdings, and to this end he allocated state funds to purchase any Polish lands that came available. He said he wanted to eliminate the 'schlechtes polnisches zeug', the bad Polish stuff, and he claimed that the Poles had brought this upon themselves by refusing to accept the new Prussian authority with good grace.

More by luck than good judgement Frederick's policies were effective. As the Polish–Russian grain and timber was diverted away from Danzig, the number of Polish bankruptcies grew and the number of Polish estates on the market climbed steadily. There was a drastic shift in the ratio of Polish to German nobility in and around Danzig. In 1772, when Frederick had admitted to the Danzig Chamber that the population of Pomerania was mainly Polish, it is estimated that the German speakers formed only about 13 per cent of the Pomeranian noble element. By 1800 they made up nearly 50 per cent of the total.[3]

It is almost impossible to judge the attitudes of the non-noble Poles of Danzig and Pomerania at this time – and even less so the attitudes of the Kaszubians. Numerically both the Poles and the Kaszubians were declining; socially they were at best second-class citizens. Politically, the Danzig Poles and Kaszubians were leaderless and the departure of the gentry left them in the indifferent care of a German Catholic hierarchy. They were also out of sympathy with the Protestant Germans who, though faintly alarmed at the poverty of the Polish peasantry, seemed unable to realise what part they themselves might have played in creating and maintaining these conditions. The confusion and lack of leadership among the Pomeranian and Danzig Poles – and the almost total failure of the Polish peasantry to identify the Polish cause as their own – can be seen in the Pomeranian response to the 1794 Polish uprising, led from Kraków by Tadeusz Kościuszko. Poles from the other areas of partitioned Poland rose up and fought for over eight months in support of his efforts to halt the dismemberment of the Polish state. Only in Pomerania was there no such support.

Without a Polish middle or burgher class in Pomerania there was an enormous social and political chasm separating the Polish peasant and the noble Polish *szlachta*. This gulf made the formation and manipulation of a specifically Polish identity in

Pomerania very difficult. The two social groups had almost nothing in common: they lacked any common shared sense of a Polish past; they did not share a sense of common identity; and historically and geographically Warsaw was far too remote, and contact with it too inconsistent, ever to exert any power over the Pomeranian peasant imagination. Grudging Polish promises to end serfdom, made when the *szlachta* thought this was the only concession that would rally the peasantry to them against foreign aggression, came too late and in any case lagged far behind the pre-emptive Prussian declarations ending serfdom. In Pomerania, where in practice serfdom was to last almost a generation longer than in any other corner of Europe, the Prussians were able to prevent even a narrow coincidence of interests between the Polish nobles and peasants by inviting the nobles to leave and by inviting the peasants to become Prussians. There was virtually no Polish middle class to act as a rallying point for the upper and lower classes, to act as a focus of opposition to Prussian policies. Under these circumstances it was highly unlikely that the Poles and Kaszubes of Danzig would rally to the Polish cause.

Although technically the Treaty of Vienna guaranteed the Poles autonomy within Prussian law and government, in fact in Pomerania the idea was never put into practice. For the Kaszubes and Poles of Danzig Poland was a distant idea only. Most of them would never set eyes on the place and few felt any loyalty towards it. For illiterate and landless serfs and peasants the language of their landlord made little difference to their lives. Conditions of service on the estates were arduous and whether the landlord came from Berlin or Warsaw, whether he spoke German or Polish, it was certain that his agent would always make himself understood.

In 1797 the young Poles of Danzig did stage a street demonstration, but that was the limit of their effort to revive the Polish state, and the limit of their willingness to parade a Polish identity. Warsaw was simply too distant and the Polish nobility too self-interested for the peripheral and unregarded Poles of Pomerania and Danzig seriously to consider dying for them. Also the material benefits of Prussian citizenship had begun to show in improved living standards and educational opportunities. The years 1794–1806 were something of a honeymoon for the Prussians and their Poles: a spirit of co-operation flourished as the Prussians sought to secure the affections of their Polish subjects. Poles were appointed to administrative posts in local government, and the law courts attempted to accommodate requests for the use of the Polish language. Some Polish judges were even appointed to district courts. It was not uncommon for German children to be taught in Polish, and there was a principle in Pomerania of bilingual education. Official notices were published in both languages until the 1870s. By the time of Napoleon's war against Prussia and his defeat of Frederick William III's armies at Jena and Auerstadt in 1806, the people of Danzig were far from disloyal to the Prussian cause, far from willing to throw off Prussian rule, lest they be handed over to some form of Polish domination. Rather than rise against Prussia, Danzig endured a 20-month siege by Marshal Lefebvre's Franco-Polish army. After the siege there was a rapid polarisation of opinion within the city, which resulted in the absorption or departure of the remaining Polish gentry, so that by the end of the Napoleonic Wars Danzig and Pomerania, though still containing a very substantial number of Poles and Polish-speakers, were considered loyal to Prussian ideals and identity.

Ironically, by absorbing huge new areas of strong Polish identity in the years 1793–1807, the Prussians probably helped extend the idea of a Polish identity to Poles who up to then had simply thought of themselves as Polish-speaking Prussians. In Kaszubia, Mazowia and Silesia the peasants referred to themselves as *Kaszuby*, *Mazury* and *Ślęzaki* rather than as Poles: *Polak* was a term reserved for the Polish nobility. In most of the territories they occupied, the Prussians, by putting pressure on the peasantry to Germanise themselves, concentrated rather than diluted a Polish identity. The way in which Germanisation was carried out gave to the newly released serfs, the put-upon peasantry, the tiny Polish middle class which felt itself to be discriminated against, and the ambitious and inflexible Polish nobility a rallying point – probably their only rallying point.

The Poles had nurtured the hope that the French would restore the old Polish state with Danzig attached as before, but Napoleon had other ideas. He strung the Poles along to the very end in order to keep their enthusiasm for his cause and their manpower for his army. Danzig became a Free City attached to the Grand Duchy of Warsaw – a Duchy that was grand in name only. In effect Warsaw became a staging post on the road to Moscow and the Poles were little more than cannon fodder. Most of the Poles who went to Russia in the belief that this would help to restore their country's independent existence never returned: of the 82,000 Poles who made up the Grand Armée's V Corps, only 2,300 survived the retreat from Moscow. If Warsaw was a glorified recruiting post, then the same in miniature was true of Danzig. A small amount of local capital was generated by the spending power of the garrison, and by the French decision to extend and modernise the city's walls and defences, but this was all brought to nothing when the

British Navy caused incredible damage by bombarding the city with Congreve Rockets. Following the defeat of Napoleon in Russia the Russian Army laid siege to Danzig for over 10 months. When the city finally surrendered the population had fallen to less than 16,000.[4]

The Congress of Vienna returned Danzig to the Prussians, and for a short while it functioned as the administrative capital of West Prussia, with a corresponding growth in civil servants and officials. In 1819, when Danzig had been the provincial capital for only three years, and for reasons that are unclear, the Prussians moved the function of administrative capital to Königsberg. This decision, combined with the Prussian mismanagement of the waterways and consequent flooding, as well as high trade tariffs, caused rising unemployment which hit the city's Poles hardest of all.

It was becoming increasingly clear to the Prussians that they would have great difficulty in making their eastern possessions a financial success: the only way to make the eastern marches profitable was to exploit the poor natural resources to the limit and develop industrial capacity. Industrialisation and the mechanisation of farming techniques would have inevitable knock-on effects within Prussian social structure, however, and the Junker landowners – who dominated Prussian politics, the military and the agricultural economy, and who were the most entrenched and backward-looking group in Pomerania – could be counted on to resist all change. Prussia in the 1820s and 1830s stood with one foot in the feudal, agricultural past and the other foot in the new age of industry. It was an unfortunate combination.

Through the 1820s and 1830s there was increased contact with British and French industrial concerns. Prussia became aware that it had lost parity with its allies from the Napoleonic years and determined to catch up by creating a series of technical schools – later to include Danzig's Technical High School for boys and the famous Conradinum – and by beginning to investigate and research industrial techniques. They also set up a light-engineering works (one of a number throughout the Prussian east) at Dirschau (Tczew). The Prussians found that the advanced industrial nations of the West were using their colonial possessions to fuel their industrial drive, and accordingly Prussia began to seek out markets that the British, French, Belgians and Dutch did not dominate. The Seehandlung organisation, set up by Frederick the Great in 1772 to promote trade along the Prussian reaches of the Vistula, was expanded and reorganised to seek outlets for Prussian goods in Silesia, India, the West Indies, South America, China and the Balkans.[5]

Increasing industrialisation in and around Danzig did the local Poles little good, however. In 1832 the new Prussian Oberpräsident Edward Flotwell supervised the introduction of a property qualification into municipal elections – a manoeuvre that automatically increased the influence and power over the Poles of the German settlers, burghers and merchants. In the 1850s a new electoral system with a complex arrangement for the election of an electoral college for each social class further downgraded the possibility of political intervention for the Poles. By 1840 Poles were almost entirely absent from the lists of Danzig merchants, were only a small minority on the list of Danzig house-owners, and were thus almost totally excluded from public life and government of the city. The peasantry and the the labourers had no voice at all, and only the few remaining Polish gentry had any representation in the upper house of the electoral college.

The Prussians had, it is true, introduced compulsory education for all 6–14-year-olds in 1825, and by 1850 some 82–5 per cent of all young Poles in the border districts, including Danzig and Pomerania, had received an elementary education, as opposed to 24 per cent in the Russian and Austrian sections of Poland. But those who received this education did so in the German language, and those who made no progress in German could proceed no further than elementary school. The Poles had maintained a very efficient educational system under a special national commission up to the time of the partition. Polish schools were not physically suppressed, but were simply left outside the system of Prussian state subsidy. After 1870 education for the Poles was seen as a way of bringing them within the German order, of lightening their Slav darkness by opening up to them the world of 'civilisation'. The Poles did not see things this way. Increasingly they felt German education to be a way of excluding them from the experience of industrial and urban life, from the totality of modernisation. With the single exception of the Polish *Gymnazium* in Kulm, the Germans had a total monopoly on higher education. For Poles it was impossible to become educated and technically competent in the Polish language. To insist on an overtly Polish identity was to exclude oneself from polite and educated Danzig society and to disqualify oneself from any job that promised social and economic advancement. Under the Prussians education for the Poles was a mere downpayment for later, more thorough, Germanisation and absorption.[6] To cling to a Polish identity was to exclude oneself from the German monopoly on higher education and from all but menial employment in industry; given the rapid depopulation of the countryside it was also to insist on the right to become and remain part of a backward, ignorant, illiterate, inward-looking agrarian people, stuck in a rural backwater with no access to the outside world, with scant interest from that world and little hope of progress.

It was not only the Junkers who misunderstood the processes at work and who felt both contempt and fear of the 'backward' Poles. In 1859 Engels contemptuously referred to them as the 'ruins' of a people 'no longer capable of a national existence'. For him it was part of the natural order of things that a rising 'larger nation' like Prussia should absorb Poland and the Poles. The only alternative was that Poland should maintain itself as an 'ethnographic monument without political significance'.[7]

Belated Prussian efforts to improve the dock facilities in Danzig and to modernise the port were aided considerably by the Great Flood of 1840 which altered the course of the Vistula and opened up a new river mouth through the delta. The cramped dock area began to expand eastwards across the newly exposed terrain. As West European industrialisation got under way, so the demand for goods manufactured in and around Danzig also began to improve: there was increased Prussian demand for armaments, chemicals, food, timber, clothing and shipbuilding to support the growth of industry in Western Prussia. There was also a considerable improvement in international trade through Danzig. Prussian industrialisation was part of a wave of change that was sweeping over the whole of Western Europe and which was just beginning to filter into Eastern Europe. As capital was generated by French, Belgian, Dutch and British industrial power, so the new industrial middle classes began to demand luxury goods: the trade in furs from Poland and Russia improved massively and Manchester, which had previously exported cotton cloth and some Yorkshire manufactured woollen goods to Danzig in return for flax and hemp, now began to open up its own fur trade based on imports from the Baltic – Manchester's Dantzic Street (which changed its name from Charter Street by residents' petition in the mid-1860s) commemorates the trade of this period. In 1854 Ferdinand Schichau, who had constructed Germany's first steam dredger, and first screw-driven steam ship at his yards in Elbing, opened the Schichau Werft construction yard in Danzig, and this was closely followed by the extension of the Klawitter yards.

Canals and the inland waterways were of vital importance to Danzig: all of the main tributaries of the Vistula were navigable and the river trade, with its construction yards and various specialised professions, was very well developed. In 1771 the completion of the Bromberg Canal had linked the Vistula with the Oder and

Berlin; the Dniepr–Bug Canal and the Dniepr–Niemen Canal (1775–84) opened up the possibility of river trade as far south as Kiew and the Black Sea. The Augustów–Grodno Canal (1825–37) connected East Prussia and Danzig's immediate hinterland with Lithuania and the river Niemen. The König Wilhelm Canal (1869–73) opened up a connection between the Kurisches Haff and Memel. Prussian canal-building projects meant that by 1914 Danzig was linked to a network of waterways that allowed inland trade with the Rhine, Bordeaux, Le Havre, Brussels, Antwerpen, and northern Germany up to the Danish border. By 1914 it was technically possible for a Danzig bargee to visit Bordeaux and the Black Sea with roughly equal facility. However, while Danzig enjoyed these widespread trade contacts and reaped the benefit of the still massive river trade in Polish timber (16,949 log floats of 9 logs per float were rafted down the Warthe to Stettin or Berlin in 1871 alone) Western Europe had already moved on to develop its rail networks.[8]

Britain, France, Belgium and Holland had been engaged in the process of capital accumulation from the formation of overseas empires and from the slave trade since at least the sixteenth century. Prussia however had access to neither of these as a way of financing industrial change. Also, Prussia was only one of a series of German states and as such could hardly take advantage of the rapidly developing and highly lucrative Atlantic trade. While Prussia struggled to create a tariff union of German states – the first step on the road to forming a German nation-state – the Western nations were already involved in building up their as yet unintegrated but nevertheless substantial rail networks. In general, the first growth of German, French and Belgian railways was about 30 years after the first British lines. In contrast to the other states though, Germany was still a series of small states and principalities, and this made it very difficult to finance and develop the railway network. The bulk of Germany's railways were established between 1848 and 1877, but even then they served the west of Germany far better than they served the east.

Danzig's first railway connection from Bromberg to the city's Main Gate, came into operation in 1852. In the 1860s a line was built along the path of the old moat and then out to the new dock at Neufahrwasser (Nowy Port), and ten years later a second branch line went on up the coast to Koszalin. In the 1890s the Central Station was constructed, and in 1905 two more branch lines extended among the factories and workshops of the Lower City, and a third snaked its way out over a drawbridge and a railway ferry to the island of Ostrów. It was also reflected in the internal development of the city. In 1864 a horse-drawn tram service started, followed in 1895 by an electric tram system. By 1870 the old city ramparts and defensive gateways had been torn down because they hindered the greatly increased flow of traffic. Yet for all the growth of its port and shipyard facilities, the size of its herring fleet, the complexity of its transportation network, the growing popularity of the bathing beaches and Spa Cures in nearby Zoppot, Danzig was tied to a backward and unstable agricultural hinterland, dominated by the massively retrograde talent of the Junkers.

In many ways Pomerania is central to the processes that were at work in Prussia and Germany. It was a marcher territory that produced extremely loyal Germans and abused and confused Poles. What happened in Pomerania also happened elsewhere, but in Pomerania the processes were accentuated because the place was so far behind the rest of the world in its social and economic order, and because its mixed Polish and German population accentuated the clash between the rural and industrial identities and social orders. Bismarck, chancellor, prime minister and architect of the German Reich, was a Protestant. As such he was deeply suspicious of all Catholics, and especially of Polish Catholics. Bismarck said he sympathised with the Polish position, but nevertheless believed that Germanisation meant the Poles would be emancipated and enriched by contact with German language and culture. He believed that Germanisation would bring the Poles security and a place in the world that they could not otherwise expect. He identified totally with the Prussian cause, and if to remain exactly as you are is an ambition, then he identified with Junker ambition too. He had been born on a Junker estate at Schönhausen in Brandenburg in 1815, and his family had moved to Kniephof in Pomerania soon afterwards. Bismarck held Pomerania in most particular regard all his life. In 1876 he said the nationality problem in Eastern Europe was not 'worth the healthy bones of a Pomeranian musketeer'. It was an interesting remark on many levels: A.J.P. Taylor has said that the phrase was more revealing than Bismarck intended: 'When he wanted to define Germany it was Pomerania on the Baltic, not the Rhineland, Bavaria or Austria which came into his mind.'[9]

That the German leader should choose an area of mixed nationality as somehow typical of Germanness is interesting in itself. It does not necessarily indicate the physical absence of Poles, but rather their invisibility to the Germans – even to those who lived there. At the same time it also indicates a polarisation of national identities. Perhaps the essential point to make is that of the ambiguity embodied in this Junker position. If Bismarck could overlook the Poles, how could a people whose political profile was so low, and whose organisation was so poor, possibly be a threat to German identity? The answer was that Pomeranian Polish identity was no threat unless the Junkers decided that it was convenient for it to be so; the identity of the Pomeranian Poles was so peripheral to Polish national identity that politically these people were no threat at all. In time the Pomeranian Poles would have undoubtedly been absorbed into the German-language community as their forbears had been in previous centuries. However, the Junker need for an external threat required that a sense of otherness, of not being Prussian, of not speaking German, when it was not altogether invisible, should be a threat.

From about 1860 the European agricultural sector entered a period of crisis in which the baleful influence of the backward Prussian agricultural system and its links with the politics of the Prussian east were made abundantly clear: the mechanisms which the Junkers managed to hide from the German populace were at last revealed. In Prussia the agricultural crisis was to reach its climax in the 1880s and 1890s, but its effects were still to be seen and felt well into the twentieth century. All across Europe there was a movement of population from the country to the city, from the south to the north, from the east to the west. In Eastern Europe this movement was related to the ending of serfdom and the growth of industry in the western regions of Germany.

The abolition of serfdom was staggered through the different parts of Poland. The bulk of the Prussian peasants were released from service in the years 1811–50. In Pomerania the general impoverishment and the already poor Pomeranian soil meant that very few peasants could gather together enough money to buy their own farm equipment – a necessary prerequisite for purchase of their land from the estate – nor could they ever manage to garner a purchase price that was often the equivalent of over 25 years' rent. This, yoked with the survival of unpaid feudal service on the lord's land, the lord's continued control of woodlands, common land, open fields and meadows used for grazing, and the continued obligation of the tenant to consume only alcohol which had been distilled through the lord's own stills, meant that while in theory Prussian serfdom was abolished by 1850, in practice it was not really seriously undermined in Pomerania until the agricultural review of 1865. Even then abolition was not completed until the early 1890s when the number of landless and dispossessed peasants and rural labourers increased dramatically. During this period the population of Danzig rose from about 50,000 in the 1830s to about 70,000 by 1860. A large number of people released from bondage simply emigrated: between 1870 and 1914 1,200,000 Prussian Poles left Europe for America, Brazil and Canada.

Throughout the 1860s Poles and Germans had probably existed in roughly equal numbers in the border districts. But by the 1880s the Poles outnumbered the Germans by two to one. In Prussia as a whole there was a discernible and understandable population shift, an *Ostflucht* (literally: East flight) from the poorly developed Spartan provinces of the east to the more 'civilised', better developed and rapidly industrialising cities of the west. By 1913 one third of all Dortmund industrial workers were *émigré* Poles.[10]

In Prussia the crisis manifested itself in a variety of ways. The Pomeranian Junkers began to complain that the end of serfdom had released the peasants they held in moneyless bondage to wander where they would. This not only disturbed the Junker sense of social stability, but played havoc with their income since it opened up the estates to the market force of unfettered labour: the Junkers were obliged to acknowledge a world that they had been desperately trying to shut out. Under pressure from the aggrieved Junkers, the Prussian government responded by pushing 30,000 Poles who lacked proof of Prussian citizenship across the border into Russian Poland in 1885.

The ending of serfdom in Pomerania coincided with Prussian efforts to increase the number of German settlers by granting land to those prepared to resist the *Ostflucht* and settle in the east. The Prussian government passed legislation designed to Germanise landholdings in the border districts, but these laws were so badly framed and so crudely implemented that they had exactly the reverse effect from that intended. A German peasant farmer moving to the east was obliged to pay one sixth of the profit of his labour to a landlord, and only those peasants who took on more than 6.4 hectares (16 acres) were given the opportunity to buy their land. In Pomerania the average holding was about 5 hectares (13–14 acres) of very poor soil, and even with Herculean effort on the part of the farmer it was clear that the payment of one sixth of profits made purchase almost impossible. Often a German settler, realising that his farm was too poor to yield the one-sixth levy required to keep his purchase, would offer instead free labour on the lord's demesne.

It has been estimated that in the years 1877–1904 70 per cent of Pomeranian farmland was held in large estates and only 30 per cent in peasant smallholdings of various kinds: about two-thirds of Pomeranian farmers were smallholders living in the most appalling poverty; their assets were non-existent or too small for them to think of trekking westwards to look for factory work; they were too poor to pay cash for their land, and too impoverished for any bank to risk giving them a loan. Their diet consisted mainly of potatoes, turnips, cabbage, beetroot, millet, buckwheat and rye, supplemented by wild fruit in the autumn and by concentrated hedge and verge scavenging to find edible grasses, wild cabbage, cress, linden leaves, horseradish, bitter-vetch, water lily, mushrooms, wild sorrel, nettles, comfrey, mallow and goose grass. They rarely ate meat, and rather than consume butter, milk, meat, poultry and eggs, preferred to send any such produce to market. Many of these people lived largely without the agent of money, and survived by bartering what excess produce they had. Living outside the money economy, they had no access to the world of manufactured goods, still less to luxury goods. The remaining one-third of Pomeranian farmers had rather larger self-supporting farms and enjoyed a reasonable degree of comfort. They covered their costs and were able to transport their grain and produce to Danzig. [11]

A tiny minority of landowners lived in enormous wealth and comfort, exacting feudal dues and enforced labour from farmers who had in effect become their tied peasants: these landowners still engaged in the grain trade as their families had done for generations, and as if they could think of nothing else to do. In Danzig it was still possible for a merchant to make a small fortune from the grain and timber trades, but it was not considered wise to invest the profits in agriculture – either the farms were too small and the returns non-existent, or the estates were too ramshackle and labour-intensive to warrant investment. As the area still had very little industry, the profit generated by trade and agriculture around Danzig was hardly ever invested locally. Danzig merchants tended to invest their money in the new and growing industrial concerns of the west.

If this was not enough, the Poles in all three partition areas were enjoying a baby boom. In 1840 there had been about 10 million Poles – by 1914 there were over 18 million. Pomerania, with a population of over 100,000 Polish-speakers, was about 35 per cent Polish, and in spite of the flight from the land and the flight of the population to the industrial centres of the west, Pomerania was one of the few Prussian provinces to show a marked increase in its population, and almost all of that growth was attributed to the Poles. In south-eastern Pomerania and the areas immediately around Danzig the Polish birth-rate was running at 36 per 1,000 of the population, which meant that by 1933 the Polish population of Pomerania had experienced a 28 per cent increase in a mere 15 years. In the predominantly German districts of north-west Pomerania, however, 14 of the 34 districts recorded a decline in their population in the same period. The Poles, it seemed, were multiplying, while the Germans were deserting.[12]

Although the number of Poles may have been on the increase there was very little sign in Prussia that they were organising to reinstate an independent Poland. Indeed, if anything, they seem to have been too demoralised politically to organise effectively at anything more than a local level, and that in itself is testimony to the devastating effect of the *Kulturkampf* and *Polenpolitik*. In 1864, after the 1863 uprising and the massive repression that followed its collapse, Julian Łukaszewski, a former Polish commissioner in the Prussian government, wrote a pamphlet despairing of the Polish people's ability ever again to control their own destiny:

> ... we don't even have the elementary conditions to start to develop our national economy on a large scale. Where is the work force? Where is the necessary capital? Where are the communications routes on land and water? Where are the credit institutions, banks, trade companies? Where are the industrial, joint-stock, and insurance companies? Where are the regulations for social relations? Where is the spirit of enterprise? Where, finally, are the people with professional education, the technicians, machinists and manufacturers to skilfully run the industries. All this must be extracted from the governments that have invaded us.[13]

The Prussians did not see, did not want to see, could not afford to see, this side of life in their border districts.

Throughout the 1870s the Prussian Lands began to restrict the use of the Polish language by removing it from schools, churches, courts and local government. In 1871 the Prussians feared that their Poles might rise up against them – partly as a late reaction to the failed anti-Russian uprising of 1863, partly in protest at the incorporation of the Grand Duchy of Warsaw into the German Reich; they deprived the Poles of the right to print their own magazines, newspapers and almanacs, and shortly afterwards banned the publication and circulation of Polish poetry. In Danzig and Pomerania, where the substantial Polish minority might have made it difficult to implement such a policy, there was a special dispensation. In spite of this, however, Polish sermons were scrutinised by Prussian bishops, and Polish prayer books were confiscated. In 1872, in an effort to eradicate Catholic influence in schools, the control of education passed to the state: the hymn 'Boże coś Polskę' was banned, and freedom of assembly and association were also severely curtailed. In 1887 Polish was banned from all elementary schools throughout the Prussian east, and German language tuition was made compulsory. Teachers were prevented from joining any Polish cultural or Catholic societies, and German language teachers were given a special bonus if they volunteered for work in Polish-speaking districts. When Polish priests protested at these measures and at the attempt by schools' inspectors to interfere in religious instruction, the government responded by arresting and exiling them. By 1876 applicants for the German civil service had to pass a special exam in German culture, and German was compulsory in virtually every aspect of public life. In 1885 Prussian Oberpräsident Möllendorf, who was widely regarded as pro-Polish, recommended a total ban on the Polish language, saying that only in this way was it possible to force the Poles to appreciate the benevolence and wisdom of German culture and administration. In 1887 Polish was officially banned even from the few private bilingual schools of Pomerania, and children heard speaking Polish were threatened with public flogging.

In response to the massive changes that were taking place throughout Germany a whole series of patriotic clubs and societies grew up in the 1890s. Hannah Arendt has linked the rise of both pan-Germanism and pan-Slavism with the 'triumphant imperialist expansion of the Western nations' in the 1880s, but it is clear that while pan-Slav ideas were confined in the main to the idea of restoring or gaining independence for the Slav subjects of Prussia and the Austro-Hungarian Empire, pan-German ideas ran in a quite different direction. In the Reich the various German patriotic societies were designed to combat 'Jewish influence', which was seen to be both ethnically alien and racially inferior, and also to be at the very heart of the economic change that at once afflicted and enriched German society. However, these organisations drew the bulk of their support from the Marcher territories, where anti-Semitism took second place to the fight against Polish influence. The National Germanic League of Clerks (1893), the Agrarian League (1893), the Pan-German League (1886), and the Naval League were all fully operational by the end of the decade.[14]

Of all the German patriotic associations that sprang up along the eastern borders in the 1890s it was the Ostmarkenverein, the Eastern Marches Society founded in 1894, that was to have the most profound impact on German border society. The Ostmarkenverein was more generally known as the Haketa, after the initials of its founders: Ferdinand von Hansemann, Herman Kennemann and Heinrich von Tiedeman. They were respectively a banker's son, a Junker and a retired army major, and between them they represented the whole range of Junker–middle-class collusion and delusion. It was Haketa that was responsible for circulating and popularising Völkisch ideas of German historians that were favourable to the extension of the Prussian state. They stressed German title to the lands of Pomerania, Silesia and central Poland, saying that German settlement had predated Slav settlement. They claimed that despite the hundreds of years of Polish independence, 'the East' owed what little civilisation it could muster to the efforts of the Germans. They claimed the Goths who had settled along the Vistula and in the Ukraine as the founders of the Polish state, saying that rule and order had been brought to these lands over the heads of the drunken, idolatrous and stupid Polish peasantry. Haketa said that the Slavs had German missionary priests to thank for their liberation from the depths of ignorance. In 1914 Emmanuel Ginschel, echoing the Haketa line on the legitimacy of the Prussian partition of Poland and its continued control of its share of old Polish territory, wrote:

> This once German land, which under Polish rule sank into misery and neglect, has been conquered for the German people by sword and plow. It has been fertilised by German blood and sweat, and owes its culture to Germans. For these reasons, we are masters here.[15]

By 1901 Haketa had a membership of 20,000 – mostly drawn from small farmers, small businessmen, craftsmen, and small estate-owners of the eastern borders. They were also recruiting among teachers and the Protestant clergy and among the Prussian civil service, employees of which were normally banned from belonging to political organisations, but whose membership was in this case overlooked. Although it was convenient for the government to appear to be quite separate from Haketa, the relationship was so close that in practice it would be accurate to describe the organisation as an officially sanctioned and sponsored 'tame' pressure group. Under popular 'pressure' from Haketa the German government extended laws forbidding the sale of land to Poles, sought out and expelled all non-Prussian Poles, and began to harass the increasingly effective and efficient Polish financial institutions with petty legalistic restrictions.

In 1901 Haketa persuaded the government to revive legislation forbidding the use of Polish in Pomeranian bilingual schools, and as the task of teaching the language fell increasingly to the Catholic Church, and the clergy felt obliged to give extended 'Catechism' lessons, so Haketa set about interfering in private language tuition too. Their interference did not pass without resistance. That same year there was a school strike in the small town of Września, near Poznań, among Polish pupils who refused to receive religious instruction or to say prayers in German. The strike was only broken when the children were publicly flogged and their parents sent to jail. The issue simmered on until 1906, by which time it was illegal for a Polish teacher to teach Polish history to Polish pupils in the Polish language: an estimated 60,000 elementary pupils refused to attend school. The strikes spread. By 1907 over 93,000 Polish pupils throughout the Prussian east were involved, and even in the normally pacific Polish community of Danzig there were street demonstrations with crowds chanting 'Polish children to Polish schools'. The strike was broken only by widespread flogging and imprisonment, but it was clear that if the Danzig Poles – by tradition the meekest of them all – were willing to protest, then Polish resistance as a whole must have stiffened considerably.[16]

In spite of Polish protest the Haketa continued and extended the range of its work. It Germanised the few Polish street, town and place names, undertook propagandist 'research work' on historical subjects, supervised the Germanising of family names among those Poles who decided to take the plunge into German identity, took down Polish-language warning notices about venereal diseases from public toilets and instituted a system of bonuses for all teachers and civil servants prepared to move and settle in the eastern provinces. Neither land nor language was the real issue, however. These were the mere surface indicators of deeper problems, the media through which the deep, internal cultural and economic pressures at work within German society showed themselves.

One of the most spectacular failures within the Prussian *Polenpolitik* was that of the *Ansiedlungskomission* or Royal Prussian Colonisation Commission. This body had been set up by Bismarck in 1886, when it was estimated that if the *Ostflucht* continued, 3 million Germans would have left their homes in the Prussian east by the start of the twentieth century. The Commission was widely believed to be the only hope of reversing the *Ostflucht* and was allocated vast sums of money by the Prussian government. Its instructions were to buy up Polish land and estates for resale to German settlers at massively reduced prices.

In general the effect of the Commission's inflated purchasing ability was to drive up the price of land in the borders. Farmers were confident that if they sold to the Commission there would be no great rush of Germans to buy it, and the Commission could not sell the land to the Poles. The inflation of land prices encouraged farmers who wanted to remain in the east to sell to the Commission only to buy the same land back again at a reduced price and pocket the difference. The Commission slowly realised that there was a second loophole in their work: on paper the scheme looked simple enough, but in fact the Prussian government had mistaken its own hostility towards the Poles for that of the general populace – with unexpected results. Polish and German farmers collaborated throughout the Prussian east to extract huge sums of money from the Commission through the sale and resale of the same property several times over – each time at an 'improved' price. A German farmer would 'sell out' to a Polish farmer who would then sell the land to the Commission; the original farmer would then buy back the property. Both German and Polish farmers made a tidy profit from the deal, and on paper it looked as if the Commission had 'Germanised' a farm.

In 1886, in direct response to the founding of the Colonisation Commission, the Poles created the Bank Ziemski to promote Polish counter-colonisation. This bank ran into financial difficulties almost immediately, and in 1892 was bailed out from certain bankruptcy by credits and low-interest loans from the conciliatory government under Caprivi. Inevitably, government help undermined the bank's ability to do the job for which it it had been established, and in 1897 the Poles opened the new Land Purchase Bank. The Commission so stirred the Poles, that while it had initially been possible for them to buy up Polish estates for German settlement, by 1898, when the Prussian Landtag voted an additional 100 million marks for the Commission's use, the Poles had already begun to see the sale of land to the Commission as a crime against the nation and had begun to organise their own agricultural co-operatives and credit unions. In the years 1880–1913 the number of land purchasing agencies and co-operatives associated with the Land Purchase Bank was to rise from about 120 to nearly 300. The crucial difference between the Germans and the Poles who profited from the efforts of the Colonisation Commission and the Polish banks through the sale and resale of farms and estates was that, while the Germans would eventually sell up for good and move away westwards to retire on money invested in Germany's growing industrial enterprises, the Poles would stay put, use their money to consolidate their farms and purchases, and deposit their savings in the Land Purchase Bank.

In 1904 the German government passed a law that forbade the construction of buildings and dwellings on any Polish-owned land which the Colonisation Commission might want to buy. The idea was to prevent the Poles who managed to buy land from being able to inhabit it. The result was that one Michał Drzymała, who purchased land in Wolsztyn, circumvented the rules only by living in a caravan for nearly ten years.

The Colonisation Commission did more harm than good even by Prussian standards. By putting pressure on the Poles and

Kaszubians to Germanise themselves, it stimulated the very sense of Polish identity it had sought to suppress. Throughout the Prussian east a wide range of specifically Polish cultural organisations sprang up in response to this pressure: the Slav Literary Society (1836), the Wrocław Flute Choral Society (1890), the Sokoł Physical Culture Society (1894), and the Association of Polish Boy Scouts in Germany (1912). In Danzig the new-found Polish identity even allowed a Polish language newspaper – *Gazeta Gdańska* – to flourish from 1891 onwards. As Polish financial institutions became more effective it was no longer necessary for Poles who fell on hard times to sell their land to the Germans. Instead, it became possible for the Poles to compete on the open market and to bid against the Commission with capital made available by the Polish banks. The fact that Poles could now compete with the Prussians 'reconciled profits with patriotism'.[17] By 1907 Polish financial institutions, though cramped by legal restrictions, had become so effective that finance flowing through them allowed almost every Polish farm in Pomerania of 5 hectares or more access to some form of farm machinery on a shared or collective basis.

The Colonisation Commission became more and more frustrated. Between 1885 and 1905 over 830,000 Germans left the Prussian east.[18] The Commission resorted to desperate, grand-scale measures: along the valley of the river Netze as far east as Bromberg it settled a solid block of 22,000 Germans in an effort to prevent Polish land purchases in the area. The Commission found that it could no longer find any Poles or Kaszubians who were willing to sell their land, and so began to turn to the purchase and resale of Junker estates. The Junkers, as usual, were badly in debt. While industrialisation and capitalist economics had advanced into the Vistula delta region, into Central Poland, Russia and the western regions of Germany, the Junkers had remained fixed in a stubbornly feudal corner of the world. Having borrowed money to maintain their vast estates they found that the estates were too inefficient to generate the income to pay back the loans. The Prussian banks found that they had been lending increasing amounts to the Junkers to maintain a lifestyle rather than to finance the modernisation of facilities and improve agricultural methods. The Junkers drained the banks to the very limit of their credit and were then forced to sell off plots of land to repay the interest on their debts and refinance their lifestyle.

By 1900 it must have been increasingly obvious that the policies of Frederick and Bismarck were not producing the desired effect. But the Germans did not relent; indeed the height of their efforts came in the years 1900–9. Competition between the Poles and the Commission had driven up the price of land in Pomerania by over 100 per cent by 1900, so that land the German farmers did not want to farm cost twice as much as farmland anywhere else in Germany. In 1912 it was estimated that since 1886 the Commission had purchased only 60,000 hectares of Polish-owned land and 100,000 hectares of German land in Poznania and West Prussia. In 1921 a report placed before the Prussian Diet revealed that of the 460,884 hectares of land purchased by the Commission up to that time, only 27.4 per cent had come from the Poles; a staggering 72.5 per cent had been purchased by the Commission from German estate owners.[19] In 1906 the Colonisation Commission estimated that it had brought over 14,000 German families to the east in the 20 years of its existence, and claimed to have removed over 40,000 Poles.[20] Yet far from cowing the Poles, the Commission had made them more nationalist and more determined to resist than ever.

In 1906 the Colonisation Commission, with the enthusiastic backing of the National Liberal Party, the Pan-German League, Haketa, the National Germanic League of Clerks and the Agrarian League, decided that the only way to resolve the issue in Germany's favour was by a policy of expropriation of Polish-owned land. In 1908, against fierce opposition from the majority of Prussian property-owners, the Catholic Centre Party and the Union of West German Liberals, Prince Bülow equipped the Colonisation Commission with the legal power to seize Polish property, and allocated increased government funding – including a substantial bribe to the Junkers to persuade them to use German rather than the cheaper Polish labour. At the same time the Prussians hamstrung Polish opposition by making the use of the Polish language illegal at all public gatherings. Yet still the Prussians delayed introducing expropriation to Pomerania until May 1912 lest they provoke an uprising, and while they bought up only four estates totalling over 6,624 hectares of land, they paid more than double the market rate. It is estimated that in the years 1896–1913 German landholdings declined by over 98,000 hectares, 20,000 of which were in and around Danzig.[21] While the Danzig Poles were thought to be docile and largely invisible, it is clear that their slumbering sense of identity had been roused by anti-Polish policies.

In spite of the obvious malice of the Prussian and German governments, the Poles still favoured a peaceful resolution rather than a bloody revolution. They insisted on fostering legal forms of opposition and on social rather than political resistance. Although the Poles participated in the Reichstag, in the Prussian Diet and in the North German Union Parliament, their main areas of activity lay in the co-operatives, culture clubs, in popular education societies, reading rooms, choirs, orchestras and libraries that grew up in the 1880s; in Catholic social organisations, in the physical culture movement and in the popular Polish-language daily newspapers like the *Grudziądz Codzienny*. It was through these avenues of expression, and through the admirably restrained quality of their protest that the Poles earned the sympathy of their German co-religionists. Opposition from German Catholics was one of the main reasons for the brutal policy of expropriation being largely suspended.

The Kaszubian people who lived along the western Danzig suburbs were badly affected by the changes of Prussian and German rule. For the most part they had been one of Europe's invisible, historyless, subject peoples. They speak a Polabian dialect of the Pomeranian group of Slav languages, closely related to Wendish (Sorbian), Serbian and the vanished Slovincian dialect, all of which are/were related to Polish. The Kaszubes are part of the ancient complex of Slav tribes who had occupied the southern Baltic shores right up to the Danish borders some time around the fifth and seventh centuries AD. In spite of everything that history had thrown at them since then the Kaszubes had remained in their chosen place. Subject to invasions and to the steady and relentless pressure to Germanise or Polonise themselves they had watched their language and culture dwindle away as the other Pomeranian cultures had done before them. By 1928 the Kaszubes numbered around 110,000, and they and the few thousand speakers of Leban dialect were the last survivors of the original Slav settlers of Pomerania.[22]

Neither German nor Polish, the Kaszubes were then (and still are) a stubbornly insular and agrarian people, thoroughly resistant to change. Sir Robert Donald, writing between the two world wars, described them as: 'a somewhat primitive community. They have no ideals. They are devoid of initiative in political action, are content to be led, and are easily exploited. They want to cultivate their fields; to live peacefully under conditions which suit their habits and characteristics.'[23] At one time the Kaszubians and their Pomeranian kin had been part of a powerful independent principality: their territory had stretched from the gulf of Danzig westwards to Słupsk (Stolp) and the river Słupia (Stolpe), where the small town of Dębnica Kaszubska (literally: Kaszubian Oaks) still survives. Kaszubia, even if it was under constant German pressure, remained an identifiable area of Slav settlement centred on Kartuzy (Karthaus) and covering the northern edge of the Tuchler Heide (Bory Tucholskie), present day Chojnice (Könitz) and Tuchola (Tuchel), Kościerzyna, Bytów (Bütow), Wejherowo and Puck (Putzig). The more fertile areas of farmland along the coast had long since been taken over by German farmers. The Kaszubes were smallholders, farm labourers, tradesmen, marketwomen or fishermen. Those that worked the land grew rye and potatoes, beetroot, blueberries, apples and cherries; they fattened pigs and kept large flocks of geese who were indifferent to the Pomeranian damp.

The Kaszubes had not been interested in the fate of Poland at the time of the partitions, and had been reasonably well satisfied by early Prussian rule. Later, as the Prussians revoked statutes governing the activity of the Jews and laws preventing usury, the Kaszubian farmers began to find themselves heavily in debt. As Frederick's policies turned into those of Bismarck's *Kulturkampf*, the Catholic Kaszubians found further cause for alarm. Their fears were not allayed by restrictions on the Polish language, since the Prussians made no distinctions between Kaszubian and Polish. In the 1890s the Kaszubians emerged from the fog of feudal serfdom and manorial labour. For them it was only very slowly that seasonal and migratory work was replaced by the idea of emigration to Canada or America. As the Poles organised themselves to combat the increasingly virulent Germanisation policies of the new German Reich, so cash flowed into the newly created and increasingly efficient Polish Land Banks. With financial backing the Poles were able to compete very favourably with the Prussian Colonisation Commission for Kaszubian land. As a result of Kaszubian naivety Polish land-dealers and banks were able to buy up 35,000 acres of Kaszubian-owned land in the years 1896–1905. Prussian law made it almost impossible for the Kaszubians who wanted to expand their holdings to do so by buying land from Germans. Kaszubian farmers felt that they could never raise enough money to compete with both the Poles and the Prussian Colonisation Commission for good quality land, and thus stood no real chance of ever turning their smallholdings into profitable concerns.

The Kaszubians came under strong pressure to Germanise under Frederick the Great, and again under Wilhelm II in the early years of the Reich. However, it took them a long time to see an ally in the Poles. Since the Kaszubes lacked any political organisation or ambition and had no recognition for their language, hardly any literature of their own and barely any sense of a common

Kaszubian identity, the Poles thought of the Kaszubians as a joke and paid them little heed. It came as something of a shock to the Poles to realise that the Kaszubians saw no difference between selling their land to a Pole or selling it to a German. Increasing pressure over Germanisation policies probably prevented any real unpleasantness between the Poles and Kaszubians, however. Hieronym Dudowski, that rare creature, a Kaszubian poet, doubtless caused much scratching of heads when he coined his slogan 'No Kaszubia without Poland – No Poland without Kaszubia', but slowly the Kaszubians did come to see their own survival as lying in the resurrection of an independent Poland rather than in the straightjacket of Prussian–German citizenship.

For the Kaszubes released from the land anchor of serfdom or property at the end of the nineteenth century, the natural focus of population drift was neither Berlin nor Warsaw, but Danzig. Their increasing presence in the city was signalled by the congregation of small traders and migrant vendors on the square between the Stadt Archiv and the main Railway Station, and in time the square became known as the Kassubischer Markt. Pomerania was still experiencing the flight from the land into the cities over 40 years after its main impact in the rest of Europe, and it was only in the years 1925–33 that the mainly German-speaking Pomeranian towns of Lauenburg, Bütow, Rummelsburg, Neustettin, Belgard, Kolberg, Köslin and Stolp expanded with the absorption of country dwellers. Danzig too was affected and by 1880 its population had risen to 109,000.[24]

In the years after the partition of Poland Pomerania had become increasingly divorced from the bulk of the Polish population; the policies of Germanisation and of steady cultural absorption had done their work. Even if the Prussian Colonisation Commission had failed to drive the Poles out entirely, many of the old Slav survivors of the original settlement of Pomerania had been drawn into the German language orbit. In 1750, although Pomeranian Słupsk had already become German Stolp, it had been possible to say that east of a line drawn from the tiny Pomeranian fishing hamlet of Rowy to the hamlet of Tuchomie, Polish or various Slav dialects were spoken. By 1830 the line of the *Slawische Sprachgrenze* or 'Slav speech border' had been pushed further east: Rowy had become Rowe, Lębork had become Lauenberg, the Łupawa river had become the Lupow. By 1850 Smołdzino had become Schmolsin, Łeba had become Leba, Wierzuchino had become Wierschutzin, Sasino had become Sarbskie.[25]

By 1910 Danzig had a population of about 175,000. The Danzig administrative district had a total population of 315,281 Germans, 9,491 Poles, 2,124 Kaszubes and 3,021 assorted bilingual and other peoples. In Danzig and the eastern parts of Pomerania combined, the population consisted of 919,102 Germans, 555,337 Poles, 106,598 Kaszubes and 20,456 bilingual and other peoples. Detailed analysis of the 1910 Prussian census returns and the 1911 survey of primary schools shows, however, that there were huge differences in the location and concentration of Poles and Germans. Danzig's northern and western districts had as high as 60–100 per cent Polish population, while south of the city the numbers fell to between 10 and 15 per cent. To the east of the city and across the Vistula delta the number of Poles fell to between 0.5 and 10 per cent. Eastern Pomerania, however, the area that was eventually to become the Polish Corridor was 60–100 per cent Polish, while the Pomeranian districts of Lębork and Słupsk were by this time only 0.5–10 per cent Polish. Western Pomerania had become almost entirely Germanised, and had a Polish population of less than 0.5 per cent.[26]

It was inevitable that the confrontation between industrial and rural cultures, German and Polish languages, between folk and high cultures, between distinct religious, social and political allegiances should produce envy, suspicion and even malice. Yet in Pomerania the Poles and most of the native Germans had come to accept the intermingling as perfectly natural and of no special significance. German and Polish peasants and farmers lived side by side without producing unendurable national conflict within their communities, without producing enduring hatreds. The real pressures on these people were not racial but political, and their real struggle was almost entirely economic. Yet even the economic tensions that existed in the villages around Danzig failed to produce results that showed any real or clear-cut and intrinsically national difference in their impact on one group as opposed to another, and failed to polarise Germans and Poles in any clear-cut political or national sense. The German middle classes and the German Catholics in particular knew that the Prussian Poles were no great threat to the state, yet in spite of their protests, the Junker-dominated Government found it essential to work through crude Völkisch opinion to maintain itself and divert the impending revolution. The growth of German industry, the flight from the land, the *Ostflucht* and the ending of serfdom had all broken the bonds of the Prussian feudal system; had caused a massive upheaval in terms of social and geographical mobility; had caused a radical change and development in German class- and national consciousness, and had created problems of identity deep within the German consciousness, precisely because they took place much later than in the west European nations. Germany's position on the developmental 'gap' between East and West Europe, between the feudal and industrial worlds, meant that Germany was subject to fear of Western competition and envy of Western colonial markets; the proximity of poorly developed lands to the East gave Germany the opportunity to rectify its lack of colonial holdings and to sink its internal problems in external conquest.

To the Colonisation Commission and its supporters the start of the First World War offered a solution to all their problems. Here at last was the opportunity for almost unlimited eastward expansion. Following the seizure of the Russian section of partitioned Poland in 1916 and the creation by the Germans of a new 'Polish state' based on the old Congress Kingdom of Poland, it was suggested that the entire Polish population of Prussia and Silesia should be expelled into this new satellite state, and that Germany should then repopulate its borders with colonists from the western districts, with recalled settlers from Russia, the Ukraine, Hungary and Romania. Only the threat of revolution and the defeat of Germany prevented the plan from being put into action, but it was a plan that was to surface again under the Nazis.

There can be little doubt that if the Prussians had not diverted social and economic pressure into anti-Semitic and anti-Polish fears along the eastern borders, the pressures of industrialisation, democracy and socialist thought would have clashed with the government's determination to support the Junkers and with the Junkers' manipulation of Völkisch opinion. It was an impossible balancing act: the Junkers were after industry and a highly developed industrial working class without democracy or social revolution and without any devolution of ancient privilege. It was a balancing act that could only be accomplished by constant recourse to the 'threat' of communist revolution, the economic power of the Jewish presence and the racial and nationalist danger of the inferior Poles. Yet the Germans, by their insensitivity in these matters, actually created the very spectres they sought to exorcise; they conjured a growing Polish national feeling where virtually none had existed before. The failure to find trade outlets in a world dominated by the French, British, Belgian and Dutch colonial holdings led Germany to penetrate the Slav east – the Balkans in particular – but there, as in Prussia, they did no more than provoke Slav nationalism. After the defeat of 1918 the policies of Frederick, Bismarck and Wilhelm II were to be taken up and extended quite logically; the search for identity, for colonial holdings, the logic of industrial expansion, the 'question' of the eastern marches would all be solved and resolved in the *Endlösung*. This 'Final Solution' of Germany's problems was to harness German industrial power to a regressive, atavistic and murderous renewal of the drive to the east under Adolf Hitler and the Nazi Party.

4
Polenpolitik und Kulturkampf

Nationalism, like capitalism, is the very bedrock of European organisation: nationalism of one sort or another constitutes the building blocks for the construction of markets, the creation of transport networks, tariff barriers, for banking systems, for economies of scale in industry and business, for defining which internal and which external markets are to exploited and to what degree. The obsession with homogeneous populations and monocultural, monolingual societies has been a feature of life only since capitalist economics forced a uniformity of workforces and markets. For the most part, when Europe was a collection of city states, dukedoms and principalities, these societies were far from uniform in their language, dialect and religion. While the phenomenon of the unitary state is relatively recent, in Eastern Europe, where the process of industrialisation and capitalist organisation arrived late, the surviving multicultural and multilingual societies were purged and simplified very late and with all the vigour that technology could muster.

It is difficult to divorce the changes taking place in the fabric of Danzig's social and political life from the wider application of Prussian policies in the eastern marches. Indeed the changes wrought by the Prussians were to have enormous consequences for the formation of nationalist opinion in the city after the First World War, and it is important to see the extent to which these policies provided the basis of German identity and political purpose in the east, and provoked the very Polish nationalist response they supposedly sought to suppress or prevent. If German anti-Semitism was the 'bastard child of the union between German nationalism and Christian anti-Semitism'[1] then it must also be said that German nationalism was the offspring of military ambition and industrialisation. German nationalism was very largely a search for a lost, elusive, mythical unity with which to bind up the German states in a re-animated, re-invented version of German history.

Napoleon's armies handled the Prussians very roughly every time they met, and at the battle of Jena in 1806 a whole series of

Prussian myths had evaporated in defeat. The Prussians lacked political, military and economic power against the might of revolutionary France. The rout of German self-opinion meant that while Britain, France, Holland and Belgium were busy shaking off the last vestiges of feudal restraint in order to industrialise, the Prussian reaction to defeat was to define their contribution to the world as *Kultur* – a commodity that was best seen as the absence of change. Progress was defined as the continued existence of a lack of change, and as far as the Junker lords were concerned the variety of civilisation represented by Western European societies was conspicuous for the absence of specifically German *Kultur*. Nevertheless, Napoleon's victories over the Prussians meant that the German states were opened up to foreign and revolutionary influences.

Napoleon simplified the great patchwork quilt of minor German states and principalities, swallowed up a series of Free Cities, abolished a series of Church states and pushed the Germans into modern Europe, whether they liked it or not. He also set about the forced emancipation of the Jews. By bringing within German identity a group that had traditionally been considered unalterably 'alien' he caused alarm and resentment against French interference in German affairs. French and Jewish 'influence' went hand in hand for many Germans and allowed Völkisch opinion on the matter to flourish: slowly but surely the word Völk came to mean not simply 'people', but also 'populist', and to imply a sense of common identity and of racial superiority over those peoples who needed the French to emancipate them.

In spite of their divided, defeated and reactionary *Kultur*, the Germans came to see themselves as people who needed no emancipation. With the defeat of Napoleon the German states reversed emancipation of the Jews. Only in Prussia and the eastern border districts was the emancipation not revoked for the simple reason that the Junkers needed the Jews to operate between the Prussian nobles and the German peasants, and as go-betweens for the Prussian Poles. With such a poorly developed social structure the Jews were very important to Prussian Poland: without their skills Prussian society could not hope to make *Ost-Elbian* society more hospitable and attractive to settlers and could hardly hope to persuade the border Poles to become Germans.

Many observers supposed that the outbreak of the French Revolution in 1789 would force the Junkers to embark on a programme of liberalisation and reform lest they should find themselves facing a similar threat. However, the Junkers, instead of facing up to the industrial, economic and social changes that were sweeping Europe, preferred instead to set about the ruthless suppression of any and every gesture of sympathy for the French revolutionaries, and they took military action against the few tiny peeps of protest that emanated from Pomerania. In 1848 Prussian peasants rose up to put an end to serfdom and to pledges of service to their landlords. Engels believed that the 'callous, narrow-minded and conceited' Junkers had learned from the French Revolution that the system they maintained was doomed, but in reality the Junkers crushed the rising and insisted on 'service' until an agricultural review had been conducted in 1865 – after which they abandoned serfdom with great reluctance.[2]

As Antonio Gramsci pointed out, the movement of 1848 failed because of the scanty bourgeois concentration in Germany, and also because the question of the renewal of the state was intertwined with the reaction to the national question. In the years that followed, the German bourgeoisie gained considerable economic and industrial power, but did not struggle against the Junkers since they regarded them as the very backbone of German society; the Junkers, even though they were already 'pensioners of economic history'[3] were a convenient rallying point for Völkisch opinion and as such had no particular reason to adapt to the changing economic structure of Europe or Germany. Instead they acted as a brake on German economic power by milking the state of subsidy as if it had been set up for that purpose alone.

Prussian reaction to the French Revolution and the advent of modernity was a headlong flight into the past, and an expression of firm resistance to the new order. In Pomerania this reaction took the form of an even tighter grip on the feudal peasantry and serfs of the great estates. Engels was at a loss to explain the Junker refusal to accept that after the French Revolution they could never again command the total obedience and respect they had once enjoyed from a cowed and illiterate peasantry. Junker resistance to the abolition of serfdom, their mistrust of the new powers of industry and their blank incomprehension when faced with the idea that their estates could be run more profitably on other than feudal lines set them on a course that was to have a profound impact on German history.

The failure of the Prussian and German people to follow the successful example of the French in a revolution from below meant that in 1870 they were forced to accept the unification of Germany by the reactionary Junker powers. That is, a revolution from above, a revolution guided not by the ambition of the bulk of the population, but by the interests of the landed aristocracy and the military. The unification of Germany protected the lifestyle of

the Prussian Junkers – indeed, the Junkers' need to protect themselves and their lifestyle from the disrupting effects of outside
economic competition through the creation and extension of a
tariff union had been one of the major components in the formation of the German state. The Junkers, by leading the German
unification, were able to enshrine their own position. They made
deals with heavy industry and government to extract huge subsidies to maintain their outmoded and inefficient estates and they
gained tariff protection for their expensive and inefficiently produced foodstuffs. The Junkers also set about diverting social
pressures that emerged from the spread of industrial and urban
society and the creation of national identity away from socialist
revolutionary solutions into naval and military expansion, anti-
socialism, and the manufacture of a threat from the east that justified the maintenance of traditional German life – a life that was,
of course, best represented in the continued existence of the
Junkers. Eventually these ideas coalesced into the belief that
Germany's rise as a new state and as an industrial power was being
hampered by uncertainty over the unreliable national loyalties of
the Slav peoples in the east, by the back-stabbing machinations of
the Jews inside Germany, and by the threat of communism that
came in both Slav and Jewish forms.

Vested interests in Germany saw only what they wanted to see:
namely that the Junkers were the traditional political and military
leaders of German society, that they had brought about German
unification and that this would make Germany into an industrial
power of the first order. The Junkers engineered the belief that any
attempt to ditch them would leave Germany prey to communist
take-over, to Jewish exploitation and subversion, and to a flood of
Slav immigrants. In a blatant lie the Junkers argued that their
massive estates were vital to the German economy and to the
country's ability to support itself. Yet the Junkers did not have
things all their own way. The growth of political parties and pressure groups meant that there was a non-socialist, non-
revolutionary challenge to their power.

The German urban commercial and industrial middle classes,
unlike the rural peasantry, were far from being the cowed, feudal
illiterates that the Junkers would have liked them to be. Yet to a
large extent it was a question of symbiosis. The Junkers tolerated
the troublesome middle classes only because they guaranteed the
Junkers their place in German society; the middle classes looked
up to the Junker traditional leadership, and regarded them as the
German image of itself. The Junker tradition gave Germany direct
contact with its historical purpose and its ancient drives. For their

part the urban middle classes tolerated the Junkers because they guaranteed the shape, content and continuance of German middle-class life and ambition over the vast bulk of the rural German population. Both the Junkers and the German middle classes created a focus for their ambition and discontent. That focus lay outside Germany and outside their own class. Together the Junkers and the middle classes located the cause of their anxieties about Germany, their reaction to industrialisation and problems with the formation of national identity as lying outside German nationality, in the threat to German nationality.[4]

The defeat of Napoleon left Germany with a problem half solved. The German states were aware of the need for change, but found that no matter how they tried, the better organised markets of Western Europe were very hard to penetrate. The successive wars between the German states and France might be seen as the result of increasing German frustration over failed attempts to reach these markets. In most of the West European colonial powers the alliance between mob and capital to form a bridge between nationalism and racism worked to ship internal pressures abroad to the colonies. The colonies in turn acted as a buffer in the ups and downs of trade. Germany, however, had no such outlet or buffer. The connection between racism and nationalism had no such outlet simply because Germany had no successful colonial holdings. The comparative lateness of German industrial-isation meant that German capital had neither outlets in the colonies nor a slave trade to generate the further capital necessary to finance industrial development. Increasingly, as penetration of the West European markets on any large scale failed to materialise, the German states looked eastwards to the less socially advanced, less well-organised societies along their borders. The German states in the years before the formation of the Reich sold largely to one another, and this brought pressure to bear on 'unfair' Jewish trade. The eastern marches were seen as a means by which internal German social and economic pressure could be relieved, where economic expansion was far more feasible than competi-tion with France and Britain. The Jews of Poland in particular were to absorb the shock of the German economic drive to the east since it was often conducted by emancipated German Jews – and this in turn fostered Polish anti-Semitism. That the Polish Jews were socially, politically and economically quite distinct from German Jews only made the business easier, since the two groups were at loggerheads with each other.

Increasing pressure on the Poles to Germanise themselves, and the corresponding Polish reaction in both compliance and defiance, were all part of the impact of capitalist industrial organisation as it spread from the first comers of Western Europe, to the second rank of industrialising nations – to Germany, Japan and Italy in particular – and through them to their potential empires and marcher territories. Industrialisation, the foundation of the German state and the growth of national identity were all closely linked. For all the surface change that accompanied the industrialisation of Prussian and German society the social and political pressures that emanated from the Junkers on these issues remained uniform and constant.

The Prussian Poles had little chance to exploit any crisis in Prussian affairs. The uprising of 1848 gave them an opportunity to alter their status, but they did not take it and by and large seem to have accepted that industrialisation meant inevitable Germanisation. However, the Junkers, military, civil service and politicians chose to react to the Polish uprisings of 1830, 1846, 1848, 1863 and 1905 – which took place in the Russian and Austrian sectors – by seeing, not a social and political movement that harked back to French revolutionary practice, and which aimed only in part at the restoration of the Polish state, but a Polish threat to Prussian and German identity. The Junkers determined to suppress political protest by reference to a mysterious external enemy whose nationals – ungrateful wretches! – were to be found on Prussian and German soil.

The suppression and control of internal and external enemies became a useful safety valve for German society, but in practice there was little in the way of a genuine Polish threat for the Prussians to fear. The Poles of the Prussian marches had been under pressure to Germanise themselves for centuries. Partition had cut off the Pomeranian Poles from the areas of Poland that might have sustained a more confident sense of Polish national identity. There can be little doubt that if the Prussians and Germans had not attempted to force them to become Germans, then in time the Pomeranian Poles and probably the majority of Prussian Poles would have allowed themselves to become Germanised. Germany was too desperate about its own sense of identity and too bound up in attempting false solutions to its internal problems to realise this.

The flight of large numbers from the German east to the increasingly industrialised western districts revealed, for those willing to see, the entrenched problems of the Prussian eastern marches. Without industry and rapid social development, the eastern lands were simply too unattractive and severe to Germanise with any ease. The Prussians could not industrialise the east because local commerce did not generate profits large enough to finance industrial investment, and because local agriculture could not support the bulk of the population at more than subsistence level. Increased agricultural production was only possible by using intensive farming methods, rather than the traditional method of leaving fields fallow one year in three. Yet it was clear that intensive farming was not possible on the poor Pomeranian soil. The Prussian government could have forced agricultural change by opening up its borders to competition from cheap Russian grain, thus undercutting the Junkers and forcing them to modernise and/or change over to dairy farming. The Junkers, predictably, wanted none of this and their interests in the government, civil service and the military persuaded the government to continue shoring up the ailing *Ost-Elbian* estate system through continued tariff protection, artificially high grain prices and a policy of grants and loans.

After 1870 the German Reich, dominated by Prussia, proved equally incapable of cutting subsidy to the Junkers. It must have been clear to the Prussian government that if it had not been for government subsidy the Junker estates would have collapsed under their own weight long ago, but they were nevertheless incapable of striking at what they saw to be the basis and guarantor of their state and society. Instead, as officials realised that the failure of agriculture, the failure to industrialise and the continuing *Ostflucht* were combining to produce a massive crisis in the east, they cast around for an external enemy on whom to project the cause of their misfortune. German officials decided that the Poles of Pomerania, Posen, East Prussia, West Prussia and Silesia should all be Germanised. Rather than face the revolution that was simmering under the surface of German political life, they were more than happy to divert attention away from the real cause of the problems in the east and to let the Poles appear to be the troublemakers. Indeed, after 1870, under the new administration of a united Germany, there was a sudden and remarkable intensification of the struggle against the Poles of the border districts. The success of German industry in the west only made the people in the east more desperate and paranoid.

The period 1860–90 was crucial for Germany: as the German state emerged and the German self-image was formed, Prussia–Germany went through a chaotic period of social and economic transformation: a boom in canal and railway building, in the steel industry, in banking, engineering, scientific research and in developing industrial techniques had been accompanied by a war with France; this was followed by a slump, financial collapse and a steady move to the right in political thinking. Bismarck, who had relied upon liberal support to create the Reich, now moved towards despotic absolutism, insisting on the centrality of the Junkers, the *Kulturkampf* against Catholicism and the unnecessarily aggressive *Polenpolitik*. Kaiser Wilhelm II came to the throne in 1888 and, after forcing the ageing Chancellor to retire, took his belligerence several steps further by bolstering the German military, by promoting the growth of pan-Germanism and by demoting and suppressing the voice and interests of the non-German peoples within the borders of the Reich. The German middle classes had lost heavily in the slump that followed the Franco–Prussian war, and many, ruined by the collapse, now looked to the Junkers to restore their standing. Lower-ranking civil servants, small farmers, craftsmen, independent traders and small businessmen all feared that the growth of German cities and the development of foreign trade and heavy industry would somehow undermine traditional German values, and would render them homeless and jobless. Völkisch opinion on these subjects came increasingly to the fore with simplistic solutions that fitted in well with the Junker status quo. It became far easier to identify Jews, communists and Poles as the cause of their misery.

In the closing years of the nineteenth century, just as the eastern Germans were leaving the land and deserting the east, at the very time that the Polish population of the border districts was on the rise, the theoretical and practical policies of both the *Polenpolitik* and the *Kulturkampf* were hardening around the drive towards industrial and imperial expansion – if not overseas, which was almost impossible – then in the eastern borderlands. It was by no means a simple set of feelings: many longed for the straightforward solutions that apparently lay in the golden-age reign of the Emperor Charlemagne when unity, conquest and expansion to the east had surely indicated racial superiority. Many looked to the new Germany to recover the supposed certainties of a pre-industrial superiority. In part the German obsession with woods, forests and mountains was a sentimental reaction against urbanisation, harking back to a restless, tribal existence. Yet to a very large extent German efforts were contradictory: Völkisch opinion wished Germany to remain as it was and yet somehow to return to the past; they wanted to return to the past yet at the same time wished for the power to behave as they pleased. Only the military power conferred by industry could help them do this. Industry was seen as both the cause of German distress and Germany's salvation.

Germany, hampered by its tardy arrival at nation-statehood, had begun to industrialise early, but still in general rather later than Britain and France. Although Germany had steel mills as early as the 1780s and a railway line by 1847, it was still able to learn from the mistakes and avoid the dead-ends of its competitor neighbours. In 1872 Britain, caught up in the complacency of overseas empire, had only 12 students reading for the Natural Sciences Tripos at Cambridge, while Germany already had 11 technical universities. In Britain government finance for schools and universities did not become available – and then only in piffling amounts – until 1890. The Prussian government's minister of finance, Peter Beuth, had been forced to offer subsidy to encourage industry in the years 1818–45, when it was realised that the kind of large-scale enterprise that Prussia would need to enter the international market was already beyond the pocket of most individuals, and beyond the imagination of the Junkers, who might have supplied finance if their estates had been more productive.

By the 1840s the Bank of Prussia – which was to become the central bank for the expanding joint-stock and credit banking system – had been established with capital of over 11 million thalers. Through this bank the Prussian government controlled investment, trade and the issue of paper money. By the 1870s, when it became clear that very little investment capital was going to flow from private sources or joint-stock ventures, and that the German people as a whole now viewed the development of the economy as part of the business of creating a strong and unified Reich, the Bank of Prussia became essential to all major German long-term investment plans. Because the development of the economy was bound up with the growth of the nation, Germany was far more tolerant than Britain, France or the US of monopoly capital, of government subsidy, and of cartels. German business ventures were, from the very start, far more closely tied to an efficient funding system and to government policy than in most other industrialised European countries. In Germany this proximity was seen to be entirely natural.

Building on the old Prussian foundations, the Reich set out to break into the world coal and steel markets. Unlike her major competitors, however, Germany lacked both a well-developed economic hinterland for agricultural and commercial support, and helpful overseas colonies. For the most part the cosy partners of Atlantic Trade saw German industrialisation as a hugely disruptive affair. America, already tied to markets in Britain, France and Scandinavia, saw the rising tide of German manufacture as a threat to its own burgeoning industries, and in 1897 raised a tariff barrier against German coal, steel, iron and textiles. In spite of this

German industry expanded rapidly: between 1870 and 1913 the UK economy was growing at an annual rate of about 2.2 per cent; the French economy at 2.6 per cent; the US economy at 3.2 per cent; and the German economy at a staggering 4.3 per cent.[5]

Precisely because it lacked access to captive overseas markets for cheap raw materials and for the sale of manufactured goods, the German economy had been forced into developing high-quality competitive produce for cut-throat international markets. The combination of modern production methods, the application of modern accounting and business practice, the rapid growth of a disciplined industrial workforce, coupled with huge state subsidy, produced staggering results. Although company policy, especially among the larger cartels, was seen as politically neutral, in practice the links between German business and political life were very close indeed. Unlike Britain and France, where profits were leaked abroad to colonial landholdings and estates, and where profits did not automatically become industrial investments, Germany had been forced to embark on a series of massive and successive re-investment programmes and re-equipment drives. The French were sufficiently worried by the rapidity of German industrialisation and by the quality of their wares that by the 1890s they had begun to invest in Russian railways, coal, steel and textiles as a way of controlling and reducing German competition. In the years 1860–1913 German coal production leapt from a mere 17 million tons to 277 million tons. German iron and steel production in the same period went from 2.1 million tons in the 1870s to 30 million tons by 1913.[6]

For many observers it was as if German industry sprang out of nowhere. By 1914 Germany had established a massive lead over Britain in traction and diesel engineering, in dye manufacture, motor engines, mining technology and in optics. Yet while monopoly capital and government subsidy played a large part in this rise, it is important to set this development against the total picture of German industrial effort. Germany, though it produced massive quantities of coal, steel and iron, was still a very backward place. While Germany as a whole might well be described as a capitalist state with feudal trimmings, Pomerania and the long arm of East Prussia remained feudal with modest capitalist trimmings. More than a third of the German population lived on the land, the east was still dominated by the huge Junker estates and the south by the highly conservative small- and middle-scale farmers and their labourers. Of the 11 million German workers less than 1.5 million worked in enterprises employing more than 1,000 people. However, the new cartels were growing rapidly. In 1900 in the Ruhr town of Hamborn, three enterprises between them employed 10,000 people; by 1913 these same enterprises employed 30,000.[7] German industry was seen to be a major threat to the European powers and to established patterns of Atlantic trade.

But where could the new, economically powerful Germany find outlets for its production? The Far East, US, and European markets were very difficult to penetrate. German industrial expansion was forced to cultivate markets elsewhere. With no history of effective colonial rule or overseas empire building, German efforts at slave trading and colonialism in Africa proved an unmitigated disaster with whole stretches of Africa laid waste and depopulated. They turned increasingly to those areas where the British and the French had not made much progress: to the Balkans, Turkey and South America. In the Balkans the arrival of capitalist modes of production as the gift of foreign nationals provoked – just as they had in Poland – a rise in Bosnian and Serbian nationalism. Balkan aggression was directed at the Germans and Austrians for much the same reason that Polish nationalism was directed against the partitioning powers, but unlike the Poles, the Serbians and Bosnians were supported by the Russians.

The long history of contempt for the Poles fostered by the Prussians was given greater depth when, as a result of German defeat in 1918, Poland – against all the odds – was revived. What had previously been a safety valve for German economic change now assumed the aspect of a threat to an already shaken German identity and sense of purpose in the world.

The paraphernalia of capitalism – the banks, mortgages, money-lenders, credit, exchange rates, inflation, Jewish competition, Polish labour – these were all things that German small business had learned to fear and mistrust as its economy had, without the buffer of empire, ridden the rollercoaster of boom and slump between the Franco–Prussian wars and the Great War. If these were things that could not be fully understood or controlled, then they were all the more menacing because they could not be avoided. It is true that Germany between the wars spawned industrial giants like IG Farben (founded in 1925), which had interests in metals, chemicals, coal, explosives, film, pharmaceuticals, armaments and synthetic fibres, and which with 120,000 workers, 50 subsidiaries and more than 100 factories was the world's fourth largest industrial combine. However, it was to the small farmer and small businessman, the very people who had failed to colonise the east, individuals who felt themselves beset by Poles, Jews and communists in ways they could not articulate, that the

Nazis were to make their main appeal. The limitations of this class were clear: they were the opportunists whose sense of failure and sense of grievance could be nicely manipulated through their sense of German identity and nationalism. These were the people most at risk from foreign agricultural policies, the failure of banks, under-capitalisation, the closure of foreign trade, tariff barriers and a whole range of xenophobic fears. The SS and the other security services became the cutting edge of German racial and economic policies, but only, as it were, on licence from the middle and lower-middle classes who stood to gain by their activities. For thoroughly understandable reasons, however, it was not to these people that Hitler turned for his image of the German: he did not want the average German for the SS, he wanted supermen for the conquest of the east.

Militarisation worked for the Nazis as it had for the Prussians in that it helped control large numbers of people, allowed a cheap and easy growth of populist emotion and nationalist identity and became the mainspring of industry by providing demand. It satisfied business by backing competition with force.[8] However, in terms of the logic of German society there was only one direction in which that force could go. The vertical and the horizontal structures of Germany were locked into a system of finance, into a particular sense of 'Kultur' and the drive to expand eastwards, that were all connected with the development of industry and the logic of capitalist modes of production.

In 1886 Paul de Lagarde, a leading Völkisch theoretician who was already disillusioned with the idea of a Reich dominated by the Junkers and an industrial bourgeoisie, wrote:

> The Russians should have the courtesy to move over for some miles into middle Asia, where there is an abundance of space that lies close to them but far from us: let Russia give us sufficient coast on the Black Sea so that, from there we can resettle our beggars and peasants in Asia Minor ... We need land at our doorstep ... if Russia does not want to give it to us, she will force us to undertake an expropriation proceeding, i.e. a war, for which we have long stored up the reasons ... The land we have to take from Russia, whether she is willing or not, must be large enough to allow us to resettle, in Bessarabia or northwest of there, all the Rumanians now living in Austria and Turkey (minus Rumanian Jews, who together with those of Poland, Russia and Austria, should be packed off to Palestine, or better yet, to Madagascar) ... The Germans are a peaceful people, but they have a right to live, and to live as Germans, and they are convinced of the fact that they have a mission for all the nations of the earth; if one hinders them from fulfilling their mission then they have the right to use force.[9]

De Lagarde's work is clearly a product of the mentality created by the eastern marches. The bulk of his writing appeared in the 1870s but enjoyed a revival in the 1890s, mainly because of its open display of virulently anti-Semitic and anti-Polish attitudes. By policing the mental and the physical borders of the newly formed Germany the Völkisch ideologists wanted to create a new and pure German identity. De Lagarde wanted to restore Germany to 'unity'. The unity he had in mind was, ironically, that which had existed before Germany became a nation-state, the unity of the disunited rainbow of German states and principalities, the state of unity when Jews were legally inferior to Germans, when Poles were not a numerical threat, when expansion to the east had been easy, when the German people had not been a rising industrial power, when the massed levy of conscripts had been enough to rout their opponents. That all this was long gone and impossible to recover, except through industrialisation, social change and arduous struggle with a resilient and increasingly nationalist foe only made life in the eastern borders even more frustrating.

The eastern solution to Germany's problems was to create an area of unified language, unified identity, unified wealth and settlement, a bulwark against the barbarism and poverty of the Poles. Yet all this was a direct response to the same basic insecurity that drove the German people to support Völkisch opinion and later to support Hitler. Eventually National Socialism, which was deeply rooted in this national complex, was felt to be a way of withstanding the impact of unfettered foreign capitalism on German society, a way of organising the country's own resources and of competing on more equitable terms – by force where necessary. Also, as West European capitalism filtered across Germany and set in motion the inevitable homogenisation of markets and language within the customs union, the reaction of the Polish subject people, who were after all not the primary, nor even secondary, beneficiaries of capitalist modes of production and the spread of profit, and who had behind them a different set of cultural and political orientations, was similar to that of the Germans.

As Germany was to use state finance to a remarkable degree in launching German industry, so in the 1920s and 1930s Poles working through the Bank Polski were to use state finance derived from France to build their own industrial projects like the new port at Gdynia. The rise of Polish nationalism merely confirmed German opinion. The Germans could never imagine that they had provoked the Poles, and yet by German standards Polish nationalism was a remarkably mild affair. Haketa and the rest worried that the Prussian Poles were disloyal to the Prussian state, yet the

Germans' behaviour more or less guaranteed Polish disaffection. Even so, open hostility towards Prussia or the German state was largely absent from Polish public pronouncements. For all the fears of a Polish revolt, it is worth emphasising just how moderate and tractable the Poles of Prussia were for most of the nineteenth century: they did not rise up in 1815, nor in 1848, nor in 1863, nor during the Franco–Prussian Wars, nor even during the 1914–18 war. Between 1871 and 1907 there is not one recorded case of a Prussian Pole being convicted of treason or anti-state activity.

In its many pamphlets the Pan-German League habitually referred to the Germans as the *Herrenvolk*, the master race. Opinion such as this was well established long before Hitler rose to power and there can be little doubt that Germanisation was one of the many items of baggage the Prussians left behind for the Nazis to snatch. The ideology of Hitler and his cronies derived from a long history of pseudo-philosophical state thuggery. It was a tradition that avoided any real contemplation of the root causes of German unease; their preference for 'action', rested secure in the knowledge that everything they did was for the good of the nation, sanctioned by law and sanctioned by the German people.

After the defeat of 1918 the conservative German government lost ground to the legatees of the Haketa, the Colonisation Commission and the Pan-German League. Both Haketa and the NSDAP sought to resolve and dissolve the internal German class and social conflicts brought about by attempting to maintain a feudal nobility and at the same time to industrialise a newly formed country by projecting their energy into false imperialist and colonial solutions in their eastern borderlands. The inter-war German democracy was precarious precisely because it was grafted on to a social order that had failed to create the very basic social and political conditions that would allow a democratic system to flourish, but also because while German expansion in the east had been halted, the drive to the east was still seen as a tantalising solution to all of Germany's problems. In 1918 the Western Allies had neither accepted nor totally crushed German economic competition: instead they had pushed it back in on itself like some kind of demonic and lethal jack-in-the-box. Worse, by stripping Germany of much of its industrial wealth, its merchant fleet and its colonial possessions; and by resurrecting Poland, and making inroads into the German sense of security over Danzig and the Polish Corridor, they gave further cause for grievance and hardened the most unpleasant facets of the German identity fostered by the marcher lands.

There can be little doubt that Hitler's conquests were ideologically bankrupt, but they were built on a profound understanding and wilful exploitation of German fears and ambitions. Germany between the wars felt a sharpening of the internal contradictions by which it lived, but it is doubtful that the people concerned ever had a clear understanding of what was happening because the tensions were buried deep within the very fabric of the Reich and because the form and pattern of struggles that resulted from these tensions were always far removed from the real heart of the matter.

Hitler's idea of *Lebensraum*, living space, though derived from the ideas of an earlier period, was in practice total nonsense. The *Drang nach Osten*, or drive to the east, so beloved of Nazi propagandists was a fiction maintained in the face of scientific evidence to the contrary. The Teutonic Knights had indeed penetrated eastwards, but their influence, when it was not military, had been to spread a lifestyle and set of material, cultural and linguistic bearings rather than set in motion the bodily removal and resettlement of vast numbers of Germans. If anything, by the end of the nineteenth century it was the expanding Polish population of the partition areas that needed living space, and the German *Ostflucht* might well have given it to them had it not been that Germany desperately needed to maintain the spluttering fiction of the drive to the east to divert and subvert internal political pressures.

The logic of German attitudes to the east was very much that outlined by Rosa Luxemburg:

> The historical process of the accumulation of capital depends in all its aspects upon the existence of non-capitalist social strata ... Imperialism is the political expression of the accumulation of capital in its competition for the possession of the remainder of the non-capitalist world.[10]

Hitler's solutions were an extension of this capitalist logic working through National Socialist mechanisms: he bodied forth the traditional Prussian remedy for all ills, but pressurised and extended by Versailles, backed up by industrial technology. It was a set of problems that were problems to no-one but Germany, and the solutions were calculated to satisfy no-one but Germany. The Poles were well aware that they had been classed as *Untermenschen*, or sub-humans, long before the Nuremberg Race Laws made it official. By 1945, German 'solutions' in the east had become so much a part of the German view of the world and 'German historic destiny' that the Russians and the Poles, who had played human safety-valve to German ambition throughout their long joint histories, saw dismemberment of German territory in the east as the only possible long-term solution.

*   *   *

To be isolated and relegated is ever likely to be the fate of those whose state authority falls prey to a stronger power. The dynamics of history are such that one nation's strength is another's weakness; nothing is constant; both strength and weakness may be part of some process as yet unrevealed. The only certainty is that those nations that are victorious will write what is later termed 'history', and will do it in such a way as to justify their actions. The inheritance of those on the losing side will be that of mistrust, and the peculiar scars, fears and obsessions that run through their later political and cultural life and which never disappear entirely, but reappear in constantly changing guises.

Poland had not been a particularly Polish entity before partition. Its lack of a well-developed indigenous middle class to act as a focus for a national identity meant that the failure of the nobility to resist partition was seen as exactly that: not a failure of the Polish people, but a failure of the Polish nobility. Poland had been penetrated with comparative ease by the partitioning military powers because its social structures made most of its population marginal in one way or another. The internal contradictions of Polish society were revealed by external invasion, and – particularly in Pomerania and Danzig – people who felt themselves to be marginal to Polish life either succumbed slowly and reluctantly or embraced the new identities on offer with enthusiasm. Some – particularly in the Polish heartlands around Warsaw and Kraków – reacted against the new identities. They reacted to the threat of absorption into the German scheme of things by clinging tenaciously to their Polish identity, often in direct proportion to the 'threat' they felt. Slowly, painstakingly, these people set about preserving and promoting Poland's folk-life, while attempting to assimilate Polish *szlachta* culture and cultural values for themselves.[11]

After the partitions Poland became invisible for over a century, its character dissolved, its history overlaid with that of the partitioning powers. For the most part the mechanisms of the growth of capitalism and the development of a lay state passed Poland by. Industrialisation took place on old Polish territories and involved Polish people, but it was conducted in someone else's name, and in general a generation after the rise of German industrial power. In Britain the railways began in the 1800s, in Germany in the

1840s, but in invisible Poland the railways were not so much a network as the far flung provincial extensions of three distant empires. It was only in the 1850s, while Prussia was 'filling in' the gaps of its network by connecting up places like Danzig, that Warsaw received its first major rail connections. The main effort of railway work in Poland came between 1880 and 1900 – considerably behind the bulk of Prussian rail building. In general this was the pattern for Polish industrialisation as a whole – a phenomenon that took place when there was the least chance of Poland ever regaining an independent existence.

Polish nationalism, like its artistic counterpart, Polish Romanticism, was a specific reaction to the material underdevelopment of partitioned Poland. The music of Chopin, the poetry of Mickiewicz – both produced in exile – and the paintings of Jan Matejko are all powerful emotional and political responses to the reality of life in a country whose people were denied their own forms of government, and whose culture was relegated to nothing more than a set of quaint country ways. Polish Romanticism differed from German Romanticism in the same way that German and Polish nationalism differed. In both cases the German provoked the Polish response. German Romanticism was a set of feelings and way of seeing the world, that reacted to and reflected on the fact that Germany was beginning to flex its intellectual and industrial muscle. With its longing for nature and the life of the spirit it reacted against industrialisation and the growth of capitalism. But German Romanticism could not sustain itself against the blandishments of urban existence, and as the nineteenth century progressed the movement lapsed into sentiment and kitsch – the absolute artistic opportunism that insisted on 'moving' people emotionally.[12]

This was the reverse face of German culture that underlay the barbaric treatment that Prussia and then Germany meted out to the peoples of the east. Germany's higher level of economic development allowed it to show a cultured and sophisticated face in the west. And, regarding itself as a cultured nation, the eastern bastion of civilisation, the bringer of culture to the poor benighted Slavs of the east, Germany conducted a *Kulturkampf* that was intended to destroy and subdue the peoples on its margins. The fact that parts of Poland were virtually indistinguishable from parts of Germany in terms of social complexity, levels of absolute poverty and economic success, that the Polish *szlachta* and the German Junker had more in common with each other than they did with either Berliners or Warsawians, that the average Polish and German smallholders and peasants had more in common with each other than they did with their social betters and political masters – all this meant nothing, except perhaps to make the Germans more convinced that the Poles would eventually drag them down to the Polish level of degradation. None of this dampened German feelings of superiority. If anything the proximity of a revived Poland after 1918 was to intensify German passions.

Polish nationalism and Polish Romanticism grew up hand in hand. Both were part of an urge to fight back, to resist, an urge to power and safety, an expression of identity forged under enormous pressure. In Polish Romantic art there was a frustrated urge to responsibility and national independence accompanied also by an indolence that grew out of the crushing knowledge that the resurrection of Poland would not arrive in the artist's lifetime. The Polish Romantics had no option but to celebrate the will to resist – no matter how compromised and battered – to celebrate the persistent and resilient folk ways of rural Poland. Rural Poland was the old, pre-partition Poland; anything that came after that was hardly Poland at all. The poet, playwright and painter, Stanisław Wyspiański (1869–1907), saw himself as the bridge over the confused gulf that separated the Polish intelligentsia and the peasantry, the perfect representative of the Young Poland movement that contained all the bitterness of repeated national defeats, all the resignation of patriots who felt they could change nothing, and all the compromised hopes for material change that the Positivists saw in Poland's potential industrial wealth under foreign rule. Wyspiański wrote: 'You could pay the wide world a visit / Watch it grow and grow / But Poland you'd never find.'[13] Alternating euphoria and despair, intense struggle and the depths of apathy are found in Chopin's piano music, which from exile in Paris celebrated Poland's folk music and at the same time elevated it to the role of a respectable and specifically bourgeois art form.

Polish nationalism, as Rosa Luxemburg pointed out to Lenin on several occasions, was unusual in that it was not primarily a bourgeois phenomenon, but rather a substitute for ideology taken over from the *szlachta* by the Polish peasantry as they and the lower ranks of the gentry coalesced to form an industrial working class and a commercial bourgeoisie.[14] An important component of Polish political life, and part of the damage wrought by partition, was the continuing failure to produce an ideology that went beyond the purely national to link the aspiration to exist as an independent nation with either capitalist organisation or a socialist vision of society. The search to find and restore the Polish state led Polish politicians to mistake the restoration of the state for a decision as to the social and political form the state should take. The highest goal was national rather than ideological.

Poland reappeared in 1918 with its wounds and hurts unbound, the pain of partition vivid and undimmed. Poland had been trapped in a time capsule, and try as it might to struggle free, the parameters of its political and spiritual life had been set firm for years to come by the humiliation of invisibility. Specifically Polish ways of looking at things – their fear of the Germans, contempt for the Russians, their intensely inward looking, ghetto-like literary culture, their almost unbounded and largely unfounded faith in the Catholic Church – are all manifestations of nationalism wrought by alien rule.

Poland emerged from the feudal soup of partition to the bright light of history and to the ongoing crisis of capitalism, which had apparently reached a peak in the horrors of the First World War. Yet most of the content of this crisis had passed Poland by: the Polish state had not been in existence. Poles had experienced the crisis as a series of personal events; they had not experienced it as a nation through institutions and organisations they saw as undeniably their own. The failures of capitalism were not Poland's failures. For all its efforts to make good the loss of over 100 years, Poland was not invited to join the club of industrialised nations. The Allies, having revived Poland as part of their anti-German strategy in 1918, had absolutely no intention of equipping Poland beyond what was strictly necessary to keep Germany occupied and at bay. Such French capital as Poland managed to secure was for specific projects like the new port at Gdynia – which was encouraged by the French to discomfort the Germans as much as to aid the Poles. Just as Britain and France had fought repeatedly to prevent German competition from developing, so Germany in its turn tried to restrict Polish economic growth and rivalry.

Part II
1918–1945

5
Danzig and Versailles

In 1918 the 47-year-old Reich created by Bismarck found itself in an increasingly difficult situation. The Reich's attempts at industrialisation had been contradicted by the effort to retain a semi-feudal social and political structure. At the same time the desire to catch up with more advanced industrial neighbours in Western Europe, to found an overseas empire and to break into the lucrative Atlantic Trade system had led Germany into conflict with the British and French. Its efforts to find new markets in the Balkans had provoked intense nationalist feeling among the smaller peoples of the region. With the assassination of the Archduke Ferdinand by a Serbian nationalist in Bosnia, Germany found itself at war with its trade competitors in the west, and at war with its nationalist rivals and its potential empire in the east.

Germany never had the slightest chance of winning a prolonged war on two fronts. As the military situation had deteriorated, so social and political unrest inside the Reich began to threaten a Russian-style socialist revolution. In case any such revolution should unseat its ruling class, the German leaders were prepared to cease hostilities against their external enemies in order to concentrate on defeating their internal enemies. For their part, the Allies were happy to see the Germans turn their aggression upon the revolutionary socialists. They feared lest Germany should become a socialist state and the revolution spread to France and Britain. The Germans negotiated an armistice and redirected their military effort at containing the German revolution.

It was not a decision that was understood or desired by all Germans. Adolf Hitler was at a military hospital in Pasewalk in Pomerania, recovering from burns to his eyes after a British gas attack at Ypres, when on 10 November 1918 a pastor brought him news of the armistice. Later, in *Mein Kampf*, Hitler was to write:

> I knew that all was lost. Only fools, liars and criminals could hope for mercy from the enemy. In these nights hatred grew in me, hatred for those responsible for this deed ... Miserable and degenerate criminals! The more I tried to achieve clarity on the monstrous event in this hour, the more the shame of indignation and disgrace burned in my brow.

What was all the pain in my eyes compared to this misery? ... My own
fate became known to me. I decided to go into politics.[1]

The moment was to have fateful consequences for the whole of
Europe.

For a while it looked as though Germany were going to sidestep
all the unpleasant consequences of going to war against its neighbours – the most predictable being the payment of reparations –
by avoiding a full surrender. The Allies, however, had no intention of letting the armistice arrangements slide by default into a
full-blown peace. On 7 May 1919, without prior consultation or
warning, the Allies announced the terms of the Versailles Treaty
and Hitler's fears were realised.

Germany was to lose Alsace–Lorraine to France, and northern
Schlesswig to Denmark. The German navy was restricted in its
construction of both battleships and submarines, and the army
was reduced to a puny 100,000 men. In the months that followed
the Allies stripped Germany of all its overseas possessions and colonies, 13 per cent of its territory in Europe, 10 per cent of its
population, 75 per cent of its iron-ore deposits, 45 per cent of its
coal fields, 10 per cent of its industrial capacity, 44 per cent of its
pig-iron facilities, 38 per cent of its steel facilities, 72 per cent of
its zinc sources, and 12 per cent of its farmlands. The British confiscated the entire German merchant fleet and then imposed a 33
per cent tax on all German goods imported to the Empire. The
French imposed import quotas. The Allies then presented
Germany with a bill for US$32 billion to be paid off at a rate of
$500 million dollars per year. And to top it all the Allies then
imposed a 26 per cent tax on all goods and materials imported
into Germany.

The German High Command was scandalised by the treaty and
considered offering armed resistance to its implementation.
However, given the demoralised state of the army, the growing
dissatisfaction of the officer class, the bitter social and political
polarisation that followed the defeat of the Spartacist uprising,
and the clear numerical and logistical superiority of Allied forces,
the High Command abandoned the idea. The Weimar Assembly
protested to the Allies that the terms were too harsh and there followed a series of street demonstrations. The Allies remained
unmoved. The victors, the senior members of the European industrial club and their main transatlantic trading partner, were
determined to put a permanent cramp in Germany's economic
and military potential. These measures were designed not just to
prevent Germany waging war, but to cripple German industry.

While the Treaty as a whole was deeply humiliating to Germany, it was accepted for the most part with a sullen resignation and silent disgust. There was one section of the Treaty, however, that occasioned deep anger and resentment. Enormous areas of eastern Germany were to be handed over to Poland. This was a newly independent state formed by the Allies around the nucleus of the Polish puppet state set up by the Germans in 1916. Poland reappeared on the maps of Europe not so much through its own efforts to liberate itself – though over the years these had been prodigious but unsuccessful – but through the collapse of the partitioning powers that had held Poland in check.

In 1918 Europe lay overwhelmed by the ruin and destruction it had wrought. Poles had fought both for and against Germany, and, partly because their state had not been involved in the war, Poles were ready – unlike the other participants in the war – to fight again, this time for something in which they had a stake. Although aware of the twentieth century, Poland's feelings and emotions were trapped in the experience of partition, and it had to struggle to catch up, not just in industrial and economic terms, but socially, artistically and emotionally. Polish independence, which had been unthinkable in 1916, was now a fact. That there had been no time to prepare for a gradual hand-over of power, to make plans for social, political, economic and military integration, only made things worse. Those who still thought in terms of a rural peasant Poland dominated by the feudal power of the *szlachta* and the Church had little time to adapt their vision. Poland was not even in the same shape or place as it had been, and virtually the only thing that now united the Poles of the different partition experiences, religious beliefs and political outlooks was a new found sense of Polish national feeling.

The leaders of the new state – Ignacy Paderewski and Roman Dmowski – were campaigning vigorously for an even bigger allocation of German territory. For most Germans it was bewildering that they should suffer such losses at the hands of a country that had not existed for over 100 years. For the East Germans the Poles had been objects of contempt for most of Prussian history, and the loss of land to them was an insult that was not to be swallowed, but would instead produce a festering sense of indignity, shame and anger. Throughout the Paris Peace Conference the Polish leaders heard tales of hunger and violent disturbance. The Poles found that they could not impose any kind of law and order until they knew the exact borders they had been given, and as each day passed they became more and more desperate for a final decision. On 28 June 1919 the Treaty was put into effect and

plebiscites were set up in Warmia, Mazuria and Silesia to determine the exact areas of land to be allocated to Poland.

The precise formula for the problems that beset the complex
area around Danzig between the wars is to be found in the terms
of the Versailles Treaty. In January 1920 Poland was awarded a
Corridor to the sea through West Prussia to the Baltic coast. On 20
January 1920 a detachment of Polish soldiers in greatcoats and
four-cornered caps waded out knee-deep in the icy Baltic. They
paraded national and military flags, recited ancient poems, sang
hymns and the Polish anthem 'Still Poland is not lost as long as
we are living'. Then they raised their hands in the air and gave
three cheers. The ceremony was called 'Ślub z morzem', the betro-
thal to the sea. Poland had access to a coastline for the first time
since the early seventeenth century. This direct and effective
control of the coast – compared to access through the vassal state
of Danzig – was probably the first in Poland's history. The only
problem was that the coastline awarded to Poland lacked a single
port larger than a fishing village along its entire length and was
therefore virtually useless to a modern state.

The Corridor through which Poland had access to the sea ran
almost exactly through Pomerelia and the area occupied by the
Kaszubes – who were now considered to be Polish. The Corridor
totalled some 16,295 sq km, was 230 km long, 230 km wide at its
base, and narrowed to less than 30 km near Danzig. To the north
the Corridor had a sea coast of 76 km; to the south it had the river
Notec and the Notec canal. The Corridor had a mixed German,
Polish and Kaszubian population. The figures from the 1910
German census show the ethnic and linguistic complexity of the
Corridor in some detail: in Pomerania as a whole there were
919,102 Germans, 555,337 Poles, 106,598 Kaszubes and 20,456
Bilingual people. In Danzig itself there were 315,281 Germans,
9,491 Poles 2,124 Kaszubes and 3,021 Bilingual.[2] In some parts of
Pomerania the Poles and Kaszubians together may have outnum-
bered the Germans, but along the river Notec there were no
Kaszubians at all, and German settlers planted in a block by the
Prussian Colonisation Commission outnumbered Poles by two to
one. The situation was further complicated by religion. Most Poles
were Catholic, but not all Germans were Protestant and there were
also German Jews and an increasing number of Polish Jews.

German defeat and the arrangements at Versailles revealed just
how complex the political, social and economic balance around
Danzig had become. To the south-east of the city, around Elbing,
there was some pig- and horse-breeding and the main farm produce
was sugar-beet; there was some shipbuilding, light engineering and

munitions works – all in German hands. On the Vistula delta the Mennonites bred black and white Friesian cattle just as their ancestors in Holland had done, and grew sugar-beet, tomatoes, rye, and a resilient variety of wheat on the rich alluvial soil. Like their ancestors, the Mennonites still shunned buttons and pockets, relying on hooks and eyes; they refused cars and engines, preferring horsepower; the Mennonites nevertheless reclaimed land from the river and sea, regulated the flood planes and wanted as little as possible to do with the evils of the outside world.

To the south and west of Danzig lay the Tuchler Heide and Kaszubia, an area of damp, sandy forest, marshy scrub, brackish lakes and poor farmland. There the Kaszubians occupied smallholdings; all the better farmland towards the coast had long since been taken over by the Germans.

To the east there was now the great long arm of East Prussia, an area occupied by German settlers planted on the remains of the Baltic Borussian peoples after the 'civilising' work of the Teutonic Knights. Cut off from the Reich by the Polish Corridor these people felt themselves to be German and to be threatened by the new Polish state. Traditionally they had looked to the Reich to trade their lumber, wheat, furs and amber, and they had every intention of continuing to do so in order to spite the Polish state. German influence in East Prussia had been so strong that over the years the southern strip of East Prussia, which was occupied by a large number of ethnic Poles, had become increasingly Germanised. Many Poles in East Prussia still clung to a Polish identity, but very few of them wanted to become part of a Polish state.

National rivalries were all the more intense and confused in these districts precisely because it was often not possible to tell who was which nationality, or where a person's loyalties lay. There were German Catholics in Pomerania, Protestant Poles in Mazuria; there were large numbers of ethnic Poles and Kaszubians in both the southern districts of East Prussia and in Pomerania who spoke German rather than Polish and who had even Germanised their family names. The Germans, where they thought about it at all, regarded Poles of all varieties as uncivilised upstarts whom they loathed for their backwardness, presumption and ambition, and this was a judgement that many East Prussian Poles accepted. Indeed there were also sizeable groups of Poles in Pomerania, East Prussia and Silesia who saw very clearly that passing under the administration of the new Polish state would mean a severe drop in their standard of living and who preferred to remain as second-class citizens under German administration.

Even though the Germans were demoralised by the end of the war and by the Versailles arrangements for peace, the Poles did not have things all their own way in setting the new borders. In disputed territory plebiscites were held in which both Germans and Poles brought proceedings into disrepute by menaces, abduction, blackmail and by outright thuggery on such a massive scale that the term 'border warfare' would be appropriate – even if there was as yet no actual border. In Silesia both Poles and Germans brought in thousands of 'relatives' and 'in-laws' to swell their vote. When the vote went against them the Poles simply marched in and took by force the areas they considered rightfully theirs. In Warmia and Mazuria, two of the districts that made up East Prussia, the Poles suffered serious reverses, gaining only 3 of the 28 disputed villages. In the Allenstein-Marienwerder district, just south of Danzig, there was a massive vote of 460,000 to remain with Germany and only 16,000 to move under Polish administration. Although the Poles could have exercised a military option in the north just as they had done in Silesia, by this time their involvement in a war against the infant Soviet state, over territories and borders in the eastern provinces, made this a logistical impossibility.

Since the days of Frederick the Great the Germans had been brought up to believe that the Poles were drunken, brutish and in every way inferior. Polish behaviour in the plebiscite areas, though no worse than that of the Germans, did little to dispel German prejudice and fear. In the Corridor and those areas ceded to Poland before the plebiscite, the Poles set about a land reform and began expropriation procedures, to dispossess German farmers of land and homes. Between 1919 and 1923 about 700,000 Germans living just inside the Polish border, in Poznania and the Corridor were forced to abandon their homes and trek west into the Reich. Between 1921 and 1931 the German population of the Corridor fell from 177,942 to 109,696, while the Polish population rose from 935,643 to 1,080,100. In 1939 the Poles published figures showing that their part of Pomerania was now 91 per cent Polish. By 1939 two-thirds of the German inhabitants of the areas ceded to Poland by plebiscite had been forced out.[3] The drastic and often brutal Polonisation policy showed that the Poles had studied very carefully Prussian methods of Germanisation.

On the question of Danzig there was no possibility of a simple answer to the problem of attachment and government. The French and American negotiating teams at the Paris Peace Conference wanted the city to be incorporated into the new Polish state. Even though its population was overwhelmingly

German, the politicians rightly considered that its position made it vital to the Polish economy. Lloyd George said that if the Conference was to adhere to President Wilson's established principle of National Self-Determination, the idea of placing such a large number of Germans under Polish rule was unacceptable. In general the Paris negotiators were keen to emphasise solutions to the 'national minority problem' of eastern Europe, rather than reveal that their main aim was the creation and resurrection of neighbour-states to control and limit German power and influence.

The final decisions affecting Danzig were left in the hands of Lloyd George, M. Clemenceau and President Wilson. The French, with Polish support, believed that the Peace Treaty ought to smash German industrial power and territorial ambition by dismembering as much of the German state as was possible. President Wilson had no particular policy except a vague notion that National Self-Determination was a good thing – a notion that owed more to America's position in the world and the nature of its own historical development than it did to the realities of European life. Wilson had made National Self-Determination the central plank of his 1916 election campaign for a second term in office. His use of this notion was in effect an extension of America's own aggressive domestic policy into foreign policy.

The US's solution to the problem of its own borders and indigenous peoples had been to expand until stopped by force, to renege on all treaties with native peoples and to conduct a policy of genocide and dispossession which, though it reached a peak in the years 1860–90, continued well into the 1920s. While this solution lurked in the consciousness of a large number of US citizens and was eventually to appeal to Hitler and the SS, it was not the kind of thing the Americans admitted or believed about themselves, and was certainly not the kind of solution they wished to offer to their 'civilised' European cousins. The result was that Roman Dmowski, one of the two Polish leaders in Paris, was reduced to despair and frustration by Wilson's attitude over Danzig. The Poles hoped at least for the award of Danzig, the nearby town of Elbing, the Vistula delta and the tiny republic of Memel. But a bitterly disappointed Dmowski was moved to complain again and again that Wilson simply did not appreciate the importance of Danzig to the Poles, and was incapable of 'thinking like a European'. Even President Wilson's negotiating team had problems in reconciling their leader's various directives. If Wilson's 'Thirteenth Point' was to be observed – that Poland should have access to the sea – then the principle of National Self-

Determination, so dear to the President's heart, must inevitably be compromised. Danzig was the most obvious port to hand over to the Poles, but the Danzigers were German.

The Allied politicians tried hard to find a solution, to resolve the conflicting demands of their own economies and ambitions along with those of the Poles and Germans. In fact the Allies were ill-fitted to assume this responsibility and unlikely to find solutions to problems that were largely of their own making. Lloyd George made a stand on the issue of a plebiscite for Upper Silesia, saying that he would no more give the place to the Poles than he would 'give a clock to a monkey'. But on the issue of Danzig Lloyd George was prepared to compromise. He suggested that Danzig should become a Free City and a ward of the League of Nations. Polish historians blame Lloyd George for the unstable and unworkable arrangements imposed on Danzig; they emphasise, quite rightly, his hostility to the Poles and his susceptibility to German pleas. And yet, although Lloyd George was the author of the Free City proposals, they were approved by the Americans and the French, and had the Poles not been so heavily engaged against the Soviets by this time, they might still have attempted to seize Danzig by force – there was certainly little the Germans could have done to prevent such a move.

Without doubt Lloyd George had a very poor record on national issues. Even so, his compromise on Danzig was not malevolent. It was designed, naively perhaps, to minimise the grievance to Poland and Germany by depriving them both of Danzig. Instead, the compromise proved to be a lasting source of grief to both parties.

Unlike 'un-historical' nations, Poland had a long history to recall and refurbish. But it was a history that was now informed by the lengthy experience of partition, *Polenpolitik* and *Kulturkampf*. As such it was a history that was perceived and shaped in terms of feelings, legacies, fears and foes. Modern Poland needed to accomplish certain tasks in order to stay alive, and it searched a pre-nationalist, pre-nation-state Polish history to find the seeds of action, historical necessity and national logic. Poland's claim to Danzig was part of the mythologising in which the new state indulged, part of its creative compensation for the years of partition. In so far as Poles began to claim Danzig on grounds other than those of practicality, then the claim was one of nationalist reaction. To insist that Danzig was 'Polish' on any other grounds than practical economics was to enlist some very uncertain history.

Danzigers had good reason to be apprehensive about the Versailles Treaty arrangements, and they were not alone. The whole of eastern and central Europe was affected by the Treaty. Germany in particular felt abused. The redrawn boundaries left over 8.5 million Germans as national minorities in Hungary, Romania, Lithuania, Poland, Italy, Czechoslovakia, Yugoslavia and the Soviet Union. Poland, too, was unhappy about the Versailles borders. Over 6.5 million Poles had been left outside the Polish state – 1.5 million of them in Germany. Also, in contrast to the golden years of the multi-racial, multilingual, multi-ethnic Commonwealth, Poland was unhappy about the number of non-Poles who now resided within its borders. According to the 1931 census more than 30 per cent of the population were not Polish.[4] But after hundreds of years of colonisation and settlement, of population shifts and absorption, how could it have been otherwise? Given that the massive exchange of populations was out of the question, it was clear that the Versailles politicians could not hope to solve the problems of forming homogeneous nation-state identities in Eastern Europe. Still less could they do this while trying to disperse the economically powerful German population of the east among the various neighbour states without aggravating the problem still further.

Articles 100–108 of the Versailles Treaty detailed the exact arrangements by which the new Free City of Danzig would be governed. The city would be under the protection of the League of Nations; its territory would include Zoppot and the surrounding farmlands. Poland would have guaranteed rights of access to the port, but Danzigers were offered fragile assurances by the League that the Poles would not interfere with the internal affairs of the city-state beyond running the railways, maintaining a Post Office, a customs service, a small garrison and munitions dump on the Westerplatte peninsula, and exercising nominal control over the city's foreign policy. In a last bid to gain full control over the port the German government offered Poland guaranteed rights of access if the Poles would allow the city to revert to the Reich. The Poles, however, already had a guarantee of access from the League of Nations, and felt that as the city depended to an enormous extent upon trade with Poland there was no advantage in surrendering the 'Jewel of the Baltic' to Germany. The offer was declined.

For their part, however, the Poles saw their only access to the sea through a port that they did not fully control, and in which there was already a a swell of anti-Polish feeling. Accordingly, they made a bid to gain command of the Danzig Harbour Board. The League of Nations rejected their offer, ruling that the Board should comprise equal numbers of Poles and Germans with a neutral chairman. The Polish effort to gain control faded out.

In spite of some very idealistic pronouncements and general high hopes, it soon became apparent that the best efforts of the League of Nations were to be frustrated with ease by the fundamental and unresolved differences of opinion as to the exact meaning of Free City status. In spite of their limited presence in the city the Poles worked to deny its sovereignty, pressed their 'historical claim' to the place by promoting its 'Polishness' and tried to gain increased control of Senate procedures. While Danzigers remained unimpressed by Polish 'historical claims', Germany, too, longed to deny sovereignty, but found it more convenient in practice to encourage notions of the Free City's independence, since this discomfited the Poles without direct confrontation.

In truth the government of Danzig had become a labyrinth sown with pits for the unwary. By 1922 the city had no less than four separate charters establishing and defining the limits of its powers: the Treaty of Versailles, the Danzig-Polish Accords, the Danzig City Constitution and the Covenant with the League of Nations. It had at least seven governing bodies and watchdogs set over it: the Danzig Volkstag, the Danzig Senate, the Polish Commissioner General, the German Commissioner General, the Danzig Harbour Board, the League of Nations High Commissioner, the Council of the League of Nations at the High Court in the Hague and finally, the League itself sitting in Geneva.

The historian N.N. Brailsford, echoing German opinion, called the Poles a 'primitive unschooled race' and went on to say that no matter how hard they tried, the Allied politicians would never manage to replace the industrial and intellectual skills of the German workforce with the likes of the Poles.[5] Danzigers felt with some justification that they had been left to the mercy of the Polish military and were now chained to what Molotov called 'the monstrous bastard of Versailles' – the backward Polish state and economy.

The new Polish republic faced enormous difficulties. It lacked industrial power, but alienated its neighbour and allies alike by attempting to rectify this; it failed to maintain a democratic government, yet under the circumstances it was highly unlikely that any state could have done so. Poland was condemned because it was not a proper nation-state, but it was condemned for its efforts to become one. Poland was set up by the Allies to help subdue Germany, but was then criticised for taking German territory. If Poland was backward it was not because the Poles wanted it so, but because Germany and the other partitioning powers had made it that way, and because the Allies had failed to provide the necessary capital to finance Poland to do the job they required. The level of economic development varied; eastern Poland was appallingly backward; in comparison the western provinces were not so bad. Only 16.5 per cent of the Polish workforce was classified as agricultural labour, and another 4 per cent as industrial labour, yet in the east as much as 87 per cent of the population scratched a bare subsistence from agriculture. In the west the average number of those involved in agriculture fell to around 74 per cent. One observer estimated that between the east and the west – that is, between the old Russian provinces and the old German provinces of partitioned Poland – there existed a socio-economic gap of experience and development of 50–100 years.[6]

In the new Poland barely two-thirds of the population was Polish, and of these barely two-thirds could read and write. In effect literate Poles constituted less than 44 per cent of the population. Predictably, the anti-Polish legislation and the policies of *Kulturkampf* and *Polenpolitik* meant that by far the worst areas of inherited Polish illiteracy were the old German territories. And there the highest level of illiteracy was to be found in Pomerania: between 1921 and 1931 the Poles reduced illiteracy in Pomerania from 5.2 per cent to 4.3 per cent. On a national scale there was a reduction from 33.1 per cent to 23.1 per cent in the space of ten years. Although by 1931 some 5,543,700 Poles were still officially classed as illiterate, the level of illiteracy in Poland compared very favourably with Italy (27 per cent) and Spain (47.5 per cent).[7]

Although it was clear that Poland would need massive industrialisation if it were to become a modern European nation, it was hampered in its efforts at every level by the legacy of partition. The integration of its railway system – it could hardly be called a network – was a major problem. Old Congress Poland, the section controlled by the Russians, had about 1,000 miles of track by 1890; the Austrian and Prussian sectors had a very highly developed system with over 50 lines running up to the old Russian border. Yet of those lines only 10 actually crossed the border into Russian Poland, and even as late as 1918 there was no direct railway link between Poznán and Warsaw.

The Polish government set about a land reform as soon as it felt able. Among the first victims of the reform were the larger German-owned estates that now fell within Poland. After the German estates came some 2,000 Polish estates of 3–4,000 hectares (about 8–10,000 acres) totalling some 20 per cent of agricultural land. These were broken up into 10,000 farms of not less than 2 hectares (5 acres). The reform was intended to affect all farms and estates of more than 180 hectares (450 acres) but in

Pomerania – the Polish Corridor – the soil was so poor that the lower limit was set at 400 hectares (1,000 acres). However, in Pomerania, where more than 30 per cent of all farms over 400 hectares were owned by Germans, such a reform could only add to the tensions and aggravations that already abounded in the border districts. Without doubt the Germans constituted the most wealthy stratum of border society.[8]

While the Danzigers could ignore neither Poland's claims to 'historic rights', nor the Versailles arrangements, the fact was that Danzig was sitting on a potential goldmine. Once again Danzig had a virtual monopoly of Polish international trade. While the Germans presented their situation as a disaster, they overlooked the fact that one of Danzig's major and continual problems had been that it could not grow or thrive purely on the traffic of its immediate Prussian hinterland. Pomerania, the Vistula delta and East Prussia had little in the way of natural resources or industrial centres; worthwhile manufactured goods and raw materials for export were located some 250–500 kilometres inland in areas that lay south of Poznań, Warsaw and Lublin. The restoration of Polish influence in the area should have returned the flow of trade from this distant hinterland to Danzig. Danzigers might have rejoiced that as Poland's industrial wealth increased, their city would have a monopoly of Polish international trade. Instead, nationalist argument and continual bickering between nation-states played on the fears and worries of the borderlands. Danzigers were far too busy protesting and petitioning, nursing wounded pride to realise the potential of their situation. They preferred to connive with Germany against Poland and never really assessed the value of co-operation at all. Bloody-mindedness on all sides soon began to show in the economic performance of the region.

The river Vistula had been one of the great European water highways. It reached, through a series of canals, linked rivers and tributaries, a hinterland that more or less defined the limits of Danzig's trading potential. In the immediate vicinity it linked Danzig with Stettin and Berlin via the rivers Notec and Oder and the Bromberg Canal; via the river Nogat and the Frisches Haff it linked up with Elbing, Marienburg and Königsberg; via the river Pregel and the river Dieme and the Kurisches Haff it reached out to Memel and Tilsit. It stretched out to Warsaw and Kraków and and beyond that into Galicia, the Ukraine and regions bordering the Black Sea. The Polish Corridor, with its customs barriers, check-points and crossing places cut right across the Vistula trade complex. It effectively disrupted the old established patterns but prevented new and more sensible patterns developing.

In the first few months of independence the Poles came to realise that the lower reaches of the Vistula waterway – their economic lifeline to the coast – had in fact been badly neglected by the Germans. Constant silting and the collapse of flood-banks now threatened Polish trade along its whole length. The cost of maintaining the waterway through the war on reduced Polish trade from the Russian and Austrian partition lands had been so high that the waterway had gone into decline. After 1918 the small shipbuilding industry at Elbing almost collapsed as a result of the creation of the Corridor simply because the cost of maintaining the river was compounded by the cost of negotiating the tariff barriers. Elbing's shipyards were kept going after the war only as a result of massive subsidy from the Reich. Now the cost of restoring the lower reaches of the river were simply too high for the East Prussian authorities to contemplate without revenues from Polish trade.

The effect of the Polish Corridor was to send the East Prussian economy into an abrupt and dizzying nosedive as it lost its traditional markets for beef, grain, timber, fur, sugar-beet and alcohol. These markets had either disappeared into the new Poland, or they were screened off by the Corridor. The feudal Prussian Junkers, whose estates had limped on for as long as anyone could remember, were hit particularly hard by the Corridor. In 1928 the *Preussen Kasse*, the Prussian Office, estimated that within a year almost 75 per cent of the surviving East Prussian estates would be bankrupt.[9] Almost all of these estates had been mortgaged and German banks were unwilling to lend more money at the rates the Junkers requested. Even those Junkers who managed to secure loans were already heavily in debt. New loans went to pay off the interest on earlier loans rather than on buying new farm machinery or modernising farming methods. In effect the Berlin banks who loaned money to the Junkers were paying themselves through an agricultural clearing house in East Prussia. The overall effect was to speed up the disintegration of the larger estates, but to leave the smallholdings virtually untouched but constantly threatened. Germany was forced to donate massive subsidy to East Prussia by laying new railway tracks across the Corridor, by starting new air services and by offering finance to the Baltic shipping lines operating out of East Prussian ports, whose trade had been damaged by the Corridor and who might otherwise have collapsed. Items of trade destined for southern Germany now had to be transported across the Corridor and then down the length of Germany. Expensive though this was, it was still cheaper than trying to transport freight by the more direct route, across Polish territory. In spite of German efforts, traditional East Prussian trade with Silesia almost ceased entirely.

In Danzig itself the sugar, sweets, chocolate, tobacco and match industries, as well as the famous Danzig Gold Water business were all badly affected by the Versailles arrangements. Local Danzig consumption of these items was taxed heavily – 7 per cent of revenue going to Poland – while consumption of these items and their raw materials was duty-free in Poland. Also it became clear that the local currency was a problem. The Danzig *gulden* was tied to the Gold standard, but the Polish złoty (in spite of the fact that the word means 'gold') was not. Though the city's finances were supposed to be independent, Polish control of the railways meant that any citizen wishing to use the trains had to change Danzig currency into Polish currency before buying a ticket.

Problems with the city's finances ran right through the local economy. By 1928 over one-third of the city's population depended on the administration for employment, unemployment relief, income or pension. A great many civil posts – postal officials, customs officers, policemen, street cleaners – were duplicated and this led to a serious imbalance between the non-productive bureaucracy and the private sector production workers. Nevertheless, in these inter-war years unemployment moved swiftly upwards: 10–17 per cent of the population were unemployed or dependants of the unemployed.[10] The financial strain upon the Danzigers came from other directions too. The city had to offer higher than average wages to attract civil servants from the Reich and was also forced to make a contribution to the salary and expenses of the League of Nations High Commissioner to the tune of £44,000 per year. Finance was a constant source of tension within the city, and increasingly the city's problems in this area were seen to be the fault of the Poles.[11]

Both Poland and Germany took delight in giving hurt and discomfort to no great purpose. Under the terms of the Versailles Treaty the Munsterwalde bridge at Kurczbrak was ceded to Poland. The bridge was one of the largest of its kind in Europe carrying a two-lane highway, railway and a footpath. Even though it was the only route for Polish–German transit between the towns of Graudenz and Dirschau – a distance of 120 kilometres – the Poles closed the bridge as soon as it came under their control. The traveller was forced to make an enormous detour. The closure of the bridge did not make good economic sense for the Poles, but their demolition of the bridge in 1928 made even less sense. This, however was a mere pin-prick compared to the actions that lay in store.

Throughout the years 1918–23 Poland was fighting to reestablish itself. It used every means at its disposal: it argued and pressured the Versailles politicians; it cheated in the plebiscites; it engineered uprisings in Silesia and Wielkopolska; it skirmished and then went to war with the Red Army for territory in the east. Poland was surrounded by neighbours who were contemptuous of its existence and anything but trustworthy, and Poland treated them as such. In the fight to regain both its old territories and some viable modern form, the link with the sea was of crucial importance.

The fragility of Poland's access to the sea was brought home with devastating clarity in 1920. Poland had taken advantage of the chaos in revolutionary Russia to launch an offensive to seize Kiev in the Ukraine. At first the Russians had been driven back in disorder, but in the months of July and August they had begun to recover and had driven the Poles back on their tracks until finally the Red Army was at the gates of Warsaw itself. The Poles stood with their capital at their backs while the Russians prepared for the assault that would end the war. It was at this moment that the Danzig dockers' union, inspired as much by anti-Polish sentiment as by fellow feeling for Soviet 'brother-workers', decided that they would no longer handle supplies and munitions destined for Poland. In a battle that the Poles called the 'Miracle on the Wisła' the Red Army was defeated and chased out of Poland. The Poles eventually settled for territory far short of their initial ambitions. No matter what part divine intervention had played, the Polish government had learned a very practical lesson, and it was one that the Danzig dockers would come to regret most bitterly.

The Polish government realised that the action of the Danzig dockers might have lost them their independence. They also realised that it might only be a matter of time before Poland's enemies used the same tactic as part of a concerted effort to wipe the country from the maps again. The French, who throughout the latter part of the nineteenth century had used investment in Russian railways as a way of discomforting German industry, now provided the Poles with capital to continue the work the Russians had started. With French backing, the Poles began to develop the tiny fishing village of Gdynia into a modern harbour. They drove huge concrete piers (totalling 13 kilometres in length) straight out from the beaches into the shallow Baltic. Behind the sand-dunes, schools, offices, churches, a market, a railway station, a radio station and hundreds of homes began to spring up with all the rapidity of a cow-town on the American prairie. The Poles constructed 200 kilometres of dockside railway and a new line from Gdynia to Bydgoszcz that avoided use (and payment) of the old

German railway. They offered very favourable rates to industry to move into the area, and the whole venture enjoyed massive success.

In 1924 the infant port of Gdynia handled just 90,000 tons of freight. In 1933, just after the port was completed, it handled 2,700,000 tons, was second only to Copenhagen among Baltic ports and was ranked the ninth largest European port. In 1927 only 33 per cent of Polish trade went by sea, but by 1936 the figure had risen to 77 per cent. In 1927 only 3 per cent of Polish sea trade went through Gdynia, the rest went through Danzig. By 1936 Gdynia handled 46 per cent of all Poland's foreign trade and handled almost all of Poland's sea trade.[12]

The effect on Danzig of the development of Gdynia was enormous. In 1931–2 Danzig's trade with Poland dropped from 8,300,000 tons to 5,400,000 tons. In 1934–5 Danzig's share of Polish trade dropped from 47 per cent to 37 per cent.[13] No city could absorb such a body-blow without showing the effects, and by 1937 Danzig was in severe financial difficulties. Not only had the Poles removed the bulk of their trade, but even the remaining Polish trade went to the Polish shipping firms who still operated out of Danzig, rather than to German concerns. Danzig found that whether it liked it or not, its life was dominated by Poland. Local farmers, too, were forced to face up to the unpleasant fact that they could no longer compete with the Poles because of the low cost of Polish labour and the high Reich and Polish tariff barriers. No matter what they did, Polish produce in the Free City and in Poland was always cheaper than Danzig produce. Kaszubian farmers in particular – scattered right across German Pomerania, the Polish Corridor and in the Free City – were hard hit. They found that neither the new port at Gdynia nor Free City status was of much use to them. The growth of population in Gdynia provided another market outlet, but now the Kaszubian farmers were in competition with the Polish farmers of the Corridor who had identical produce for sale.

The Kaszubes in Danzig and Germany found that they could not export their produce to Poland economically simply because Polish produce was cheaper, and in the Corridor they could not export their produce to Germany effectively because, as far as the Germans were concerned, the Kaszubes were Polish. Kaszubian produce, though initially cheaper than German farm produce, was much more expensive by the time levies and taxes had been added. As usual the Kaszubes were piggy-in-the-middle and found their sales restricted almost entirely to local markets and the bigger markets in Danzig, Oliva and Zoppot.

By the mid 1930s it must have been abundantly clear to the Danzigers that their 'independent status' was a millstone round their necks. But it was a situation that had problems for both Germany and Poland. The Poles bore the massive burden of state subsidies and international debt repayments first to create Gdynia and then to run it at rates that would undercut the Danzig trade. The whole Gdynia venture was only possible because of massive government preference, and there is little doubt that the port could not have been run indefinitely at such favourable rates. However, in the short run, Gdynia was more than capable of causing the Danzigers severe economic distress and genuine hardship. As the Danzigers saw it, Gdynia was just a very expensive way of ruining them; it proved just how hard-hearted and merciless the Poles could be, and that feeling helped to foster the growth of the Nazi Party in the Free City.

If the economic situation of Danzig was complex and in decline, then the ethnic and linguistic changes in the city reflected these alterations. In 1910 there had been 315,281 Germans, 9,491 Poles, 2,124 Kaszubians and 3,021 others living in the area that was to become the Free City. In 1921 the population of the urban districts was about 195,000, and of these only 5,000 were Poles. In 1934 the population of the entire Free City area was about 400,000 and of these 50,000 were Polish or Kaszubian. By 1935 the population of the urban districts had grown to 295,000. Although there was some overlap – Polish Poles, Danzig Poles, Polish Jews, German Jews, Polish, German and Danzig citizens – the vast bulk of the population was German. By 1937, as a result of migration from rural Kaszubia, an influx of unemployed people from nearby Elbing and Marienburg, and the large number of Jews in transit through the city who had become trapped there after a change in US immigration policy, there were about 17,000 Poles – including Kaszubians, Danzig Poles, Polish immigrants and Polish Jews – living in the urban districts. The total population of the Free City in 1937 was 375,972.[14]

The rich ethnic mix gave massive scope for discontent, disruption, tension and victimisation. In spite of the fact that most of the Völkisch parties in the city blamed the Poles for all their problems, relations between Poles and Germans in the city were spikey but surprisingly good.

It is true that we didn't speak Polish – well, a few words maybe: Tak, nie, dziękuje. But we had no need to speak it. There were only a few Poles in the city and they all spoke German. All of them. It was very rare to find a German who knew Polish or even thought they should ... Frederick the Great said that Poland was all heath, moor and Jews, and

that the Germans had tidied it up a bit and turned it into a garden. I
don't know if that's true. Many people thought it was. We used to say
that the Poles were all fur coats and dirty knickers. I remember we went
on a visit once to the newly opened Polish Post Office. We were surprised to see this fantastic marble everywhere – on the table tops, on
the benches, on the counters – but when we went back there three
years later the place was a total mess. Everything was filthy and broken.
Even the marble was damaged.[15]

The Polish presence in the city may have been small, but they
made the most of it. Indeed they made a significant contribution
to the life of the city and took every opportunity to demonstrate
their existence. They had a remarkably dense network of social
organisation – probably in reaction to the overwhelming
'German-ness' of their surroundings. While the Danzig Poles were
not keen for the city to come under Polish rule, they were nevertheless determined that they should not be penalised for being
Polish, and in their own way they were proud of their identity –
even if it did not quite amount to 'nationality' in a conventional
sense. Of the 50,000 Poles in the Free City, almost 40,000 were
members of the Community Association of Poles. The Poles had
20 nursery schools, a music school, 7 primary schools and 13
other schools; speech days, sports days and prize-givings were big
events in the local calendar. There were still 40 Polish shipping
firms in the city. There were several Polish newspapers. The
Gdańsk Society of Friends of Science and Art published an annual
yearbook.

On Westerplatte peninsula the Polish military had an ammunition store, their own port, brick-built barracks, guard huts and
concrete bunkers. Inside the spacious military depot the soldiers
kept several cows for fresh milk and grew vegetables under glass.
The Polish military had close links with the Polish community;
soldiers' rowing, football and handball teams often played against
local Polish and German teams. Polish officers attended both
League of Nations and Danzig official functions in full dress
uniform with swords at their sides. They maintained close contact
with the League of Nations High Commissioner and with the
Polish Commissioner General. It was common to see Polish soldiers walking on the Hel peninsula, on day trips to Świbno or out
courting local girls. On Sundays a detail would march out to the
nearest Polish church to attend mass.[16]

Polish control of the railways and customs, and the presence of
a Polish Post Office and military garrison, were a constant
reminder of Danzig's fragile economy and expensive independence. Indeed, by 1933 Danzig needed Poland far more than

Poland needed Danzig. Ironically, while the post-war Polish communist regime was to seek desperately to legitimise its seizure
of Danzig in 1945 by reference to history, ancient settlement
and archaeology, the inter-war Polish Communist Party (KPP:
membership approximately 16,000) under J. Herryng and J.
Leszczyński, decided to oppose the continued existence of the Free
City and campaign for its return to the Reich by attachment to
East Prussia.[17] The KPP recognised that the city's economic difficulties were fertile ground for a German nationalist reaction, and
that the Versailles solution was unworkable. Indeed, since Poland
now had its own port, the Versailles solution and the continued
existence of Danzig as a Free City were no longer relevant, and the
KPP considered the Polish military presence in Danzig an unneces-
sary provocation.

The KPP argument made sense, but they compromised this position by claiming that the Ukrainian and Silesian territories seized
in the first years of independence should also be returned to their
respective 'owners'. The KPP, whose membership included Rosa
Luxemburg and the young Isaac Deutscher, was continually at the
mercy of Russian nationalist machinations masquerading as the
theories of the world's first socialist state. Later it was found that
its policies in relation to Polish territorial claims had been formu-
lated for it by the Comintern as a way of weakening Poland. The
Soviets hoped that the prospect of reunited German lands would
somehow help the German revolutionary left.

The KPP, clearly influenced by Rosa Luxemburg, believed that
national self-determination was impossible under capitalism, since
the logic of capitalism led to bigger combinations, bigger markets
and bigger conflicts fed and fuelled by ever-increasing military
and industrial complexes. It believed that under socialism all
nationalism would be irrelevant since there would be no need to
organise market forces against one another in competing nationalities. The KPP made two mistakes. First, it defended Trotsky
against Stalin. Second, it supported Marshal Piłsudski's May 1926
coup d'etat in the belief that the Marshal was still a socialist. The
Russians could not forgive the Poles for supporting their internal
and external enemies, nor for their independence from Moscow.
Even if Piłsudski had been a socialist, he would still have been an
independent Polish socialist in Moscow's eyes. As things developed Piłsudski was to mix his own highly individual style of
socialism with Polish nationalism in a manner reminiscent of
James Connolly's Irish socialism, and was to remain hostile to the
Soviet Union until his death. While Piłsudski was to accuse the
KPP of undoing his own hard work as military leader and of trying

to dismember Poland by 'Trojan horse methods', Moscow decided to rein in the free-thinking Polish socialists. In 1938 the KPP was accused of factionalism, intellectualism and misguided patriotism. The Soviets claimed that the party was riddled with fascist and Trotskyite agents and initiated arrests and executions. The party disintegrated and with it went one of the very few sensible perspectives on the Free City's position.

6
The Growth of the NSDAP in Danzig

In the Reich the elections of 1930 were the turning point of Nazi Party fortunes. The insecurities of life in the border districts, maturing over a period of 14 years, had produced Poles who were very Polish, and Germans who were very German. But one of the ironies of life in the border districts was that it also produced Poles who became more German the more nearly they were incorporated into the Polish state, and Poles and Jews whose political opinions were so far to the right that only their ethnic, religious or national identity stood between them and the Nazi Party.

In East Prussia and Danzig the effect of being 'cut off' from the Reich was to compress ambition, exaggerate opinion and tune emotions to a remarkable pitch. The solutions offered by the Nazi Party were no less simple than in the Reich, but isolation, the proximity of Poland and the effects of the Depression gave the hopes and fears of the borderlands a personal intensity and meaning quite different from those in the Reich. Thus, when Hitler landed at Danzig's Saspe airfield on a whistle-stop tour of the east for his 1932 election campaign, the entire Danzig SA, along with a uniformed company of the local police force, turned out as a guard of honour. Hitler was pleasantly surprised to see thousands of cheering Danzigers waiting for him. But as he progressed on into East Prussia, towards Tannenberg, the full impact and consequence of the Depression and partition were borne upon him, and so also the full potential of the Nazi Party was impressed upon him. Otto Dietrich, Hitler's Chief of Press Bureau and link with Rhine and Ruhr businessmen, recalled Hitler's tour:

> ... here in the Masurian border districts, Adolf Hitler had the vast majority behind him, already at the time of the first Reich Presidential election. But on this journey it seemed as if the whole land of Masuria was faithful to the Hooked cross.
>
> Here the nation's poorest children were the most true of all. Hitler flags lined all roads, pictures of Hitler decorated all houses, and garlands draped the entrance to every village; hope and loyalty were prevalent everywhere!
>
> Wherever our Führer approached, every man and woman came out.

Crowds lined all streets. Grandmothers, on whose distressed faces the direst poverty was written, raised their arms in greeting. Wherever we stopped, the women stretched out their children toward our Führer. There were tears of joy and emotion.[1]

The growth of the NSDAP in Danzig followed that of its growth in the Reich, but it did so with a slight time-lag – a phenomenon of border districts everywhere. The high-point of the Danzig Nazi Party's electoral success came in 1935, though it was never as massively successful as the Nazis had hoped. One of the reasons for this was that while the border districts bred massive ambition for simplistic solutions, it also bred an open cynicism about the effectiveness of all solutions. Many Danzigers felt that the Nazis could not help them, and at the same time that only the Nazis could help them; they urged the Party on while at the same time distancing themselves from it. Even though the NSDAP was to achieve its majority in the Danzig Volkstag with a very clear mandate from the electorate to do what it thought necessary, most Danzigers were prepared to reap the benefits of being on the winning side without pondering too deeply the significance or morality of their own personal support for a party they did not entirely trust or like. In this they might have taken heed of the Reich's experience, but instead they went ahead and repeated that experience in miniature.

In the period 1928–32 Hitler had gained about 13 million votes. About half of these had been won from the moderate middle-class parties and were augmented by the vote of about 6 million new voters, half of whom were young people voting for the first time, and the other half of whom were people who up to now had been too weary, cynical or lacking in hope to vote at all. But the vast increase in the Nazi vote came primarily from the impoverished middle classes who had seen their savings and living standards smashed in the wake of the Versailles Treaty and the Depression. Perhaps half of those who had previously voted for the middle-class parties now voted for the NSDAP. The People's Party and the Democrats had between them polled over 5,500,000 votes in 1928, but in 1932 they polled less than a million.[2]

With their insistent anti-Polish, anti-Jewish and anti-Communist propaganda, their apparently radical economic policies, their contempt for the 'weakness' of Weimar democracy, their emphasis on military virtues and their theories of racial supremacy, the Nazis appeared to have solutions for the problems that beset the Reich. It seemed that they were determined to carry these solutions through. Nevertheless, in Danzig these policies took longer to establish themselves as specifically Nazi ideas because there were already several local political parties with a similar outlook, but with less ruthless and less violent leaders.

Also, since to a large extent the promise of Nazi solutions was false and depended upon the Nazi ability to create the problems it intended to resolve by force, matters in Danzig had to move much more slowly because the city was subject to massive foreign observation through the League of Nations. In Danzig it was not possible for the Nazis to proceed as they had in the Reich. This fact meant that Danzigers had far more opportunity to mull over Nazi propaganda and assess for themselves the extent of the Polish, Communist and Jewish 'threats'. The more isolated rural Free City population gave its support to the NSDAP at an early stage, but by and large the city dwellers could give the lie to much Nazi propaganda. It was obvious to them that Danzig, up to the advent of the Nazis, had been far freer from racial strife and entrenched national rivalry than might have been expected in such a complex and explosive economic and political environment. There was certainly far too little tension between the Poles, Danzigers and Jews than was convenient for Nazi recruitment.

The Danzig NSDAP was founded by a minor tax office clerk called Albert Hohnfeldt, who had served with both the Erhardt Brigade and the Freikorps – organisations famed for violence fuelled by spectacular beer consumption. When he joined the Party in 1922 he was the only member in Danzig, and had to wait until after Hitler was released from the Landsberg prison and the Party was re-launched before he could become active on its behalf. By the end of 1925 NSDAP-Danzig boasted 130 members. Hohnfeldt's leadership left much to be desired. He had no notion of how to create, channel or exploit the frustrations of this retrograde and embarrassing nook of dismantled empire. He lacked imagination and, like most of those in the right-wing Völkisch parties, was not noted for the subtlety of his political thought. His 'confrontation' with the Reds in the workers' district of Emmaus ended with the tiny Nazi Party surrounded by a sea of Red Front members, who, to the intense discomfort of the Nazis, did nothing more violent than bellow endless verses of the 'Internationale' at them.[3]

In these early years the Reich Treasury was unwilling to offer any subsidy to the Danzig Party, presumably on the grounds that with such poor leadership it would be money wasted. If this is so then the Danzig Volkstag elections of 1927 would have confirmed this opinion, since the NSDAP polled a total of 1,400 votes to obtain only one of the 120 possible seats. Following their disastrous showing at the polls, there was a period of time-consuming and bitter recrimination followed by a round of resignations. So intense was the internal struggle that the Party actually missed a magnificent opportunity to display itself to the public: the tenth anniversary of the Treaty of Versailles – the seat and source of all their misery – passed without the Nazis mounting even a token demonstration. Recognising that the local leaders were incompetent dimwits, the NSDAP put the area under the control of *Gauleiter* Erich Koch of East Prussia, and he appointed Bruno Fricke as Danzig's new business manager. Under Fricke's guidance membership began to increase: from 300 members in 1926 to 800 by 1930.[4] But this was not achieved without stirring up local feeling.

As the Reich Nazi Party moved towards its own internal revolution so tensions arose within the Danzig Nazi Party too. However, while dispute in the Reich centred on the political control of Ernst Röhm's brownshirt empire within an empire, in Danzig the affair had more to do with petty jealousies and spite, through which the hazy outline of some dispute about the future and direction of the Party was just discernible. The year 1930 saw a bewildering and rapid sequence of events: Bruno Fricke was arraigned for court martial, there was a string of resignations, public rows and even expulsions. Finally Hermann Göring intervened to dissolve the Danzig Party. Almost immediately the party was reconstituted, but this time Göring kept a watchful eye on the Danzigers.

In the three years that followed, the Danzig Nazis became better at governing themselves and at developing strategies to exploit the increasing economic difficulties of the Free City. As the NSDAP in the Reich moved nearer to its electoral victory of 1930, so the Danzig Nazis shifted their thinking from the idea of seizing power in the city state to the altogether different business of returning Danzig to the Reich. The man to whom this task fell was Albert Forster.

Forster was a Bavarian who had joined the Party in 1923. He had been an associate of Julius Streicher, the editor of *Der Stürmer*. In 1930 he was the youngest member of the Reichstag and was considered by all to be a high-flyer. It was Göring who suggested to Hitler that Forster should be appointed *Gauleiter* of Danzig in time for the forthcoming elections. Certainly Forster's powers of demagoguery were equal to the city's economic distress. Unemployment – mainly a result of the opening of the new Polish port at Gdynia – had risen in 1930 to 25,000, and would rise to over 30,000 in the next three years. Forster made use of this in a way his predecessors had not been able to. He organised huge torchlit rallies on the Langemarkt, uniformed marches through the city, military displays on the Maiweisse, and an impressive list of speakers from the Reich. The result was gratifying to Göring. His man had increased the Nazi presence in the Volkstag from a single seat to 27 seats. And just as in the Reich, on the back of electoral success rode increased party membership; between June 1930 and December 1932 membership increased from 800 to 9,519.[5] The Danzig Party leapt into the political struggles of the Volkstag with renewed energy and Forster settled down with confidence to work at his leisure the rich vein of economic discontent that ran right through every strata of Free City society.

The discriminatory policies of Poland, which had been prompted by Germany's boycott of Polish coal in 1925, had by this time developed into a fully-fledged trade war, and this, combined with the effects of the new port at Gdynia, the increasing Jewish population, the irritating presence of Danzig Poles and the continual clucking of the League of Nations, all helped to shift the political perceptions of the local population towards simplistic, populist, nationalist and ultimately racist solutions – namely those offered by the Nazi Party. The economic crisis reached into every corner of city life. It was impossible for any society to absorb without hardship a shock like that of the massive loss of trade to Gdynia. At the same time it was widely known that unemployment relief, while inadequate, could only be paid at all as a result of direct subsidy from the Reich. Even Catholic sympathy for Polish co-religionists was wearing thin, and, in spite of the efforts of Bishop O'Rourke, there was considerable hostility towards the Poles from within the Free City's Catholic hierarchy.[6]

With their increased membership and improved position on the Volkstag the NSDAP felt confident enough to begin behaving badly in public. An article appeared in the Nazi newspaper *Danziger Vorposten* claiming that the Danzig Harbour Board served only the interests of the Poles and should therefore be abolished.[7] Artur Greisser, a Nazi and the Danzig nominee on the Harbour Board, went to the office of one of the Polish engineers on the Board and threatened him with a revolver. The Danzig Senate dismissed the incident as a joke. The Poles took the matter seriously, but the League of Nations, saying that no-one had been hurt and perhaps the revolver had not been loaded, took no action.

Tempers flared again later that year over the renewal of the Danzig–Polish Accord on the use and access to the port facilities. According to the initial agreement, any foreign warship putting into the port was to be greeted by a Polish warship and escorted inside the port canal for an exchange of courtesies. In the spring of 1932 the British announced that a flotilla of three destroyers was to grace the city with a visit. The Danzig authorities immediately began to drag out the renewal of the Accord and, hoping perhaps to stop the visit altogether, told the British that all procedures were in temporary suspension and that this would prevent the Poles from greeting the British in the agreed manner. The Poles reluctantly asked the British to cancel the visit but the British insisted that the visit should go ahead as planned. Marshal Piłsudski ordered the Polish destroyer *Wicher* to greet, salute and escort the British as if the Accord were still in effect, and Tadeusz Morgenstern, the commander of the destroyer, was instructed that if the Danzig authorities insulted the Polish flag or tried to interfere with the visit in any way, he was to bombard designated targets in the city centre. Mercifully, the event passed off without incident. Afterwards the Danzig Senate lodged a complaint with the League of Nations about the behaviour of the Poles, and the Poles lodged a similar complaint about the Germans. The two sides were still arguing when the League of Nations endorsed the Accord in Geneva the following September.[8]

In 1933 the Nazis increased their number of seats on the Volkstag to 38, and were present for the first time in sufficient numbers to have an effect on the business and workings of the chamber. As in the Reich, it seems that they had gained votes at the expense of the middle-class Centre Party. The biggest Nazi vote came from the rural districts, and the lowest came from urban areas, where the SPD, KPD and DNVP were still firmly based. Regardless of where their support came from, the fact was that possession of 38 seats in the Volkstag meant they could now rule with little or no reference to the other parties. The Danzig Nazis celebrated their electoral success by journeying to Berlin to share coffee and cakes with Hitler. He congratulated them, but at the same time insisted that, for the time being at least, they must move towards some sort of accommodation with the Poles. Hitler had no wish to provoke an armed conflict that he was not certain of winning. This left the Danzig Nazis in an awkward situation since they had specifically whipped up anti-Polish feeling as part of their election campaign. They felt that they had a much stronger position than before and that a certain amount of muscle flexing was now unavoidable if they were not to lose face with their supporters.

When the Danzig Polish Accord came up for ratification, the Nazis ordered that all Polish Harbour Board officers should be replaced by German and Danzig officers. The Poles were furious and determined to resist any such move. On 16 March 1933 they brought in armed Polish police to protect their Harbour Board officers, and saying they feared the Nazis were planning an armed raid on the Polish ammunition dump, they reinforced their garrison on Westerplatte by bringing in 120 soldiers aboard the destroyer *Wilia*. The Danzig Senate denied any such plan and, after a debate, the League of Nations, in a rare display of firmness, obliged the Poles to withdraw their soldiers and police. The Danzig authorities renewed the Danzig–Polish Accord on direct orders from Berlin, and in September 1933 they signed, without fuss, the Minorities Agreement guaranteeing the protection of Poles and Polish Jews within the city. In return the Poles agreed to drop some of their discriminatory tariffs. If Marshal Piłsudski and Colonel Beck, the Polish leaders in Warsaw, were upset that France had not given them stronger backing over the *Wilia* crisis, then they were also relieved to find that Hitler was not prepared to go to war over the city – at least not yet.[9]

Even without offering provocation to the Poles the Danzig Nazis were busy enough with their *Gleichschaltung* or Nazification of the city. They imposed a ban on all unemployment relief organisations that were not run through the Nazi Party. They passed an Emergency Powers Act which, under the guise of doing anything they felt necessary to 'relieve the distress of the people', allowed them to do as they pleased without resorting to the Volkstag for authority. Their plans under this law included: the introduction of protective custody without trial; the introduction of a law to protect the NSDAP from libel, slander or defamation – which effectively meant that all criticism of the Party ran the risk of legal action; and the curtailment of the rights of newspapers, editors and journalists. They also made communism illegal. The Danzig police, who had been early to convert – almost as a bloc – to Nazism, began the ominous rounding up of oppositionist politicians, communists, activists from the Centre Party and those editors and journalists who remained hostile to the NSDAP. Even though it was against Danzig law, these people were all sent to the Reich, presumably to concentration camps. Bishop O'Rourke organised a petition complaining of the illegality of the move, but all this achieved was to get those who signed (and later re-signed) beaten up.

The Nazis also set about preparing their version of history for public consumption. Danzig's first Nazi Senate President Rauschning recorded a conversation he had with Himmler, probably at the end of 1933:

> Himmler called me to account about a professor who lectured on prehistoric times at Danzig and Königsberg. This man, he said, had been criticising current ideas about the origin of the Teutons and the age of their civilisation, and had condemned these ideas from allegedly scientific points of view. At the time a sensation had been created by an

exceedingly silly book, a manifest forgery, the *Uralinda Chronicle*. The book traced back the history of the Teutons to an infinitely remote period: and it proved once more that the original German-Teuton race was the true creator of European civilisation. The professor had treated this book with proper severity, and Himmler wanted me to dispose once and for all of this type of scientific mischief-making. He himself would put the fear of God into the professors of Königsberg and Breslau; I was to do the same thing in Danzig.[10]

The Nazis now had little need of the Volkstag, and it met only rarely. Yet the Nazis knew that they could not behave too outrageously because there was always the threat that the League of Nations might call in the Poles to annex the city and suppress the NSDAP in the name of European peace. Hitler's instruction to curb anti-Polish activity meant that what they could not accomplish by open violence or legalistic chicanery they would have to accomplish by stealth and skulduggery. The odd balance of power within the city was almost destroyed entirely when on 12 November 1933 Adolf Hitler announced that Germany was leaving the League of Nations. Only his swift conclusion of a non-aggression pact with Poland saved Danzig from a final resolution of the city's problems in Poland's favour.

During 1934 the tensions within the Danzig NSDAP were most evident in the hostility between *Gauleiter* Forster and Senate President Hermann Rauschning. Rauschning was an ex-Prussian cadet who had been wounded in the First World War. Although he was a leading member of the Danzig Party it would probably be fair to describe him as a misguided liberal who only realised his mistaken alliance when he saw the brownshirts pulling on their kicking boots. Rauschning had tried to bring about some sensible appreciation of Danzig's rapidly fading monopoly position vis-à-vis Polish trade and to effect a policy whereby the city would realise its unique position on the Baltic by quietly penetrating the Polish, Lithuanian and Russian markets. In many ways this was a sensible policy since even if Danzig had not been made a Free City and had remained within the long arm of Prussia, the local economy was too poor to maintain it for long; a German Danzig would still have been forced to rely upon a distant Vistula hinterland. *Gauleiter* Forster, on the other hand, had been using the threat of Russian communism and Polish nationalism as the basis for the development of the NSDAP. Without these threats the party would cease to exist. While Rauschning emphasised reconciliation, understanding and harmony through balanced trade, Forster had been saying that reconciliation with the Poles was impossible and endlessly repeating that a return to the Reich was essential, but was prevented only by the intransigence of the vengeful Poles. It took Rauschning a long time to realise that his standpoint was exactly opposite to Forster's.

Rauschning also began to realise that *Gauleiter* Forster had been using the economic reforms initiated by the Party in 1933 to line his own pocket. Forster's holdings in real estate and fine art, his lavish lifestyle and frequent 'entertainments' were common knowledge within the Party and a source of embarrassment to Senate President Rauschning. Opposition leaders had long since satirised the Nazis as 'all new cars and gold braid'. Unlike in the Reich, where the Nazis had sealed off the German people and the NSDAP membership from foreign scrutiny, and where investigative journalism, hostile comment and moral concern were all about to disappear into the camps, leaving the party accountable to no-one, Danzig was never able fully to apply these principles simply because the city remained a ward of the League of Nations. Danzig, even if its own journalists and citizens were harassed and threatened, was open to all the observation and criticism the world could muster. Rauschning, though he hardly seems to have understood, could complain about the *Gauleiter's* lifestyle precisely because they lived in the Free City. Inside the Reich Rauschning's moral scruples would have appeared foolish, even suicidal. If anything Forster was restrained compared to the excesses of other leading Nazis.

Rauschning made the mistake of taking his complaint to Hitler. And while the Senate President was away in Berlin, Forster and his cronies concocted a simple plan to remove him from office. In September 1934 the Danzig Nazis charged a Latvian Jew with communism and violation of the Press Laws. Under 'pressure of interrogation' the unfortunate man named two of Rauschning's closest associates as his accomplices. Rauschning returned to face a whole series of issues and policies he felt he could no longer support or accept and to find himself cited in an investigation of both Jewish and communist influence in the city. Failing to find support from within the Danzig party or from Berlin, Rauschning had little option but to resign from both his post as Senate President and from membership of the Party. He withdraw on sick leave to his farm at Grosses Werder and later, by a roundabout route, emigrated to the US where he wrote various books warning about the Nazi menace and lamenting his involvement with them.[11] The departure of Rauschning was significant because it meant that the last liberal conscience, the last internal barrier to the complete and violent Nazification of the city had now been removed.

Their 'soft' attitude to the Poles lost the Nazis a great deal of support in the 1935 Volkstag elections. The business sector of the city was also upset by the circumstances of Rauschning's departure. As a local – he was from Thorn – and as a farmer with business interests in the Free City, they had trusted his leadership far more than they trusted Forster, whom they saw as a boorish Bavarian appointed by Berlin. Rauschning's departure had brought to the fore worries that Danzig was not sharing in the economic recovery about which the Reich newspapers – strictly controlled by the NSDAP – trumpeted so loud. As if to reassure the Danzigers, on the first day of the election campaign Hitler announced his intention to renegotiate the Anglo–German Air and Naval pacts. Even so, this was nowhere near enough to win over the Danzig voters. That Forster and the local Nazis knew as much is evidenced by the fact that the 1935 election was the dirtiest and most dubious of the Danzig NSDAP's victories.

At this stage of their takeover the Nazis needed a massive vote of confidence from the electorate to justify the virtual disappearance of the Volkstag and their assumption of Emergency Powers. The Nazis also needed a mandate to proceed with their policies. The election was required by law, and if anyone thought it odd that there should be such trouble over elections to a chamber that now met only to ratify decisions taken elsewhere, then they kept the notion to themselves. When it looked as if the Danzigers would not oblige the Nazis with an overwhelming vote of confidence, the Nazis set out to help themselves.

The election campaign included forcing all newspaper sales off the streets, widespread use of violence and thuggery, arson attacks on offices and homes, the takeover of the local radio station by the NSDAP and exchanges of gunfire on the streets. Miraculously no-one was killed. The Poles, in an effort to re-elect their own representatives, drew money illegally from outside the city. But the amounts the Poles spent were dwarfed by the way the Nazis used state funds as if they were from the Nazi Party cash box. Goebbels visited the city to give the campaign a boost, and toured around in a series of noisy, impressive and carefully stage-managed motorcades complete with motorcycle outriders. He reviewed the massed ranks of the uniformed SA and SS on the Langemarkt and made violently anti-Polish speeches from the Artushof and from the Zoppot Cure-House – speeches that left what remained of the opposition staggered at his vehemence and fearful of the consequences. But his words and attitudes heartened the Danzig Party, who had begun to feel that Berlin no longer cared for the city's struggle against Poland and Polish trade.

Expectations that the vote would repeat the Saar plebiscite of the previous year and that the Nazis would make a clean sweep of the Volkstag were dashed. The NSDAP gained only 43 of the 72 seats and polled less than 60 per cent of the vote. Forster was so smitten by the result that he could not trust his voice to announce the Nazi gains on the radio, and is said to have spent the night at home weeping uncontrollably. Even though they had failed by their own standards, the Nazis had reduced and contained the power of the communists, DVNP and SPD. Technically, they still did not have total control of the machinery of state, but in practice their use of the Emergency Powers and willingness to use violence meant that, subject only to the threat of a Polish invasion, they could do more or less as they pleased.

Ambassador Lipski had begun to complain to Göring that German newspapers like *Der Stürmer* and *Der Gessilige* from Pila were stirring up resentment against the Poles throughout the border districts by referring to the forcible separation of Danzig from the Reich, and by referring to the Polish Corridor as land ceded to Poland. Lipski was able to point to several passages in school textbooks containing similar references. He also complained that the consistent use of the word *Pomerellen* in German texts was offensive to Polish residents of the Corridor. Lipski made the point that these and other examples of anti-Polish sentiment occurred with greater frequency in the areas bordering the Polish Corridor than they did in other parts of Germany. Pomerania in particular was rapidly approaching hysterical anti-Polish feeling. Lipski cited three German publications from the previous year in which the generally intolerant attitude of the border districts was not only present, but had clearly been sanctioned and licensed by the energy and policy of the NSDAP in Berlin. In short Lipski said that the Germans were manipulating a crisis in order to renege on their debts to Poland.[12]

There was a great deal of truth in Lipski's comments. The Reich's rearmament programme and the continued high level of subsidy to Danzig had caused a severe drain on German gold reserves and had upset the balance of payments. The Poles calculated that Germany owed 29,500,000 złoties to Poland in transit fees through the Corridor, but was dragging its feet over payment.

Early in 1935 Göring assured Ambassador Lipski that, far from stirring up trouble in the border, Danzig was quiet only because the Nazis were in control. He said that if they had not gained the upper hand then the old Völkisch parties would certainly have picked a fight with Poland. Lipski had to agree. Even if Nazi domestic policies were worrying, it did look as if the Nazis were maintaining a friendly stance towards Poland. Hitler's instruction that the flags should be flown at half mast to mark the death of Marshal Piłsudski on 12 May 1935 was also taken as a reassuring gesture.[13]

Göring, of course, knew more than he told Lipski. In late April 1935 *Gauleiter* Forster, Hitler, Göring and the Reichsbank president Hjalmar Schacht had met and discussed the city's desperate financial situation. Failure at the polls had exposed Danzigers to the true state of the city's finances. Looking at the account books – the real ones, not the fabrications served up to the Poles and the League of Nations – it was clear that Danzig's projected budget for 1934–5 would run at a deficit of over 44 million gulden, which, when added to the employment projects the Nazis needed to keep their supporters in Danzig happy and faithful, would leave the Reichsbank to pick up a bill of over 110 million marks. The Reich had been injecting money into Danzig to make it appear that Forster and his pals were able to find the resources to create employment projects through their superior management skills. Reich subsidy to the city had now reached its limits and Schacht was in favour of cutting off all further aid.

In Berlin it was agreed that with the depression eating away at Danzig's own tax revenues, the city's only possible course of action was to devalue the Danzig gulden by 57.5 per cent to achieve parity with the złoty. The announcement of the devaluation and the attendant massive fall in the standard of living caused total panic at every level of society. Huge queues formed outside shops as people tried to spend all their savings before they were devalued. Prices rocketed to anticipate the devaluation and speculation was rife. Danzig's already depleted currency reserves dropped steadily. Local banks faced massive demands for withdrawals which they could not possibly meet and promptly declared several bank holidays in a row. Local businessmen felt that all their worst suspicions about the Nazis had been confirmed, though some suspected that the Poles had engineered the crisis in order to introduce the złoty as the new Danzig currency. By the end of April 1935 Danzig's currency reserves stood at less than half of their 1933 figure; by June the reserve had dropped to less than one-eighth of that figure.

Bankruptcy stared the Nazis in the face, and for a while they were so desperate that they actually considered introducing the złoty as a way of stabilising the currency and restoring calm. They abandoned this idea when they realised that it would mean the end of the NSDAP in Danzig. On 11 June 1935, without consulting the Poles, the Danzig Senate imposed currency and exchange controls – a move that was in direct contravention of the Danzig–Polish Accords. In Warsaw the move was seen as a strike against Polish business interests in Danzig. Ambassador Lipski hastened across Berlin to speak with Hjalmar Schacht, who was on his way to Danzig to help sort out the mess. Schacht made soothing noises and promised Lipski that there was no real crisis at all – merely a psychological one. He said that in fact the gulden was very healthy, that no cunning ploy against Polish business had been intended, and that everything would be well again within two months.[14]

The Poles were nevertheless alarmed. Their revenues from Customs Duties were affected by the imposition of exchange controls. They stopped all trade entering Poland via Danzig and re-routed traffic through Gdynia. They also decided to levy duty in Poland rather than in the Free City. These measures put many of the dockworkers out of work. The port never recovered from this blow and about 10 per cent of the trade lost to Gdynia during this crisis never returned. The Danzig Senators argued that the only way forward now lay in an immediate return to the Reich, but they were still afraid that this would provoke an invasion of the city and war with Poland. Eventually the Senate decided to admit tax-free food and medicines destined for use in Danzig. The Poles responded by refusing entry to all goods (mainly matches, beer and chocolate) made in Danzig. On 2 August 1935 Ambassador Lipski spoke with German Secretary of State von Bülow, but still could not effect a solution. It was only after the personal intervention of Göring, who spoke with Lipski by telephone on 6 August, that it was agreed Danzig would return to a fixed currency levy. Göring, much to Hitler's annoyance, also managed to persuade the Danzig NSDAP of his point of view. After lengthy phone-calls between Berlin and Danzig on 8 August, Forster announced that a fixed currency levy was now in operation and everyone breathed a sigh of relief.[15]

In spite of evident satisfaction that the crisis had been resolved, the Poles were increasingly alarmed by the instability of the Danzig economy and the Nazis' failure to control the city's financial arrangements. While the Poles were largely indifferent to the internal problems of the city – which they reasoned were the result of German agitation and would never have arisen if the Versailles politicians had made some more workable arrangement – they were very sensitive to any disturbance in their trade through the Corridor and the Baltic ports. Poland, too, was hard hit by the Depression and, in spite of the developing trade war, Germany had taken advantage of the weak Polish mark to trade at advantageous rates and to become Poland's main trading partner. In 1918 the exchange rate had stood at 1 US dollar to 9 Polish marks; by 1923 the rate was 1 US dollar to 15 million Polish marks. The currency reform of 1924 had introduced the new Polish złoty, tied to the newly created central Bank Polski, but a stable currency was maintained only at terrible social and political cost.

The British General Strike of 1926 had given both Germany and Poland a new sense of the gains that might be made through co-operation, and while they explored this unexpected windfall, the effects of the Polish currency reform were hidden. Both countries poured out millions of tons of coal to make good the orders of the international coal trade. The Poles filled every available truck and train with Silesian coal and sent it north; for weeks a fine drifting cloud of coal-dust hung over Danzig and it seemed the port was to become a coal-opolis fit to rival Cardiff, the coal capital of the world. But after the settlement of the dispute Danzig–Polish co-operation lapsed as if it had never existed. The currency reform had been intended to halt inflation and end the inequality in the terms of trade. In this it was a great but short-lived success and provoked Germany into refusing to buy Polish coal, which in turn provoked Poland into putting an embargo on all German trade.

In many ways it was the currency reform and the severance of trade with Germany the following year that had paved the way for the military coup in Poland that installed Marshal Piłsudski as head of government in May 1926. By the time Piłsudski took over, the Polish economy was in a desperate plight and it was only with centralised planning introduced in 1936 under the guidance of Eugeniusz Kwiatkowski and the left wing of the *Sanacja* ('moral cleansing' regime) that the Polish economy began to show signs of recovery. The new state had so far relied heavily upon French, American and Italian finance to integrate its railways, rationalise its industry and build the new port at Gdynia. But after 1936 – a turning point for Poland – only the French continued to supply finance (over 2,600 million francs) and roughly half of the trade credits and finance that flowed through the economy came directly from the state. Even so, by 1937 40.1 per cent of all remaining capital in joint-stock ventures was foreign-owned. Companies in which foreign capital amounted to more than half of the total capital constituted 63.1 per cent of all joint-stock companies.[16]

The Polish economy showed signs of economic recovery and of rapid industrialisation in the years 1936–9. Nevertheless Poland was still encumbered by a poorly developed industrial sector, a primitive, almost feudal, agricultural system, an under-funded banking sector and a poorly integrated railway system, and was hampered by the fact that it paid out 40 per cent of Gross National Income (approximately 28 per cent of all government expenditure) to maintain an army that was second in size only to that of Russia. Under the ageing Marshal Piłsudski the Poles had become very hard-nosed about the problem of Danzig and trade with Germany. They had no choice; their economy had very little room for manoeuvre, the German threat meant heavy military investment at the cost of social and industrial improvement; yet any halt in the country's ability to trade was tied directly to the continued life of the government, the existence of the state and the possibility of a military solution to all its problems.

Throughout 1936 Danzig teachers, trade unionists and politicians who were unsympathetic to the Nazi Party were beaten up or suspended from their jobs. The League of Nations appeared to have washed its hands of the city, and the general attitude was that it was a matter for Poles and Germans to decide between themselves. It was only with the greatest of difficulty that the League could be persuaded to do its job in Danzig. In June 1936 the Danzig SA attacked a DVNP meeting, and in the brawl that followed one of their men died. Rejecting medical evidence that he had suffered a heart attack brought on by stress and aggravated by a syphilitic condition, the Nazis used the funeral to turn the dead man into a Nazi martyr.

The year's prize crisis occurred just a few days later, when the German battleship *Leipzig* visited the city. At an official reception the captain of the ship pointedly ignored Sean Lester, the League of Nations High Commissioner, and later excluded him from the list of official courtesy visits. Lester summoned Senate President Artur Greisser to explain this breach of etiquette and protocol. Greisser said that the previous year the German battleship *Admiral Scheer* had put into Danzig, and on that occasion the ship's captain had been introduced socially to anti-Nazi members of the Danzig Senate. This, Greisser said, was a breach of courtesy, and as Lester had been responsible, there would be no apology for the German reply.

Greisser was summoned to the High Council of the League of Nations in Geneva to repeat his explanation. When he arrived Greisser gave the Hitler salute, and by his pompous language and ridiculous bearing reduced journalists, observers and officials to helpless laughter. Upon leaving the League's Palace Greisser said loudly: 'This place is nothing but wind.' He accompanied this with a rude gesture – some say it was a noise, others that he stuck out his tongue, or even that he made a sign with his forearm. Whatever it was, the meaning was clear. When he returned to Danzig Greisser was treated as a conquering hero, and was greeted by cheering crowds at the railway station. The League of Nations and the Danzig Senate exchanged notes of protest, but that was as far as the League pursued the matter.[17]

On 31 October 1936 armed Nazis attacked a Polish home at Schönbrun, near Danzig, and Marian Chodacki, the Polish Commissioner General in Danzig, had to intervene to try and get the police to bring the trouble-makers to court. A week later the Senate created the *Landesarbeitsamt* – a kind of labour exchange, but one which refused to cater for the Polish unemployed of Danzig. There were continual violent clashes between the SPD, DVNP, Centre Party and the Nazis. The Volkstag hardly met at all by this time, so those anti-Nazis who had not fled and who were not under arrest had no voice in the government of the city. By Christmas all three main opposition parties had dissolved themselves.

Nazi Party membership was still climbing steadily. In June 1934 membership had stood at 21,861. During the electoral and economic crisis of 1935 the Party had accepted no new members, but when it opened its books again in September 1936 membership shot up to 29,819. In proportion to population there were now more NSDAP members in Danzig than there were in the Reich.

In February 1937 Marshal Göring visited Marshal Śmigły-Rydz in Warsaw and assured him that Germany had absolutely no territorial claims on the Polish Corridor and that Danzig, though 'eternally bound' to Poland by trade, would remain a Free City. In August Ambassador Lipski wrote to Colonel Beck, the Polish Foreign Minister, to say that von Moltke, the German Ambassador to Warsaw, had informed him that 80 per cent of the 300,000 Germans living within the Polish borders were now unemployed. Lipski and von Moltke agreed that Berlin understood its Poles about as well as Poland understood its Germans.

On 5 November 1937 Hitler made a public speech in which he said that Germany had no claim on Danzig and that he did not want to change the city's status: 'Danzig ist mit Polen verbunden – Danzig is with Poland bound.' Yet had he decided the reverse it was already clear that the League of Nations lacked the will-power to say him nay. At this stage Hitler's plans were still fluid, but the last thing he wanted was for the useful Danzig problem to be solved. It was in any case too late for the League of Nations to move against the Nazis since they were in power as a result of legal democratic electoral procedures. To attempt to suppress the

Party in Danzig would probably have united the Danzigers against the League. In any case, Germany had already removed itself from the control and sanction of the League of Nations.

On the same day that he declared he had no intention of altering Danzig's status, and after meeting Ambassador Lipski at the Reich Chancellery to make the same assurance, Hitler went to a private meeting with a small group of Nazi leaders. At that meeting he said he hoped that if Germany occupied Czechoslovakia the move would paralyse Poland at the same time. He warned that if war in the west should break out, Polish neutrality – guaranteed by treaty with Germany – would end abruptly. Hitler predicted that, if given the opportunity, Poland would strike out to take over Silesia, East Prussia and Pomerania. It was clear that Hitler was mentally preparing himself and his assistants for all possible configurations of alliance and animosity. Notes from this meeting were kept by Colonel Hossbach and later fell into Allied hands. Several commentators are of the opinion that the 'Hossbach Papers' mark the beginning of Hitler's practical planning for war in the east.[18] In spite of his plans, as late as January 1938 Hitler told Colonel Beck that he considered the Danzig arrangements binding, that he thought it possible to accommodate Poland and that he had no territorial claims to make.

As Hitler's preparations for war gathered pace, so the atmosphere in Danzig became increasingly tense. In the late summer of 1938 the local campaign against the 'Jewish problem' received public attention. In August Göring told Lipski that certain anti-German incidents along the Polish border were poisoning the atmosphere and that Poles were conspiring to interfere with the work of the League in Danzig. Göring added that it was widely believed that Poland intended to annex East Prussia and Danzig in the near future. By September 1938 it was clear that Carl Burckhardt, the Swiss League of Nations High Commissioner, was not prepared to do anything to prevent the drive to Nazify the city, and that he saw his position to be that of 'observer' or, at most, intermediary. The Poles and the Jews were uneasy about Burckhardt. He failed to do all he could for the Jews and socialised with the Nazis too easily for the Poles' liking. Only later did it emerge that the Germans had supported his candidature for the post of High Commissioner in Danzig, and that he had since 1920 been on very friendly terms with Baron Ernst von Wiesäker, the head of the political section of the German Foreign Office.[19]

In Colonel Beck's terms, the appointment of Burckhardt meant that the League was now 'bankrupt'. Accordingly the Poles instructed Ambassador Lipski to seek assurances from Hitler that his statement of 5 November 1937 still applied. On 16 September 1938 Lipski reported to Warsaw that Göring had said that without Poland Danzig could not expect to survive on trade from East Prussia. Poland had by now withdrawn most of its trade through the city to its own port at Gdynia, and the Reich could hardly be expected to maintain or guarantee for an indefinite period the subsidy the city required.[20] Lipski and Göring agreed that Germany and Poland should draw together in an understanding that they would jointly stabilise the city if the League should either collapse or decide to withdraw from Danzig. Later events proved this 'understanding' to be a smokescreen of Göring's invention.

On 24 October 1938 von Ribbentrop had dinner with Ambassador Lipski at the Grand Hotel in Berchtesgaden. Von Ribbentrop said that if Poland would allow Danzig to return to the Reich, Germany would be happy to guarantee Poland access to the road, rail and port facilities. He also said that if Poland would agree to an extra-territorial railway line to run across the Corridor, linking Stettin, Danzig and Königsberg, Germany would agree to guarantee Polish borders for a period of 25 years. Lipski was both shocked and impressed by the offer. Only six weeks before, the Germans had said they had no claim on the city. Now they had a claim. Lipski said he would repeat the offer to Colonel Beck in Warsaw, but that he was sure the answer would be 'no'.

The Germans began to put on pressure. In November 1938 there was trouble over the installation of several Polish postboxes in Danzig. As fast as the Poles installed them, the local Nazis tore them from their mountings and heaved them into the Radaune canal. Following hard upon this came the issue of a set of stamps to commemorate the anniversary of Poland's rebirth in November 1918. On 11 November 1938 (the twentieth anniversary of Armistice Day and therefore a very sensitive date on the German calendar) the Poles released a set of 15 *groszy* stamps. The design on one of the stamps recalled the victory of the armies of King Jagiełło and Queen Jadwiga over the Teutonic Knights at Tannenberg (Grunwald) in 1410. Another stamp showed Polish and Danzig merchants trading grain. The Danzig Senate complained to the League that the stamps were offensive to Germans and pointed to a pair of crossed swords incorporated in the design as indicating particular ill-will on the part of the Poles. The Poles, through Commissioner General Marian Chodacki, said that what went on to their stamps was their business, and they were genuinely mystified that Danzigers whose ancestors had risen up against the Teutonic Knights should feel offended by stamps that celebrated their victory. Also, as the Poles pointed out, many of the Knights had not been German. The Senate then took exception to the legend on the stamps: 'Polish Post Office: Port of Gdańsk'. Again the Poles were mystified. They had a post office in that location; it had been there protected under Treaty and by the League of Nations for nearly 20 years, and that was where the stamps had been issued. The Senate then took offence at the picture of the grain merchants. They felt it emphasised the Polish presence in the city. The Poles replied that the design was based on a painting by the Dutch artist Van Der Block dating from about 1608, that the original painting hung in the Danzig Main Town Hall in a room which the Nazis used for frequent social and political meetings. They had not taken exception to it before, so why start now? The Senate retreated in sullen anger. The Poles withdrew the stamps and reissued them without the crossed swords. The only people to benefit from the clash were the philatelists.

The Polish government debated von Ribbentrop's proposals and decided that, if granted, concessions to Hitler would start rather than end with Danzig, and would lead to demands for the return of Mazuria, Poznań and Silesia. While the Poles appreciated German fears about the threat posed to Central Europe by a rise of Soviet power they did not see that they would be serving Poland's interests by agreeing to Hitler's demands. The Poles were well aware that they were a kitten between two cats, but they preferred to persist in Piłsudski's strategy of keeping both Germans and Russians at arm's length while trusting to Western capital and military alliances. Germany's offer may have appealed to anti-Russian prejudice, but then the Polish state had fought and beaten the Soviets once, and compared to that Hitler's offer sounded to Lipski like the opportunity to become a mere German satellite. Certainly there seemed little point in giving either side the initial advantage; invasion by one might be precipitated by an agreement with the other, and if Germany and the USSR came to blows, it would inevitably be on Polish soil.

On 19 November 1938, with the row over the postage stamps still simmering in the background, Lipski and von Ribbentrop met again. Lipski explained that the proposals had met with no enthusiasm in Warsaw, and that while Foreign Minister Colonel Beck was prepared to discuss the removal of the League from Danzig, he was not prepared to hand the place back to Germany. Nor was Beck prepared to discuss improved road and rail links across the Corridor unless they were 'territorial' – that is, under Polish control.

Von Ribbentrop reported back to Hitler, and on the evening of 24 November 1938 Adolf Hitler added Danzig to the list of military targets for the forthcoming campaign in the east. It was clear that in spite of the NSDAP's grip on the local population and the conciliatory attitudes of British and French politicians, he would be unable to bargain Danzig back into the Reich. For the first time Hitler's policy of threat and bluster met with a loud, clear and firm rebuttal. It was something of a gamble. The Nazis must have known that the Poles would not release Danzig without a struggle – indeed, they had asked for something they knew the Poles would not give. The Nazification process thrived on an air of constant tension. If by some chance the Poles had agreed to hand over the city it is quite possible that even at this late stage NSDAP support in the city would have evaporated. The Nazis could only thrive on being seen to be refused, and the Poles had just obliged.

The Nazification drive had been remarkably successful by this time. According to the Party's own population estimate there were 375,972 people resident in the city.[21] In December 1937 Party membership stood at 36,475 – or 9.7 per cent of the population. In that year Nazi posts of responsibility, membership of voluntary organisations and services totalled over 254,389.[22] Though many of these posts overlapped and the bulk of the membership were passive, it is clear that almost every avenue of expression or opinion – from welfare to warfare, from motoring to flying – was controlled, regulated and policed by the NSDAP. Only the Catholic Church stood a little to one side from this network. But even there, after the departure of Bishop O'Rourke in June 1938, his successor Bishop Splett released the pent-up tensions of the German hierarchy in a ferocious anti-Polish campaign that blocked the promotion of Polish clerics and administrators, harassed Polish priests and closed Polish Catholic schools.

The Danzig NSDAP was a floundering, brutal beast for most of its existence. Its importance within the city lay not in the speed of its rise – which was hardly spectacular – nor in its violence – for it could only do what Berlin sanctioned, but rather in the social and national spirit it fostered within the community. Its real achievement lay in slowly but surely creating and manipulating opinion to create a border mentality where one had not existed in such crude form before. By and large the Poles and Germans of the city had shown very early in the Free City's existence that they could rub along together. The discrepancy between the large number of Party members and the Party's poor performance at the polls indicates clearly that while Danzigers were prepared to take advantage of it as a social refuge, they were by no means as convinced by it as Forster and Hitler desired.

The failure of the League of Nations in Danzig was a failure of nerve and understanding on the part of the member states: unforgivably they minimised the difficulty and frustrations of the position they had carved for Poland – a country emerging to modernity after over 100 years of partition, a country without financial capital, with hostile neighbours, border problems, huge minorities but without a port of its own. The League also failed to understand the humiliation of the defeat and dismemberment inflicted on Germany and failed spectacularly in its appreciation of the unworkable arrangements made around Danzig. In the abstract the Free City arrangements might have worked, but they failed to take into account the hostilities they provoked; failed to take into account the fears and prejudices unleashed by the sudden alteration of patterns of trade and allegiance; and failed to take into account the long years of humiliating Polish partition, Prussian *Polenpolitik* and the rise of revolutionary Russia.

For both Poland and Germany, Danzig became an isolated node of half-realised ambitions, of pointless and wasteful economic competition, of half-understood fears, of provincial prejudice and wilful stiff-necked pride. These elements were part of a long and complex history of German restlessness and Polish insecurity – ideas that the British, French and Americans, secure in thoroughly different kinds of national, linguistic and cultural identities, could not even begin to chart. The Allies' aim in 1918 had been to leave Germany shorn of its military and industrial power, to make sure that it would never again be capable of waging war or threatening the established pattern of Atlantic trade and European industry. To help them do this the Allies had, among other measures, resurrected Poland to stand as a barrier to the reunification of the German eastern lands. But that was as far as their thinking took them. Western Europe hardly appreciated the cultural and economic complexities of the German drive to the east, nor the nexus of ideas lodged in its collective polity used to fuel that drive. They did not understand, or gave no thought to, the ethnic, national and ideological conflicts that their arrangements would create within Germany, nor the internal and external targets Germany would come to identify as the causes of its misfortune. The Allied politicians lacked understanding, and yet they did not hesitate to place a barrier to Germany's growth, and having placed that barrier, did not think to support it effectively in the years to come.

Mikos, in his study of the League of Nations' actions in Danzig, attempted to apportion blame by counting up the number of important decisions made by the various High Commissioners. The British – who had dreamed up the Free City idea in the first place – came out of the exercise very badly, while the Dutch and Italians did rather better. And yet it is much more complex than that. The British made some bad decisions, as did the Irishman Sean Lester. Yet at a time when decisive action against the Nazis might still have been effective the Swiss Carl Burckhardt made very few decisions at all.[23]

In a carefully balanced account of the pressures at work H.S. Levine has written:

> Try as the Danzig government might, the free city's ethnic and economic difficulties were dependent on forces almost totally beyond its control. Some small amelioration of the economic catastrophe might have been gained by a programme of thoroughgoing compromise with Poland, but the success of such a policy depended on the reasonableness of Polish demands and on the good sense of the Danzig electorate. Unfortunately so sensitive were the Danzigers on the issue that no serious Polish demand appeared reasonable. The voters turned to those parties that promised a fight against the Polish enemy. Given the weakness of the free city, this fight could not possibly succeed. On the contrary, it invited effective Polish economic retaliation. The political anger created by economic fears was diverted by nationalism away from the only course that stood even a small chance of success. The anger of the electorate, denied an outlet in successful political action, became hysterical. The Nazis made themselves the beneficiaries.[24]

In the long run the Nazis made the Danzigers their willing victims. The Danzigers went along with them – slowly at first and then with greater enthusiasm. They agreed to support policies most of them knew to be damaging, misguided and inhuman. They went along with populist solutions to problems that if not actually created by the Nazis, had certainly been worked on and exaggerated to the Nazis' own advantage.

After the voluntary enslavement of the Reich it was the failure of the Danzigers that opened up Eastern Europe to the murderous policies of the Nazis. The Danzigers, in spite of the clear example of what was happening in the Reich, tolerated the Nazis in their city because they were 'strong' on Poland and the Polish threat. And they did this against all common and economic sense. While Danzigers were most definitely on the sharp end of Polish–German relations they were also historically and personally in a unique position to give the lie to Nazi manipulation and simplification. This they did not do. Instead, to their own imagined advantage, they fell in with the renewed *Drang nach Osten*.

7

The NSDAP and the Danzig Jews

Up to 1918 the Jewish community of Danzig was remarkable only in the extent to which it was entirely unremarkable. Jews had settled in the area during the Middle Ages – possibly as early as the tenth century – though strict laws prevented them from dwelling inside the city walls. In the fifteenth and sixteenth centuries regulations relaxed a little and they were allowed to buy entrance to the annual city trade fair. Appeals to the Polish King Sigismund III Vasa failed to secure them the right to settle in the city, and it was only with the Prussian revision of Jewish legal status in 1869 that they became fully equal citizens before the law.

The Prussians, anxious to catch up with their rival industrial neighbours – England, France and Belgium – found their efforts hampered in Pomerania by the entrenched system of serfdom and by a class system in which virtually no bourgeoisie existed to mediate between the Prussian Junker and Polish *szlachta* landlords and the vast impoverished and illiterate mass of the peasantry. Prussian rule allowed the Jews to enter the full range of commercial and cultural life as a way of creating a middle class in the Prussian east. Prussian relaxation of anti-Jewish legislation allowed the Jews to move out of Altschotland, and Hoppenbruch – their traditional settlements, and to buy and occupy property in the city centre. Almost as a gesture of confidence in the Prussian regime the Danzig Jews agreed to close down their outlying synagogues in Langfuhr, Weinberg, Altschotland, Danzig-Breitgasse and Danzig-Mattenbuden and to build a new Central Synagogue within the city walls.[1]

The completion of the massive and alarming Byzantine Temple of United Communities in 1887 could not disguise, however, the community's problems. As the local Poles responded to the *Kulturkampf*, and as industrialisation put them under increasing pressure to 'Germanise' themselves, so the Poles dug in their heels and became more and more defiantly Polish. Between 1905 and 1912 the Poles responded to the Prussian efforts to turn them into Germans by making good the deficiencies in their own class structure as best they could. Their intention was to put a halt to the activities of the Prussian Colonisation Commission, which had been buying up Polish land and estates for re-sale to German settlers. These were the peak years of the Polish effort to create their own banking and credit facilities to rival those of the Jews and the Prussians, whom they saw as in collusion. Such was the growing paranoia of those years that the Jews were increasingly cast as the agent of the opposing national interest by Pole and Prussian alike.

The creation of the Free City of Danzig, sandwiched between the great amputated arm of East Prussia and the slim extrusion of the Polish Corridor, changed the situation of the Danzig Jews completely. The Versailles settlement created a tiny city-state whose very existence exaggerated and exacerbated national tensions and left the Danzig Jews trapped between the rival powers. Danzig, though ethnically and linguistically German, depended upon trade not with its immediate hinterland – for Pomerania was agriculturally and industrially very poor – but with the most far-flung corners of the Polish state, reached via the course of the great river Vistula and its connected waterways. It was a situation ripe for exploitation.

After 1922, when the Versailles politicians finally fixed the Danzig, German and Polish borders, social pressure and conflict within the Free City became increasingly complex, and the internal life of the Jewish community was no exception to this. Not all the Jews in the city were German. After 1922 a flood of *Ostjuden* (Eastern Jews) had arrived from Poland, Lithuania, the Ukraine, Hungary, Czechoslovakia and Russia. All were intent on emigrating to Canada, the US or Palestine. In contrast to the urbane, sophisticated, assimilated, German-speaking Danzig Jews, the *Ostjuden* were mainly *shtetl* dwellers, villagers who spoke Yiddish rather than German or Polish, were desperately poor, and were of Zionist, and often socialist, opinion. The liberal Danzig Jews, in spite of a long history of protecting East European orthodox Jews from persecution, found that in these circumstances the orthodox Jews' long gabardines and kaftans, fur hats, untrimmed beards, side-locks, phylacteries, country manners, 'medieval' beliefs and outspoken Zionist opinions were an embarrassment and a source of conflict.

Between 1920 and 1925 over 600,000 *Ostjuden* passed through Danzig. The city authorities were forced to open up a transit camp for them amid the lumber yards on the island of Troyl. In 1922 the US realised that in creating the Free City of Danzig it had helped create a stepping-stone for would-be immigrants, and it abruptly tightened up its immigration procedures. The British, too made, legal entry to Palestine more difficult, and illegal entry more dangerous. The result was that a large number of *Ostjuden* found themselves trapped in Danzig – unable to proceed further on their journey, and unwilling to return. In 1910 there had been only 2,717 Jews in Danzig. By 1929 there were 10,488.[2]

Easy entry into Danzig meant that the *Ostjuden* revived orthodox practice in the city. In 1923 an orthodox rabbi – Jakub Sagalowitsch – was elected to the Mattenbuden synagogue. It was the first orthodox appointment in the city for over 63 years. The rabbi, who belonged to the Zionist *Mizrachi* movement, almost immediately antagonised the Danzig liberal Jews, the League of Nations and the British Foreign Office by performing marriages whose clear intent was to circumvent British restrictions on entry into Palestine. Such were the antagonisms generated that his contract was not renewed when it expired in 1932. Further evidence of the strains and tensions within the community can be seen in the decisions to build new synagogues in Zoppot and in the suburb of Langfuhr.

The orthodox and liberal Jews were divided on the best way to combat the growth of anti-Semitism that marked the inter-war years. The unstable borders imposed by the Versailles Treaty had acted as a catalyst upon the fearful Polish and German populations and had formalised a 'Jewish threat' for both sides. But the Danzig Jews faced a particular dilemma. In the Reich it was possible to combat anti-Semitism as part of the fight to secure and maintain democracy. But in Danzig the pressures were slightly different. Nominally the Polish Jews were under the protection of the League of Nations but any complaint about anti-Semitic activity in the city could be seen as serving the interests of Poland and characterised as unpatriotic – one of the crimes the Jews were accused of anyway. The idea that the Danzig Jews were somehow unpatriotic was a slander that even casual enquiry would demolish. Many had been decorated for military service and a plaque on the wall of the Central Synagogue commemorated 56 Danzig Jews who had given their lives for Germany in the 1914–18 war. For most of its existence the League was dithering and ineffectual, so the Danzig Jews met the rise of anti-Semitism with their traditional low-key strategy of apologetics and economic pressure on the business community. German resentments found expression in the growth of Nazi power. In practice what protected the Jews in Danzig – many of whom were Polish Jews leaving Poland – was the fear that any open move against them would precipitate a Polish invasion.

Neither the Danzigers nor the *Ostjuden* wanted to see a Polish takeover in the city. Poland was involved in a long trade war against Germany and against Polish Jews. Unassimilated Jews in Poland were barred from holding state employment and from a whole range of private enterprises. Although press reports of pogroms were later discredited, the actual level of anti-Semitic violence coupled with the devastating poverty of rural Poland was such that between 1919 and 1939 some 400,000 Polish Jews decided to emigrate. Doubtless there would have been even more if entry to Palestine or the US had been easier. There was certainly no advantage for these people in provoking the Poles into an attack on the city. The Zionists, however, found the Danzigers to be intolerably timid in their defence of the Jewish identity and presence. While the Danzigers tried to limit the influence of the Zionists in the Jewish community's decision-making processes, it was the Zionists who had the ear of the Danzig Nazis and the local police force. The Nazis and the Zionists agreed that the only way to help the Polish and Danzig Jews was for the entire Jewish community to emigrate to Palestine.

The rifts in the Jewish community were gradually brought to a halt by the success of the Nazi Party in the 1933 Danzig Volkstag elections. While the city was slower than the Reich to Nazify, by 1935 it was far more of a Nazi stronghold than most places within the Reich: NSDAP membership accounted for one person in every 18.6 (compared to 1:26.4 in the Reich), while one in every 11.1 was a Nazi voter (compared to 1:18.5 in the Reich). By 1938 the NSDAP had a membership of nearly 10 per cent of all Danzigers.[3] Nazi electoral success did not mean that the city was suddenly subject to violent confrontation, however, as the Nazis were bound by the same considerations that bound the Jews. Rather than the weight of the League of Nations it was the constant threat of a Polish move to incorporate the city that held the Nazis in check.

This external brake on Nazi power was helped by the presence of the 'moderate' Nazi, Senate President Hermann Rauschning. But his sudden understanding of the content of the Nazi revolution – the 'revolution of nihilism' as he was later to call it – and his consequent departure from politics in 1934, removed the last internal barrier to unrestrained Nazi ambition and saw the start of a campaign that operated quietly and effectively to isolate and exclude Jews from every aspect of public life in the city. The Nazis declared that they would stick to the very letter of the Danzig–Polish Accords, but privately they removed and demoted Jewish judges; doctors found their practices transferred, their hospital consultancies withdrawn; artists, technicians and writers found that their contracts for work at the local radio station, or at the

Opera-in-the-Woods were not renewed. Also the various Jewish physical culture associations – most notably *Bar Kochba* – were banned from using public recreation and gymnasium facilities. Very soon the atmosphere was such that parents started to withdraw their children from state schools in favour of separate Jewish community schools: for the younger children there was Sam Echt's primary school, and for the older children there was Dr Ruth Rosenbaum's High School. In spite of the difficulties both schools maintained impressive standards of education.

The Nazi leadership denounced repeated assaults on Jews, but the criminals went unpunished, and the hideously anti-Semitic newspaper *Der Stürmer*, the Nazi paper *Völkischer Beobachter* and a wide range of equally racist and propagandist pamphlets were still sold openly on the streets. In July 1935 local shopkeepers announced a campaign against 'unfair Jewish competition'. They did not specify in what way Jewish competition was unfair, but then, as they had the muscular backing of the brownshirted SA, such niceties were hardly necessary. As the campaign progressed, so the NSDAP felt need of reinforcement and began to bus in brownshirts from the nearby town of Elbing. The brownshirts patrolled the beaches carrying anti-Semitic placards. The League of Nations intervened to prevent the Elbing Nazis from parading in the city centre, but felt that this was the limit of legitimate action. The League may have felt that it needed to do only a very little because the Nazis did not get the reception they had hoped for. Where they were not laughed off the beach as primitives, they met with a stony indifference: many of the tourists were Poles who did not think it necessary to advertise anti-Semitic opinions, and many of the other bathers were wealthy Polish Jews who, unaware of the situation in Danzig, were attending the Zoppot Cure House on the Beach or the Wagner Festival at the Opera-in-the-woods.

The Nazis were forced to change tactics and began to haunt the night. They seized and beat up unwary Jews – local and tourist alike. Yet before very long this activity was halted by *Gauleiter* Forster, who pointed out that Danzig was in the middle of a trade recession and badly needed tourist revenues. The boycott of the Jewish tourist trade may have ended badly but the Nazis pressed ahead with other projects. In 1936 they made illegal the kosher slaughter of animals within the city, and banned all Jewish traders from the Central, Langfuhr and Zoppot markets. By the end of that year some 3,000 Jews, scenting perhaps what was in the wind, had left Danzig. Carl Burckhardt, League of Nations High Commissioner, calculated that some 7,479 remained.[4]

By this time the League of Nations was little more than a phantom moral conscience. The Swiss High Commissioner Carl Burckhardt was thought by many to be a Nazi sympathiser, but more probably was a careerist and confused Puritan with an authoritarian cast of mind. His refusal to stand against the Nazis publicly, and his decision to counsel the League to pursue a policy of restraint in Danzig certainly played into the hands of the Nazis by allowing the NSDAP to improve its hold on the city both by stealth and by electoral success. Having given the Nazis some leeway, his failure to influence them behind the scenes was only revealed when, after a violently anti-Semitic speech by *Gauleiter* Forster on 23 October 1937 the Danzig Nazis ran amok and attacked over 300 Jewish homes.

The violence of these attacks was such that Marian Chodacki, the Polish Commissioner General in Danzig, not a man noted for his Jewish sympathies, was moved to complain about the treatment of Polish Jews. He made it clear that while he was not turning *'Judenfreund'* he was determined to protect Poland's commercial interests in the city, and these now lay largely in the presence of some 2,000 Polish Jews, whom he was taking under his personal protection. When Chodacki's charges were brought before the Danzig Senate, the Nazis pooh-poohed Polish 'concern' and had plenty of mud to sling in return over Poland's treatment of its Jews. Though it was no more than a gesture, Chodacki's interest alarmed the Nazis who suspected that the Poles were looking for a reason to invade.[5]

In May 1937 the bathing beaches opened again, but this time bathing was segregated, and the brownshirts were not ridiculed. Over the summer a series of raids on Jewish hostels and Jewish-owned hotels were conducted. In September Jewish doctors in the Free City were relieved of their practices, with the exception of two who were restricted to treating only Jewish patients. In October two people were arrested for 'racial pollution'. Although the Nuremberg Laws did not yet apply in the city, the local police imposed a fine saying that it was a political matter and did not need to come before the courts. In November Jews were banned from all cinemas.

On 9 November 1938 Herbert vom Rath, Third Secretary to the German Ambassador in Paris, died of gunshot wounds after Herschel Grynszpan bungled his attempt to assassinate the Ambassador. The date of his death was most unfortunate since it was also the anniversary of Hitler's failed Munich *putsch*. The combination of events unleashed a well-organised and probably pre-planned wave of anti-Semitic violence – later dubbed Kristallnacht

– throughout the Reich. Danzig, always a little out-of-step with the Reich, spread its demonstration over several days. Between 12–23 November the synagogues in Langfuhr and Zoppot were burned down and over 300 homes were destroyed. Only an armed guard of First World War veterans protected the Central Synagogue from the Nazis.

On 23 November *Gauleiter* Forster announced that the Nuremberg Race Laws had now been ratified and adopted by the Danzig Senate for application in the Free City. It was now illegal for Aryans – including the Poles – to have sex with Jews, or for female Jews to be employed in domestic service at an Aryan household. All private Jewish enterprise was abolished. In spite of Marian Chodacki's promise of protection, the city's 2,000 Polish Jews decided that perhaps it was marginally safer to return to Poland after all.

The decision to return was a mark of desperation since life in Danzig at this point can have been only slightly worse than the situation that awaited them in Poland. When farm prices fell in the Depression, the *Sanacja* regime of Marshal Piłsudski had made an alliance with the *Endecja* (NDC or National Democratic Party), and rather than embark on land reform to ease the burden of the Polish middle class and the peasantry, had encouraged Poles of all classes to see the Jews as the cause of their misery. Some writers have tried to minimise the anti-Semitic content of events:

> ... as agricultural co-operatives developed in Poland, these middlemen were no longer needed and the Jews were deprived of this means of livelihood; they were left destitute, with no means of support. This had nothing to do with anti-Semitism; it was a natural economic development.[6]

But this hardly explains the nature of the 'development'. Starting in 1935 there had been a well-orchestrated series of pogroms; credit to Jewish firms was blocked; Jewish students, when they did not have to stand for lectures were forced to use a Jewish bench; in schools and universities it was not uncommon to hear of Jewish girls who had been attacked by fellow students wielding razors to their hair and face. The *Endecja* campaign to boycott all Jewish trade had caused thousands of bankruptcies. Thousands more Jews lived on the edge of starvation. In Warsaw *Endecja* organised anti-Semitic marches at which members gave the Nazi salute.[7] Yet for all this, the situation of the Jews was rather better in Poland than it was in Germany or any of the East European states at that time.

After all those Jews who could had left Danzig, or had made plans to do so, 3,000 still remained. These were Danzigers by birth, citizens of the Free State. They had nowhere to run to. It was clear that some desperate measures were called for if they were to avoid the fate of Reich Jews. On 17 December 1938, some 2,000 of those remaining assembled in the Central Synagogue to debate the possibilities and resolve upon a course of action. Zvi Hermann Segal had voiced a plan for the massed emigration of the entire community to Palestine over a year before, but then his good connections with the local police and his membership of the Zionist Revisionist Party had made him a figure of suspicion to the conservative Danzigers.

Their hesitation was not entirely unfounded. The Revisionist Party was an extreme right-wing Zionist group led by Vladimir Jabotinsky (sometimes written Zabotinsky), a man widely regarded as a Jewish fascist. The military arm of the Party, *Irgun Zvai Leumi*, was made up mainly of Polish Jews armed and trained by the right-wing Polish government of Marshal Śmigły-Rydz and Colonel Beck in the hope that military action by this group would force the League of Nations into setting up a Jewish state in Palestine to which the Poles could then expel their 3,300,000 Jews. The Revisionists were later to provide a 'sizeable proportion' of the *Ordnungsdienst* – the Jewish ghetto police who assisted the SS. Even within the tiny Jewish resistance movement in the Warsaw ghetto, the Revisionists had a bad reputation for maintaining contacts with the Polish right wing and for refusing to share arms or accept direction from those who were not Party members. From 1937 onwards *Irgun* was directly involved in bloody reprisals against Palestinian Arabs and was in direct confrontation with the Jewish Settlement Agency and their military arm, *Haganah*. Revisionist policy insisted that the whole of the Emirate of Transjordan should be made part of any Jewish state – by force if necessary.[8]

That the Danzig Jews should one year later see Segal and his party in a different light is a measure of their desperation. Segal's connections with the local police and his Zionist opinions were now a positive advantage. In language that was clear and direct Zvi Hermann Segal told the assembly in the Central Synagogue that to stay in Danzig meant certain poverty and probable death. Other speakers backed this with stories from the Reich. At the end of the day it was agreed that Segal would arrange with the authorities for the evacuation of the entire community. They were going to Palestine.

Gerald Shepherd, the British Consul in Danzig, knew almost immediately of the plan to enter Palestine and became increasingly frustrated when, in spite of his best efforts, he failed to convince the Foreign Office of the gravity of the situation facing the Danzig Jewish community. He also worried that Carl Burckhardt and the League of Nations had not done all they might to help. Burckhardt was still advising the League that they ought to compromise with the Nazis. British, French and American interests in the League seemed unwilling to go against Burckhardt's advice by offering assistance to the Jews lest this be taken as tacit acknowledgement of the failure of the League's policies. While Shepherd's relations with Burckhardt, the local Nazis and the Foreign Office deteriorated he was nevertheless obliged to dissuade the Jews from any attempt to enter the British Mandate of Palestine illegally. Shepherd fulfilled his obligations with increasingly obvious distaste before being replaced as Consul by his brother in the summer of 1939. The Nazis meanwhile, ever keen on tidy legal fictions, obliged each departing Jew to sign a document stating that they were leaving the city of their own free will.

Zvi Hermann Segal, after lengthy negotiations with the Nazis, had agreed to sell the little property the community owned in common to help finance the exodus. The fire-damaged synagogues of Langfuhr and Zoppot, the Central Synagogue, three cemeteries, a lodge and a vacant plot of ground were valued on the open market at around 500,000 Danzig gulders. Unfortunately there was only one buyer for the property and the Nazis refused to pay more than 300,000 gulders. Segal had totally failed to raise any money from other Jewish communities in America and Western Europe – probably because of his membership of the Revisionist Party – and so was forced to conclude a deal for the sale of property to the Nazis.

It is doubtful that even after the sale of all its property the community would have had enough money to accomplish its task, but at this point the American Jewish Joint Distribution Committee in New York came to their aid and offered to buy all the community sacred objects and records, including the unique art collection of Lesser Gieldzinski, which had been bequeathed to the community in 1904. This sale would acknowledge that the community was about to be broken up with no hope of recovery. But there was no choice; they had to accept. Accordingly the 342 separate items of interest, weighing a total of over two tons, were packed into 10 crates and on 8 February 1939 were shipped to the Jewish Theological Seminary in New York.

The Danzig Senate informed Segal that he had until 31 May to complete his evacuation. By mid-April the Central Synagogue had been surrounded by a high wooden fence. Over the main entrance fluttered a banner which read: 'This synagogue for demolition.'

On the fence someone had lettered in large, clear Sütterlin script the words: 'Come dear May and make us Free from Jews.'

Against an atmosphere of increasing political tension Segal's plan began to unfold: 150 children would go to England for 'educational purposes'; 50 people were planning to go to Shanghai; 12 families were planning to emigrate to Bolivia. By the end of March the first 500 people, none of whom had entry permits from the British, were ready to begin the journey to Palestine. They left the city by bus and went first to Marienburg; there they entered a sealed train which took them via Breslau, Vienna and Budapest to Reni. At Reni they took ship for Varna, Istanbul, Cyprus, Rhodes, Zoa, Libire, Heraklion – a zig-zag course designed to confuse the British. On the journey they were attacked by British fighter planes, and there was a hunger strike in protest at the appalling conditions on board. They finally arrived in Palestine on 1 July 1939. These were the lucky ones; they were allowed to stay. Those who came after found that British opinion hardened against them rapidly with the outbreak of war.

Lord Lloyd, the British Colonial Secretary, who was generally regarded as pro-Arab, worried that the new arrivals might include German spies. With the precise gift of hindsight it is possible to see what an unlikely idea it was that any Jew would spy for Hitler, but Lloyd's knowledge of what was happening in Hitler's Europe was neither detailed nor extensive. Since the Nazis appeared to have actually helped the Jews to leave Danzig with the specific intention of entering Palestine illegally, Lord Lloyd's worries might be understood if not excused. Indeed his fear that the Jews were being used against the British in the Mediterranean was not entirely misplaced. The Germans had encouraged the Jews to head for Palestine as a way of discomfiting the British war effort in the Middle East, and both German and Italian radio had been broadcasting in Arabic that the British had invited boatloads of Jews to settle in Palestine as a way of driving out the Palestinian Arabs. Listeners were invited to believe that the Axis powers would support an anti-British uprising. Under these circumstances Lord Lloyd decided that all those attempting illegal entry to Palestine would be interned on Cyprus or Mauritius. The majority of those who arrived after the first transport from Danzig escaped the Final Solution to spend the war amid the boredom, pestilence and disease of British transit camps and were not permitted into Palestine until after 1945.[9]

The last of the Danzig Jews to arrive in Palestine were aboard the 800-ton paddle-steamer *Atlantic*, which docked in Haifa on 24 November 1940. By this time the British military were admitting no newcomers and set about transferring the refugees to the steamship *Patria*, which was moored nearby, for immediate shipment to Mauritius. *Haganah*, the military arm of the Jewish Agency, had decided, in spite of the British attitude, that no ship carrying would-be immigrants was to be allowed to leave port, and they had planted a bomb on board the *Patria* with the intention of disabling it. In the event something went seriously wrong – perhaps the ship was older and more frail than anyone had realised, or perhaps the bomb was too powerful – the explosion tore a huge hole in the ship's side and it capsized and sank in less than two minutes, taking with it over 200 refugees. The very people *Haganah* had sought to protect had been its victims.

The deaths were not without effect. Although British officials tried to hustle the survivors off to Mauritius as quickly as possible, the British Cabinet ruled that the survivors of the sinking should be allowed to stay in Palestine. British officials protested that the Jews could now assume that they had established the precedent of unlimited settlement and uncontrolled entry to the Mandate territory. General Wavell, whose troops were preparing to give battle with the German and Italian forces in the desert around Sidi Barani, said that the Jews had been seen to challenge and beat British authority, an example which he felt was not calculated to boost the morale of his troops, which would drive the Mufti further towards sympathy with the Nazis, and which would cause the British great difficulties in Iraq, Syria and Egypt as a result.[10]

The 1,580 Danzig Jews who had not been aboard the *Patria* at the time of the explosion were not subject to the mercy of the British Cabinet. They were kept at a camp in Athlit until a ship could be found for them. Many began to suspect that Britain had made a deal and that they were being sent back to Germany. Thus, when on 9 December 1940 Alan Saunders, Inspector General of Police, arrived at the camp at 5 a.m. in the morning, accompanied by 150 armed British police and troops, the inmates refused to move, scattered their possessions across the floor, took off their clothes and lay naked on their beds. Chaim Weizmann, a Jew from the Polish town of Pinsk who was at that time an influential London Zionist later to become Israel's first President, wrote a letter of protest to the Foreign Office quoting two anonymous eye-witness accounts saying that the women had rolled in the dust half-naked, that the men had been severely beaten and that the police had laughed and jeered at the refugees.[11]

An official inquiry by Harold MacMichael, the High Commissioner, failed to resolve the allegations and ended up by questioning the validity of evidence from anonymous informants. The

British had little idea that its policemen could resemble the dreaded Nazi security services in the eyes of grieving and fearful Jewish refugees. The Foreign Office was only concerned lest tales of brutality should alienate British and American Jewish influence friendly to the war effort.

By 1 September 1939 there were still about 1,700 Jews in Danzig – most of these too old or too sick to travel. The Nazis nevertheless picked out 450 as fit for work and sent them to the newly opened labour camp at Stutthof. In November a further 50 were allowed to leave for Palestine. They first went to Vienna, then they were marched to Bratislava, put into a camp, taken by river-steamer to the Hungarian border, taken back to Bratislava, put on board a paddle-steamer and taken to the town of Kladovo and interned in the camp at Sabac. It was there that the German invasion of Yugoslavia found them in October 1941. One man escaped to Switzerland, two were released after immigration papers arrived admitting them to Palestine. The rest were shot by firing squad.

Surprisingly a further transport of 500 Danzig Jews left the city in August 1941, but these were intercepted by the British and sent straight to Mauritius. After this, the few who remained in Danzig were confined to a series of grain warehouses on Mausegasse. Some were transferred to the Warsaw ghetto, others to the Lublin ghetto, from which they passed into the obscene maw of the Majdanek death camp. A few were sent to the concentration camp at Theresienstadt. Of these there were no survivors.

At the end of March 1945 Russian and Polish forces finally managed to take Danzig by siege. They found a few Jews – some say 20, others 100 – who had lived in the city right through the war, protected because they were married to important Aryans or because they had useful skills in armaments manufacture.

International scrutiny of the Free City of Danzig may have helped preserve the Danzig Jews from the worst the Nazis could do, but it did precious little actually to help them. British, French, American and Polish policies might all be blamed; the finger might also be pointed at the international Jewish community who failed to help. Certainly all these people share the responsibility for pushing normal, ordinary Danzig citizens, who happened also to be Jews, into a massive emigration to a land that none of them had ever seen. The process by which conservative assimilated liberal German Jews – who previously had shown no interest in Zionism – were pushed further and further towards a Zionist solution to their problems is also instructive. Under these circumstances Zionism – even the extremism of the Revisionists – took on a new meaning and a new urgency. However, when it comes to

apportioning blame, those Danzigers who watched their neighbours and fellow citizens harassed, intimidated, expelled and even
liquidated in their name and the name of the Party they had
elected – or at least failed to oppose – must surely carry an enormous burden.

Now, nearly 50 years after the destruction of the Jewish community in Danzig, there is precious little to remind us of their
presence in the city or their fate. The artifacts and sacred objects
sold abroad can be seen in exhibition at the Jewish Museum in
New York, but in modern Gdańsk barely a trace remains. The
Central Synagogue was demolished as soon as the Jews had
departed; the site is still a vacant lot at the back of what is now
police headquarters. The Langfuhr Synagogue has been refur-
bished as the Wrzeszcz School of Music. There is no plaque to
mark what the building once was, but the high front windows and
the false suspended floor sit oddly with the building's current use.
The caretaker is a cheerful, kindly Danzig Pole who remembers
how the place used to look, and is delighted to show visitors
around. The rear of the building is now a delivery area for the
local supermarket. There, amid the peeling paint, a crumbling
plaster sculpture of the Tablets of the Law still clings to the high
gable-end and reveals the original purpose of the place.

8

The NSDAP and Danzig: 1939

5 January: Polish Foreign Minister Beck went to see Hitler in Berchtesgaden. Hitler claimed that Danzig rightfully belonged to Germany and should be returned to the Reich. Hitler said that if Poland would grant extra-territorial road and rail links across the Corridor, he would be prepared to guarantee Poland's borders. Beck saw very little for Poland in such an arrangement but agreed to take the proposal to Warsaw.

10 January: Hitler assured Beck that there would be no German military action to seize Danzig.

13 January: German Foreign Minister von Ribbentrop ordered *Gauleiter* Forster to delay the formal introduction to Danzig of the Hitler salute, the formation of a local SS unit and the use of the German flag until at least the end of January.[1]

25–7 January: Von Ribbentrop and Beck met in Warsaw. Both agreed that if the League of Nations collapsed or withdrew from Danzig, both Germany and Poland would issue statements saying that Danzig would remain a Free City until Germany and Poland could resolve their difficulties and differences.

29 January: Polish students from the Danzig Technical High School were drinking and chatting in the Café Langfuhr when German students interrupted and told them not to chatter like apes in Polish. A fight broke out. The proprietor wrote to the Polish Students' Association announcing that in future Poles were banned from the café.

12 February: Polish students returned to the Café Langfuhr but found a notice on the door which read: 'Dogs and Poles not allowed. Poor Dogs.' A fight broke out and was followed by further violence in the lecture halls of the High School. All classes were cancelled. Over the next few days Polish students in Germany, in Kraków, Poznań and Warsaw demonstrated in sympathy. The Germans sent a Commission of Inquiry to Danzig, but nothing came of it.[2]

13 February: Count Edward Raczyński, Polish Ambassador to Britain, visited Beck in Warsaw. He thought 'the problem of Danzig would shortly demand solution as a result of the abandonment by the League of Nations, and especially by Britain, of its role and obligations as guarantor of the Free City.'[3]

25 February: Warsaw students threw stones at the German embassy in protest over the Café Langfuhr incident.

1 March: Polish Ambassador Lipski spoke with Göring, who was still weak from losing 45 pounds weight in a purge. Lipski felt that the Danzig Nazis were putting pressure on the Nazi leadership, but Göring assured him that there would be no military conflict over Danzig.

20–1 March: Von Ribbentrop taxed Lipski again on the matter of extra-territorial road and rail links with Danzig. Next day there was frantic activity among British and French diplomats as they tried to establish a policy on Polish–German relations. In Berlin Lipski called on von Ribbentrop. He was told that Hitler was very angry at Poland's intransigence over Danzig. The return of Danzig was, he said, to be a precondition of future friendly relations between Poland and Germany. The Germans wanted the Poles to consider the idea of a possible pact against Russia, and von Ribbentrop said that Danzig was to be a security for this co-operation. Much to Lipski's annoyance he pointed out that Poland could not hope to steer an independent course between Germany and Russia indefinitely, and he urged Lipski to go to Warsaw and tell Beck that Hitler was convinced the Poles were not taking him seriously. Lipski left for Warsaw at once.

23 March: The previous day *Gauleiter* Forster had announced that the Danzig Volkstag so perfectly reflected the opinion of the Danzig public that he was suspending that year's elections – current deputies would serve for another four years. The League of Nations, in a panic after the German seizure of Memel that same day, made no reply. Although technically the Lithuanian government had ceded Memel to Germany, it was clear that the Germans had pulled off a very successful political and military coup. The Poles saw that this operation had implications for them and for Danzig. They began to feel that time was running out.

24 March: Hitler spent the day closeted with General Brauchitsch, Chief of the German Army. Clearly the Polish government had no intention of giving away its rights to Danzig, and Hitler wondered whether a German military coup in the city

might not make re-possession easier for the Poles to accept. The following day Admiral Canaris, head of the German Intelligence Service, reported that the Poles had mobilised the first three categories of their reserve army. He estimated that there were 4,000 Polish soldiers in Gdynia.[4]

26 March: Lipski returned from Warsaw to say that the Polish position was unchanged. While improved road and rail links between Danzig and the Reich were in order, there was no possibility that these could be extra-territorial, nor would the Poles allow Danzig to return to the Reich.

27 March: There were anti-German demonstrations in Bydgoszcz. Von Ribbentrop complained to Lipski that atrocities had been committed against Germans living in Poland. The following day Beck summoned the German Ambassador, denied that any atrocities had taken place and warned that any attempt to alter the status of Danzig would be seen as a hostile move against Poland. In Warsaw Kennard met with Beck to put forward a British proposal that Poland, France and Britain should sign a mutual assistance pact. Beck accepted the idea at once.

31 March: Chamberlain announced the unconditional British–French guarantee of Poland's borders against German aggression.

1 April: In Warsaw Beck called a meeting of government ministers to discuss the danger of a possible German coup in Danzig. Beck worried that a German move in Danzig would signal an invasion of Poland from East Prussia, but thought on balance the Germans would prefer to seize the city and then negotiate a ceasefire in order to bargain for a peace settlement from a position of strength.

3 April: Hitler issued directives for Case White. Commanders were ordered to consider three possible plans of action: (a) a war with Poland; (b) the defence of the German frontiers; (c) the seizure of Danzig – an aggressive war, a defensive war and a local action with limited objectives. If it were possible Hitler wanted to exploit a 'favourable political situation' to grab Danzig without going to war. By 11 April Case White Appendix III, the plan for military action in Danzig, was complete.

28 April: With no sign of the British or French backing out of their guarantees to Poland, Hitler decided to fire his own warning shots: he told the British that if they went to war against him they would almost certainly lose their empire and he urged Britain to give him a free hand to solve the Danzig problem as he saw fit. He

said his offer of a negotiated settlement over Danzig was a 'once only deal'. If the city were returned to the Reich then Germany would willingly negotiate Polish access to the port, but only after the Poles had abandoned their treaty with the French and the British. This left the Danzig Nazis in a very difficult position. They could not publicly declare that they were planning to return to the Reich lest this provoke the Poles into an invasion under the protection of the League of Nations. Indeed in practical terms it would have been far easier for the Poles to take the city than it would for the Germans. While the Poles controlled the city's railways and the seven highways into the Free City area, their garrison on Westerplatte overlooked the whole port area and had a dock of its own. For the Germans, on the other hand, the city was cut off from East Prussia by the Vistula and the only bridge was at Tczew (Dirschau). The Poles could easily block this route by destroying the bridge. One thing was certain: whoever made a move to take Danzig, if they were to succeed it could not be any half-hearted effort.

23 May: At a senior military staff conference in the New Chancellery Hitler talked with his generals about his ambitions in the east. It was not a question of seizing Danzig, he said, but of 'expanding our living space in the east, of securing our food supplies and of settling the Baltic problem ...' He added: 'There is no question of sparing Poland.' Throughout the month preparations for a German move in Danzig went ahead at a considerable pace. The local brownshirts openly paraded and drilled with arms, while at night guns and ammunition were smuggled through the port or across the Vistula. Wehrmacht officers 'on holiday' lectured the SA on street-fighting techniques and hand-to-hand combat. They also gave additional training sessions for the cadets, high school and scout companies. By the end of the month there were 168 German officers of the High Command in the city for 'study purposes'. There were also 12 light and 4 heavy artillery pieces secreted about the place.

17 June: Goebbels, Reich Minister for Enlightenment and Propaganda, on a visit to Danzig, gave an alarming and violent speech at the Artushof. He said that Poland must allow Danzig to return to the Reich, and uttered dire warnings if Poland dared to refuse.

20 June: In spite of British protests to the League of Nations the Danzig Nazis celebrated the fifth anniversary of their electoral success by arriving at the Volkstag clad in the brown uniforms of

the SA. The only two members who were not in Nazi uniform were the two Polish deputies. It had been Forster's intention to use this rare meeting of the Volkstag to formally introduce the German flag and the Nazi salute and also to announce the introduction of the Nuremberg Race Laws, but in view of British protest the German Foreign Office advised that these things be deferred. This was virtually the last time that any member of the League of Nations managed to exert any power over the Danzig Nazis, and for all practical purposes the League's regulation of city affairs ceased at this point. Two days after this, Hitler asked the military to draw up plans to secure the bridge at Tczew.

27 June: British Ambassador Kennard wrote to Foreign Secretary Lord Halifax from Warsaw to say that the Danzig Freikorps now numbered about 4,000 men and was located in new barracks at Praust. He observed that the smuggling incidents in the port which had been frequent in the previous two months had now ceased and he supposed that this meant that the Freikorps were now fully armed.[5]

28 June: Gerald Shepherd, British Consul in Danzig, wrote to Lord Halifax describing the preceding week as 'increasingly eventful'. All members of the German Automobile Association had been obliged to answer a questionnaire about their vehicles. The owners of trucks and lorries had been required to submit them for inspection at the military police depot in Langfuhr, where each was given a military registration number. All draught horses had been taken for inspection too, and car-loads of saddles had been delivered to the local police. The previous night the city had been on a full invasion alert; the border with Poland had been closed while the Poles installed anti-tank ditches along the road to Gdynia. Shepherd noted that the Germans had constructed pontoon bridges across the Vistula and Nogat rivers to bypass the Polish-controlled bridge at Tczew. All students and civil servants had been told that they must spend their vacation inside the Free City area. A sports contest between Danzig and the Reich had been organised, and 1,000 'sportsmen' who just happened to be Reich-SS men stayed on after the meeting, living in the crowded police barracks.[6]

1 July: The previous day the workers on the early shift had arrived at the Danziger and Schichau Werfts to find armed guards wearing Nazi insignia patrolling the gates and perimeters. Less than five minutes' walk from the League of Nations building troops were hidden in the world's largest Youth Hostel, and the

area was fenced off with barbed wire. There were by now between 900 and 1,800 SS-men from East Prussia, 1,000 Wehrmacht regular soldiers, 800 'holiday-makers', SS sportsmen, the entire staff of General Eberhardt's headquarters, three armoured cars, 450 machine-guns and 30,000 rifles in the city. The Freikorps alone was estimated to be in divisional strength. *Pravda* reported: 'Danzig is teeming with German military trucks from Königsberg ... Danzig is invaded by hordes of "tourists".'[7]

19 July: Interviewed by Carl Burckhardt, *Gauleiter* Forster strenuously denied rumours that German soldiers had been brought into the city and said he knew of only four officers on holiday in Zoppot. He complained that the Poles, on the other hand, had illegally reinforced their garrison so they now had over 300 soldiers on Westerplatte. He also claimed that the Poles were trying to intimidate the city and had over 3,000 troops camped along the Free City boundaries. Three days later Consul General Shepherd wrote to Lord Halifax that the atmosphere in Danzig was so poisonous it justified wearing a gas mask.

27 July: Ambassador Lipski reported from Berlin that German attitudes were hardening rapidly on the issue of Danzig. Polish language newspapers in Berlin, Gleiwitz and Allenstein had been heavily censored; the Gestapo had arrested several Poles in Westphalia. In the border districts of Warmia 20 Polish schools – 40 per cent of the Polish schools in Germany – had been closed down on the grounds that they were a health risk. Lipski's patience with the Germans was wearing thin and he recommended that German schools in Poland should be closed in retaliation at a rate of 8 German schools for every Polish school.[8] In Berlin the High Command presented Hitler with its revised plan of campaign against Poland – including an action to gain control of the bridge at Tczew. Hitler approved the plan but left the date for action blank.

11 August: On 4–6 August the Danzig Nazis had refused to allow Polish customs officers to work without German supervision. The Poles had taken this as direct aggression against Poland itself. Hitler and the Polish government exchanged notes of protest, but the language of both was so intemperate that neither side had made the notes public. In the wake of this exchange *Gauleiter* Forster visited Hitler in Obersalzberg. Hitler was absolutely furious and when Forster returned home he told Burckhardt that on the matter of Danzig the Führer had reached the end of his patience with Poland. Burckhardt had a chance to see Hitler's fury for

himself when he went to Obersalzberg on 11 August. Hitler fumed
that the situation was now so precarious that the slightest provocation could bring destruction down upon the heads of the Poles.
William Shirer, who was then an American foreign correspondent,
arrived in Danzig to note that the hotels were full of German officers, the streets thronged with military vehicles hastily fitted with
local civilian licence plates; the roads along the border with
Poland had been blocked with logs and tank traps and he was told
that Czech machine-guns and anti-aircraft guns were still being
run across the river by night. As far as he could see the German
public had become completely isolated from world opinion: 'Any
fool knows that they don't give a damn about Danzig, It's just a
pretext.' He felt that the Danzigers' mentality was 'blinkered'; they
wanted Polish trade, but they did not want anything to do with
Poland. The Berliner *Zeitung* and *Der Führer* both claimed that
Poland was threatening to invade Germany. He concluded that
the city, like the Reich, was completely Nazified. He spent most of
the next day trying to persuade the Nazis to let him use the local
radio station in Langfuhr to send a report to America. At first they
were cool, then they refused outright. Shirer abandoned the leafy
shade of Langfuhr's Jaschkentalerwald to try the Polish radio
station in Gdynia. However, the taxi drivers refused to take him
saying the Poles would fire on any car with Danzig number
plates.[9]

14 August: During the night three Polish customs officers in
Danzig port saw a German vessel without lights. They suspected it
of gun-running and instructed it to heave-to in mid channel. It
ignored the order and berthed. When the customs officers landed
nearby to board it, they were immediately arrested by German
police. In a second incident a Polish border guard was shot dead.
The Poles announced that anyone attempting to cross the border
without authorisation would be shot without challenge. Four days
later *Gauleiter* Forster announced that the SS-Heimwehr Danzig
was to be formed. It would consist of 1,500 men and 42 officers.
The announcement was a fake since those who joined up were the
Wehrmacht and SS 'holiday-makers'. It is no surprise that the unit
was fully operational in less than a fortnight.

23 August: Much to Polish annoyance and against the Danzig
Constitution, *Gauleiter* Forster declared himself State President. In
Berlin Ambassador Henderson delivered a letter to Hitler in which
the British government expressed its willingness to discuss any
and all issues relating to German minorities in Poland. It was too
little and it was too late. Hitler flew into a rage and said that such

was its incompetence he expected Chamberlain's government to fall that night. That evening Hitler filled in the date on Case White plans for the invasion of Poland: 26 August. The German High Command sent a coded telegram to alert the German Consulate in Danzig. The following day the Russians signed the Molotov–Ribbentrop pact in which they agreed to carve Poland in two along the line of the Narew-Vistula and San rivers. On the same day the British ratified the Anglo–French Treaty guaranteeing Polish borders. Hitler had not expected this and the High Command sent a second coded telegram to Danzig, cancelling the first message. In Warsaw Ambassador Kennard was sifting evidence that Poles had been beating up Germans, and finally decided that German claims were grossly exaggerated. In a letter to Lord Halifax he said that Beck had tried to control anti-German resentments by ordering the press not to report anti-Polish violence in Silesia and East Prussia. Such acts, he said, had 'increased beyond number' in the preceding six weeks.[10]

25 August: German and Polish troops clashed in the early hours at the border village of Pelta (Pełta). One German soldier was killed. German newspapers magnified the clash into a major conflict and had farm houses in flames, passenger aircraft fired upon and German farmers castrated. In the town of Marienwerder the German police occupied the Polish Consulate. The newspapers reported that one-and-a-half million Polish reservists had been mobilised. It was clear to Hitler that his move would have to be made before the October rains turned the Polish fields into an impassible quagmire, and preferably before the Poles had completed their massive and ponderous mobilisation. Foreign businessmen began to pull out of Danzig.

28 August: The German battleship *Schlesswig-Holstein* put into Danzig. The Polish Commissioner General, Marian Chodacki, went aboard and inspected a guard of honour without realising that the bulkheads under his feet were secretly crammed with 250 German soldiers. The battleship was ushered to its mooring in the port canal by the tug-boat *Albert Forster*.

31 August: Ambassador Lipski cabled Beck that according to Ambassador Henderson the Germans wanted Danzig but were prepared to let Poland keep Gdynia so long as there was a plebiscite in the Corridor.[11] Meanwhile elsewhere in Berlin Hitler issued Directive Number One, detailed orders for the attack on Poland. A coded telegram was sent to the German Consulate in Danzig telling them that 'military operations' would commence next morning.

1 September: At 2.15 am, F.M. Shepherd, the acting British Consul in Danzig, who had been packing all night, was told by an American colleague that German newsreel cameramen were out on the streets with their cameras wound, waiting for something.[12] At 4.45 am, Action Stations sounded aboard the *Schlesswig Holstein*. The huge 11 inch guns swung to face a target less than 200 yards away. When they fired the air pressure was so great that windows throughout the port were shattered. Before long the petrol dump began to burn and a huge greasy pillar of smoke and flame curled high over the peninsula. At 5.15 am, German troops occupied the railway station, the Polish Customs Inspectorate and a Polish student hostel in Langfuhr. Carl Burckhardt was aware that his residence had been under Gestapo surveillance all night. In the early hours he received a visit from *Gauleiter* Forster who informed him that his function in the city was ended. After two hours of hasty packing, Burckhardt was put in a Gestapo car and driven to the Lithuanian border. He arrived in Kovno next day.[13] Later that morning Forster sent a telegram to Hitler announcing the successful return of Danzig to the Reich. He then went on local radio to make a special announcement: 'Men and women of Danzig! The hour for which you have longed for 20 years has come. This day Danzig has returned to the Greater German Reich. Our Führer Adolf Hitler has freed us!' The battle was not as easy as Forster made it sound. Innate German superiority refused to manifest itself in easy victory and German racial pride took a while to show any determination as impressive as that of the Polish army and navy. It was nearly three weeks before the fighting in and around Danzig was finished. Ilse Kohl was to recall:

I remember seeing a lot of planes flying over us, and a man in the street shouting that they were enemy planes. Suddenly everybody was running into the forest and shouting for gas masks. When we realised we were at war with Poland we were very worried because our house on Anton van Obbergen Weg was less than an hour's march from the Polish border. I had four children then, the youngest only a week old, so my husband took us over the Weichsel to the old flying boat station. From there we could see the Stukas dive-bombing the Polish troops on Westerplatte. The noise was unimaginable. We put our babies in a pram and walked round and round the building. Towards the end of our time at the flying boat station all the women gathered to discuss the situation. We noticed *Gauleiter* Forster's wife in the crowd. She was very nervous, and she was complaining: 'My husband likes pudding, but there's no milk, so I can't make him any.' We knew that she would never go short, but we had to laugh at her stupidity. I said: 'You should keep goats.' After that she kept away from us. She was very angry ... We stayed at the flying-boat station for about eight days. Even then the army were still firing over our house at the Polish positions towards Gdynia. My son sitting on his potty in the garden would imitate the sound of the guns: Boom! Boom![14]

The local police had drawn up plans in July 1938 to seize the Polish post office. Although SS-Heimwehr Danzig under SS-Obersturmbannführer Bethke deployed two armoured cars, two anti-tank guns, a 105 mm howitzer and a detachment of sappers, the mainly civilian Polish postal workers embarrassed the Nazis by holding out far longer than had been anticipated. Only when the Nazis brought up flame-throwers and the city fire brigade began pumping benzine into the basement did the defenders surrender.[15] The 38 survivors were imprisoned in the Napoleonic fort on Bischofsberg. On the recommendation of Dr Gizecko, the head of the military courts in Danzig, the postal workers were tried at a special military tribunal and, as none had been in military uniform at the time, were all condemned to death as agents provocateurs. On 5 October 1939 they were taken to the City Cemetery at Saspe and shot by firing squad. Their bodies were later removed to an unknown location.

After five days of incessant air and sea bombardment the Westerplatte garrison surrendered. Cut off and hopelessly outnumbered the Polish army north of Gdynia held on. William Shirer watched their final hours through binoculars from Zoppot pier; battered from land, sea and air they were overrun on 20 September.

A few days after the last Polish opposition in Danzig had been suppressed, Hitler visited the city. He was to have made a victory speech in Warsaw, but Warsaw was still fighting and the Poles refused to oblige him by surrendering their capital on time. He had to make do with Danzig. Hitler and his entourage entered the swastika-bedecked city in triumphal motorcade. He distributed angular salutes at the cheering, flag-waving crowds thronging Langgasse and the Artushof to greet him and hear his speech, but in truth he was in a filthy temper over the failure to crush Warsaw. Later he, Albert Forster and Martin Borman, looking like a bunch of Chicago hoods, posed for photographs on the Langen Brüke, and then went on to inspect the impressive artillery damage at Westerplatte.

Britain and France found themselves committed to war for an ally about whom they knew little, understood less and who had in any case disappeared from the maps within a few short weeks. They had demonstrated again, just as they had at Versailles, that they had little understanding or sympathy for the complex problems of the Polish–German borderlands. Unfortunately, ignorance did not prevent them from interfering, nor did it help them intervene in a way that would prevent bloodshed. British diplomacy had been responsible for throwing away a possible Russo–British alliance against Hitler which Poland might just have been persuaded to join. Britain and France had instead encouraged Poland to stand up to Hitler knowing that there was little they could do to help. British and French diplomacy encouraged Polish intransigence.

It may well be that A.J.P. Taylor was right when he argued that Hitler blundered into a war with the west, but his war in the East was another matter altogether. There was no doubt that Germany would eventually come to grips with its national, industrial and ideological rival in Soviet Russia. There was some question as to whether it might not have been in Poland's interest to side with Hitler in such a conflict but, given the history of German expansionism towards the east and the nationalist rivalry set up by the Prussian state and exacerbated by the Versailles Treaty, there was very little chance that the Poles would view German ambition sympathetically and little doubt that German nationalism would clash with Polish nationalism. Even if by some odd freak of history the Poles had sided with the Germans, the war with Russia would almost certainly have been fought on Polish territory.

Hitler's belief in German racial supremacy grew out of a complex historical intertwining of the German drive to the east, the need to finance industrialisation without recourse to long-established colonial sources of finance and cheap labour, and the rival national ideologies that resulted from the spread of capitalism and the nation-state. These things found their particular expression in National Socialism, a form of government that was distinguished not for its brand of state capitalism, its demagoguery, its thuggery, nor its ambition, but rather by its preparedness to recognise openly its state and national ambitions, the lengths to which it was prepared to go to achieve those ambitions, and the power and ability of its leaders to shape, direct and give voice to the far from inchoate fears, prejudices and suspicions of the German people. Hitler's policies were designed to bring to triumphant conclusion an ever-present trend in German history, a trend that had become increasingly central to Germany's image of itself and its place in the world: Nazi propaganda about the Master Race and the *Untermenschen* of the east was an exact expression of that belief and the hope for military and racial victory.

A.J.P. Taylor has remarked that in terms of international affairs there was nothing wrong with Hitler except that he was a German

– which is to say, that Hitler did what any other politician would have done for his country, but that he was licensed by a Germany whose sense of its own identity had been arrived at late, incompletely and imperfectly, and whose grievances had multiplied with its progress in industrialisation.[16] Germany did not have and did not want any perspective on the nature of its eastern ambition and its sense of German identity other than its own. Hitler was no lunatic aberration in German political history. He and his party were the logical outcome of a long series of internal developments that sought release, fulfilment and resolution in a specifically German identity in the east. Hitler had made his aims abundantly clear in *Mein Kampf*; he could have done little or nothing with only grudging acceptance from the German people, but did a great deal more with their acquiescence and much more still with their willing participation. The end result was obscene folly, but the path to that end is perfectly clear.

9
Wartime Danzig: Germanisation

The turn of the century had seen the rise of German nationalism, but also the rise of German scientific method. This was the direct outcome of German educational and technical investment in the universities and high schools of the nineteenth century – organisations that promoted the growth of research on projects that ranged from areas that interested Krupps and Siemens to those of Adler, Jung and Freud. The sciences of archaeology, ethnology, anthropology, philology and etymology were all taken up, extended, developed and shaped primarily by German theoreticians and field-workers. However, precisely because these sciences were still in their infancy, their findings were open to popular misrepresentation, and the professions themselves were open to all manner of quacks and cranks whose aim was not necessarily to extend scientific knowledge but rather to bolster nationalist opinion and thought through bogus learning.[1]

It is a relief to know that most of the Nazi racial classification was just pseudo scientific hocus-pocus, but it is a pity that a great deal of pathfinding German work in ethnology and anthropology should have become contaminated by the use to which the Nazis put it – a use for which it was never intended. Not all German scientists were Nazis, or even proto-Nazis, and though they measured heads and ears and noses, it should not be supposed that this was done solely to determine who was a Jew, or who should be consigned to the gas-chamber. There is a body of evidence – much of it in existence before 1939 – that flatly contradicted Nazi racial claims, and which gave a very different picture of Pomeranian settlement and ethnography from that preferred by either Germans or Poles.

In 1906 the results of a survey of the height of recruits to the German navy indicated that the average stature of the Pomeranian was about 5ft 6½ ins. A survey of German prisoners of war confirmed this. Archaeologists had already determined that the 'Nordic' skeleton of the old Scandinavian invaders stood at around 5ft 8ins, so that while Pomeranians were generally taller than the average German (5ft 5ins), they were certainly not pure

'Nordic'. Scientists posited the possibility that their average height indicated a general base population of Slav and Baltic origin with a significant later addition of the Nordic element. While the men of northern Germany were taller than those of the south, the 'contour line' of 5ft 6¹/₂ ins was found to coincide almost exactly with the borders of Pomerania.[2]

The conclusion of a far from 'Nordic' population for German Pomerania was backed up by research on the German cephalic index. This is a classification obtained by measuring the breadth of the skull, multiplying the figure by 100 and then dividing the result by the length of the skull. The lower the index figure, the more 'Nordic' a skull was thought to be. Careful measurement of 'Nordic' skulls had revealed a long skull with an average index of about 79. In Britain, where there had been considerable Scandinavian settlement the cephalic index never went above 80 and often tended to be as low as 74. In Pomerania the cephalic index averaged at around 81.6–82.4, too short and too wide to be 'Nordic', but indicative of considerable cross-breeding between long-headed 'Nordic' and round-headed Slav and Baltic peoples. When Polish scholars checked these findings against the Polish Corridor they found that, far from being a vastly different race from their German neighbours, the Pomeranian Poles were as tall and had an almost identical cephalic index (81.0). In these terms the Poles and the Germans of Pomerania were almost identical; that is they were not pure 'Nordic', nor were they purely Slav.[3]

German scientists also studied the incidence of blond hair and blue eyes, but since 'Nordic', Slav and Baltic peoples all had a high incidence of both, these were not useful in ethnological research. The scientists also considered the shape of Pomeranian faces. The Baltic and Slav peoples had predominantly round skulls and round faces, whereas the 'Nordic' peoples had long faces to match their long skulls. Research indicated that where long-faced people interbred with round-faced people the result would be a high incidence of pointed faces – that is, faces too wide to be 'Nordic' and too long to be either Slav or Baltic. The whole of eastern Germany had a very high incidence of pointed faces, and in parts the appearance of the pointed face coincided with the old *Limes Sorabicus*. In Pomerania there was an incidence of pointed faces that ran between 25 per cent in the west to 35 per cent on the edge of the Polish Corridor, but which rose to as much as 55 per cent in the Corridor itself. Taken with the information about Polish height and cephalic index, this might have indicated that the Poles of Pomerania had inherited a slightly higher proportion of the 'Nordic' element than the Germans. This might at first seem surprising, but those Poles and Kaszubians who were the descendants of the original Slav settlers in the area had tended to remain where they lived throughout the Prussian period, whereas the Prussians, like the Teutonic Knights, had brought in settlers from parts of Germany where there had been very little 'Nordic' influence.

The German scientists measured the width of cheek-bones and produced very similar results. Pomeranian Germans averaged 142 mm–143.5 mm, and this fell between the extremely narrow measurement of the southern Germans and Austrians, and the extreme width of the Slav and Baltic peoples. Even in the measurement of nasal profiles the result indicated a mixed population. The ratio of Slav and Baltic concave noses to 'Nordic' convex noses was between 1.3:1.6 in Pomerania, rising to between 1.7:2.4 along the block German settlements of the Netze valley.[4]

In a survey of north European house types it was found that while villages along the shores of Pomerania were mainly of 'Nordic' origin – resulting from Scandinavian and Dutch settlement in the twelfth and thirteenth centuries – these were confined to a very narrow coastal strip which ran from south of Rügen to the edge of the northern end of the Polish Corridor. Immediately inland and throughout the remainder of Pomerania the villages were predominantly of the Slav type known as *Angerdorf* or *Owalnica* (spindle-shaped). Further inland there were belts of Slav-styled street villages and in the area of the Polish Corridor to the south of Danzig and west of Dirschau there were isolated Slav hamlets and single dwellings. Overwhelmingly the villages and settlements were of Slav origin.

These findings were echoed in surveys of rural architecture. Along the coastal strip the buildings were mainly of the East-Elbian Old Saxon type – a barn-like structure with animal stalls and living space along each side, and a central passageway and work-space running right through the building. Inland, in the area of the Slav villages, the buildings were known as the Old Saxon Middle-German Mixed Form (the name is slightly misleading: it refers to something between the Saxon and the Slav styles). This, though still a barn-like structure, had a different internal layout with an entrance hall and immediately adjoining living space: animal stalls were kept to the rear of the building. In the area of the Polish Corridor and around Danzig – overlapping with the area of the Mixed Form – a second mixed form of Middle-German and Lithuanian styles was to be found. These generally consisted of an L-shaped block with residential space of two or three rooms at one end and animal space at the other, with several outhouses and barns. It was clear that early Baltic and Slav forms had survived to dominate: in Pomerania and the Polish Corridor the farm buildings may have been of mixed forms but those forms had their origins in Slav and Lithuanian (Baltic) styles. Saxon architecture was restricted to the area of the Saxon settlements along a narrow coastal strip.[5]

Even a survey of rural women's headgear confirmed the basis of the racial mixture of the areas around Danzig. Women throughout Pomerania wore the Slav kerchief. In the Polish Corridor and the German territory bordering it the women wore either the Slav kerchief or the Slav hood.[6]

Much later, linguistic evidence could also be brought to bear to show that 'Nordic' influence in Pomerania had been of a social and political nature rather than ethnic or racial, and that there had been a sharp distinction between the ruling classes of successive waves of Scandinavians and the bulk of the Slav population. If the area of Pomerania had ever been subjected to massive immigration and settlement by Scandinavians, then words from Danish or Swedish languages would have survived into the Polabian vocabulary of loan words. That is, where the social and political pressures transmitted words downwards rather than upwards. It seems that only one such word has so far been identified. Polish took '*witeź*' from Polabian, and that word is thought to have derived from the Scandinavian word '*hvitingr*' meaning viking. In its Polish and presumably in its Polabian usage, it described a mounted chief, a warrior or knight – proof enough of the relative social standing of the peoples involved.

One word is slim enough evidence on which to base a theory, but in this case the evidence supports other material and helps clarify the nature of the 'Nordic' element in Pomeranian settlement and in the national and racial identity of the area. The Scandinavians were in Pomerania as lords and rulers, rather than as settlers. But those who settled under them, who passed under their power and those who were absorbed into their language and way of doing things were not necessarily Scandinavian at all.[7] The findings of the German researchers flatly contradicted Nazi propaganda and were certainly not the kind of thing that Völkisch politicians wished to hear. They preferred to believe that the 'Nordic' races were all conquering on the eastern borders, and yet at the same time believed that the German presence there was threatened by the Poles. What German research revealed was that most Germans in the east were not ethnic 'Nordic' stock at all.

The base population of eastern Germany, running from Russia right through Lithuania, Poland, Pomerania, Brandenburg, and on to the Elbe, were part of the same spectrum. The east Germans were not part of a separate Germanic, 'Nordic' people, but were for the most part Germanised Slavs and Balts. The ethnographic and anthropological data spoke most eloquently of a population continuum where settlement was still overwhelmingly Slav, even though the Slavs now spoke the German language and thought of themselves as German nationals. The real divide that emerged from German research was that there was no sharp distinction between the Poles and Germans, but that the river Elbe and the old *Limes Sorabicus* showed a very sharp divide between Germans who were ethnically of Scandinavian origin, and Germans who were assimilated from other races. Of the much vaunted 'Saxon' and 'Nordic' influence beyond the Elbe there was but little sign, while of the despised Slav there was an embarrassing proliferation of evidence. Where there was evidence of Scandinavian influence – in settlements along the Pomeranian shores – it was seen to be very limited, and in matters of physical racial characteristics, the study of the height of the Pomeranian Poles in the Corridor tended to suggest that they, rather than their 'German' neighbours, had absorbed Scandinavian genes.

Perhaps the Pomeranian Poles were more 'Nordic' than the average Berliner or Austrian, but rather than accept all this as evidence that the pursuit of a 'Nordic' appearance for the German people as a whole was a mere historical nonsense, the Nazis took this research as evidence of how far the German race had fallen from its 'Nordic' ideal, and how desperately it needed help before its descent into total racial hodge-podge. The revelation that Germany, like every other European nation, was already a racial mixture made the Nazis even more desperate. After 1923, when in the light of such research it became increasingly apparent that the Germans were not all tall, fair, blue-eyed and long headed – that, as one observer put it, a large proportion of Germans 'were almost indistinguishable on the one hand from the populations of Switzerland, Belgium and Northern France, and on the other from the despised Slav' – Völkisch and then Nazi opinion made it increasingly difficult for scientists to conduct research of this nature unless the Nazis could turn the results of the work to their own advantage.[8]

*   *   *

In September 1939 the Danzig Germans had yet to learn that it was one thing to feel threatened by the Poles and seek security from the Reich, but quite another matter to put themselves totally in the hands of Hitler and the Nazi security services. Like other Germans, the Danzigers had watched as the Jews departed either into exile or into the camps, as the communists and opposition politicians were intimidated into silence or arrested, while their political parties were forcibly disbanded, and then while the Poles at the post office were defeated, arrested, imprisoned and shot. As long as it was someone else, as long as it was for the good of the race, the good of the Reich, then everything, or at least nearly everything, was permissible. So effectively had Hitler's policies come to reflect the fears and ambitions of the German people that the details of exactly how the Master Race treated sub-humans did not bother those who already knew, and did not stir the curiosity of those who did not. It was a double bind: if you were not with the Master Race in body and spirit, then you must be against them – with the *Untermenschen*.

In order to promote the German cause in the east it was necessary to demote the history of early Slav settlement and achievement. The only effective way of stopping 'scientific mischief-making' was by destroying the evidence on which the scientists worked. It was by this time well established that the Slavs had settled the Odra-Vistula basins long before the Germans – with the exception of the Goths – had arrived. But now the Nazis thought it necessary to destroy all evidence of early Slav settlement. In the late 1920s a series of prehistoric Slav settlements had been found at Biskupin near Poznań, and at a series of Pomeranian sites – at Grabowo, Wielka Wieś and Oksywie. In October 1939, as soon as the Poles had been defeated by the German and Russian armies, the Nazis moved in groups of 'specialists' under Professor Petersen of Rostock University and *Ahnenerbe* (the Ancestral Heritage Society) to examine the archaeological sites around Danzig. It was a process that was repeated throughout the German east.

The Nazis supposed that the Slavs had been culturally and intellectually incapable of creating anything as socially and politically complex as the archeological remains indicated, yet after careful examination, the German experts said that the sites were indeed early Slav. Himmler ordered the SS to destroy the evidence, to raze the sites and level them. The Slavs were a people without a future, so their history would be of interest to no-one. In Hitler's Reich the intention was to resolve the issues between the Germans and the Slavs by creating a state where there were only Germans and slaves.[9]

Hitler had said in *Mein Kampf* that Germanisation was a process that could only be applied to soil, not to people. What then was to become of the people on the soil? In the autumn of 1939 Himmler spelled out what Nazi victory in the east would mean:

> The removal of foreign races from the incorporated eastern territories is one of the most essential goals to be accomplished in the German East ... In dealing with some members of the Slav nationality we must not endow these people with decent German thoughts and logical conclusions of which they are not capable, but we must take them as they really are ... I think it is our duty to take their children with us ... We either win over the good blood we can use for ourselves ... or else we destroy that blood. For us, the end of this war will mean an open road to the East ... it means we shall push the borders of our German race 500 kilometres to the East.[10]

Himmler made his intentions for these people plain in a pamphlet published in August 1940 entitled: 'Some thoughts on the Treatment of the Foreign Populations in the East':

> This population will be available as a leaderless race of labourers and workers on special projects (road building, quarrying, construction work); they will have more to eat and will lead a better life than under Polish rule, and with their lack of culture, and under strict, consistent and just leadership of the German people will be called on to co-operate in the latter's everlasting cultural achievements.[11]

In spite of the fact that racial policy was so central to their rise to power, to their ambition and continued existence both as a political and military force, the Nazis were ill-prepared to implement their policies. The public pronouncements of Hitler and Himmler have combined with the Hollywood image of the super efficient black-clad supermen who set out with ruthless efficiency to rule the world and who were only prevented from doing so by weight of numbers. It is often assumed that the Nazis had real, detailed plans for their conquest of the east, when in fact what they achieved – hideous though it was – amounted to little more than day-to-day improvisation.

The Nazis were incredibly inefficient in every area of their eastern policy, and it could well be argued that their refusal to put the German economy on a proper war footing, to get women into the factories on a large scale, and their obsession with tying down huge numbers of men, material and rolling-stock, to guard, transport, and exterminate the millions of *Untermenschen* contributed very largely to their defeat in the east. There never was any Nazi study to ascertain the resources available in the territories annexed to the Reich, nor in the *Lebensraum* conquered further east. Although RuSHA – *Rasse und Siedlungshauptamt*, the Head Office for Race and Settlement – had been working on the matter for years, there was no adequate policy or definition of exactly who was to become part of the Reich's labour force and who was to go to the camps. There was no recruitment of staff and no special training to enable the Nazi fantasies to be carried through in a rational, systematic and economic manner.

Even in relation to the German population there was no survey of exactly how the east was to be colonised or the borders to be re-Germanised. The result was that right up to the end Nazi officials ran about distributing a blizzard of contradictory, uneconomical orders that sapped the powers of the military, tied up the railway network and which could only be accomplished effectively with the aid of a willing or at least cowed civilian population. Again and again the 'Nordic' racial purity of the SS was made into even more of a nonsense by the acceptance of Belgian, Cossack, Yugoslav and Ukrainian units, and then by the declaration that the Japanese were, after all, Aryan.

*   *   *

Himmler, the Reich's senior policeman, had massive ambitions for his work of racial salvation. He was aware that most Germans (like the leadership of the Nazi Party) were not 'Nordic' in appearance, that they were a mixture of Celtic, Hungarian, Mediterranean, Slav and Jewish peoples. Only a small percentage of the population, located for the most part in the north-west corner of Germany, came anywhere near the Nazi ideal. Accordingly, Himmler wanted to populate Germany with 120 million 'Nordic'-looking Germans by 1980, so that Europe as a whole would have 250 million 'Nordic' Germans to guide it by the turn of the century, and that eventually 500 million 'Nordic' Germans would populate the *Lebensraum* the German army was about to conquer. In order to fulfil his plans Himmler intended to bring back settlers from the Far East and South America and from old German colonies in Africa. He planned to appeal to the 'Nordic' Germans who had emigrated to Canada and America to return or at least to send their sons and daughters back as settlers for the east. Himmler even contemplated the massive transfer of Norwegian girls 'of the correct physical type' as 'breeding material'.

Even if all these actions had been feasible it was clear to Himmler that it would take many years to accomplish the task. He set up a series of interlocking agencies whose aim was to foster and secure the Reich's racial policies for the future. Under the control of RuSHA, the security services and welfare associations were to implement three main directives: they were to expel Poles from Danzig into the area of the General Gouvernement – the dumping ground for the Reich's slave labour force and extermination site for unwanted mouths; they were to foster selective breeding of approved Germans of suitably 'Nordic' appearance through the provision of maternity homes, clinics and foster homes; they were to make a selection of any 'racially useful material' they might find among Polish children. Where the Poles would not co-operate in rendering up the 'material' the security services had the power to effect a solution by force.

Aside from the business of extinguishing the Poles and the German opposition, the main work of the security services lay in helping with the purification of the German race and the re-establishment of the correct 'Nordic' look. RuSHA relied chiefly on a highly selective reading of German anthropological research, on the works of H.F.K. Günter and on Wilhelm Schallmayer's book *Inheritance and Selection in the Life of Nations* (1903) – which had been instrumental in the formation of the Society for Racial Hygiene in 1904, which had been awarded a prize from the Krupp Foundation in 1908, and which had become the standard text on the subject for the next 20 years.[12]

RuSHA set up the SS-Lebensborn organisation specifically to bring together suitably 'Nordic' men and women for breeding purposes. Lebensborn homes acted as centres for specially selected, racially approved SS-men and young women who, in the parlance of the day, had decided to 'give the Führer a child'. SS-Lebensborn also provided maternity and foster homes for the offspring of these encounters. The organisation was supported by the NSV – the National Socialist Welfare Organisation – and Himmler's wealthy friends in the Reichsbank, Deutschbank, Dresdnerbank, IG Farben, Siemens and Krupps also gave direct financial support to the organisation's work of racial purification and salvation.

The main SS-Lebensborn home in Pomerania was opened at Bad Polzin in 1933, and it was here that children of attested 'Nordic' parentage were born in privacy and secrecy. The children born in such homes were either kept by their natural mother or were put out to good foster Nazi parents in and around Danzig and Stettin. While the fathers of these children were carefully chosen local SS-men, approved by their commandant and by an *SS-Rassenprufer*, the children they sired remained embarrassingly average in looks and intelligence. Children born with physical or mental defects were not kept by SS-Lebensborn, nor were they put up for fostering. A club-foot, a cleft palate, deafness, any serious early illness like meningitis, scarlet fever, water on the brain, all these meant that the child would be sent to the special SS-Lebensborn clinic at Bad Görden near Potsdam. There the child would be given 'special treatment' and would die of measles or pneumonia and its body would be dissected for medical research.

As well as bringing together 'Nordic' parents RuSHA also organised a programme designed to salvage 'racially useful material' from among the subhuman races of the east. The intention was for the SS, Gestapo, Sipo, local police, SA, NSV, the League of German Women, doctors and hospital staff to help RuSHA to steal Slav children of 'good appearance' for Germanisation. Between 1940 and 1944 special units of RuSHA, acting on information received from a wide variety of sources – often neighbours – would raid schools, parks and kindergartens in search of suitable material. RuSHA combed the Danzig city archives, local government and registry records for information about children born to German parents but adopted by Poles. They sifted through the intake of children to the concentration and forced labour camps, they inspected the children born in the camps, sifted through children whose parents were taken into custody for misdemeanour or minor offences – they even took away 'Nordic' German children whose parents were unsympathetic towards the Nazi cause.

The Germans began their war against Polish and Pomeranian children on 25 August 1939 when Gestapo, SS and local police officers raided Polish schools at Kwidzyn and Bytom. They selected only a few of their captives, the remainder – some 172 teachers and children – were sent to the camp at Hohenbruch.[13] After November 1939 it was required by law that all Polish families should bring children under 16 years for inspection by RuSHA officers. If a child was judged suitable for Germanisation it was often taken away from the parents immediately and sent to the SS-Lebensborn centre at Kalisz where it was issued with a false birth certificate. With remarkable lack of imagination the Nazis put little effort into creating new names for the kidnap victims and preferred simple translation: Kowalski became Schmidt, Twardowski became Hartmann, Gęs became Gänser. This laziness made the job of tracing the children after the war slightly easier.

From Kalisz the children were sent to the Germanisation centres at Jabłonowo, Lubawa or Potulice or to the home at Bad Polzin. SS-Lebensborn also abducted a number of suitably blonde, blue-eyed girls who were rather older than the children they normally stole. These girls were injected with hormones to bring them rapidly to puberty. They were impregnated by SS-men, allowed to give birth to two or three children and then killed.

The RuSHA Germanisation centres were little different from concentration camps and it is difficult to imagine what success the Nazis expected their methods would bring. The regime was fierce:

Hell began the day we were forbidden to talk Polish. We were accommodated in groups of about forty boys, aged between six and thirteen, in a big hall. The daily routine was as follows: We got up at six o'clock, did gymnastics, then washed and made our beds, and had breakfast at 7.30. Then there was roll-call, and we started work in the garden, digging, watering and so on. The work was very hard, and it was not unusual for a boy to fall ill through exhaustion. We were punished for the smallest mistake or act of disobedience by being beaten or not being allowed lunch, or having to work an extra hour. I could not reconcile myself to denying my nationality, so I went on talking Polish. For this I was often tied to a post and beaten, but as I was strong and refused to give in, I managed to stand it. In winter it was worse, because we were only lightly clothed in the Hitler Youth fashion. Germans often came to the camp and picked out boys they liked. The child would be told that his parents were dead and that he was going to get new ones ...[14]

SS-Lebensborn also organised the adoption of Polish children under the age of six who showed that they were open to re-education in German ways. Like the selective-breeding programme this policy was not a spectacular success. After September 1939 RuSHA was so overwhelmed by the number of blue-eyed blond children in Poland that it was forced to set up a special reception centre for them at Jabłonowo. The centre proved inadequate however, and many of the children were sent to the Bad Polzin home or to the transit camp at Kalisz. In all the SS-Lebensborn establishments Polish children were measured and then graded into those who were desirable, those who were merely acceptable, and those who were found to be unacceptable upon closer examination. Children in the first two categories were kept by RuSHA for about six months, in which time they were taught uniform and insignia recognition, how to march in step, how to bow at every German uniform, how to salute and how to stand at attention when a German addressed them. At the end of this time children deemed suitable were told that their real parents were traitors, were given faked birth certificates and put up for adoption by approved German families.

RuSHA decided that over 200,000 children of less than six years old were to be 'salvaged' in this way: in fact less than 10 per cent of these children were accepted for Germanisation; the remainder were sometimes sent home, but more usually were dumped in Stutthof – the local concentration and extermination camp. Those who failed any stage of the Germanisation process were also sent to the camps. Large numbers of the children who fell into the hands of RuSHA perished at every stage of their processing. At the Potulice camp near Danzig over 5,000 children aged 1–14 years died of malnutrition, neglect, maltreatment and backbreaking labour before the RuSHA officers had even seen them.

In 1945 it was calculated that over 2,025,000 Poles under the age of 18 had died during the war. A further 250,000 children and young people were thought to have survived Germanisation and adoption to be taken west to the Reich to live as Germans. By 1948 the Polish government began to despair of restoring these children to their parents and complained that its efforts were being frustrated by the British, French and American authorities. While 20,000 such children were traced in the Russian sector of Germany, only 6,000 were ever found in the British, French and American sectors combined. A Polish newspaper was moved to conclude: 'The British not only tolerate German war crimes against humanity – crimes that include robbing a nation of its children – but now they also co-operate with the criminals.'[15] In 1949, with the formation of an independent West German state, the International Refugee Organisation announced that it would no longer attempt to trace these children. It must be assumed that many of them survived the war, and that though ethnically Polish, they still live in Germany, believe themselves to be German and now have children and even grandchildren of their own. It is another ironic layer of Slav identity that underlies a substantial slice of the ethnology of Germany.

*　　*　　*

In Danzig the Nazis had very firm ideas on how and where the local Poles should live. Even before the fighting of September 1939 had finished, the police and security services set about evicting Poles from the better homes. Poles were forbidden the ownership of motorbikes, cars, radios, telephones and gramophones; their access to parks, post offices, cinemas, theatres and schools was severely restricted and eventually abolished entirely; they were not allowed to use civic sports centres or to attend public concerts and recitals; they were forbidden to attend the Danzig High School or to travel to university in any other city. They needed special permission to travel outside Danzig. In August 1940 Himmler decreed that Polish children could be taught to read and write their own name, and to count up to 500, but this was to be the absolute limit of their learning. Since the long-term policy of the Nazis was that all Poles along the borders of the Reich should be expelled, and that these people were to become a mobile, leaderless and illiterate labour force, the education of Polish children could hardly have been considered a priority.

RuSHA had drawn up guidelines of racial classification as early as 1931, and it was on this basis that Himmler issued a directive in November 1939 saying that all Poles thought hostile to the Reich should be expelled at once to the General Gouvernement. Under this directive all Poles who had moved to Pomerania and Danzig since 1918 were to be uprooted and returned. Indigenous Poles in Pomerania and Danzig, along with the Kaszubians of the Polish Corridor, were allowed to stay, presumably because their identity as Poles had been less overt and they were deemed almost by tradition to be more tractable than Polish Poles. There may have been another reason too. The researches of German scientists had shown that these people had inherited a high level of the 'Nordic' element in their physical make-up, and that, accordingly, they would produce large numbers of 'racially useful' offspring, suitable for Germanisation.

Himmler later clarified the selection procedures determining those who would be sent south to the General Gouvernement, and those who should be sent straight to the camps. He gave priority to the destruction of the Polish intelligentsia and intellectual community – artists, teachers, writers – but also included the incurably ill, the mentally ill, the aged, owners of enterprises marked down for seizure by the Germans, veterans of the Wielkopolski and Silesian uprisings of the 1920s and the entire membership of the Union of Western Poles. The membership of no less than 23 Polish cultural and political organisations and associations were listed for liquidation. The SS and Gestapo made a start on his instructions by raiding the mental hospital at Kocborowo and executing all the Polish patients.[16]

The expulsions began almost as soon as the Polish military around Danzig had surrendered. Polish families were often given less than 24-hours' notice to quit, some were given less than half-an-hour to pack and get out. The military police, local Danzig police, SA, SS and the NSK (National Socialist Drivers' Association) all helped in the expulsions. The Poles were allowed to take with them only 30 kilos of luggage and 100 złoties per person, but many found that having been robbed of their apartments by their neighbours, they were robbed of their few valuables by the security services before the journey south had even begun. It was a chaotic and ill-organised business, but nevertheless in September–October 1939 some 30–40,000 Poles were expelled from homes in Danzig, Pomerania and the Polish Corridor. The bulk of these people were sent to displaced persons' camps at Potulice, Smukała, Thorn, Dirschau and Radzim. There they were sifted and candidates thought suitable for Germanisation were sent to the camp at Jabłonowo.[17]

In March 1940 the Nazis declared that all Poles would soon be expelled from Opole, Lubusz, Warmia and Mazuria because their proximity to other Slav peoples of a more tame disposition – the Czechs, Lusatian Sorbs and Wends, and the Kaszubians – was infecting these minorities with a sense of their own identity that was at odds with the intentions and ambitions of the Reich. The wholesale expulsion of Poles from areas annexed to the Reich was designed to speed up the process of Germanising the border districts. In total the Germans had hoped to expel 80,000 Poles between September and December 1939, with a further 600,000 the following year, and another 800,000 in 1941. In practice, though, it was not possible to effect the expulsion of the Poles from these areas because of the Reich's growing labour shortage. In total over 110,000 Poles were sent to Stutthof; at least 5,000 of these were Poles from the Danzig area. A further 124,000 Poles were expelled or taken for forced labour from Danzig, Gdynia and the area of the Polish Corridor: the expellees were farm-workers, housewives, children, factory-workers, fishermen, railway-workers and at least one old man of 80.

In spite of repeated attempts to make Danzig and Pomerania 'Pole-free', by 1944 there were still very large numbers of Poles living and working there. In addition, over 176,425 Polish forced labourers were brought in: Danzig-Pomerania alone had 32,274 forced Polish labourers at work in September 1944.[18]

On paper, German plans for expulsion, kidnapping and Germanisation looked fine to the Reich's theoreticians, but in practice the business of Germanisation and expulsion stirred up enormous resentment and promoted a Polish nationalist reaction among the previously more pliable sections of the Polish community in Germany. The Poles and Kaszubians of Danzig resisted Germanisation at every level and the Nazis found that the process was a great deal more complex than simply teaching a four-year-old how to salute and march in step. As the war progressed and weapons slowly came available through RAF supply drops to the AK (London-backed Home Army) and the AL (Moscow-backed People's Army), the Poles and Kaszubians could even, on occasion, resort to violence to defend themselves and their children.

Himmler and Hitler repeatedly called for more than 2 million German settlers to re-colonise the German eastern borderlands, but, as under the Prussians before them, the Germans did not want to live in the primitive and underdeveloped rural eastern lands. They much preferred the comfort and sophistication of the urban west, and there was little the Nazis could do about it, apart from resorting to enforced resettlement. Between 1939 and 1941 approximately 551,000 Germans were uprooted from their homes in Latvia, Lithuania, Ukraine, Hungary, Yugoslavia and Russia by the resettlement agencies, and 'planted' in the German eastern borderlands. However, less than 100,000 of these people agreed to stay in their new homes. By 1944 over 404,000 settlers had volunteered to seed the borderlands, but compared to the Nazi plan for over 2 million settlers, this figure was minute. A mere 51,000 Germans had been persuaded to settle in Pomerania.[19]

The failure of the resettlement and Germanisation programmes may well have fed directly into the decision to expand the death camps. The large-scale indifference of the German people towards the *Drang nach Osten* helped push the Nazis into feeling that the only way they could Germanise their borders was by exterminating all non-German populations and then through the slow process of settling reluctant German colonists.

* * *

Danzig's terror apparatus – the machinery that made all this possible – was no different from any other in that its speciality was the midnight raid. On the night of 31 August 1939 the Danzig police, SS and Gestapo rounded up over 1,500 'undesirables'. The prisoners, mostly Polish men, were taken from their homes under armed guard and hustled off to the barracks at Neufahrwasser or to the Viktoria School on Holzgasse. Next morning, while the guns of the Schlesswig-Holstein blasted away at Westerplatte, these civilian prisoners were sorted into two groups. Those with building experience – about 250 – were packed into lorries and sent off to the little village of Stutthof. The remainder were sent to Danzig prison.

The camp at Stutthof is probably one of the least known of the death and concentration camps set up by the Nazis. The camp lies to the east of the Vistula delta village of Stutthof, near the base of the Frisches Haff (Mierzeja Wiślana), the long sandbank that runs east to west almost from the mouth of the river Vistula towards Königsburg. In the summer of 1939 the birch and pine woods sheltered nothing more sinister than the Stutthof Old People's Home. In August of that year, however, the peace was shattered by the arrival of SS-guards and prisoners who set about clearing a small area of trees to construct a set of long, low wooden cabins. The official date for the foundation of the camp was 20 September 1939, but the decision to build the camp on this site had been taken on 27 August of that year. The choice of this particular site was nothing if not logical. The village lay at the end of both the road and rail spur, so there would be no through traffic, and all local traffic could be strictly controlled. With the Baltic to the north, Frisches Haff to the east, river Vistula to the west and river Nogat to the south the camp was isolated and easily policed.[20]

The guards assigned to the camp were from SS-Wachsturmbahn Eimann (named after their first commandant) which had been set up in July 1939 with specific instructions to 'solve' the Polish problem in and around Danzig. On the night of 14/15 September 1939 these guards and the local Gestapo conducted a series of raids and 'special actions' to arrest the 250 remaining Poles regarded as possible trouble-makers, or who were known to hold strong religious, nationalist or political opinions opposed to Nazism. At short and predictable trials all those arrested were found guilty and sentenced by a Gestapo court to internment at Stutthof. These were the first official prisoners, and they were followed on 17 September by 450 Danzig Jews, and, after the surrender of the Polish army in Gdynia, by over 6,000 soldiers. In the first four months of its existence the camp also received Poles from the Gestapo prisons in Thorn, Bydgoszcz, Płock, Graudenz and Elbing. A large number of Gdynia's boy-scouts were sent there.

During the course of the war, as the Nazi leaders expanded their own little empires and extended their definition of those who were undesirable, so the security services considerably enlarged the area of the camp, and it recorded the growth in the powers of the security services. From the original site of about 4 hectares (11 acres) the camp grew to over 120 hectares (300 acres). From an initial intake of about 250 prisoners, it grew to become the primary extermination centre for the whole of Pomerania and northern Poland.

At its busiest Stutthof held over 100,000 prisoners, among them local Poles, Danzig and other Jews, prisoners-of-war from Britain, Poland and Russia, Polish resistance workers, teachers, priests, lawyers, trade-union officials, oppositionists, Bible students, Jehovah's Witnesses, Evangelists, Gypsies, homosexuals, deserters, the Latvian and Lithuanian governments, German communists, Danish communists and a variety of other prisoners from Austria, Belgium, Holland, Czechoslovakia, France, Greece, Spain, Romania, Serbo-Croatia, Slovakia, Estonia, Finland, Norway, America, Hungary and Italy. After the abortive attempt on Hitler's life in July 1944 a number of German suspects and their families were ushered into the camp bunker, bricked-up alive and left to starve.[21]

The camp railway station bore the innocuous legend Waldlager Stutthof: the Forest Camp. At first Stutthof was listed as a *Zivilgefangenenlager* – a civilian prison camp – up to September 1941. After that it became an *SS-Sonderlager*, and then in January 1942 became a *Konzentrationslager*. The distinction is one of subtle grades of hell and is largely meaningless since very few of those who went in ever came out again. Up to 1942 the camp buried its dead in the old Danzig city cemetery at Saspe. However, packing over 14,000 corpses into the tiny graveyard had more than exhausted the available space. The Stutthof accountants were against transporting the bodies such a long distance and argued that, rather than transport them for burial, it would be quicker and more economical to burn the bodies at the camp. This way the SS could sell the ash for fertiliser, or just dump the remains in the Baltic. A furnace was installed in a small wooden hut at the eastern end of the camp. This later burned down as a result of overloading during the typhus epidemic of 1944, but during its operational period it was deemed successful enough for a more modern oil-burning oven to be installed. The oil-burning ovens survived the war intact. When the gas-chamber was built in 1944, the ugly, squat, red-brick, shoe-box affair was located right next to the crematorium for convenience.

In Danzig the SS and the Gestapo were most active in combatting domestic dissent during the period 1940–1, when over 2,000 Danzigers – Germans and Poles – were arrested for 'security reasons'. After this the SS and Gestapo directed their attention to suppressing the growing strength of the Polish resistance movement in Pomerania, Danzig and particularly around Gdynia (now renamed Gottenhaven). There was a steady flow of Poles from the Gryfa Kaszubskiego, Armia Krajowa, Związek Jaszczurczego and Szarych Szeregów organisations to the Gestapo prison at 27 Neugarten, and then, after torture, into Stutthof. Many of the Polish resistance workers died in the Gestapo prison, where a guillotine with a 56-kilo blade had been specially installed.[22]

By the end of the war over 14,000 Poles had been tortured and then taken out to the Piasnica or Szpęgawskie woods to receive a bullet in the back of the head. By far the most active period for Stutthof was from October 1944 to January 1945, when, as well as the captives already present, the camp had to absorb thousands of prisoners from the Warsaw uprising. As the eastern front began to crumble Stutthof also had to accept thousands of prisoners evacuated from the eastern concentration camps too.

Throughout its existence Stutthof was an essential part both of the German war effort as a whole, and the local Danzig economy.

It had become accepted that it was possible to work Jews and others to death for the benefit of the Reich and the profit of the SS. The main camp at Stutthof had workshops for gunsmithing, locksmithing, cobbling, shoe-making and leatherwork, painting, carpentry, joinery – all of which were available to local businessmen and firms on a sub-contractual basis. Local businesses also made use of cheap slave-labour from the main camp and from a series of sub-camps spread all over Pomerania.

The building firm of Dehler and the construction company Rommel both used slaves from Stutthof for the heavy physical labour of road construction and maintenance; Fokke-Wulf and the German navy also used labour hired from the camp; Delta Halle, Holzbau AG and DAW all had workshops in the camp for the manufacture of weapons, machine parts, naval armaments, submarine parts and aeroplane engines. Prisoners went to the synthetic petrol plant at Police; to the Schichau Werft in Danzig; to the Elbing docks and railway wagon works; to the Deutschen Erd und Steinwerke (an SS concern) at Hoppehill, to the brickyards and quarry at Graniczna Wieś; to the Deichverband des Kreises in Elbing to repair the dykes and waterways; to the Allgemeine Elektricitäts Gesellschaft; to the five military airfields around Pomerania, to the poison gas plant at Brzeg Dolny, and to the explosives plant at Kędzierzyn.

In Danzig itself large numbers of prisoners in groups of 70–1,600 worked at the Danziger and Schichau Werfts, at Matzkau, on the islands of Troyl and Holm, on Westerplatte and in the Langfuhr brick factory. In their flimsy blue-and-white striped pyjamas and crude wooden clogs these half-starved, half-frozen wretches could hardly be mistaken for anything other than what they were. Even if the Danzigers who saw them for the first time did not know exactly what they were, subsequent encounters must have made it clear; workers at the various sites where the slaves were employed must have known all there was to know about them. At their most numerous, in 1944–5 there were at any one time over 2,400 Stutthof prisoners working on details within the city; there were 25,000 other Stutthof prisoners located at 60 sub-camps and worksites around Danzig and Pomerania, and by that time the security services did very little to hide or disguise them.

* * *

The Nazis were not as accomplished or as efficient as popular mythology would have them. They were at all levels interested in lining their own pockets and creating small empires for themselves.

The Nazis institutionalised the mentality of the petty criminal and gangster by giving ordinary people almost unlimited scope for personal action and aggrandisement in the name of a social order. Whatever Himmler, Hitler and RuSHA had decreed on the subject of racial purity, the men who actually implemented the policies found that the machinery of state allowed and even encouraged them to profit from this state-terrorism: they enhanced their own positions and personal fortunes while ostensibly about their Führer's bidding. On one occasion, however, the Danzig Nazi Party Treasurer was dismissed for embezzling Party funds which was, at least in the eyes of the Danzig Nazis, applying the logic of the Nazi system in the wrong quarter.

Danzig *Gauleiter* Albert Forster and ex-Danzig Senate President, *Gauleiter* of Posen, Artur Greisser, had been sniping at each other since their early days in the Danzig Nazi Party. Greisser felt that as ex-Danzig Senate President, the position of Danzig *Gauleiter* should have been his after the victory of September 1939 and the return of the city to the Reich. He had been furious to learn that Hitler had promised that Forster could continue in the position, and his appointment to the post of *Gauleiter* of the Posen-Warthegau had done nothing to mollify him.

Posen and Danzig had now been incorporated into the Reich, and under Himmler's edicts, both Greisser and Forster were therefore obliged to make their territories 'Pole-free'. At his trial in Poland after the war it was said that Forster had been intent on transforming Danzig-Pomerania into a purely German province where no Pole would be allowed to live except as slave-labourer.[23] But brutal boor though he was, Forster was never as single-minded as the charges against him suggested. Forster was indeed intent on turning the place into a purely German territory, but he was equally intent on doing it his own way. Himmler, the SS and RuSHA were all impatient at the speed with which he was transforming his Gau, but it was Greisser who took every opportunity to point out to Himmler just how tardy Forster was and who sided with the SS in a number of attempts to interfere with the running of the Danzig Gau.

If Forster disliked being told what to do by the SS, he disliked Greisser's meddling even more. In the Posen-Warthegau Greisser pursued a policy of ruthless expulsion and fiendishly brutal Germanisation. There is little doubt that, left to his own devices, Forster too would have run a similar policy since each Gau had a specific quota of Poles to Germanise every month. However, the effect of Greisser's interference in Danzig affairs was to make Forster dig in his heels. When it seemed likely that Himmler would try to have Forster removed from office for his failure to create a Pole-free Danzig-Pomerania fast enough, Forster created a Pole-free Gau almost overnight by declaring that he had achieved a remarkable success rate and had over-fulfilled his Germanisation quotas by discovering a huge amount of 'racially useful' material among the Pomeranian and Danzig Poles. He began to issue certificates showing that Danzig and Pomeranian Poles had been successfully processed and that they were now Germanised. It was a Nazi administrative solution to a specific administrative problem.

Forster's sloppy attitude to Germanisation and matters of racial purity did nothing to endear him to Greisser, Himmler, RuSHA or the SS, but it was very difficult for them to make a move against a Gau that had achieved such spectacular 'progress' without undermining the Nazi propaganda of success. The different racial policies of the two neighbouring Gau territories made for a series of odd problems both for the subjects of racial classification and also for the people who tried to administer this nonsense. In Greisser's Posen a child might be classed as Polish because its parents were Pomeranian Poles; but if for some reason that child was sent to Danzig, it was suddenly eligible for a higher category on the *Volksliste*. 'German' parents from Danzig-Pomerania might have a lower category if they went to live with their 'Polish' child in Posen. Movement from one Gau to the next entailed a change of papers, a change of identity and a great deal of friction between the two administrations. Nazi racial policy was never anything more than convenient, lethal gibberish, but it was something that individual Nazis were prepared to subvert when it suited them and when they thought they could use it to their own advantage.[24]

* * *

From the filth and degradation of Stutthof, the brutality of the Germanisation process and the squabbles and empire-building of the Nazi officials, one man stands out as uniquely disgusting. The work of Professor Spanner at the Danzig Medical Academy's Anatomical Institute was very much a part and product of the Nazi world. His work had been the cause of unpleasant rumours throughout the war, but it was only in 1945, as the protective screen of German military power crumbled and the security forces evaporated, that the truth about his work was revealed.

The Institute of Anatomy stands as an annex in the courtyard of the Baroque main building of the Medical Academy. It is a modest, unplastered brick building of no architectural merit.

Behind this unassuming façade Professor Spanner ran a special research unit to turn human bodies into soap.

Spanner, accompanied by a half-witted Danzig Pole, travelled to Königsberg, Elbing, all the Pomeranian jails, Stutthof and its sub-camps, and to the Danzig mental asylum to purchase corpses and transport them back to his workshop. When Danzig prison installed a guillotine, Spanner had bought and paid for the first body before the blade had fallen. The half-witted Pole was later to reveal that on one occasion over 100 bodies had been delivered from the prison and that it was only as a result of this technical innovation that Spanner was able to procure a steady supply of bodies for his work.

Spanner was very fussy and took special care that every corpse, headless or otherwise, was delivered before it began to 'spoil'. He refused to accept the bodies of those who had been shot by the Gestapo or SS, or those executed by firing squad because, he said, these bodies spoiled too quickly. Spanner's vats, located in the basement of the Institute, could only take a very small amount of human material at a time. Each body had to be shaved, dismembered, skinned, cut in half. Spanner had installed a special machine to separate flesh and sinew from bone. The treated remains were boiled down according to a special recipe his assistant had given him 'from the countryside'. The recipe, framed in wood and dated 15 February 1944, was found hanging on the basement wall when the Russians and Poles took the city in 1945: 5 kilos of human flesh, 226 grams of caustic soda per pound, 11 litres of water; the mixture to boil for 2–3 hours before cooling. Spanner had great difficulty in getting his soap to set properly or to lather sufficiently and a great deal of his budget went on perfumes and scents to make the soap smell acceptable.

Spanner's work was of interest to a wide range of high-ranking Nazi officials, and his staff allocation reflected this. As well as his Polish assistant, Spanner had a senior female assistant, two German manual workers, a deputy – SS-Professor Wohlman – a senior male assistant called von Bergen, and the compulsory help of a number of anatomy students whenever it was necessary to separate large amounts of fat and tissue from bone, or to fire up the incinerators.

On 5 May 1945, with Berlin about to fall, the International Committee for the Investigation of Nazi War Crimes found the remains of over 350 bodies in various stages of preparation in the Institute basement. The Polish novelist Zofia Nałkowska (1884–1954) was one of the members of the Committee and she has left a memorable description of the sight that greeted them:

In the oblique light which fell from the distant, high-placed windows the dead lay the same as yesterday. Their creamy-white, naked young bodies, resembling hard sculptures, were in perfect condition, although they had been waiting many months for the time they would no longer be needed.

Like in stone sarcophagi they lay lengthwise, one body on top of another, in long concrete tubs with open lids. Their hands were not folded across their chests according to funeral ritual but lay alongside their bodies. And the heads were cut off from the torsos as neatly as though they were stone.

In one of the sarcophagi, on top of the dead lay the headless 'sailor' already familiar to us – a splendid youth, huge as a gladiator. The contours of a ship were tattooed on his broad chest. Across the outlines of two smokestacks appeared the inscription to a vain faith: God with us.

We passed one corpse-filled tub after another ... Fourteen corpses would have sufficed for the needs of the Anatomical Institute. Here there were 350 of them.

Two vats contained only the hairless heads severed from those bodies. They lay one on top of another – human faces like potatoes heaped up haphazardly in a pit: some sideways as if pressed into a pillow, others turned face down or up. They were smooth and yellowish, also excellently preserved and also chopped off at the nape as though they were stone ...

With the two professors we later passed to the little red house and saw there on the now cold fireplace a huge vat full of dark liquid. Someone familiar with the premises lifted the cover with a poker and drew to the surface a dripping human torso, cooked to the bone ...

The Committee interviewed the two senior professors of the Medical Academy who claimed they knew nothing at all about Spanner's work, that neither of them had ever been inside the Institute and that the only people who knew what Spanner was doing were his own staff. As far as they were concerned, Spanner was known as a hard worker, a good German and a loyal Party member. The Committee were not convinced. Out in the courtyard stood the charred remains of no less than three of Spanner's incinerators – all of which had caught fire as a result of overloading. On each occasion the fire brigade had been called out. It was difficult to believe that the Academy's two senior professors had not investigated the cause of the blaze in each case. Likewise it was difficult to believe that the professors, who had authorised the expenditure of scarce funds for the purchase of the incinerators, had done so without asking questions. Also it was impossible to believe that they had not been aware of the stench of burning flesh whenever Spanner used the incinerators. Certainly it was known that the Dean of the Academy had received complaints about the stench from nearby residents and had asked Spanner to burn flesh only very late at night. From Spanner's half-witted-Pole the Committee learned that the Reich Minister for Health, the Reich Minister for Education, *Gauleiter* Forster, the Dean of the Faculty of Medicine and a string of visiting professors from every corner of the Reich had all visited Spanner's section of the Institute. The Committee found it difficult to believe that the professors who ran the Institute had not been informed of the purpose of these visits and that they had not taken part in the formal reception of distinguished guests.

When asked whether he might not have guessed what Spanner was doing in the basement, one of the professors said: 'Well, yes, I might have supposed that – because Germany was suffering from a great shortage of fats. And consideration for the economic situation of the country, for the good of the country, might have induced him to do so ...' The other professor replied: 'Yes, I could have supposed that, had I known that he had received such orders, for it was well known that he was a disciplined member of the party.'[25]

In their answers the professors did not show any indignation at what had been done in their name at their institute of learning; there was no hint of moral condemnation. The curious blend of economic and loyal Party-member reasoning, the underlying belief that if this was for Germany, then it was allowable are testimony to the effect that the Nazi system had worked on ordinary German lives, on the extent to which it had sanctioned and legitimised these ambitions and behaviour. The years of isolation from the values of the outside world had produced a fundamental change in the moral standards of the German people – even in those of the highly educated and privileged professors of the Danzig Medical Academy. The damage affected the very language these people used to explain what they had been doing, and thereafter it affected the way they thought about themselves. The Nazis covered over their brutal reduction of human variety with banal clichés of administrative jargon; they removed the burden of responsibility from each individual concerned. In doing so they made the unthinkable a daily event, and made normal moral revulsion and protest a question of disloyalty and race betrayal.

If what happened in Danzig was anything like a microcosm of what happened in Germany, then what happened in Spanner's workshops was a microcosm of the indignity – even in death – of Germanisation and the camps. Spanner's Institute was an image of the Nazi vision of the world – run on state subsidy, using SS staff, compliant academics and the co-operation of ordinary students. By the most economic means possible, it turned

Untermenschen and enemies of the Reich into a commodity that was useful to the German people.

Professor Spanner left Danzig to give a lecture in Halle an der Saale in January 1945. His last message to his team was that they should adhere strictly to his recipe and not allow the incinerator to overheat. He was never seen again.

10

1945: The Last Days of Danzig

Up to the autumn of 1944 Danzig's war had been a very quiet affair. For the most part it consisted of the same dreary round of rationing, queuing, conscription, and the inevitable telegrams bearing news of casualties. Around Pomerania there were various military airfields, poison-gas and munitions plants; in Gotten-haven there was a torpedo factory; but Danzig's main contribu-tion to the war effort was through its work as a centre of U-Boat manufacture. This function was of particular interest to British military intelligence during the Battle of the Atlantic.

In April 1943 Admiral Karl Dönitz and Albert Speer, the Reich's Industry and Armaments Minister, were informed by specialists that current rates of U-Boat production would not produce enough submarines to stave off the impending Allied invasion of Europe until 1946. Up to this point Germany had barely managed 30 U-Boats per year. Hitler, Speer and Dönitz agreed that U-Boat production should in future be given top priority, and they appointed the engineer Otto Merker to speed up and streamline the production process in order to finish 30 boats per month.

Merker developed a system whereby the U-Boats were con-structed as a series of prefabricated sections at inland factories. The assorted hull assemblies were sent to special yards where gears, engines and pipes were installed, and then the assemblies were rafted down rivers and canals to Danzig, Bremen and Hamburg. Once in Danzig the parts were assembled, launched and sent out into the convenient and ideal deeps of Danzig Bay for trials. Later they were manned by crews from the Naval Training Division stationed in Danzig and Gottenhaven before being sent out on operations. As Merker's system became more efficient, so Allied interest in the submarine yards grew. Air reconnaissance showed the U-Boat sections standing on the quayside, waiting on barges, disguised under huge canvasses or covered by long assembly sheds. Analysts of the aerial photographs surmised that the length of a given shed gave an accurate gauge as to the readi-ness of the U-Boat it housed. The appearance of a new shed meant a new assembly had been started; the extension of an existing shed meant an assembly was one step nearer completion. This was a game that two could play though, and it is likely that there were always more sheds than U-Boats.

In spite of British interest in Danzig, the RAF mounted only one significant raid, on 11 July 1942. Although aerial photographs clearly show submarine assemblies, it is probable the RAF were also aiming to destroy the fleet of invasion barges assembled there. The plan was to use 44 Lancasters from Bomber Command's 5 Group in a daylight precision attack. At the time this was the heaviest raid the RAF had ever launched, and was against the most distant target attempted. The raid was not a success. The crews had no proper training or experience of navigating over long stretches of water – for most of the journey they were over either the North Sea or the Baltic – and as a result more than a third of the bombing force failed to find the target. Those that arrived at all did so after dark, and hence lost the ability to pinpoint their target. The RAF pressed home the attack against a formidable array of searchlights, flak and night-fighters. Some bombed from 600 feet, as planned, but others released their bombs from 15,000 feet. The raid did little damage to the submarine yards, and only slight damage to the city. Submarine production was not affected at all, and U-Boats were assembled in the yards right up to the end of the war. Indeed, Danzig's ability to maintain U-Boat production was the only fact about the city that interested Hitler.[1]

The security services waged war on Poles, communists, the resistance, schoolchildren, the mentally ill, trade-unionists, Church leaders, Jews; the camps continued their work as the dustbins and incinerators of the Reich; Nazi racial policies were pursued now with enthusiasm, now with indifference; local industry and the military wrung the last ounce of profit from slave labour while Professor Spanner used the corpses to perfect his process of turning the enemies of the Reich into soap. Yet all this hardly touched the Danzigers. The skies over the city remained clear, the property of the expellees and camp inmates was appropriated and redistributed, but without the majority of Danzigers giving much thought to the meaning of these things or their possible consequences. In general the Danzigers reaped all the advantages of being part of the Reich and part of the Master Race. As long as the Russian front stayed in Russia and the Allied bombers struck at the big industrial cities of the west, then Danzigers saw no particular need to question their allegiances. And if they wished to question, then the whole weight of the Nazi system – the camps, the disappearances, the rumours – all made sure that these questions

remained unvoiced. The idea that the *Untermenschen* might overcome the *Übermenschen*, that Danzig might be lost, that the Red
Army would make no distinction between a citizen of the old Free
City of Danzig and a Reich German – these were thoughts that
simply did not occur until in the autumn of 1944 the Red Army
crossed the old East Prussian border, less than 150 miles to the
east of Danzig.

After the attempt on his life in July 1944 Hitler's personality
underwent a rapid deterioration. Whatever military competence
he had had seems to have deserted him. Gehlen's intelligence
service had gathered information indicating a Russian attack
across the Vistula and Narew rivers in early January 1945, but
Hitler was convinced that the Soviets were planning to attack the
Reich, not by the shortest route through Poland, but in a long
southern sweep. Accordingly he moved 20 divisions from Poland
to Hungary.

The formation of Army Group Vistula must have seemed a more
sensible response to the threat, but in reality it consisted of two
very battered armies, the 9th and 15th, and the remains of the
shattered 3rd and 4th armies. Around Danzig it had the as yet
undamaged 2nd army. Many of the units of Army Group Vistula
were made up of ageing *Volkssturm* men, Luftwaffe ground-crews
who now lacked planes to tend, naval surveyors, sappers and boy-
scouts. Often these units had no artillery, no anti-tank weapons,
no signals, no supply system, no transport. Frequently there were
no officers above regimental level. *Volkssturm* men lucky enough
to have anti-tank rocket launchers generally had only one projec-
tile apiece: the grandest thing about Army Group Vistula was the
name. General Guderian quietly ordered the formation of local
Volkssturm units in Pomerania and recommended that tank traps
be dug around Danzig as soon as possible.

On 9 January 1945 Gehlen informed Guderian, who in turn
informed Hitler, that a Russian attack into Poland should be
expected in the next two or three days. Gehlen estimated that the
Russians would outnumber the Germans 11:1 in infantry, 7:1 in
tanks, 20:1 in artillery and 20:1 in aircraft. Hitler raged that
Gehlen was an idiot and threatened to have him locked in a
lunatic asylum. On 12 January the Russians launched their offensive and within five days had smashed their way through the
German defences. By 29 January they held a line that ran roughly
from Breslau to Posen, to Thorn, and on to Elbing and the Baltic.
North of Posen the situation was described as 'fluid', which is a
euphemism for chaotic. Russian units had reached the Oder at
Wriezin, and only a sudden thaw had prevented them from

attempting an infantry crossing over the river-ice to establish a bridgehead. The Russian advance to Elbing had cut off 25 German divisions in East Prussia, but had also outrun Russian supply lines and fuel reserves.

Predictably Hitler blamed his generals for this mess, and in a superb piece of mental midgetry, declared that the new commander for the eastern front should be Heinrich Himmler. Just a few weeks before this Himmler had reduced his Rhine army to a bloody shambles, but in the nightmare of the Reich's final days this did not bar him from a repeat performance in the east. By the time Himmler arrived at his new HQ in Deutsche Kroner on 24 January, the roads from Pomerania were already choked with refugees heading westwards. Army Group Vistula was an army in name only, and precious little of it was left on the Vistula: 2nd Army was now committed to the defence of Danzig, while the 9th army had simply ceased to exist. Himmler's knowledge of the units at his command was scanty, but it is doubtful that further acquaintance would have improved his general-ship. After a counter-attack around Schwedt and Freiwalde, Himmler – without consulting Guderian, Keitel or Jodl – ordered the withdrawal of the garrisons at Thorn, Kulm and Marienwerder, and at a stroke surrendered the staging grounds for any possible German counter-attack to relieve Danzig. After this the siege and eventual capture of Danzig were inevitable.

In the bitterly cold winter it was one thing to order an evacuation, but quite another to carry it out. The Thorn garrison left the city and began to make its way north to Danzig on 1 February. They loaded the sick and wounded onto sledges and travois, divided the 600 civilians accompanying them into small groups and set out into a raging blizzard with temperatures well below freezing. Of the 32,000 soldiers who started that journey, only 19,000 survived. The rest perished along the way, victims of the cold, ambush by the resistance and Soviet air attack.

If Hitler and Himmler did not appreciate the weakness of the German position, other clearer heads had already made their own estimates:

> I had all my children with me and my mother and sister too. The daughter of the military commander of Danzig, who was the sister of one of my pupils, managed to get us train tickets. We left on 1 January 1945, and it took us five hours just to get from Zoppot to Danzig Central Railway station. When we got there we were told that our train was leaving from Saspe, so we had to go all the way back there through deep snow. When we found the train we realised that it was a military transport. They asked us to get off, but we refused. I think I would have

attacked them if they had insisted. The journey from Gdynia to Rostock normally took a few hours, but it took us several days and there were constant air raids. Then I fell ill, along with my children. We all had Scarlet Fever. The guard kept saying that it was too dangerous for us to travel, that Polish engine drivers were taking trains full of refugees through the lines into the hands of the Russians. Of course we panicked when we heard this and we wanted to get off, but a soldier near me said: 'Don't lose your nerve. We are all in the same boat.' He managed to calm us down. It took us six days to get from Danzig to Stettin. When we arrived in Rostock I had to wait before I could get permission to go any further, as only military traffic was allowed. Finally I managed to get us all onto a train for Hamburg. Normally the train didn't stop, but for some reason that day it did. It had people hanging on all over it: on the roof, in the doorways, on the buffers, from the windows. Somehow I got my family aboard and then my mother said she wanted to get off to go to the toilet. It was impossible; if she got off she would never get back on again. I said: 'Do it in your pants'. So she did. She was very wet and she cried. But what could I do? The Russians were coming.[2]

Late in January 1945 German radio announced that in future Danzig ration cards would be honoured anywhere in the Reich – a sure sign that the Danzigers were fleeing in numbers. Those who left the city early – without waiting for the official evacuation – were the lucky ones. It was still Nazi policy to label all talk of flight as defeatist, but it is clear that even Albert Forster had his doubts. In mid-January he phoned Goebbels in Berlin to ask for reassurance and instruction. Goebbels said that 'Fortress Danzig' would certainly hold out against the Russians. When Forster asked Goebbels what he was to do about Stutthof there was a long silence; Goebbels did not know what Forster was talking about. Forster explained that it was the local concentration camp. Goebbels said that the proximity of the Russians might tempt the inmates to stage a mass break-out. Forster waited. There was a long silence. Forster began to think Goebbels had hung up, then Goebbels said: 'Sort it out yourself.' Unknown to both men, the Polish resistance had been listening in on the call.[3]

In spite of Goebbels' assurances that Danzig would resist the Russian seige, Forster decided to liquidate Stutthof and remove the surviving inmates westwards. He contacted the camp commandant, Paul Werner Hoppe, on 22 January and it was agreed that the camp would be evacuated 3 days later. As early as 20 January the inmates had begun to suspect some such move. Through the snow squalls they caught glimpses of panicky SS-men carrying cardboard boxes and index cards, filing cabinets and armfuls of documents to waiting trucks. The whole camp administration was active. Russian artillery could be heard to the south and east. Over the next few days the gas chamber and the crematorium were in action round the clock. The incinerators could not cope with the huge number of bodies. Special details were sent out into the woods to the north of the camp to set corpses on slow burning funeral pyres. When the wind dropped a dense, sickly smell hung over the camp; inmates and guards alike retched.

Fears that the inmates might stage a break-out were not unfounded. About 200 prisoners – mostly Poles and Russians – were armed with a variety of primitive weapons made in the camp workshops. They had decided to meet with force any attempt to move the prisoners away from the advancing Red Army. Unfortunately their efforts were frustrated by the speed of the German evacuation. In the three days before departure began the Polish and Russian prisoners in particular were watched constantly, and were not allowed to meet or congregate. On the day of departure the Poles and Russians were divided up and mixed in with other nationalities to prevent any concerted action. Columns of 1,000 prisoners guarded by one NCO and 40 SS-men marched 7 kilometres apart. Their destination, 40 miles away, was the small Kaszubian fishing village of Wejherowo, just north of Danzig. Food for two days was issued at the start of the march, and although most groups were on the road for more than ten days, no further food was distributed.

As the first columns of prisoners left the camp there were fresh falls of snow, and they were buffeted by bitter winds blowing straight in from the Baltic. It was not long before the sub-zero temperatures began to tell on the undernourished, pyjama-clad prisoners. Hundreds simply keeled over in the roadway or crawled to the kerb where they were finished off by the SS guards. Later columns stumbled over the snow-covered bodies, but the SS drove the prisoners on at bayonet point. One survivor from the march later wrote that local civilians stood along their route:

> People gathered together along the roads, walking for hours from the most distant villages. They were not deterred by the threats, shouts of the SS-men or pistol barrels. The people stood along the roadside angry and silent, like living statues in the sad cemetery of Europe.[4]

Wherever the columns wound their way through Kaszubia – through Pruszcz, Zukowo, Łebno, Lębork – the locals turned out in their hundreds to see the columns pass. Whenever they could the Kaszubian peasants threw bread and winter apples to the moving ranks of scarecrows. Sometimes they created diversions to distract attention long enough to slip the prisoners a cup of soup, a pair of gloves, a coat, a cap, a sweater, a baked potato. Mostly they simply stood and gaped, tears frozen on their cheeks as column after column emerged and then disappeared again into the gloom and snow.

The population of Elbing, cut off by the Russian advances in January, had become increasingly desperate. They had tried to cross the 13-mile wide stretch of frozen sea between the coast and the Frisches Haff, where they hoped the German navy would be able to reach them. It was an extremely hazardous escape route since in places the ice was too thin to bear weight, and the Russians, who were aware of the escape attempt, split the ice into large floes by long-range artillery fire. Also a bitter wind sent waves a foot high running over the ice. It is estimated that a million people tried to escape across the ice. Half of them perished.

Danzig's U-Boat facilities had become something of a minor obsession with Hitler. Admiral Dönitz argued that retaining control of the yards and the deep-water training areas in the Bay was senseless at this stage of the war, and he had ordered the four cadet submariner divisions around Danzig and Gottenhaven to withdraw to Lübeck. Hitler, however, insisted that Danzig and the Pomeranian coastline must be defended at all costs. The General Staff at Zossen had told Hitler that to do this adequately the army needed the 25 divisions trapped in East Prussia, but in spite of repeated requests for their withdrawal, Hitler insisted that the divisions should remain where they were. Army Group Vistula was no longer capable of defending Pomerania: on 2 February Graudenz was surrounded; on 10 February Elbing was taken; on 14 February, after fierce street-fighting, Schniedermmuhl fell. Russian and Polish troops pushed along the shores of Lake Wdzydzkie towards Starogard, along the highway from Bromberg to Dirschau, and tested the defences along the Danzig–Stettin highway. Graudenz still held out, but on 21 February the Russians took Czersk, only 45 miles south of Danzig.

In spite of the speed of the Russian and Polish advance, it was clear to Marshal Rokossovski that German resistance was stiffening and that a headlong assault on Danzig would cost him dear. He decided to isolate the city and then lay siege. With this in mind, the assault along the Vistula delta slackened slightly and the weight of the Russian and Polish attack fell on a drive to smash through the static defences of the 'Pomeranian Wall' and push through to the coast north-west of Danzig. On 4 March Köslin fell, and two armoured spearheads moved to encircle Kolberg. The westernmost prong broke through to the Baltic on 7 March.[5]

The SS guards from Stutthof feared that the arrival of the Russians would catch them with their prisoners, after which they could expect to be handed over to the prisoners for long and grisly revenge. On the evening of 8/9 March the prisoners were being marched up to Putzig (Puck) for evacuation by sea, but on hearing that the Russians had broken through to the sea and closed off the overland escape-route one group of SS-men pushed their prisoners into the courtyard of Wejherowo jail and machine-gunned them.

The German military around Danzig was outmanned, outgunned, and now stood with its back to the sea, burdened with over a million panic-stricken civilian refugees. They had good reason to panic. There had been ugly stories about the behaviour of Soviet troops since October 1944, when a German counter-attack to recover the East Prussian towns of Gumbinen and Goldap after 15 days of Russian occupation had revealed that only a handful of the local German population had survived. The Wehrmacht found dozens of bodies: old people with their throats cut; infants only a few weeks old crushed to death; men, women and children nailed to trees, tables and barn doors; an old man with his head split by a shovel blade; and there was evidence of rape on a scale so massive that at first no-one was willing to believe it was possible.

In an incident at nearby Nemersdorf a Russian armoured column had come upon a group of German refugees in a narrow lane. The Russian tanks had driven over them, churning waggons, horses and people to a bloody pulp. After the Wehrmacht had re-taken these villages they invited neutral Swiss and Swedish observers to inspect the sites of the massacres. French and Spanish reporters were also allowed to visit the area, and a special commission reported that all the women aged from 8 to 84 had been raped before being bayoneted to death. Some of the women had been nuns. While thousands of Danzigers had departed as soon as they heard that their ration-cards would be honoured elsewhere, thousands more had stayed on. Many believed that their status as erstwhile citizens of the Free City would protect them from Russian excess, and that after an unpleasant siege and occupation the Allies would restore their pre-war standing. However, as refugees poured into Danzig from Memel, Pillau, Königsberg, Osterode, Allenstein and Elbing, they gave the Danzigers a very clear picture of what lay in store. The folly and delusion of such a belief must have become increasingly clear.

Gauleiter Forster had made meticulous plans for the emergency evacuation of Danzig, but the sudden encirclement of 2nd Army and the massive influx of refugees swamped his plans utterly. His early attempt at evacuating Marienwerder had been sabotaged by Nazi die-hards. They tattle-taled to Martin Borman, the Party

Minister, and he ordered Forster to cancel the move since it smacked of defeat. Whatever Borman said, the fact was that with or without Forster's orders, the flight from Marienwerder to Danzig was already well underway.

That Germans and Danzigers alike had vastly underestimated the scale and ferocity of the hatreds they had provoked and fuelled through their racial policies. This was made abundantly clear to Army Medical Corps Major Jänecke as he made his way south from Danzig to 2nd Army positions above Graudenz on 20 January:

> Behind Marienwerder the roads were so congested that for a time we tried to make headway across country and along field paths. But even there, refugee treks were blocking the way. People of all kinds, on foot, leading fantastic vehicles, stragglers – an indescribable ghostly procession, bundled up so that you could see only their eyes ... Near a small village which, strangely enough, was already entirely deserted, I saw for the first time a trek that had been destroyed from the air. Many wagons had caught fire in spite of the wet – perhaps from phosphorous bombs – and were entirely burned out. The dead lay around in strange positions, among them children pressed against their mother's breasts ...
>
> Soon afterwards we were stopped by a man waving desperately ... he had seen the red cross on our car. His excitement nearly choked him. He was pale as death, and raised his right hand in an imploring gesture. He kept pointing to a waggon that stood out in the open field. His left arm, probably broken, hung limply from his shoulder.
>
> His wife would bleed to death, he managed to groan, if I did not help immediately. A Russian tank crew had caught them, two days ago, while they were resting in a village. Later they got away. But now she was dripping blood. She hardly breathed anymore – no-one could help her.
>
> I have performed some difficult operations in the field, under impossible conditions.But this was the first time I tried a tamponade of the uterus, on a snow-covered field over which an icy wind was blowing, with the patient lying in a filthy waggon in her blood drenched clothes. I shall never know if I helped her. Some other women stood around. By the patient's head cowered a befuddled boy of about fourteen, all the while close to tears. 'He had to watch it,' the man said while I was giving the woman two injections I happened to have with me. 'When the fifteenth man was on her they knocked me down because I dropped the light.' He had to hold the light till they were all through.[6]

Refugees from all over Pomerania, Warmia and East Prussia had the same story to tell. The Russians were repaying the Germans for three years of genocide, maltreatment and rape in like measure.[7]

Refugees from nearby towns began to arrive. Those from Allenstein said that their town had been taken more or less intact with hardly any fighting, but had been totally destroyed in the orgy of drunken violence, looting and rape that followed. The Gliewe family – a mother and two sons – fled the town of Stolp on 6 March. Mrs Gliewe obtained permission to travel on a hospital train from a friend whose husband was a Medical Corps Major. They found the train jammed full with wounded SS troops, many of whom were also ill with malaria after recent service in Greece. Hans Gliewe spoke with a woman who had been in Marienburg when the Russians arrived. Her father had been shot; she had been raped. She said:

> I thought they were through now, and the next wave will take a little while. I just wanted to stay between the two waves. I walked and walked. Tanks kept coming, and the Mongols on them, and then it started again. My Joachim [her baby] lay beside me, crying all the time. When it was over we went on walking. [8]

When the Gliewes arrived in Gottenhaven they found the railway yards packed with hospital trains full of wounded. The city streets were impassible with thousands of refugees camped in makeshift tents or under wagons, and thousands more milling about in an attempt to get a place on a boat leaving port. After spending the night huddled in a doorway the Gliewes managed to get on a special workers' train to Danzig, but when they arrived there it was clear that the same chaos reigned. Over 1.5 million refugees and 100,000 wounded soldiers from the fighting in Courland and East Prussia were packed into every available space in the port and dock districts. The situation was greatly aggravated by almost constant air-raids. Danzigers, upon hearing the sirens, would dive for their shelters only to find them crammed with refugees from the Reich. At Saspe airfield refugees had taken over the hangars and barracks and, in spite of constant air attack, refused to leave. The Gliewes found a room that night but were evicted next morning by SS soldiers who confiscated the house to turn it into a defensive strong point.

> We went from door to door looking for a place. Many people slammed the door in our faces when they heard we were from old German territory. They called us Nazis and blamed us for everything that had happened to Danzig.[9]

As the situation deteriorated the Danzigers forgot that they had become far more Nazified than most towns in the Reich in the years before the war, and began verbally to insult and then physically to abuse Reich Germans. Shopkeepers also refused to honour Reich ration cards:

Just before I left Danzig I was queuing in a butcher's shop to collect my ration. A Reich German was also there and the assistant was slicing him some sausage. He watched her precise cutting and measuring, and finally lost patience with her: 'Come on, don't be so stingy. Don't forget we Reich Germans pulled you Danzigers out of the shit in 1939.' The assistant pointed at the sausage with her knife and said: 'Reich German, I would have given you three whole sausages just to leave us in the shit in the first place.'[10]

But it was too late for the Danzigers to rectify their mistake, too late to distance themselves from the Reich and the policies they had embraced, or at least tolerated, when the going was good.

There were many shameful scenes in the final days. As the last military transports departed, corruption and profiteering reached new heights: fortunes were made and exchanged in the sale of petrol, food and forged evacuation papers. Men hid themselves in trunks, disguised themselves as women – even as pregnant women. They stole babies, posed as the sole surviving relative of a child already on board. If you had the money it was possible to 'buy' a child already on board. And through the milling throng stalked the SS and the military police, sniffing out deserters, searching people and luggage, carrying off those whose act was not good enough.

By mid-March virtually all official shipping had departed and there was little chance that the huge fleet of paddle-steamers, pleasure cruisers, barges, dredgers, tugs and river-ferries would willingly return for a second cargo of refugees. The Danzig harbour officials announced that there would be no more sailings from Danzig and that those still wishing to take ship should go to Gottenhaven. The announcement brought about a near riot among the desperate people who still remainded. Local yacht-owners made it clear that they were for hire to the top bidder. When Nazis stepped forward with huge sums of money, heir-looms, pearls and quantities of gold, the dockside crowd became incensed and the Nazis had to run for their lives. It took a detach-ment of military police wielding truncheons to restore order. The Gliewe family made their way north to Neufahrwasser in the hope of finding a boat. They pooled their money – a total of 800 marks – but were devastated to learn that boat-owners were charging 1,000 marks per person for passage. After a while someone took pity on them and smuggled them aboard a ship from Königsburg.

Escape seawards did not mean safety though. The Soviet air force roamed the skies, and Soviet submarines now patrolled the Danzig deeps. Between January and March 1945 the Russians sank 12 clearly marked German hospital-ships in the Danzig roads, including the *Steuben*, which went down with 3,500 wounded on board. On 30 January the *Wilhelm Gustloff*, packed with 7,000 refugees from Pillau, was torpedoed and sunk – fewer than 900 survived. On 16 April the troop transport *Goya*, carrying over 7,000 Danzigers, was torpedoed – there were only a handful of survivors.[11]

Throughout the city, preparations were in hand for a desperate defence. The SS, Wehrmacht, Luftwaffe auxiliaries, sappers and local *Volkssturm* units began work: bridges and viaducts, roads, pumping stations, lock-gates, goods yards, railway stations, piers, cranes, landing stages, jetties, private houses and apartment blocks. If a position could be held, it was turned into a strong point. If it could not be held or if it might prove to be of use to the enemy, then it was mined.

It was at about this point that Captain Walter Girg, an officer of Otto Skorzeny's 'special unit', caused panic and confusion by driving into Danzig with several Tiger tanks crewed by Germans and 'White' Russians disguised as 'Red' Romanians. They refused to stay and assist in the defence of Danzig, saying that they were on a secret mission through enemy lines to the French SS Charlemagne Division defending besieged Kolberg. They would not give any details. It was a surreal episode, and by this stage a few tanks could not have made much difference. Perhaps in response to this, *Gauleiter* Forster made a sudden appearance at the Führerbunker in Berlin. He was in a thoroughly defeatist mood and determined to see Hitler to let him know the plight of his Gau and the hopelessness of the coming struggle. Forster estimated that over 1,100 Russian tanks were poised to attack Danzig, against which he could pose only four Tiger tanks. He wanted permission to abandon the city without a fight. However, after a 20-minute interview, Forster emerged beaming, saying: 'Hitler has promised me new divisions! Danzig will be saved!'[12]

As well as boosting Forster's sagging morale, his visit to Berlin had some practical results. General Dietrich von Sauken was appointed to command the defence of Danzig. Von Sauken arrived at the Führerbunker to hear of his appointment from Hitler personally. The General was aware that he was unlikely to return from such a mission. With monocle firmly in place and his iron cross prominently displayed on his finest dress uniform, von Sauken scandalised the bunker inmates by giving the military rather than the stiff-armed Nazi salute. Hitler noticed the gesture of insolence but made no comment. Von Sauken shocked the assembly a second time by refusing the appointment if he were to be subordinate to *Gauleiter* Forster. Borman and Guderian tried to dissuade him, but von Sauken insisted he must be free to act as he, a professional soldier, saw fit. Eventually Hitler gave in. For what it was worth, the General could have complete control in Danzig.

In Moscow it was reported that Soviet and Polish forces were now only 7 miles south of Danzig. Dirschau and its bridge fell and with that the Russians gained access to the Vistula delta. To the north in Kaszubia, Russian and Polish motorised units were 14 miles from Gottenhaven. On the night of 14 March, tanks, followed by motorised infantry, self-propelled guns and motorcycle troops, brushed aside the city's outer defences and announced their presence by shelling the Gottenhaven centre. Shells hit the main market where a small herd of cattle were penned. The terrified beasts broke loose and stampeded through the icy streets scattering and trampling the crowds. In the docks sappers had mined the quays, cranes and warehouses along the whole waterfront. As the sappers finished their work Polish boy-scouts made contact with the leading Russian and Polish armoured units. The scouts guided the armour past the prepared German defensive strong-points and in a matter of minutes tanks were racing along the main street. As they turned into the dock area, their tanktracks struck sparks from the cobbles. The German sappers, who had promised to blow the place to smithereens rather than hand it back to the Poles, were true to their word. As the lead tanks reached the waterfront the sappers threw the switches and the port disappeared in a series of mountainous explosions. To complete the work of destruction the 32,000 ton battleship *Gneisenau* was sunk across the harbour entrance.

While the Russians and Poles dodged falling debris in Gottenhaven a peculiar ceremony was taking place at Kolberg – which had already been renamed Kołobrzeg. On 18 March, in a repeat of the 1920 ceremony that followed the award of a coastline to Poland, Polish soldiers paraded battle flags with the Warsaw mermaid down to the shore. Once again they took a solemn oath never to forsake the Baltic.

On 24 March Russian planes flew low over Danzig dropping leaflets in which Marshal Rokossovski exhorted surrender and offered guarantees of life and property. The defenders had no faith in such offers. That evening Forster received a telegram from Hitler which read: 'Each square meter of Danzig-Gottenhaven area must be defended to the last.' Nobody, it seems, had dared to tell Hitler that Gottenhaven had again become Gdynia.

The latest news was that Polish troops had reached Zoppot and were now pushing along the beaches, down the main highway, into the northern edges of Langfuhr. The Nazis used an old Wehrmacht printing press to produce pamphlets full of slogans, war cries, Hitler's promises of a counter-attack and detailed descriptions of Russian atrocities. The pamphlets were intended to stiffen German resistance, but there were many among the exhausted and terrified Danzig women for whom the pamphlets were the final straw. The appearance of the pamphlets was followed by a rash of suicides: a few women had access to cyanide capsules through doctors and husbands in the SS or the upper ranks of the Party; some drank bleach or slashed their wrists; one ran through the streets begging soldiers to shoot her; another swallowed razor blades.

Most of the 4th SS Police Division had been evacuated by sea for the defence of Berlin, but on Forster's request 450 had remained in Danzig to help him maintain discipline within the perimeter of the beleaguered, city. The SS Police had already seen hard fighting in Western Pomerania where they had taken heavy casualties. By the end of March they were in a mean and ugly mood. Now they patrolled the rear of the fighting line, where, as road, rail and telephone links within the perimeter were cut or overrun, it became increasingly difficult to keep track of troop movements or maintain discipline. Most of the victims of the SS Police were *Volkssturm* men aged 14–80, many of whom felt entitled to go home for lunch; *Hitlerjugend* armed with nothing more offensive than swastika brassards; messengers travelling without written authority; stragglers, deserters, wandering victims of shell-shock, unarmed and untrained Luftwaffe auxiliaries who had begun to desert in large numbers. All were taken to a tribunal set up in the waiting room of the central railway station. Those found guilty were hung from the trees of the Hindenburg Allee, their crimes written on placards pinned to the bodies: 'I hang here because I left my unit', 'I betrayed the Fatherland', 'I am a cowardly traitor'.

On 25 March – Palm Sunday – the first Russian artillery shells fell on Danzig. The previous night there had been a massive air-raid on the Old Town, where the wooden buildings became kindling for flames that were to burn for several days. There had been air-raids every night since 19 March, but this was by far the heaviest. Gusting wind carried dense clouds of smoke and threatened to spread sparks to the remaining buildings and to ammunition and petrol dumps. In the confusion of the barrage Polish and Russian troops edged forward into the suburbs.

In Ohra housewives hastily unpicked the swastika from the red Nazi flag and hung them out of their windows as an ambiguous gesture of welcome. In Oliva Polish tanks thundered along the raised and open road from the Zoo towards prepared German anti-tank positions. Although perfectly sited to massacre the Polish advance the guns did not fire because the gunners had no ammunition. Without pause the tanks smashed their way through the barricades, into the market place, past the Cathedral gardens and on to the main Danzig highway. In Zaspe the sewage pumping station took a direct hit and human excrement rained down on the defenders. Russian elements were already reported at the Johanneskirche and on Langenbrüke, though fires still raged there. One Danziger wrote:

> We had to get out of the cellar because our house was on fire and we thought we would be crushed or burnt. We didn't want to get caught. When we got into the open air we saw that everything was burning and the smoke nearly choked us. There was street fighting on Milchkanengasse and low flying aircraft were strafing the streets ...[13]

On the evening of 25 March, with Russian shells still falling and German units in retreat all around the perimeter, news came in that Ohra, Emmaus, Langfuhr and Oliva had fallen. Von Sauken knew that since he had neither the men nor the guns to deny them, it was now only a matter of time before the Russians seized the Bischofsberg and Hagelsberg hills. Once Soviet artillery was placed on those hills observers could direct fire with great accuracy on the city and on targets moving east of the city. If he delayed too long movement would cease and a withdrawal would become impossible. Von Sauken reluctantly ordered the withdrawal. But a withdrawal to where?

The only possible line of evacuation lay eastwards on to the Vistula delta some 19 miles east of the city. Russian armour had crossed the bridge at Dirschau a few days before, but von Sauken had ordered his engineers to destroy the lock-gates and pumping stations that drained the fenlands. This had flooded over 100,000 hectares (40 square miles) of the delta, placing a massive water barrier between the opposing forces. For the Russians, the only line of advance was along the dykes and embankments, where, outlined against the sky, their tanks made superb targets for the German gunners. For the next two days German sappers toiled without rest to construct piers from the delta shores into the Baltic. Bands of weary bloodstained soldiers, their eyes red from smoke and fatigue, struggled into the icy waters to lend a hand while German destroyers came close inshore to give fire support to the defenders.

By the flickering light of the burning city the hospitals began to evacuate all the patients who could be moved. Ambulances took them as far as possible, but when the bomb craters and the rubble blocked their path, stretcher bearers and civilian volunteers had to carry the patients as best they could. Thousands of civilians joined the evacuation too. Slowly they picked their way eastwards along the banks of the 'dead' Vistula or the road to the village of Schiewenhorst, and then across the river to Nickelswalde. There they made their way out to the salt marshes to wait in tiny, frozen, waterlogged scrape-holes in the sand while the sappers finished the piers. In the distance they could see and hear the roaring bonfire of the city that had once been the 'Jewel of the Baltic'.

As the remnants of the 2nd Army retreated through Danzig they too had to abandon their transport. On foot, making frequent detours to avoid the roaring bonfire of the city centre, the soldiers spilt into smaller and smaller groups. Those coming from Langfuhr found their way completely blocked and were forced to thread their way through allotments and back-yards until they came to the long straight Danzig highway, only to find it under constant air attack. They moved eastwards skirting the shipyards, looking for boats and rafts – anything that would float long enough to get them across the shipyards and docks, and perhaps even as far as the comparative safety of the Vistula delta.

Russian troops crested the rise of Bischofsberg in the gathering gloom of late afternoon on 26 March. The battle to dislodge the German infantry in the old Napoleonic fortress took only a few minutes. As the victors emerged from the fortress the whole grim panorama of destruction lay spread out before them. Through binoculars they could pierce the smoke to see the central railway station; molten lead spilling from the roof of St Mary's Church, the smoke-blackened finger of the Town Hall tower. A last trickle of Germans could be seen away to the east, moving towards the Vistula. The Russians hastily called for artillery, and by midnight a battery of guns had been moved in to control any further German efforts to escape.

At 2.00 in the morning on 27 March the guns on Bischofsberg fell silent. A loudspeaker played a string of sentimental German tunes, and then a voice said: 'Now come out. You will not be hurt.' Nobody moved. The artillery fire started again. At dawn the Red air force attempted to bomb the city's last standing bridges. By the end of the day the Russians had flown 2,000 sorties over Danzig. On 29 March the firing and the bombing ceased.

Slowly, cautiously, the Danzigers emerged from their shelters, blinking in the light and the smoke. They emerged to occupation and to an unrecognisable landscape. The streets, where they existed at all, were littered with the debris of battle and hasty flight: shattered wagons, maimed horses, abandoned vehicles, torn tram-tracks, twisted guns, burned-out tanks and bodies – bodies everywhere. Opposite the main station a wall had collapsed to reveal the body of a young woman who had hanged herself from her living-room door lintel.

At some stage during the fighting *Gauleiter* Forster had left the city by submarine. At the radio station a pre-recorded tape of his voice played his last message: 'Danzig is, and will remain, German. Heil Hitler!'

On 30 March General Berling's 1st Polish Army hoisted their red and white flag from the gaunt, still-smoking ruin of the Town Hall, and then set about finding enough sober soldiers to stage a march-past. As the Poles in their four-cornered caps and long great coats marched by, the Western Allies were informed that the post of *Wojewoda* (voivode – Provincial Governor) of Gdańsk had been created. The significance of this was missed by the British, but on 8 April the Americans realised that this was the first move in the creation of a Polish administration for the city and that it prefigured the incorporation of the city into the Polish state. The Western Allies had known since the Tehran Conference that the Poles had been promised eastern German territory – now protested through their Ambassador in Moscow. Stalin assured them that the Poles would not incorporate the city without international agreement and that the present move was merely a way of establishing some sort of order in their rear area to ensure the smooth passage of war materials and supplies and to combat werewolf groups. Apart from this, said Stalin, some sort of Polish administration was necessary simply because, apart from werewolf groups, all the Germans had run away westwards at the approach of the Red Army.

With their insatiable thirst for statistics the Russian High Command announced to Western correspondents that in Danzig they had captured 10,000 German soldiers, 140 tanks, 84 planes, 358 artillery pieces, 566 mortars, 1,397 machine guns, 15 armoured trains, 6,665 railway wagons, 45 U-Boats, 214 ammunition- and fuel-dumps. And somewhere beneath the smouldering rubble lay 39,000 civilian dead. The Polish 1st Army alone lost 4,050 dead and 5,400 missing in the Pomeranian campaign. The Russians have never given figures for their casualties.

The war was spluttering to a finish. Yet one tiny fragment of this enormous drama had still to unfold. On 5 May, three days before the German surrender, a ship crammed with survivors from Stutthof, still under SS guard, arrived at Admiral Dönitz's headquarters in Flensburg. By this time Hitler was dead and Dönitz was the new Führer. In the past he had been the victim of some very shoddy British propaganda about his U-Boats, and had consequently dismissed rumours of Himmler's death camps as yet more enemy propaganda. In the closing hours of the war he was forced to face the truth about the regime he now led. Shocked by the arrival of the prisoners, Dönitz purged his cabinet of Nazis and set up an inquiry into the camps in the hope that this would soften Allied attitudes.

It was too late to help most of the Stutthof prisoners . Those who arrived in Flensburg represented only a tiny proportion of all those who had been sent to the camp. Of those who set out on the evacuation march in January there were a number of stories. Some had been marched all the way to the Hel peninsula and evacuated after a night spent in the open in sub-zero temperatures. They had been packed into four barges and towed out to sea. Two of the barges made it safely to Klintholm, another was sunk by RAF fighter-bombers who mistook it for a troop transport. There were no survivors from the fourth barge which was scuttled at sea by the SS. The boat that arrived at Flensburg was a late column from Stutthof that had only managed to get as far as Nickelswalde before Russian advances forced the SS guards to march the column to the sea and commandeer whatever transport they could find. Dönitz was embarrassed by their arrival: he certainly did not want concentration camp survivors at his HQ when the Allies arrived. He ordered the barge back to sea, to head for Malmö in Sweden. It arrived there in June and the prisoners were handed over to the Swedish Red Cross.

Stutthof itself did not officially surrender until Russian soldiers arrived there on 10 May – two days after the German surrender. Of the 120,000 prisoners that had entered the camp since its inception in September 1939 less than 30 per cent – 35,000 – had survived.

Von Sauken's plan to evacuate his command via the delta, though born of desperation, was well executed. By the time Germany surrendered on 8 May, the German navy, in one of the most hazardous and least-known episodes of the war, had snatched 1,200,000 civilians and soldiers from the hastily improvised jetties. On 9 May von Sauken too surrendered.

*   *   *

After the firing died down, the initial cautious street patrols gave way to massive occupation. Military traffic into and through the city increased, and where access was possible, Red Army policewomen appeared at the main street corners and intersections directing the flow with crisp brightly coloured flags. As well as the huge self-propelled guns and tanks, the Dodge and Chevrolet trucks and jeeps, there was a vast amount of horse-drawn transport: wagons rolled into Danzig piled high with straw, food, munitions, gasoline and loot: feathered caps, brassières, cami-knickers, corsets, bed-caps, top hats, tail coats, chains of office, theatrical powdered wigs and chain-mail costumes; pianos, double-beds, rocking-chairs, toilet bowls, lamps, writing desks, bicycles, typewriters, chamber pots. The Russians also looted livestock from the courtyards and allotments. It was not unusual to see soldiers with rabbits, chickens, ducks or even goats slung around their necks. One Danziger wrote:

> You must have heard what happened here. Of your things I'm afraid there is nothing left. I managed to save a few pieces of your furniture, but everything else is lost. I hardly managed to save my own possessions. It really doesn't bear repeating.[14]

This colourful and acquisitive anarchy does not hide the less savoury activities of the conquering forces. The story of Mrs Siedler is probably typical. Driven from her home by the shelling of 25 March the widowed Mrs Siedler, her aged mother and some family friends sought shelter in the nearby church but found it full of refugees. They could not return home because of the spreading fire and so took refuge in a house. When the house was hit they tried to get into a bunker, but again it was already full. Just after they left the bunker it took a direct hit from artillery fire. The group abandoned their luggage and took shelter with over 2,000 others in the basement of the gasworks offices. They stayed there all the next day until at 2.00pm on 27 March Russian soldiers arrived and the occupants of the basement promptly surrendered. They emerged to be met by a drunken Russian aged about 18 who pushed the elder Mrs Siedler into a telephone booth and raped her. While this was happening, the younger Mrs Siedler saw a Russian soldier kill three small children by smashing their heads against a wall. As soon as these Russians moved off a another group arrived and took it in turns to rape the old woman. Before they managed to get home a Pole and his girlfriend stopped them and threatened to cut off the younger Mrs Siedler's finger if she did not give them her wedding ring. That night the Siedlers and their friends decided to move out to the suburbs as soon as possible. When the shelling started again they hid in a cellar only to be discovered by Russian soldiers who, even as the bombardment continued over their heads, took the women into a hallway, raped them and bit their breasts. The younger Mrs Siedler escaped violation by pretending to have cholera.[15]

Russian and Polish troops were simply out of control in some parts of the city. In Emmaus and Praust, two districts that fell early to the Russians, several women died of exposure in the ruins rather than risk being found again in the shelters by marauding soldiers during the hours of curfew. The following statement derives from 17 eye-witness reports of events in Danzig and Oliwa:

> The Russians entered every shelter, cellar and basement and under menaces, demanded and took watches, rings, and other valuables. Nearly all the women were raped – among the victims were old women of 60 and 75 and girls of 15 or even 12. Many were raped 10, 20 or 30 times. Most of those who suffered in this way contracted venereal disease. All the houses left standing were ransacked – according to one eye-witness, the Russians gave orders that the doors should remain unlocked. Furniture, wireless sets, pianos, sewing machines and so on were taken away.
>
> There was much drunkenness amongst the Russian troops, and offi-cers, many of whom took part in the excesses, seemed to have little control, though some showed consideration for the civilians and tried to exercise authority. The excesses went on for days. Boys trying to protect their mothers against outrages were shot down. There were many suicides.
>
> Danzig cathedral was plundered of all movables and left in a condi-tion of indescribable filth. It was reconsecrated by Dr Behrendt.
>
> There were similar scenes in other towns. At Oliva the Russian offi-cers lost control of their men, all of whom seemed to be drunk. One Russian officer went to several shelters and advised the inmates to take refuge in the church. They did so and remained unmolested for a night and a day. The next night the church was invaded and became a scene of wild outrage; while some of the soldiers played, or tried to play, the organ, others tolled the bells. The inmates took refuge in the vicarage, where they were undiscovered for two days. On the third day they were again subjected to outrage – amongst the victims were the Sisters of Mercy and a girl of 13.
>
> The principal hospital in Danzig was looted of everything. The nurses and women doctors were outraged.[16]

This last sentence is hardly adequate to describe what happened at Danzig's main hospital. The Russians broke into the store-rooms and drank the surgical spirit, they machine-gunned valu-able and very scarce medical supplies and set fire to bandages and dressings. In the central operating theatre, where operations were still in progress, the Russians raped nurses over the bodies of the unconscious patients. In the maternity ward the soldiers raped all the women regardless of their condition. Doctors who attempted to intervene were shot. Soldiers passed out in heaps from drinking neat spirit. Later, when the Russian medical units arrived to plunder the place systematically for their own wounded they found that virtually everything they wanted – anaesthetics, drugs and equipment – had been destroyed.

If anything the Polish militia who arrived in the wake of the front-line troops seem to have been worse than the Russians:

> One morning, Polish soldiers came in on horseback. Some time before them, the Polish militia had made an appearance in the villages. They had looted so wildly that even the Russians, who had now had their fill, stopped them here and there.[17]

Polish militiamen arrived. They were on bad terms with the Russians and stole the little that was left to steal. Women in particular would often find protection from the Poles with Russian officers.[18]

Regardless of whether the militia or the soldiers were the worst, those elements of the Polish 1st Army who were engaged in the fight for Danzig were not fit to resume the drive on Berlin until the end of April 1945.

In conditions such as these it was not surprising that fires throughout the city should become uncontrollable. In Oliva, which had been taken with very little damage at all, drunken Russians and Poles, angry at not finding the women they believed to be sheltering in the cathedral, set fire to the place, destroying one of Europe's finest and most distinguished churches. In the Nederstadt the Russians mounted guns on the backs of lorries and rode around shooting up the few remaining buildings. In spite of this, the East Prussian Fire and Life Assurance building, the Danzig police headquarters and the Danzig prison all escaped serious damage while all around them was reduced to desolation. The miraculous survival of these buildings may be attributed to the fact that they had already been taken over by the NKVD. The Russian security service was particularly interested in the records of land-holdings, farm ownership, criminal and political archives and police files, and they needed a jail for their own purposes. Not even the most drunken Soviet troops wanted to fall foul of the NKVD.

The remaining men of Danzig – old and young, sick of heart, soldier and civilian – were rounded up and confined:

> One eye witness relates that he was locked up in a stable with 30 others. There they were kept for five days without food or drink, except for fouled water they could scoop up from the runnel. Several contracted dysentery. He himself was released because of his illness and went home. But his home had been completely looted. He stayed with his sister-in-law who nursed him. She cooked for some Russians and was decently treated. They came every evening for a meal and gave

him some of their food. Other Danzigers who were arrested by the Russians were asked if they had been members of the Nazi Party, the Gestapo, or the Werwolf. Their denials were followed by such terrible beatings that they were ready to admit to anything. Many were sent to a concentration camp at Matzkau. The rooms were so overcrowded that the inmates could not lie down to sleep. Twice daily 800–1,000 prisoners were sent to Russia.[19]

Some of the prisoners died before they could be sent to Russia:

As well as teaching physics at the Conradinum my husband worked at the torpedo factory in Gdynia. They took him prisoner and kept him in Danzig for a while. Then they marched him to Graudenz, and then back to Saspe. He died at Saspe from dysentery.[20]

Russian and Polish scholars have been extremely reticent about what happened in Danzig, and very reluctant to enter into any discussion of the widespread raping and looting that accompanied the move on to German territory. Artillery Captain Alexander Solzhenitsyn was a witness to events a few miles east of Danzig:

Yes! For three weeks the war had been going on inside Germany, and all of us knew very well that if the girls were German they could be raped and then shot. This was almost a combat distinction. Had they been Polish girls or our own displaced Russian girls, they could have been chased naked around the garden and slapped on the behind – an amusement, no more.[21]

Alexander Werth, the *Sunday Times* correspondent in Moscow, recorded the comments of a Russian major:

Any of our chaps had simply to say: 'Frau komm', and she knew what was expected of her ... Let's face it. For nearly four years, the Red Army had been sex starved ... but the looting and the raping in a big way did not start until our soldiers got into Germany. Our fellows were so sex-starved that they often raped old women of 60, or 70, or even 80 – much to these grandmothers' surprise, if not delight. But it was a nasty business, and the record of the Kazakhs and other Asiatic troops were particularly bad.[22]

With Asiatic troops who barely spoke Russian, let alone Polish or German, blue-eyed blondes of either nationality were indistinguishable. There was considerable tension between Polish and Asiatic troops when it was found that the latter made no 'combat distinction' between German and Polish women.

Cornelius Ryan, writing of the battle for Berlin, where the incidence of rape matched the total number of Russian dead, has said:

Soviet historians admit that the troops got out of control, but many of them attribute the worst atrocities to the vengeance-minded ex-prisoners of war who were released during the Soviet advance to the Oder. In regard to the rapes the author was told by the editor Pavel Troyanskii of the army newspaper *Red Star*: 'We were naturally not 100 per cent gentlemen; we had seen too much.' Another *Red Star* editor said: 'War is war, and what we did is nothing in comparison with what the Germans did in Russia.' Milovan Djilas, who was head of the Yugoslav Military Mission to Moscow during the war, says in his book *Conversations with Stalin* that he complained to the Soviet dictator about atrocities committed by Red Army troops in Yugoslavia. Stalin replied: 'Can't you understand it if a soldier who has crossed thousands of kilometres through blood and fire has fun with a woman or takes a trifle?'[23]

The overwhelming scale of the raping in the German east has been attributed to a pamphlet written just before Russian troops crossed the German borders. The pamphlet is mentioned by most commentators on the campaign, but so far nobody has been able to produce a copy of it. In his memoirs Admiral Dönitz quotes part of it:

> Kill! Kill! In the German race there is nothing but evil. Stamp out the fascist beast once and for all in its lair! Use force and break the racial pride of these German women. Take them as your lawful booty. Kill! As you storm onward, kill! You gallant soldiers of the Red Army.[24]

The confusion between killing, rape and the accumulation of property is illuminating here and surely represents something of the pain and confusion of the Slav reaction to German material superiority, as well as the more predictable reaction to grief and slaughter. These are not simply the responses of people made callous and indifferent by war. They are the precise responses of those whose friends and relatives had been the victims of Nazi racial policy, of genocide and unlooked-for war on a massive scale. In resisting calculated German aggression Russia suffered over 20 million dead and the Poles lost over 6 million.

In effect, rape was an officially sanctioned method of degrading Germany in the womb: it was an act that refuted Nazi racial policies in the most direct, intimate and brutal manner possible. For the first time since Hitler came to power, the German people – women in particular – were forced to appreciate the sheer terror, pain and enduring misery they had inflicted on the *Untermenschen*. For the first time they experienced conditions and feelings which for the bulk of the non-German population of central and eastern Europe had become absolutely normal. For the first time they felt on their own skin, in their own nerve ends, the reality of what they had been doing to other people.

* * *

Sollman, Ebner and Tesch, the leaders of the Lebensborn operations in Danzig and Pomerania, were never accused of kidnapping or killing any of the missing 200,000 'racially useful' Polish children, merely of belonging to an illegal organisation.

From Stutthof a total of 17 SS guards and 5 block supervisors were executed; 58 other camp guards were given prison sentences ranging from 3 to 15 years. Sturmbannführer Max Pauly, the second commandant at Stutthof, was executed by the British, but Paul Werner Hoppe, his successor, was given a 9-year jail sentence by a West German court. Fritz Selonke, a Stutthof guard with a reputation for sadism was given a two-year sentence by a Hamburg court. Otto Knott, the man whose job it was to climb on to the roof of the Stutthof gas chamber and scatter the Zyklon-B crystals on to the prisoners below through a special aperture, was acquitted by a court in Tübingen.

Heinrich Himmler, the initiator of RuSHA, head of the SS and main architect of Nazi racial policy, killed himself on 23 May 1945. Richard Hildebrandt, head of the Danzig SS, was executed by the Poles. The British caught *Gauleiter* Albert Forster and handed him over to the Poles. After a trial he was hanged. Artur Greisser, ex-Danzig Senate President and *Gauleiter* of the Posen-Warthegau, was paraded in a steel cage through the streets of Posen – which had by then become Poznań – before execution.

* * *

The war was over, but for those Danzigers still alive in the ruins of their once beautiful city the ordeal was far from finished.

Part III
Post-war Perspectives

11

Winning the West

By the spring of 1945 the whole of Eastern Europe lay in ruins, and across those ruins wandered the millions: displaced persons, liberated prisoners of war, camp inmates, refugees, both London and Moscow-backed resistance workers, Red Army and Polish soldiers, militia, disguised SS-men, camp guards, deposed Nazi officials, bandits, civilians of more than a dozen different nationalities, incoming Polish settlers, dispossessed Germans, and commissars fresh from the USSR.

Danzig was no different from anywhere else in Eastern Europe. Recovery was slow, but it began even before the rioting Polish and Russian soldiery had been brought under control. On 3 April Polish railway workers arrived from Bydgoszcz (ex-Bromberg) to start clearing the tracks between the towns now called Gdańsk and Gdynia. By May they had cleared the line as far as Wejherowo. On 13 April Polish schools opened throughout the city. By mid-May the electric pumping-stations had been repaired and limited quantities of fresh water became available for the first time since the end of March. The Poles had already appointed a *Wojewoda* to Gdańsk, and in Warsaw it was officially announced that henceforth all previously German land now under the jurisdiction of the Polish authorities was to be known as the Recovered Territories. On 3 May the Poles and Russians assembled the city's entire population of German men from the various prisons and camps where they had languished since their arrest at end of the siege, and marched them in a huge parade down the Allee of Victory. When word got out that their menfolk were being taken away to imprisonment in Russia the German women ran to watch the departure. They strewed the roads with spring flowers and watered them with their tears. Most of the men never returned.

In mid-June working parties of both German and Polish women were organised to help clear rubble from the streets, to sort out re-usable bricks and lay the bedding for track repairs. By the end of June liberated Jewish prisoners from Stutthof were at work restoring the elaborate façades to the main town hall. By 11 July four of the enormous dockside cranes had been repaired and the

205

first cargoes – from Finland – were brought ashore. By mid-July the damaged tram system had been cleared and repaired and had a single-track service operating between Wrzeszcz and Oliwa Gate. Almost at once teams of sappers began to clear the field fortifications of booby-traps, barbed wire and mines. The whole of the Danzig defensive perimeter had been thickly sown with mines and the task of clearing them was not fully accomplished until late in 1947. The task of making safe some of the outlying districts of the old Free City area was to take even longer.

By the end of May 1945 a special commission was at work to change all the place- and street-names from German into their Polish equivalents. The district of Langfuhr – literally 'far cry' – became Wrzeszcz, which in Polish is the imperative: 'You scream!' It slowly began to dawn on the Western Allies that although the Poles had been offered these lands at Yalta, they were not going to wait for the formal ratification of possession through any peace treaty but were going to press ahead with immediate incorporation.

Reconstruction was a slow painstaking business. What had been destroyed in seconds took years to repair fully. It was estimated that 85 per cent of all industrial plant was damaged, and 35 per cent of all roads and 60 per cent of all railways were unusable. In the surrounding countryside something like 94 per cent of the livestock had been killed. In Danzig city-centre more than 60 per cent of the buildings had been destroyed, including 33 schools; 20 of the 36 major bridges and viaducts had been destroyed; half the city's rolling stock was out of use, the other half was damaged beyond repair; 15 per cent of all tram tracks had been destroyed; only one of the nine water-pumping stations was operative; and none of the sewage works was capable of working. The gas and electricity plants had both been seriously damaged, and damage to the gas and electricity networks made the use of such services extremely hazardous. In the Danzig dock area 30 per cent of all buildings, 15 per cent of the quays, 90 per cent of the warehouses and 70 per cent of all dockside machinery, including cargo-handling installations, had been demolished in the fighting. The port entrance was blocked by the wreck of the ship *Africana* and some 60 other smaller ships. To the south and east of the city the dykes and pumping stations had been destroyed so that over 72,000 hectares of farmland were flooded, while tens of thousands of hectares of adjoining land had been turned into semi-swamp.

As if things were not bad enough, recovery was seriously hampered by the activities of the Red Army. They had set about stripping the city of all its assets – not merely looting light bulbs, cami-knickers and wristwatches, but heavy industrial equipment, raw materials, stores, supplies, tram-tracks, machinery, automobiles, tram-cars and even lengths of railway line. They tore up the railway lines that the Poles had just repaired. They even took the statue of Gutenberg from its sight in the Langfuhr woods. Although the Poles had repaired and were operating the dockside cranes in Gdańsk, the Russian soldiers attempted to dismantle those too, and there were several clashes between Polish militia and Russian soldiers. The Poles then sealed off the whole of the dockside area with an armed cordon and in this instance, the Russians went elsewhere. In general the Poles learned that if there was nothing they could do to prevent the destruction, then the best they could manage was to keep away from the area where the Russians were scavenging.

Arthur Bliss Lane, US Ambassador to Warsaw 1945–7, visited Gdańsk and was appalled at the thoroughness of the scavenging.[1] Stanisław Mikołajczyk, premier of the London based Polish government in exile, and vice-premier of the first post-war government, visited the city in the summer of 1945 and wrote:

> The process of hammering all of Poland to a lower standard of living than it had known in generations was aided by the burning of houses – and in some instances, entire villages. It was accelerated by Russian seizure of Polish factories and other assets as 'war booty'. From that part of Poland which had been incorporated into the Reich, the reds removed two synthetic oil plants, near Oswięcim and Gliwice. They also denuded the new western territory of its railroads and factories. In Danzig one day I watched three floating docks being loaded with Polish machinery and supplies and then towed off.[2]

It is perhaps worth pointing out that that the 'Polish machinery' had only recently been confiscated from the Germans. The Poles were nevertheless furious. They had expected to inherit a badly damaged but still workable strip of highly industrialised Germany, but the Russians were active throughout the Recovered Territory. In Silesia they took away mile after mile of the Silesian rail network, rendering impossible transport and full economic recovery in that region for years to come. In a fever of acquisition, the Russians were busy denuding the entire area of western Poland of the little industrial wealth that had escaped damage in the fighting. If a piece of machinery could be dismantled, then the Russians dismantled it. If it could not be dismantled, then the Russians set-to with blow-torches and crow bars to send the item home in rusting and frequently useless pieces.

An industrial wasteland would be of little use to the post-war Polish economy and on several occasions the Poles made a stand.

Hilary Minc, the third most powerful man in the post-war Polish government, frequently intervened on the subject in Moscow. Jakub Berman – who in the immediate post-war period was a member of the Central Committee and the Politburo; an under-secretary-of-state to the praesidium of the Council of Ministers; under-secretary-of-state in the Ministry for Foreign Affairs; and Deputy Premier 1954–6 before being expelled from the Party – complained to Molotov about the destruction of factories in Police. Years later Berman, while doubting that the Russians had gained much by their activities, described the situation as follows:

> Nevertheless we protested against the transportation of factories and tried to prevent it; we considered this our main task. The Soviets treated the Recovered Territories as their personal spoils of war and considered the wealth contained there to be not ours but German, and thus their claim to it incontestable. They created their own Spoils of War Divisions, whose main task was to aid in the rebuilding of their country by pinching as much as possible. They were particularly successful in this during the first few months, when we were not yet entirely in control of the situation and the liberated territories were governed by Soviet military commanders. That was when they managed to bring out quite a lot ...[3]

If there was any Russo–Polish agreement about the business of seizing war payments from Germany, then, as far as the Russians were concerned, it took precedence over the business of establishing the new Poland on a sound economic footing. It was to be more than ten years before First Secretary Władysław Gomułka denounced Russian behaviour towards the Poles in the Recovered Territories, but by then the damage had been done. It must have been clear to the Poles right from the outset that their position as Soviet ally was that of an untrustworthy inferior, and that the alliance was far more a matter of geographical necessity than of some deep Slavonic fraternal feeling.

Speaking of her arrival in the city shipyard, worker Maria Komarowska said:

> I arrived to find a heap of scrap metal and rubble. People were living in there, among machines that were destroyed and burned. We began by putting the place in order, by cleaning out the shipyard. The first sheds were rebuilt, the first machine tools dragged out of the debris, and the old ships repaired. This was in 1945 and it took us a good six months to restore some semblance of normal life.[4]

In practical terms the Poles arriving in the shipyards of Gdańsk had almost a free hand in organising the recovery work: there were very few managers or accountants, and the Party was still too busy with the civil war in the south, with policy organisation and with the coming referendum to take any real interest in the detailed business of the workplace. In many workshops and factories the workers formed their own self-managing 'teams' and 'brigades'. Initially, the formation of workers' self-management and independent workers collectives had been sanctioned by a decree from the 'Lublin' government in October 1944, but this was only to recognise a situation that the authorities were powerless to alter. In May 1945, however, as the strictly vertical arrangements of Leninist practice were imposed, grass-roots organisations lost their powers and independence; instead, their rights to bargain for their own wages, to set production norms and alter working conditions were fixed by the tame unions of the government's one-way transmission belt.

Count von Lehndorf, a doctor who lived in the East Prussian village of Rosenberg, a few miles east of Danzig, has left a description of the arrival of Polish settlers in his village which cannot differ very much from their arrival in the city itself:

Round the ruined core of the town the Poles have moved into any house left standing, but only a minority appear to be really settled. The majority are in a state of perpetual unrest, and the train that runs once or twice daily over this section of the line is crammed with adventurers who come and go because they haven't yet found anywhere to stay or are on the lookout for better openings. They come from every part of Poland, and represent the most diverse types, eastern and western, who have hardly anything in common with one another as regards disposition and mentality ... all they have in common is the fact that they have lost their roots, otherwise they wouldn't come here of their own free will, to a country lying in waste, and with which they have no connection, except for the few that worked here on the land during the war, and are now trying to build up a new existence for themselves on the deserted farms. The others first arrived here a year and a half ago, immediately behind the Russian Army. They are relatively best off, because they were able to secure a lot of things that had been overlooked in the original looting. They are more or less clothed, and already represent a sort of social stratum, if a somewhat loose one.

Every newcomer tries to take up some sort of trade, or to assume an office. We already possess a burgomaster, a priest, a doctor, a lady dentist, a solicitor, a forester, a postmaster, a station master, a chimney sweep, a hair-dresser, a shoe-maker, a tailor and so forth, although none of them appears to be particularly well-versed in his profession. Tradesmen too, of all kinds, from baker, butcher and innkeeper to simple matchseller. They make a living, and their activities are limited only by the general poverty and the presence of the militia and UB [Urząd Bezpieczęstwa – Department of Security], who discharge their dreaded offices according to the most primitive and temperamental points of view.

There are only a few Germans still living in the town, they can be counted on the fingers of both hands: two old men and a few women and children, who clean the streets, remove the rubbish and do domestic work in Polish households. Any other Germans left in the district live on estates, mostly under Russian surveillance and in closed communities. Separately they would hardly find the means to live, and would be at the mercy of every despot's caprice.[5]

Von Lehndorf's account would probably serve as an accurate description of life throughout the Recovered Territories.

For many Poles who had lost their homes and families the new Polish western territories were a kind of promised land. In his novel *Ashes and Diamonds* Jerzy Andrzejewski described some of the chaos that reigned at the end of the war as Poland tried to adapt itself to a new territorial base, set about repairing the material and human damage and at the same time fought a savage civil war. The seizure of German lands was probably one of the easier tasks that confronted the Communists. One of the characters in Andrzejewski's novel says: 'Now is the best time. Everything's in confusion, the land doesn't belong to anyone. A man can take what he wants.'[6] In that comment lurk all the simplifications that the Germans had worked upon the Poles and which the Poles were now visiting upon the Germans.

The new lands were coming to assume awesome importance in the mythology of the new state, and their primacy was acknowledged very early by the Communists. In the referendum of June 1946 Stanisław Mikołajczyk, Peasant Party leader who wanted the old Poland rather than the new, was defeated by a vote of 91.4 per cent on the issue of whether or not Poland should retain the Recovered Territories. The defeat was a false one, however, as the ballot had been rigged to a massive degree: in 10 per cent of the 11,070 voting districts the Communists failed to rig the ballot effectively and it was revealed that 83.54 per cent of the voters had decided they did not want to keep the new lands. Yet Mikołajczyk could not exploit the discrepancy. Harassed without mercy by the security services and accused of spying for the Western powers, he left Poland the following October declaring that his country had been raped by the Communists. He never returned.

Those Poles who headed westwards into the new lands may have believed that they were about to start a new life in a land of unlimited promise and wealth. That belief hardly survived the first encounter with the Recovered Territories. Polish farmers took one look at the devastation and headed straight back to old Poland. Even those Poles native to Gdańsk, Pomerania, and

Wrocław were deserting these places as fast as they could. The government's promises were fine; the growing mythology of recovered ancient Polish territory was also very comforting for the nationalist ego, but to actually live there was another matter.

The Poles may have gained the west, but, given the devastation and the absence of any treaty or guarantee of continued possession, each waited for someone else, for some other Pole to go and make the place habitable again. And who could blame them? It is clear that taking on a farm successfully under these circumstances was practically impossible. It seems that during the first few years, people were leaving Pomerania and Gdańsk faster than they were settling. In 1939 the total population of the city of Danzig had been about 300,000. By April 1945, after enormous civilian war casualties, the flight of refugees, imprisonment of the German men, the expulsion of remaining Germans and the influx of settlers displaced from the east, the total population stood at slightly more than 70,000. By 1946 the figure had risen to 117,000, and by 1950 had reached 194,600. But it was not until 1960 that the city regained the level of its pre-war population.[7]

Repatriation and resettlement were handled initially by the *Państwowe Urząd Repatriacyjny* – the State Bureau of Repatriation – an organisation set up in 1944 by the 'Lublin' Polish government. The bulk of those people who eventually settled in Gdańsk and in the central sections of Pomerania came from the old Polish city of Wilno and from nearby Bydgoszcz. In southern and western Pomerania the immigrants came mainly from the USSR, Poznań and Kielce, while along the edge of the old Polish Corridor, the settlers came from Bydgoszcz. However, even with the offer of land and work it was not easy to persuade these people to settle. The Polish government offered special free railway passes to all those who expressed a wish to settle in the Recovered Territories, but there were few real settlers. A radio broadcast from Warsaw on 10 September 1945 is one of the few official indications of the scale of the problems the Polish government had with its new territories:

> Until the Poles come in masses it will not be possible to expel the Germans. A violent depopulation of the area (i.e. by militiamen) depriving it of its labour, would do more harm than to allow the Germans to stay there for the time being. Our fellow countrymen from central Poland, however, are not in a hurry and keep finding new reasons against a rapid settlement ... great masses are wandering to the west for 'gleanings'. This unhealthy post-war phenomenon may be called a social disease; and the extent of this disease can only be realised by those who are going to settle in the regained territories ... Why

is it so difficult to find room in trains westward bound? Good citizens think this overcrowding is caused by settlers going to the west. Every one of these settlers has a pass and a settlement card entitling him to free passage. The good citizen is greatly surprised when he sees the same trains coming back ten times worse, not only with passengers but with bicycles, typewriters, sewing machines, wireless sets, etc. The 'settlers' are coming back as gleaners loaded with all kinds of goods, acquired more or less illegally ... The professional gleaners are (1) stealing from the state by travelling free; (2) overcrowding the trains; (3) causing false statistics in the settlement movement to the west, because the most expert statistician could not guess which are the false settlers; (4) denuding the area so completely that real settlers find only emptiness.[8]

The broadcast finished by promising all 'gleaners' prison and hard labour.

The arrival of Polish civilians anxious to make a new home in the Gdańsk area led to further tension. The expulsion of Germans began even before the German army had agreed to surrender, but the raping and looting of the surviving German population continued for some time. Among the other early sources of conflict between the German and Polish communities who lived in the ruins were the opening of monolingual Polish schools, the introduction of Polish as the language of administration and the use of Protestant churches by Catholics. The German language was forbidden even for German Catholics, so mass, where it was conducted at all, was in Latin with the sermon and parish notices given in Polish. It was a practice the Poles had learned from the Germans. For many Germans the behaviour of the Poles was intolerable. Czesław Miłosz was to recall:

... the few days I spent in a certain village near Danzig left me with feelings of loathing and sadness. Germans were being evacuated from the area then. Some woman named Müller, who had tried in vain to defend herself by pointing out that she had harboured allied prisoners, committed suicide there, together with her children, by jumping into the Vistula ...[9]

At a time when famine and chaos reigned over the whole of Eastern Europe, the Russian and Polish authorities insisted on carrying through land reform. The land reform had long been necessary and in truth a very similar proposal (along with the nationalisation of banks and key industries, and the provision of a national welfare scheme) had already been agreed by the non-Communist Council for National Unity. The 'Lublin' Polish government had announced its intention at Chełm on 6 September 1944, but at that time the reform could only apply to land under

Soviet control – some 9,300 estates totalling about 6 million hectares to be broken up between between 1 million peasants. As the
liberation of Poland progressed, the application of the reform was
most uneven. Eventually the whole venture had to be relaunched
after the German surrender and even then had to await the ratification of the rigged referendum of 1946 before it could be
effectively implemented, even in part.

In Pomerania, the departure of the Germans made land that had
previously belonged to either smaller farmers or to the Junker
estates available in huge, often deserted, tracts. The low number of
indigenous Poles meant that competition for the land was
minimal. However, the soil of Pomerania is poor and in general
farmers from old central Poland were reluctant to take over land
in the north, even if possession meant certain social elevation
from their pre-war status and holdings. For those farmers who
came from the eastern territories it was slightly different. In
general they were used to a harsher climate, backward farming
techniques and poor soil. Luckily this fitted in with the policies of
the new authorities in Pomerania. They were concerned to integrate as many of these eastern farmers as possible into the new
western agricultural system, and were keen to avoid setting up co-
operative farms lest these be mistaken for the start of some collec-
tivisation drive. In Pomerania, because the soil was poorer than
elsewhere, the tendency was to create family farms of between 5
and 50 hectares (13–120 acres).

Under the guidance of the political commissars, the larger
estates were broken up. Such a policy had long been necessary,
but this was not the best time; these were far from ideal circumstances and the inflexible, inexperienced Polish Communists were
probably not the ideal people to undertake such a hazardous
venture. The decisions as to which farms and estates should be
dismantled and when, to which farmers the land would be allocated – all had a random quality about them. No particular
reference was made to the experience of the farmers who were
gaining land, nor was there any consideration of the economic
viability of some of the smaller farms that were created. Many
were too small to be anywhere near self-sufficient, and too small
to produce a surplus of produce for sale at market.

These mini-farms were hardly an attractive proposition, and if
the reform had any basis at all, it seems to have lain in ideological
preconceptions and short-term political needs – to bribe settlers
and to oust the Germans – rather than in sound economic practices. In some cases, German families were dispossessed only for
their land to lie fallow for the following two or three years, either

because a farmer lacked the experience to work it, or more frequently, because lack of machinery had persuaded the farmer to give up and move on elsewhere. This reluctance to take on the Pomeranian farms was doubtless accentuated when the incoming farmers saw that the Russians had left the Polish agrarian revolution without horses, cattle, sheep, chickens, ducks, grain for feed, seed stocks, root vegetables, tractors, harrows, ploughs or even simple hand tools.

The following description of the land reform was put together from eye-witness reports:

> The inhabitants of a district would be summoned to a meeting and an agitator would ask: 'Who is for breaking up the estate of X?' If there was not a considerable show of hands, indicating assent, the question would be changed into: 'Who is against breaking up the estate?' Few, if any, would run the risk of open and, in any case, futile, opposition, and a 'unanimous resolution' was registered. The owner of the estate, with his family, bailiff and others of his men, would be evicted at short notice – sometimes an hour, or even less, sometimes 24 hours. He was allowed to take little or nothing with him – sometimes as much as he could load on a wheelbarrow, sometimes as much as he could carry, sometimes even less. Sometimes he was arrested and taken off to an unknown destination – perhaps even Siberia. If not arrested, he was ordered to leave the district and forbidden to come within less than a certain distance – usually 20 kilometres – of his old home. Some of the Pomeranian landowners were sent, with their families, servants and tenants, to a concentration camp. The landowners of eastern Germany are today a class of pariahs – they live, if they live at all (for many have committed suicide) as outlaws in complete destitution. It makes no difference whether they were supporters of Hitler or not. Even if they were well known locally for their hostility to him and all he represented, they are nevertheless 'big landowners', 'reactionaries' and 'fascists', and therefore outcasts without means of subsistence and without hope.[10]

In spite of these problems the land reform was vital to the new Polish state, and by 1947 over 22 per cent of all Polish farms had their origin in the boundary shift and the agrarian reform.[11]

The news that the Germans were to be expelled from their homes and their homeland and shipped westwards came as a mixed blessing. On the one hand many Germans were relieved that they were at last to get away from the Poles and the Russians. On the other hand the Danzigers had cherished the belief that somehow the old Free City would be restored and revitalised as an ethnically German town, perhaps under Polish control. It was a thoroughly unrealistic notion, and it was foolish of them to nourish such a hope. All Danzigers knew that the Poles had been expelling Germans westwards since the end of March 1945. That the expulsions were suddenly made official could hardly have surprised them, but there was still little warning of the exact application of the expulsion order in particular districts:

> The Russians announced that all Germans must leave Danzig. No distinction was made between Danzigers and Germans proper. In the first half of July (1945) the Polish militiamen cleared Danzig of all its inhabitants street by street, without any regard for the sick and aged. On July 26th the Polish Vice-Voyevod informed the Bishop of Danzig that all the German clergy must leave. The Bishop said he presumed the Voyevod meant only Germans proper (Reichsdeutsche). The Voyevod replied: 'No, subjects of the state of Danzig also' ('auch die danziger Staatsengehörigen').[12]

By the time the militia came knocking on the door it was clear that there was precious little reason for the Germans to want to stay.

The decision to expel the Germans can be traced back to the Yalta Conference in February 1945, where it was accepted by all the Allied forces represented that the massive transfer of German population would be one of the major problems following an Allied victory. The meetings of the Allied foreign ministers at Malta, Yalta and Potsdam had all assumed that the Polish annexation of German territory would entail the transfer of millions of people, and Winston Churchill in a speech to the British Parliament on 16 December 1944 had encouraged the Poles to believe that the decision to give them Danzig, Breslau and the rest of Germany east of the River Oder had already been agreed. He mentioned that Poland would now have Danzig and 200 miles of coastline in return for territories in the east: 'The Poles are free, so far as Russia and Great Britain are concerned, to extend their territories at the expense of Germany to the West ... they gain in the west and north territories more highly developed than they lose in the east.' The transfer of millions of German residents was seen as a 'satisfactory and lasting solution' to the border and nationality problems of the area.[13]

However, neither at this stage nor later did the western Allies give much thought to exactly how or when such a transfer would be carried out. Indeed, as the post-war situation began to unfold, Western politicians grew tired of hearing about the fate of a Poland abandoned to Stalin's sphere of influence. Winston Churchill summed up the reordering of priorities when at Potsdam he exclaimed: 'I'm sick of the bloody Poles.' In contrast to the British, the United States Committee on Post-War Programmes had submitted plans and recommendations for population transfer as early as May 1944, but it was clear that for most politicians the matter had a very low priority, and those who gave the matter any thought at all assumed that the transfers would take place over a period of several years, some considerable time after the war had been concluded, and that the transfers would be both 'orderly and humane'.

Even those who doubted Stalin's claim that there were no Germans east of the Oder thought that there could be no more than about 3.5 million. The Allied Control Council, set up to govern the defeated Germany, had no idea that there were still at least 5 million Germans in Poland. In 1946 alone something like 1.6 million Germans were expelled from Poland. Between 1946 and 1949 an estimated total of 2.75 million Germans were expelled.[14] These figures are estimated because the Control Council did not even begin to keep any statistics on this subject until 1949, by which time they calculated that something like 9 million Germans had fled or been expelled from Poland, East Prussia and the Russian Sector of Germany. Between 1949 and 1963, a further 2,718,661 Germans were expelled from Poland, Czechoslovakia and Hungary.[15]

George Orwell said:

A leaflet recently received from the Friend's Peace Committee states that if the current scheme to remove all Poles from the areas to be taken over by the USSR, and, in compensation all Germans from the portions of Germany to be taken over by Poland, is to be put into operation, 'this will involve the transfer of not less than seven million people'. Some estimates, I believe, put it higher than this, but let us assume it to be seven millions. This is equivalent to uprooting and transplanting the entire population of Scotland and Ireland. I am no expert on transport or housing, and I would like to hear from somebody better qualified a rough estimate (a) of how many wagons and locomotives, running for how long, would be involved in transporting those seven million people, plus their livestock, farm machinery and household goods; or, alternatively, (b) of how many of them are going to die of starvation and exposure if they are shipped off without livestock etc.

I fancy the answer to (a) would show that this enormous crime cannot actually be carried through, though it might be started with confusion, suffering and sowing of irreconcilable hatreds as the result. Meanwhile the British people should be made to understand, with as much concrete detail as possible, what kind of policies their statesmen are committing them to.[16]

Orwell's worst fears about the manner of the expulsions and the hatreds they would generate were to be realised, but on an even more massive scale than he had suspected: the figure of seven million was an underestimate, and the idea that these people might be allowed to take their property with them to their new homes was naïvely mistaken. It is estimated that over 2,111,000 Germans died in transit to the west, but such a figure does not include those prisoners of war who, like the men of Danzig, were marched off to Russian labour camps. Nor does it include the 200,000 other Germans from Pomerania and East Prussia who were transported to the USSR for various and usually unspecified reasons. And such a figure swamps the disappearance of 34 exceptionally bright children from Pomerania who were singled out by the Russians from their school reports, invited to sit a special examination and who were never seen again.[17]

The statistics mask the individual, personal terrors of expulsion. On 27 July 1945 a boat arrived at the Berlin West Port with 300 children from the Finkenwalde camp in Pomerania. The Red Cross observer who met the boat reported:

> Children from two to fourteen years lay in the bottom of the boat, motionless, their faces drawn with hunger, suffering from the itch and eaten by vermin. Their bodies, knees and feet were swollen – a well-known symptom of starvation.[18]

In August 1945 the survivors of the outrages at the Danzig Marien hospital and the Weidlerdasse Orphanage arrived in Berlin by train. The journey from Danzig had taken eight days:

> They were packed into five cattle trucks, with nothing to cover the floors, not even straw. There were no doctors, nurses or medical supplies. The only food provided when the journey began was twenty potatoes and two slices of bread for each orphan. The patients had nothing, but the train stopped from time to time so that those of the passengers who were fit enough could forage. Some of the villages through which they passed were completely deserted – the crops had not been gathered and the cherries had dried on the trees. Between six and ten of the patients in each truck died during the journey. The bodies were simply thrown out of the train. When the train arrived in Berlin, sixty-five of the patients and orphans were removed to the Robert Koch hospital, where nine of them died.[19]

The Berlin correspondent of *The Times* described the arrival of other Danzigers:

> A woman recovering from typhoid had, she stated, seen her husband beaten to death by Poles and she had then been driven from her farm near Danzig to work in the fields. Now she has survived the journey to Berlin with two young sons, and, without money, clothes or relations, cannot see what the future holds.
>
> Three orphans I saw aged between eight and twelve are still almost skeletons after ten days' treatment, owing to the almost complete lack of fats in Berlin; none of them weighed more than three stone.

Another small boy turned out of Danzig had a scrawled postcard attached to him stating that his soldier father was long missing and that his mother and two sisters had died of hunger.[20]

Time magazine aroused considerable anger in Polish diplomatic circles by publishing photographs that showed in detail the pitiable state of the Danzig orphans. Many readers mistook them for victims of the Nazi concentration camps.[21]

Perhaps the most moving account of the arrival of the Danzigers in Berlin was that given by Norman Clark:

Under the bomb-wrecked roof of the Stettiner Railway Station ... I looked this afternoon inside a cattle truck shunted beside the buffers of No. 2 platform. One side four forms lay dead under blankets on cane and raffia stretchers; in another corner four more, all women, were dying. One, in a voice we could hardly hear, was crying for water. Sitting on a stretcher, so weakened by starvation that he could not move his head or his mouth, his eyes open in a deranged stare, was the wasted frame of a man. He was dying too. Two women sanitary workers did what they could in ministering to the small wants of the dying. The train from Danzig had come in. It had taken seven days on the journey this time; sometimes it takes longer. Among other things I saw when the Danzig train came in I am bound to record. Apart from the women rocking in tears and anguish, and the famished children asleep in their arms or crying for food, there was a group of young men – all Poles – who sat apart, waiting for the next train to go out. Then they would board it, and going through the train, would force these unprotected mothers and women to give up any possessions of value, including watches and jewels. The guards on the train and at the stopping places are shot if they attempt to intervene.[22]

But the fate of the Danzigers was but one part of the fate that was unfolding for all the Germans who had lived east of the Oder. From March 1945 they were evicted, often at gunpoint and at less than two hours' notice, marched to railway stations and collection points, searched and stripped of all valuables – including jewels, precious metals, photographs, antiques, books and heirlooms. For the most part they were allowed to take the clothes they wore and food for a short journey, but beyond this they were allowed to keep very little. Danzigers, like most German refugees from the east, arrived in the west with little of use and nothing of value.

Most refugees headed for Berlin, the natural transport focus for the north German plain. But as they converged, so the staging posts along the Oder grew. Mecklenberg came to resemble a vast, sprawling refugee camp. The woods were crowded with improvised tents where young and old alike were ravaged by typhoid, cholera, dysentery, lice and hunger. In Rostock, Schwerin and Ludwigslust there was an average of ten corpses to each new train load of refugees. The hospitals were jammed to capacity. The incidence of venereal disease, even among girls as young as nine and ten, was fearsome. A shocked British army officer, just returned from a tour of the Russian sector and the Polish western territories, reported that the whole of the old German east had become 'a gigantic Belsen'.

Under pressure from the Exchange Control Committee, the Poles did agree to a halt in the flow of expulsions on 2 August 1945. Documents were signed, agreements were reached as to how much currency the expellees might keep, how much baggage they might take; delousing facilities were agreed; railway timetables were set up; rolling stock was allocated. But it all went for nothing. The flow of expellees never slowed, never faltered, never halted. The only part of the agreement that the Poles kept to was the use of DDT supplied by the British. The 'orderly and humane' transfer of the German population never materialised.

The Poles continued their expulsions at an average rate of about 5,000 people per day right up to 1947. The Allied Control Council produced a plan designed to spread the expulsions over a year from November 1945 so that they would be more or less complete by the end of 1946, but nothing like organised transportation began until January 1946. And even then, the brutality of the expulsions was still clearly in evidence. For example, in his memoirs Count von Lehndorf says he was roused from his bed in Rosenberg and expelled without notice. He spent three days at a transit camp in Deutsche-Eylau and a night in the guard house. His clothes were torn to shreds during repeated compulsory searches. He spent two more days on a train to Kohlfurt, and a further two days waiting to be deloused. He eventually arrived in Elsterhorst to find the people there were as undernourished and dystrophic as the people he had been treating as a doctor back in Rosenberg. Yet von Lehndorf's expulsion took place in the spring of 1947, when in theory transport and expulsion had become regulated.

Western journalists and correspondents strove to bring the whole matter to the attention of the public and they achieved a certain measure of success. There was a debate in the British Parliament, followed by a direct appeal to Stalin; there was an official visit to Poland by an American General; British Foreign Minister Ernest Bevin confessed himself appalled at the situation; Robert Murphy, the US Political Advisor on Germany, wrote an urgent report for the American government and Arthur Bliss Lane, US Ambassador to Warsaw, was instructed to convey the US government's displeasure to the Polish government. The US effort, however, was undercut by their ambassador's attitude. He felt that the Germans exaggerated their sufferings and he was reluctant to make any written submission to the Poles. His conversation on the subject with Rzymowski, Polish Minister for Internal Affairs, had no effect whatsoever. Rzymowski said that the Poles were only giving as good as they got, and that in any case the Poles were treating the Germans in the west no worse than the Russians were treating the Poles in the expulsions from their eastern territories.[23]

In defence of the Poles it must be said that they had endured the Nazi occupation, suffered six long years of Nazi bestiality, genocide and Germanisation: the total population of Poland had been reduced from 35 million in 1939 to 23 million by 1945. The Germans had been utterly indifferent to Polish humanity. There was no mystery about what the Nazis had done in Poland, and no uncertainty about what they had planned to do. If these particular Germans were not the ones who had carried out the killings in Poland, then they were the mothers, sisters, wives, sweethearts and children of those who had. They or their families had voted Hitler into power and had joined Danzig to the Reich; they had profited from Hitler's policies and now they must pay the price. The fact that the war was over did not stop the wounds inflicted upon Poland from hurting, and now that the roles were reversed there was no reason why the Poles should have felt the slightest pity. The autumn of 1945 and 1946 brought very poor harvests. In Poland agricultural production was running at less than half of the pre-war levels. If famine was to be a fact of life in Poland, then the sooner the Poles got rid of the Germans, the better it would be. It was a cruel decision, but one which few Poles, if any, would have disagreed with.

In November 1945 a special Ministry for Recovered Territories, with Władysław Gomułka at its head, was created to try to bring some order to the new Polish western lands. Although Gomułka was later to become First Secretary of the Polish Communist Party, it is likely that history will judge his real claim to fame as being the integration of this vast, battered tract of land into the framework of the new Polish state and economy, and in engineering the international recognition of Poland's western borders.

Gomułka was quick to realise that the business of repopulating the western lands was part of the much broader problem of putting the Polish state on a secure footing for future economic growth. He warned repeatedly that the movement of over 3.5 million Poles into the western lands could not be undertaken lightly, nor could it be undertaken too soon. Tardiness would cost the Poles dear. It was while the harvests rotted and seed stocks sat unused that the Poles began to wonder if their haste in carrying out the expulsion of the Germans had not been unwise.

Whatever the uncertainties of retaining large numbers of Germans on Polish territory, the fact was that Poland could ill-afford to lose the skills and local knowledge of these people. Gomułka's Ministry began to question whether all the Germans facing expulsion were in fact German at all, and suggested that Poland was expelling people who, although they were perhaps third or fourth generation German speakers, were ethnic Poles who had been assimilated. It became necessary to apply certain tests of 'verification' to determine their Polishness. Some of these people acknowledged Polish ancestry, others did not. Some kept up links with the Polish language, others had not even a vague knowledge of it. But at a Congress of Autochthones in November 1946 Gomułka said: 'We shall not give up one single Pole to the Germans, and we do not want among us Poles one single German.' By this time Gomułka claimed that they had already 'verified' over 1 million autochthonous Poles, and went on to say that these people were 'a million witnesses declaring by their presence before the world and history that their forefathers were the sole owners of these lands, and that the Germans were there only as second comers.'[24]

For the autochthones it was a desperate and confusing business. Many had thought of themselves as German and were stunned to hear that Poland had claimed them as its own. These people had at first been defined as Germans and treated as such by the incoming Polish settlers. Most had already been thrown out of their homes and farms; the women had been abused as Germans. Now their farms were to be returned to them and they were expected to become loyal, happy and co-operative citizens of the state that had sanctioned abuse without mercy only a few months before. Most of these people had no idea whether they were ethnically Polish or German. Very few had any kind of documentation that went back beyond their immediate personal memory, and few could say with any certainty anything more about their family origins than had been transmitted to them orally by their parents and grandparents. At best their 'Polishness' was dubious.

Years later, when Gierek realised that he could get hard currency from West Germany for the German-Polish autochthones the decision was reversed and they were allowed to leave. Many, however, still remain in Poland.

12
Saddling the Cow

Stalin said that giving socialism to Poland would be like putting a saddle on a cow. Yet when it came down to it, Poland's strategic position between Germany and Soviet Russia meant that no matter how inelegant or inefficient the mount, as far as the Soviets were concerned the Polish cow had to be saddled.

By 1945 there were several interdependent policies on which most of Eastern Europe was agreed. It was felt that to protect themselves in future, the *Untermenschen* – primarily the Slavs – needed to form some sort of union against German economic and military power and against Germany's possible future allies. Given the USSR's political ideology, massive war effort and huge loss of life in the struggle against Nazism, it was clear that the Soviets would want a major role in any post-war set-up. It was also clear that the future East European states would be nation-states, and in consequence must be made minority free – or as minority free as was practicable. In almost all cases, with the exception of Poland, the pre-war bourgeois political parties had been thoroughly discredited by their willingness to co-operate with the Nazis at the expense of the local population. In Hungary, Romania and Czechoslovakia there was a recognisable, almost irresistible urge towards socialist forms of government that was accentuated by the nationalisation of all large industrial enterprises and by the seizure of all lands and properties owned by Germans and by collaborators.

Of all the 'liberated' states of Eastern Europe Poland was the one that caused the USSR the most worry since it was the most truculent, the least tractable. Hungary, Bulgaria and Romania had been Germany's allies until the closing stages of the war, but when German defeat was imminent they had staged revolutions to break free of German control and install regimes that were far more favourably disposed to Russian influence. Czechoslovakia, the only country with any lengthy democratic tradition behind it, had never had any substantial contact with the Russian state and therefore had none of the traditional hostility that marked Poland's attitude to the Soviets.

In Poland the legacy and memory of the Russian contribution to the Partitions was still vivid, as was the Polish–Soviet war of 1919–20, the Molotov–Ribbentrop Pact and the German and Russian invasions of Poland in 1939, the Katyn massacre, the Warsaw uprising, the war against the incoming Polish Communist government and the fate of the AK or Home Army. All combined to confirm established anti-Russian prejudices. In popular mythology these things were linked with a Communist order that was set to overturn the established Polish social system, revising downwards the status of everyone from the remaining *szlachta* right through to the humblest and most impoverished peasant. Whether this was in fact the case was another matter, but the fact that it was thought to be so made the business of constructing a socialist Polish state that was both economically powerful and still friendly towards Moscow an exceedingly prickly proposition.

It was a proposition that the boundary shift and the expropriation of German property and land both simplified and complicated. It complicated matters because at a time when Poland was waging a civil war in the south and east of its territory, the state had to absorb a vast area of land in the west and north, land that was unimaginably devastated, and whose population – many of whom were not Polish – were close to starvation, and who were to remain so for several years after the war had finished.

The boundary shift and expropriation simplified matters because the Polish state found that in the post-war atmosphere of simple anti-German sentiment they could seize and nationalise German industrial and commercial enterprises on their territory without opposition, and this left both land and property aplenty for the incoming settlers in the gift of the Polish Communist authorities.

To achieve such a high degree of state control on traditionally Polish territory and over Polish-owned enterprises under other circumstances would have proved impossible without violence and bloodshed – as the civil war showed. But in the west and north this control was accomplished as part of the process of assimilating these lands into the new Polish People's Republic. The gift of land, homes, jobs and whole enterprises was something the struggling Communist regime could use to buy, if not the affection, then at least the postponement or suspension of outright hostility of Polish society right through from the surly and suspicious Polish peasantry to the dispossessed and uprooted *szlachta* and middle classes.

The fantastic, exotic, hopeful and hopeless, brave cavalcade of gentry, professional pre-war soldiers, victims of the camps, forced labourers, displaced persons, stolen children, strident and cultured bourgeoisie, right-wing politicians and diplomats in exile returned to Poland after the war. It was inevitable that these people would see the new regime as an alien imposition, would resist the implementation of any kind of Soviet or socialist rule and would attempt to restore the pre-war status quo. It was inevitable that some at least would try to wrest control of the state from the hands of the Moscow-approved 'Lublin' Poles by rekindling ancient hatreds and by fuelling them with more recent outrages.

While it was possible for the new Czechoslovakian regime to trumpet that it was reversing once and for all the events that followed the Battle of the White Mountain in 1620 – when Bohemian forces were defeated and after which the victorious Habsburgs ruled for nearly 300 years – it was not possible for the Polish Communist regime to find any such simple rallying point in their history. The Poles had been partitioned by the Germans, Austrians and Russians, but the Austrian partition regime had been fairly liberal. The Poles had little reason to lash out at the Austrians, for 'geo-political' reasons could not focus upon Russian injustices, and so struck out all the harder at the Germans. The Polish government treated its remaining German population with far greater contempt and hostility than was strictly justifiable in terms of the threat they now posed to the new Poland. It was a delicate balancing act maintained only by the massive use of censorship and strict control of the media.

In Czechoslovakia intense nationalism led to the nationalisation of key industries as a gesture of disgust at the political and moral standards of the German, Hungarian and Czechoslovak middle classes who had collaborated with the Nazis. In Poland, however, socialism was seen as the very opposite of national feeling. For most Poles all forms of socialism were abhorrent because they believed that it meant a reduction in their standard of living and their quality of life. For a country which had long regarded itself as the eastern bastion of both Christianity and civilisation, absorption by the Soviet power bloc meant reduction to the anonymous, godless savagery of the barbarian Muscovite horde. In Poland there had been no collaboration with the Nazis and the pre-war government was still widely regarded as the legitimate heir to power. In this environment, co-operation with the Moscow-backed Polish government had to be both bought and coerced. The wealth of the new territories was to be the carrot; the threat of a German bid to regain those lands was to be the stick.

It is not easy to grasp the importance of the boundary shift for the post-war Polish state. The sheer scale of the thing, in both human and organisational terms, defies visualisation. It is hard to quantify exactly, but between 1946 and 1949 about 2.5 million Germans were expelled from the lands east of the river Odra. Approximately 1.5 million dispossessed Poles from lands in the east ceded to Russia, plus a further 1.5 million Polish refugees, exiles, internees and soldiers settled in the new Polish western lands. Between 1946 and 1970 a further 7 million Poles (including a young Lech Wałęsa) left their farms and villages in old Poland to head for the growing industrial centres of the new territories. Most Poles who settled in the west were country dwellers – the preponderance of rural and village nicknames among their surnames is evidence: in Wrocław and Gdańsk rural immigrants now comprise more than 40 per cent of the population. The massive westward shift of population totally altered the basic relationship between the people and the state and it brought about a new integration at every level of society. By 1986 over 5 million Polish children had been born in the western lands, and this, coupled with the general 'melting pot' atmosphere of places like Wrocław and Gdańsk, where Poles from every corner of old Poland meet and mingle accents and backgrounds, has helped to make the remarkably homogeneous political, social, ethnic and linguistic entity of contemporary Poland.

But what was at stake in the wealth of those lands? The Polish politicians at Potsdam were sure that the proposed border changes would mean a smaller, poorer Poland. Defeated Germany lost 18 per cent of its territory to Russia, Poland and Czechoslovakia. But Poland, nominally at least a victorious Ally, lost over 22 per cent of its land (an area roughly equivalent to the whole of England, Scotland, Wales and Northern Ireland) to the USSR. The gift of German lands in the west and north (roughly the equivalent to the area of England) did not make the new Poland anything like the size of the old. In fact, when all the calculations were finished the new state had shrunk from 338,000 to 309,000 sq km – of which 116,000 sq km, about 33 per cent, was made up by German land. Some saw the change as a defeat imposed by Moscow.

The assumption of the new Polish borders was not achieved without grief. At the Potsdam Conference the Soviet diplomats juggled shamelessly with figures at Poland's expense. At least the Poles were present to see this happening – at the previous Tehran and Yalta conferences, when the 'big three' had taken decisions in principle affecting the shape and location of the new Poland, there had not been a single Polish representative present. The Poles were present at Potsdam, but their fate had been decided before they even reached the negotiating table. They soon felt that their presence was a mere salve to Western consciences and that they had little real say in their own affairs. Indeed, as the conference wore on the Poles were to wonder if they were not on the losing side after all.

The Soviets seemed keen to take advantage of the Poles at every opportunity, and Russian conversations with Milkołajczyk were little more than a string of revelations of duplicity for the poor man. The Russians announced at Potsdam that the Poles would not be negotiating a separate claim for reparations against Germany, but would accept a proportion of the claim made by the Russians, which would be adjusted accordingly. This in itself was a blow to Polish pride and independence, but after the Russians had finished their calculations Mikołajczyk was informed that their share of the damages was expected to be 15 per cent of the total Russian claim. They could expect to receive about US$500 million. Mikołajczyk recalled his conversation with Molotov:

> 'Poland is luckier than the Soviet Union', he complained. 'You get this amount in addition to the US$6 billion dollars you've already received.'
> 'What $6 billion?' I asked, startled.
> 'Don't you understand?' Molotov asked coldly. 'Poland has given her eastern provinces to Russia. The Polish property left behind there totalled $3.5 billion. But on the other hand you receive from Germany an area whose property is worth $9.5 billion. So it is clear that you have gained $6 billion dollars."
> 'Just a moment', I asked. 'You say the property in the new western part of Poland is worth $9.5 billions. Don't you remember that you stripped it of its factories, railroads, plants, homes, livestock, and everything else you could transport to the USSR?'
> Molotov scoffed at this. 'Oh that has amounted only to about five hundred millions', he said – and abruptly adjourned the meeting.[1]

Next day the Poles learned that they had agreed to give the Russians a 51 per cent share in the ownership of all industrial enterprises in the Recovered Territories. And later still, they learned that as part of the Soviet–Polish reparations agreement which came into effect in August 1945, Poland was obliged to deliver 13 million tons of coal per year to the Soviet Union for the next four years at less than one-sixth of the world market price.

The absorption of the new lands radically altered the basis of the Polish economy. Compared to 1939 levels, Polish coal production potential was raised by 152 per cent; brown coal potential was raised by 3,220 per cent; coal briquettes potential was raised by 1,270 per cent; zinc production potential was raised by 147 per cent; iron was raised by a possible 7 per cent. While Poland lost its entire potassium industry and 76 per cent of its oil

wells to the USSR, it gained the potential to develop its own cellu-
lose, nitrogen fertiliser and copper-ore industries. The Polish
border changes actually enhanced Poland's chances of becoming
a modern European nation rather than remaining simply a convenient peasant-dominated grain basket for its industrialised
neighbours.

There was still a great deal of resistance to continued possession
of these lands, though, and it was widely believed that most Poles
would gladly swap them for their old territory in the east.
The 1946 referendum was rigged on a massive scale by the
Communists. Nevertheless, the returns from the 10 per cent of
districts where the Communists had failed to rig the election adequately indicated that nearly 85 per cent of Poles voted against
retaining the western lands. This was probably a reflection of the
way Poles felt about the fate of their country, rather than an accurate or realistic assessment of the potential of their new People's
Republic. They did not want a new People's Republic; they wanted
pre-war Poland restored to them. The vote against the western
lands hardly made sense in terms of the best material interests of
the voters; it was a protest against Communist rule and the influence of Moscow.

Jakub Berman later tried both to acknowledge the ballot rigging
and to minimise the extent of the protest vote:

> Those were aberrations; that kind of thing always happens ... peasants,
> uprooted from their villages somewhere on the other side of the Bug,
> who, even though they were given better farms and excellent housing,
> still longed, quite simply longed, to return to the place they were used
> to. Those were the first years on alien soil, and they hadn't yet adapted
> to the new conditions of life there; the process of adaptation isn't
> nearly as one might wish.
>
> Was the process of proletarianizing the peasants an easy one? No, it
> wasn't easy anywhere, not in Western Europe, either. How, then,
> could the process of assimilating the peasants on the Recovered
> Territories be an easy one? It couldn't ... It may be that individual
> communities or groups came out against the Oder–Neisse border, but I
> don't think everyone, en masse, was taking a stand against it. I don't
> believe that. Many soldiers settled on the Recovered Territories; I'm
> sure they didn't vote that way.[2]

The changes for the better were soon to show in the levels of
investment that the now highly centralised Polish state could
manage. In the years 1932–5 the Polish state had invested absolutely nothing in industry; the highest figure it achieved in the
entire inter-war period was a meagre 6.8 per cent of national
income in 1938. Yet between 1946 and 1969 gross investment in

Polish industry averaged 40.7 per cent of national income per annum. The lands lost in the east had accounted for about 12 per cent of Polish pre-war industrial capacity, but the new western lands were equivalent to about 65 per cent of post-war capacity. Looked at another way, the ratio of industrial output to agricultural output in 1937 had been 1:1, but by 1949 it was 2:1. Further, while Poland had regained the port of Gdynia, it now had the ports of Szczecin and Gdańsk at its disposal: cargo handling at these two ports rose from about 11 million tonnes in 1946 to over 30 million tonnes by 1972. The possession of these ports also opened up the possibility of a Polish shipbuilding industry: production rose from 2,000 tons in 1948 to 532,000 tons in 1972. During the period 1947–9 national income rose by 45 per cent – about 36 per cent per capita, on the 1939 figure.[3] The absorption of the western lands was directly responsible for Poland's sudden ability to create and accumulate capital. They were at the heart of Poland's rise to become number 11 in the list of the world's industrialised nations by 1979.

Berman may have dismissed the unmassaged 1946 referendum figures as mere disgruntled protest, rather than considered opposition, yet the fact remains that in 1946 most Poles did not regard the new territories as the 'real' Poland. That was something that would come later and would have to be 'massaged' too. But it is clear that just as the western territories were to lie at the heart of Poland's material development, whenever policies to enhance material prosperity went wrong they were also to lie at the heart of reaction against the Communist government. And Polish economic policies have gone wrong with monotonous regularity since the mid 1950s. In almost every case the western territories have acted as a barometer of social and political pressure, measuring the exact level of both political and economic discontent.

In many ways the issue of the Recovered Territories was an absolute gift to the post-war Polish regime. Andrzej Szczypiorski, a writer arrested under Martial Law in 1981, has written:

The regaining and restoration of the lands in the west is the greatest achievement of the nation and the greatest claim to pride in the post-war history of Communist Poland. For it must be stressed that only in conditions of a new polity could this undertaking succeed and bring fruit. The centralised authorities having all the means at their disposal at the cost of other, sometimes more burning social needs, had mobilised the resources of the state and nation in order to colonise, equip and cement with the rest of the country the territories of the west. In that sector the Communists were able to set in motion the initiative of the state and its citizens, for everybody realised that the consolidation of the Polish presence in those lands is a question of national survival ... there is no doubt that the consolidation of the Polish presence on the Oder, the Neisse and the Baltic coast has been, throughout all the post-war years, not only the hinge and axis of the foreign policy of the Polish Communists, but also the touchstone for all Polish citizens. Without the support of the nation the Communists could not have been able to restore life to the lands of the west. It was the whole nation that contributed to that enormous task.[4]

The west was a place where wealth could be acquired and created, not only through expropriation, but through industry and determination. The landless, homeless peasants from the east gained both land and homes simply by moving to the west. The factories (those that survived) sought new hands, and such was the shortage of labour and skill that the lowliest worker was instantly rewarded with promotion in the west. Experience was at a premium: the pre-war machine minder became a foreman, the charge hand became part of middle management. All advancement in property and promotion passed directly or indirectly through the gift of the Communists and their tame trades unions. Though some took part in active resistance, the vast majority of the Poles, though truculent, were unwilling to contest the Communist take over by force of arms. Many were prepared to suspend their disbelief long enough to give the Polish Communists a chance to prove themselves. Poles who had survived the occupation and who remembered the uncertainties of the inter-war period felt that here was a chance to begin again on a secure economic footing. And after all, a party that had fought the Germans and expelled them in their millions, had created jobs, gave away promotion, had farms and homes and positions of responsibility in its gift – such a party could not be all bad. Membership of the Polish Communist Party rose from about 4,000 in 1942 to 15,000 in 1944, to 30,000 in January 1945 and then to 300,000 by April 1945.[5]

The Recovered Territories provided a superb focus for virtually every element of Polish society. They were an issue on which the new Communist-sponsored middle class, the various surviving political parties, the Polish military, the economists and planners were all in full accord. The issue of the Recovered Territories and the threat of German efforts to recover these lands enabled the Stalinists to take the lead in carrying though social and political reforms behind the facade of 'National Unification'. It was an issue that allowed the Stalinists to divert attention away from the crucial, underlying and still unresolved issue of just who was to govern Poland after the war.[6]

Throughout his reign as Minister for Recovered Territories, and later as First Secretary of the Party, Gomułka's constant theme was West Germany's refusal to accept Poland's western border and the loss of Danzig, Stettin, Breslau and the other cities east of the Oder. Gomułka had little difficulty in persuading most Poles that this refusal was a threat to Poland's existence and that, given the opportunity, West Germany would start a war to reunite the East and West German states as one Reich before proceeding to reclaim lands from Poland. Gomułka used the threat of West Germany as a way of justifying Poland's alliance with the Soviet Union – an alliance that needed mighty justification in the eyes of Poles who saw the new government as an imposition, who were still loyal to the London government in exile and who regarded the Russians with barely concealed contempt. For Gomułka socialism and the Soviet Union were insurance against West German claims. After their experience in the last war, he argued, the Germans would be foolish to go up against a Poland which had the industrial and military might of the USSR behind it. If Poland stood alone, however, it would be a different matter. The German threat dominated Polish domestic and international political life in the immediate post-war years.

It was a theme that Jakub Berman returned to several times in his 1981 interviews with Teresa Toranska. He was in absolutely no doubt at all about the threat to Poland's western lands: 'The new shape of Poland became our trump card.'

> For us to break away from the Soviet Union would have meant losing the Recovered Territories, and Poland would have become the Duchy of Warsaw. Yes, that's right, the Duchy of Warsaw. There's no other possibility that I can see ... America immediately placed her bets on Germany and made efforts to unite it, and if she had succeeded, a victorious Germany would have been created, and thus an aggressive and greedy Germany, ten times worse than it is now, just as Hitler's Germany turned out to be worse than Wilhelmian Germany. It would have posed a complicated problem for us, and maybe even a new threat, for a united Germany would have become a pro-American Germany, and thus hostile to the Soviet Union and to us. And the existence of a pro-American centre bordering on the Soviet Union would lead to an inevitable clash, because the whole of Europe would be in danger of being subordinated to America. In such a situation we would immediately be the first to foot the bill, since we would be the first to be exposed to the dangers of such a clash. We're in the middle, after all; we'd be crushed to bits, and then the Recovered Territories would be taken away from us. The whole Adenauer strategy was directed towards taking the Recovered Territories away from us at the appropriate moment, and that's what would have happened. I've no doubt about that. Because, look: it's been so many years since the

war, and yet the issue of Vilnius and Lvov is still alive in Polish society, so how alive must the issue of our western territories be in Germany ...[7]

Berman, like other Communist Poles of his generation was almost entirely the creation of the Soviet Union and forgot that Poland was awarded the Recovered Territories, not solely by the gift of Stalin but by agreement with the other Allies too.

The flame of revenge may have burned – there were after all some 15 million expellees and refugees from the east living in West Germany – but if it did, then the light burned exceeding dim through the 1950s and not much brighter in the 1960s. Many Germans were moved to protest at the conditions of their expulsion, and most were bitter about the experience, but very few thought of regaining the lost lands by force. Yet the sudden growth of the Cold War, the failure to sign a Peace Treaty to end the Second World War and the establishment of de facto boundaries by international accord had left Poland 'in' Germany in a state of suspended animosity. The Poles had been led to believe that their western border had the full authority of Tehran, Yalta and Potsdam behind it, but instead found the Allies feeding German hopes by claiming that Poland was merely administering a temporarily occupied sector of defeated Germany in much the same way that the British, French, Americans and Russians administered their partition areas.

Most Western countries did not recognise Poland's new borders at first because it would also signify recognition of Russian sponsorship and control over what had become the East bloc, and in particular the creation of the East German state. With such a massive electorate of exiles and refugees, the recognition of East Germany was something that no West German politician could be seen to flirt with if he valued his career. Even if the electors were unable to recover their lost lands or reverse the expulsions they were not prepared to vote for a politician who failed to condemn these things and who did not entertain some notion of a return to the east. The West German politicians were unable to recover the lost lands by force but were prevented from acknowledging them as lost by the size of the refugee population.

But this was a knife that cut both ways. The West German inability to accept their losses in the east and Poland's new western border suited both Soviet and Polish claims that West Germany was the home of Nazi revanchism. Yet had West Germany acknowledged the changes this would doubtless have endangered the fragile West German democracy by removing common ground between the leaders and the electorate. However, such a move would have also had a profoundly unsettling effect on Poland too since it would have taken away virtually the only subject on which Gomułka and the Communist government had the total support of the Polish people. The threat from Germany was one of the main props to the Communist regime. In the years of Chancellor Adenauer, it was the supposed power of the *Bund der Vertrieben* (the League of Expellees) that was the main internal block to any kind of formal reconciliation with Poland. Ironically it was to transpire later that both the Poles and the West German politicians had over-estimated the cohesiveness and power of the expellees. In 1957 the BHE – the largest of the expellees' parties – suffered crushing defeat at the polls and in the 1961 elections failed to gain even 5 per cent of the vote.

Since diplomatic relations between West Germany and Poland in the immediate post-war years were practically non-existent, the various arguments about the new Polish western lands were conducted through the medium of the Catholic Church. The Recovered Territories became a focal point for the rivalry between the Catholic Church and the Communist state. In 1944 the Polish Committee for National Liberation – in effect the embryonic Communist government – had declared in Chełm that there should be a land reform in which all estates of more than 50-100 hectares, depending on the location, should be broken up and distributed among the peasantry. The declaration included some 450,000 acres of Polish Catholic Church land, and would eventually come to include all the property and land of the Catholic Church in the Recovered Territories. The Church naturally feared the reform and had hoped that German Church property would automatically devolve to them intact.

The refusal of the Vatican to recognise the new Catholic hierarchy in the Recovered Territories was seen as a failure to recognise Poland's new western borders, and since it became possible to argue that the Catholic Church, led by the Pope, had sided with the West German Nazis and revanchists, this gave the Communists ammunition to use against the Church. Revelations that the Vatican had helped several top Nazis and wanted war criminals to escape from Europe to South America by providing them with accommodation, money and passports hardly helped either the Polish Catholic Church or the Vatican in their relations with the Communist regime. Even so it was hardly fair to argue that the Polish hierarchy was siding with the revanchists. Cardinal Hlond, Archbishop Wyszyński and the Polish bishops all argued vigorously with the Vatican that it should acknowledge the new borders and order its affairs in Poland accordingly.

The Polish flock suffered every bit as badly as its government from uncertainty and the ad-hoc arrangements of the post-war years. The Vatican position was clear and unaltered from the start: it was prepared to accept the new Polish borders just as soon as Poland and Germany signed a peace treaty. Without a treaty that signalled amity and acceptance from both parties, the Vatican would recognise nothing. The Catholic Church thus referred to property in the Recovered Territories as 'Property under temporary Polish Church administration', and the Vatican persisted in naming members of the West German Church hierarchy as 'capitular vicars' to parishes in Poland that they were not allowed to visit.

In March 1950 the Polish government revived the Land Reform decree of 1944. It nationalised all lands in the west that had not previously been reformed, and technically it nationalised all Church property while leaving the lands in the possession of the Church. For a while it looked as if the Church and state were heading for a mighty clash over the issue of the Recovered Territories, but within a couple of months the Polish Episcopate issued a public declaration that as far as the Polish hierarchy was concerned these lands belonged to the Polish state 'for all time', and that they had agreed to lobby the Vatican for the permanent appointment of Polish bishops. The Episcopate also agreed to help combat the revisionist and anti-Polish activities of the West German Church hierarchy wherever possible.

At the end of 1950, when the East German government signed a protocol recognising the Odra–Nysa border, the Polish government renewed its calls for Vatican recognition. The Vatican, however, did not recognise East Germany as a sovereign state. There was little the Polish hierarchy could do when the Polish government began to make its own 'managerial appointments' to Church property in the Recovered Territories. Co-operation, though grudging, paid dividends the following year when the Church's assistance was enlisted by the government. In return for control in the appointment of its own hierarchy the Polish Church agreed to support the introduction of a single party list of candidates for the forthcoming elections to the Sejm. The Communist Party was so pleased that it had gained the support of the Church in instituting this piece of anti-democratic chicanery that it granted the Church the powers it sought, retaining only the right of veto. The role of the Church in helping establish Communist rule in Poland, though in line with a long tradition of Church pragmatism, was hard for the average anti-Communist Pole to understand or accept.

In the spring of 1965 the German Evangelical Church made the first hesitant steps toward the Poles. First a Memorandum on Polish–German relations, followed by an exploratory visit to Warsaw. In November 1965 the Polish bishops wrote a letter of 'reconciliation' to the West German bishops, and they invited the Germans to attend the Polish Millenium celebrations due to take place the following year. The letter suggested that the Poles should now forgive the Germans for the horrors of the occupation, just as the Germans should now forgive the Poles for the violence of the expulsions. When the content of the letter was made public the Poles were deeply shocked by the behaviour of their bishops. Most could not imagine the expulsions, but the memory of the occupation was still clear. How, they wondered, was it possible for their bishops to equate these two things? Surely the one had been a punishment for the other. Why should the Poles beg forgiveness of Germans? They had not organised and executed a policy of genocide, they had not kidnapped, tortured and killed millions of innocent victims.

The Polish government at once accused the Church of allying itself with the German revanchists, and flayed the bishops for daring to equate Nazi genocide with Polish expulsions. As far as the government was concerned, as long as the Vatican refused to accept the new Polish borders there could be no reconciliation and no dialogue with the Germans. The government's virulent criticism was intended to drive a wedge between the Church and the congregation, but the policy misfired hopelessly. In a manner that was to be repeated again and again in later years, the Communist government failed to understand the strength of anti-Communist feeling in Poland: the more the Communists criticised the Church, the more ardently the bewildered Poles ran to support their priests and bishops.

When it came, the German bishops' reply was a let-down – something less than jubilant enthusiasm, but also less than brutal fascistic rejection. The West German hierarchy was caught in the same double bind as the politicians. No matter how sensible the initiative of the Polish bishops, the German hierarchy dared not appear too enthusiastic lest this alienate their congregation – most of whom were refugees. The Polish people, already beset by the peculiar darkness of censorship, hardly understood these problems, nor did their government wish them to. Millenium celebrations – a resentful, ill-humoured hotch-potch – were held separately by both Church and state and without German guests. The Church celebrated a thousand years of Polish Christianity while the state celebrated a thousand years of Poland. In Wrocław and Szczecin the government put up posters that read: 'Poland – a thousand years on the Odra'. In Gdańsk there were banners fluttering over Długy Targ, along the front of the railway station, on hotel portals and the Communist Party office on Wały Jagiellonskie, that read: 'Poland – a thousand years on the Baltic'. Perhaps it was just as well the Germans did not visit.

Although the letter of reconciliation had failed in one sense, it did open up the idea of a dialogue and indicated that elements of both Polish and German society were willing to talk. In December 1970 West German Chancellor Willy Brandt – who had spent the war as an anti-Nazi exile – knelt on his country's behalf in front of the Warsaw Memorial to the Victims of Nazism and signed the West German–Polish Treaty. Almost at once the Vatican announced 'normalisation' of its affairs in Poland. The Polish government, in return, formally granted the title deeds of German Church property in the western lands to the Polish hierarchy. The Vatican signified that after the 1970 Treaty had been ratified in 1972 it would publicly recognise the Polish Odra–Nysa border. In June 1973 the Vatican set about appointing permanent bishops and settling diocesan boundaries in accordance with the borders of the Polish state.

Given the actions of the Catholic Church it was inevitable that Poland and West Germany should talk to each other again, but trade was also a major spur. The recognition that the expellees' parties were neither as powerful nor as united as everyone had believed, coincided with pressure from the Church, and also with Poland's increasing economic difficulties. Drought, a series of poor harvests, rising prices, lack of capital, shoddy management, poor economic infrastructure and a desperate shortage of industrial technology, compounded by the legacy of the German occupation, the massacre of the Polish intelligentsia and the misguided policies of the Polish communists, were made worse by the highly centralised system of economic planning. If the Polish economy was ever to achieve economic 'lift-off', Premier Władysław Gomułka had little option but to go fishing for credit, loans and technology transfer. The obvious catch was West Germany.

The re-armed German economy, basking in the glories of its economic miracle, was still expanding at an enormous pace and was searching for new markets for its products and technology. As their markets in the emerging nations of Africa, South America and East Asia became more industrialised, more nationalist and less stable, West German bankers and businessmen – for example Bertold Beitz, chairman of the board of Krupps, his part in the wartime seizure and management of the Polish oil fields now forgotten – came to think that perhaps they should switch some of their investments to Eastern Europe where it was believed a disciplined industrial workforce would provide a good return on their investment. In relation to Poland, loans and trade credits were doubly important since they were essential to the business community and to the power of the politicians, but also because trade credits acted as a salve for the West German conscience. There was an additional element, though. If Gomułka was fishing, he had live bait on his hook. Over 19 million Germans still lived in the East Bloc – in East Germany, Hungary, Czechoslovakia, Romania, Bulgaria and the Baltic republics of the USSR. It was estimated that in 1961 there were over 1 million Germans still resident in Poland. Among other things the West Germans believed that they could use trade credits to relax Poland's grip on these people.

There were those on the German right wing, and even those on the right of the ruling centre coalition, who had pushed hard for German re-armament and who thought that if the East could not be defeated in war it should at least remain isolated – quarantined – from the world. They urged that the only real possibility of improvement in East–West relations lay in the reunification of Germany and the repossession of the lost lands. In many ways these people were the true heirs of Adolf Hitler; they felt that Germany should be in sharp confrontation with the East and that apart from the fact that it was too far to the west the Iron Curtain was a good idea since it preserved Hitler's basic ideas with regard to the Slav races and communism. Mercifully, these people were few in number. In direct contrast there was also the sane, rational hope that economic linkages might allow sensible and humane relations between the two countries to grow. This was a dream fostered by the West German Foreign Minister and later Chancellor, Willy Brandt, and supported, among others, by the Danziger writer Günter Grass.

Brandt had every reason to believe that if he could tone down the official West German line on the expulsions and hostility to communism he might be able to open up a dialogue with the Poles. Gomułka believed that if he could rein in some of the traditional hostility towards the Germans he might get, not only recognition of the Odra–Nysa border, but also trade credits and loans worth about US$500 million.

Understandably Gomułka's line on Germany began to soften. If the place was not exactly the home of Nazism and revanchism any longer, then it merely contained elements of these things within it. In the closing stages of the approach West Germany almost became a friendly state. Finally, while Gomułka was pleased to announce that after years of diplomacy Warsaw had finally reeled in this difficult fish, in Bonn the West German politicians explained that Poland was not such a communist sort of place after all, that it ought to be possible to do business with these people, and that after years of cautious negotiation the Poles had finally been persuaded to come to the conference table. The Polish–West German Treaty was signed on 7 December 1970.

Many in Brandt's Social Democratic Party felt that he was naïve about the Polish Communists. Expellees in particular felt he was not representing their best interests by seeking rapprochment with these people. The East was a place of grim memory for them but in truth most of them had put down roots in the West, had children and even grandchildren who had grown up in the West and who could not even point to Danzig, Breslau or Stettin on the map. By 1970 only a small but vociferous minority of these people still campaigned for the return of the lost lands. Some harboured the notion that they might be allowed to return and repossess their property as a German minority in a Polish state, but the advent of tourism to Poland quickly cured them of this idea: the Polish economy was already a centralised morass of bureaucratic treachery and general inefficiency. Nevertheless the loss of eastern lands remained a point of honour and until the late 1970s it was still possible to see West German school atlases showing eastern Germany as under temporary Polish administration; nightly West German TV presenters thoughtfully and with a straight face gave the weather forecast for Breslau, Stettin and Danzig.

In the years before the Arab–Israeli wars brought the Western industrial societies to the brink of collapse it seemed that the flow of trade credits and rapid industrialisation meant that the East bloc as a whole, and Poland in particular, were set to enjoy a consumer boom and a massive rise in their standard of living. Later, as West German observers came to understand the nature of these societies better, hope that there might be some profit from trade began to fade. In spite of this disappointment, and even though the West German banks kept a close watch on the downward spiral of the Polish economy in the late 1970s, the flow of West German credits, loans and hard currency never dried up. There was some talk of drawing the Polish economy into the capitalist orbit through generous terms of trade, but this was little more than a pipe dream. Western intellectuals enthused over the idea as a move towards full detente, but the military sanctioned the idea only grudgingly because they felt trade, and all that went with it, helped to take the edge off Polish Communist hostility towards NATO.

Brandt was welcomed in Poland, not because of his manifest sense of conscience and morality, but rather for the economic opportunities he made possible. As well as the loans, trade credits and technology transfer, Poland could now claim hard currency repayments for war damage, and the Poles could extend facilities still further by bargaining over the remaining 1 million Germans still living in Poland. Poland's economic situation by this time was steadily worsening, and West German credit was seen by the corrupt and inefficient bureaucracy as a way of staving off the catastrophe that was sure to result from poor planning and disastrous exploitation of the workforce for inadequate returns. Gomułka could not avoid a delay between the signing of the Treaty and the first results of the credit flow from Germany; on 12 December 1970, less than a week after the Treaty had been signed, Gomułka announced that the price of bread, flour, meat, jam, coffee and a long list other foods was to rise by an average of 37 per cent and in some cases by over 90 per cent.

The Polish people were prepared to put up with a great deal while they were threatened by the Germans, but if the Germans were no longer a direct threat they saw no reason why they should tolerate without protest the organised chaos of the Polish economy – still less were they inclined to pay a penalty for the inefficiency and corruption of politicians and a political system they did not want. Gomułka's management of the economy and his place in Cold War diplomacy had been but different aspects of the same problem – the question of who was to govern Poland, the legitimacy of communist rule. Gomułka failed to realise that when he ended the German threat he also ended the only reason that the Polish people had tolerated the imposition of communism and the alliance with Moscow. There was no longer any need for a 'wartime' economy, still less was there a need for the kind of economy where the 'whole nation' created wealth, and the state and its senior party members were the only ones to share any substantial part of that wealth. Gomułka's attempt to raise prices came at exactly the moment when Poles felt that prices should be falling. In Gdańsk, Gdynia and Szczecin there was a wave of protest strikes. In Poznań there was a riot in which 50 people were killed. In Gdynia shipyard workers returning to work were fired on by the police and upwards of a hundred people – even today nobody knows how many – were killed. It was as if a gentlemen's agreement not to question the workings of the state and the basis of that state's power had been broken. The West German bogeyman had evaporated in the light of the Treaty. That dawn had also revealed the enormous discontent of the Polish nation. Less than a month after the signature of the Polish–West German Treaty no amount of foreign currency could prevent Gomułka's deposition.

When Gomułka tried to raise food prices the workers took to the streets and occupied their factories. Among the leading elements were the shipyard workers of the Recovered Territories. On 24 January 1971 Edward Gierek, the new First Secretary of the Party, acknowledged the economic power of the Recovered Territories by turning up at the gates of the Adolf Warski shipyard in Szczecin and humbly asking to see the leaders of the strike committee. Gierek's strategy was to listen to the barrage of workers' complaints for almost nine hours and then ask the industrial workers for their assistance. The workers, identifying Gierek as a coalminer – a worker like themselves – are said to have roared: *Pomożemy! Pomożemy!* We'll help, we'll help!

Gierek used foreign credits to build up Poland's industrial strength with the aim of paying back the loans through the foreign earnings of the new investment and plant. Unfortunately Poland's highly centralised economic system failed to cope with the influx of hard currency. It was impossible for such a highly centralised economy to make efficient use of the new funds. Managers attempted to make up for the deficiencies in consumer goods by simply providing larger and larger pay rises which could not be spent on anything useful. While the investment in fixed assets rose by 69.5 per cent instead of the planned 38.5 per cent, wages rose by 36 per cent instead of the planned 17 per cent. Meat and alcohol prices were pegged at their 1967 levels, and as wages rose, so consumption of these items rocketed.

Initially the economy enjoyed a boom, but before very long the entrenched problems of the Polish political and economic system began to show themselves. Most of the money was spent on projects that the Polish economy could not sustain simply because it lacked the necessary infrastructure and management skills, and because its products could not compete on the international market. Without sales on the international market the loans could not be repaid. The dream of an industrialised, productive and wealthy Poland began to evaporate. Trade credits continued to flow but it became increasingly apparent that only those who basked in the grace and favour of the Party would benefit from the country's newly generated income. However, by 1979 it was also apparent that the wealth that the Party had boasted of so frequently had not derived from the earnings from foreign loan-investments, but from the foreign capital itself.

The Polish–German Treaty of 1970 had opened up the basic question of the legitimacy of Communist rule in Poland. The new industrial working class of Poland – located very largely in the western lands – asked fundamental questions about the nature of Communist rule. They asked those questions louder and longer than other sections of Polish society because by the 1970s they had become the cutting edge of socialist industrial society and social ambition. It was they who generated the bulk of Poland's income. As Poland entered the highly competitive markets of the industrial world the pressure to compete with the technologically advanced nations meant that the factories and shipyards of the Recovered Territories could only survive by the imposition of ever harsher workplace discipline, by setting ever higher work quotas and by ignoring basic safety procedures.

The shipyard workers of Gdańsk tried to reconcile the idea of a socialist society with the actuality of failure that they saw every day. They tried to find a way of bringing together centralised planning with workers' self-management, to set socialism within a democratic framework. Their struggle constitutes a massive monument to the Polish post-war industrial achievement but also to the complete failure of that government's economic, political and social strategies: the Polish government had created an industrial working class, but had failed either to satisfy or control it. Indeed, its efforts to foil worker self-management contradicted the notion of democratic socialism it preached so loudly. It became increasingly obvious to the well-educated Polish working class that the Polish post-war regime had followed the Soviet example in blurring and then ignoring the distinction between state ownership and social ownership, and had set about a process of 'conceptual embezzlement' whereby socialism meant the continued existence of the status quo. If the Polish Communist Party had made promises to Poland, then it was in the western lands that the failure of those promises was most keenly felt.

In Gdańsk in particular the sense of opposition and resistance was particularly strong because when the Soviet Union cleared its jails in the amnesty of 1956, over 25,000 political prisoners, all with a deeply ingrained and thoroughly understandable grudge against the Stalinist system, were sent back to Poland and settled by the authorities in and around Gdańsk. As a result the ground-swell of industrial unrest in and around Gdańsk has always been coloured by a steady and well-informed anti-Stalinist opposition. Since 1945 Gdańsk alone has suffered an estimated 400 dead in protests and demonstrations.[8]

By the 1970s Gdańsk was part of Trójmiasto – the three city con-
urbation of Gdańsk–Gdynia–Zoppot – which had a total population of over 700,000, and was home to shipyards employing
directly and indirectly over 28,000 workers. The 1970s' wave of
foreign capital had hit Poland as a mania for 'gigantism' – giant
plants producing on a massive scale: West German trade credits
arrived in Poland to be channelled into the shipyards of Gdańsk,
Elbląg and Szczecin and their related support plants; the coal
mines of Silesia; the steel works at Nowa Huta and Huta Katowice;
the giant Ursus tractor factory in Warsaw; the Berliet bus factory;
the manufacture of Fiat cars under licence; the PVC factory at
Włocławek, and the Ethylene plant at Płock. Gomułka had been
able to engineer toleration for the poor performance of the Polish
economy by using the threat of German revanchism and the
promise of the western lands. For Gierek, there could be no such
cloak for his communism. He tried instead to buy legitimacy for
the regime with foreign trade credits and the development of
industrial wealth.

By 1976 it was clear that Poland's massive investments were not
going to pay off, that as far as the Party was concerned the
workers would have to be reined in, and that the plant and investments would somehow have to be made efficient. In June 1976,
without warning, the government removed the subsidy that had
kept food prices low for so long. It was calculated that across a
wide range of foodstuffs prices would rise by 60–69 per cent.
Polish workers saw no reason why they should pay for the inefficiency and corruption of the bureaucracy, or why they should
subsidise a variety of state capitalism they had not willingly
chosen. The workers of the Baltic shipyards went on strike, closely
followed by workers in Warsaw and Poznań. In Radom a large
crowd set fire to Party headquarters. That night the Party
announced that the subsidy had been renewed and the price rises
had been withdrawn for further consideration. In the months that
followed the Polish debt began to climb steeply from US$10
billion towards $17 billion. By 1979 the debt stood at $20 billion,
with a staggering 92 per cent of the country's hard currency earnings being spent on servicing this debt.

The consequences of this international debt reverberated
through the lives of Polish workers. Although the shipyards of the
coast were showpieces of modern industrial endeavour they
existed in sharp contrast to the increasing poverty and hardship of
the workers who struggled in them. Workers in the major industries came to see themselves as the first victims of state mismanagement and of state capitalism; they saw their standards of

living eroded in order to prop up management and planning systems that had quite clearly, and by every conceivable test, failed. It was in the industrial centres of the Recovered Territories that the contradictions showed through most clearly. Along the Baltic Coast in particular the discrepancy between industrial investment and social investment was massively in evidence in the contrast between the newly started Port Północny (North Port) and the widespread housing shortages. The highly developed, well organised and disciplined, remarkably homogenous working class of the western territories found itself facing a backward, centralised, self-seeking bureaucracy.

During the period 1978–80 real wages fell by 2.6 per cent (officially) and yet the state still tried to increase productivity by making workplace discipline harsher and more punitive, by increasing work norms and shift targets, by cutting back on safety procedures and health services. One commentator said:

> Working conditions in Szczecin's main industries – the shipyards, docks and chemical plants – are very harsh. Dockworkers suffer from lung disease and bone diseases – dockers working on the conveyor belt are like broken men by 45. The welders and other workers in the shipyards are prone to terrible industrial accidents through non-enforcement of safety standards and the pressure to earn extra money on overtime. The chemical workers also face serious health hazards.

In terms of physical health Alina Pieńkowska, a nurse in the Gdańsk shipyards and one of the founder members of *Solidarność*, had no doubt about the general trend. She said that as well as more widespread European illnesses like cancer and heart disease, tuberculosis – an illness that had almost been eradicated in the early 1960s – had risen in the years 1968–76, particularly in the 23–35 age group, to give Poland the second highest rate in the world. This, taken together with the high incidence of stomach ulcers and alcohol-related illnesses, was an accurate indication of the living standards and working conditions of Polish employees.[9]

In the late 1970s there were serious shortages of imported foodstuffs, chemicals, drugs and medicines, metallurgical products, plastics, fertilisers, seed stocks. The shortages had a cumulative effect: the shortage of cement ensured that in spite of an enormous waiting list for houses, the housing factories at Kokoszki and at Gdynia were working at between a third and a half of their full capacities. In Poland as a whole there was a housing shortfall of over 1,160,000 dwellings. Deputy Premier Jagielski admitted at the shipyard negotiations of 1980 that the Gdańsk region lacked some 7,000 nursery school and 11,000 kindergarten places. Tadeusz Fiszbach, the Gdańsk District Party Secretary, also pointed out that the 'disproportion in investment' between the social and industrial spheres had 'appeared more sharply and sooner in the Gdańsk region than anywhere else'. He took the problem to the Central Committee on 3 June 1980 and was told that the Politburo had recommended a special Planning Commission to draw up a programme of 'socio-economic development' for the Gdańsk region for the years 1981–5, but how such a committee was to proceed in a climate of economic chaos, or what the Party thought it might achieve, were never spelled out.[10]

Although the government had backed down in 1976 it was still determined to restore authority and to implement their policy. In order to do this it would have to break the increasingly organised independent power of the workers and the moves to channel worker participation and self-management through the tame official unions. In the months that followed thousands of workers active during the 1976 strikes lost their jobs. Thousands more found themselves in court charged with anti-social behaviour of one sort or another; many more were simply beaten up – sometimes by the police, sometimes by unidentified 'hooligans'. One of those sacked was a little known electrician called Lech Wałęsa who was later to estimate that he had been arrested over 100 times between 1976 and 1980. It was these legal reprisals against workers that forced the foundation in September 1976 of KOR – the Committee for the Defence of Workers. KOR included the economist Edward Lipiński and the novelist Jerzy Andrzejewski. A little later another unofficial organisation, TKN or the 'flying university', set out to explore a wide range of subjects which the 'official culture' of the Polish universities was forced to ignore. At the same time a huge unofficial publishing industry sprang up, ranging from the underground work of the large-scale publishing houses Zapys and NOWa, to the silk screen fly-sheet. By 1978 it has been estimated that there were probably more than 20 underground journals each with a readership of well over 20,000.

Dissident thinkers like Adam Michnik and Jacek Kuroń began to write that workers had no opportunity to expand the idea of democratic, pluralistic socialism within the confines of the decayed Stalinist state they had inherited. They began to urge that workers of all kinds should organise themselves outside the currently sanctioned channels of communication, bypassing and subverting wherever possible the officially sanctioned machinery of state: in short they urged an alternative Poland, an autonomous civil society for the most part beyond the reach of the Party. To a large extent this was to turn Lenin's recommendations for revolutionary conspiracy against the Party. The government – since it had mastered the vocabulary of Marxism without pondering the content – did not quite know how to handle such wilful and well organised resistance, and it was only in 1977 that it began to harass and arrest KOR members. By this time the Polish debt was almost out of control and arresting dissidents did absolutely nothing to alleviate the problems.

For industrial workers perhaps the most significant development took place in Gdańsk, where on May Day 1978 the Free Trades Union of the Coast announced itself. Among its early membership are some names which are now very familiar: Lech Wałęsa, Alina Pieńkowska, Bogdan Lis, Andrzej and Joanna Gwiazda, Bogdan Borusewicz, Anna Walentynowicz. Within weeks the tiny union was printing and distributing its own newspaper *Robotnik Wybrzeza*, aimed at providing information from the whole of Poland about workers' actions in resisting victimisation at work and fighting wage cuts. By September 1979 (when the government for the first time officially admitted that National Income was falling) the union had produced a charter of workers' rights tied in to the relevant sections of the various international agreements to which the Polish government was a signatory, but which in practice it had ignored. The authorities tried very hard to squash the Free Trades Union of the Coast. In January 1980, when members of the union demonstrated against victimisation and called a general meeting at the Elektromontaż factory, the management decided to transfer 14 employees (twelve of them union members). When the union picketed the factory the police surounded the place and the management then sacked 139 workers – a third of the factory's total workforce.[11]

By the summer of 1980 Prime Minister Babiuch was talking of cutting domestic consumption by 15 per cent in order to raise exports by 25 per cent and on 1 July the government announced price rises for foodstuffs. Almost immediately a series of small and uncoordinated strikes broke out all over Poland – including a one-day strike by Gdańsk's tram drivers. The Free Trades Union of the Coast had been monitoring the government's preparations, but it had little hope of organising any large-scale resistance to the rumoured measures. In the end they were aided by the machinery of state.

Anna Walentynowicz had worked at the Lenin shipyard as a welder and then as a heavy-crane operator since 1950 – during which time she had been awarded the bronze, silver and then the gold Industrial Cross of Merit. She had been a member of the 1970 strike committee and was a founder member of the Free Trades Union of the Coast. She had already been disciplined for distributing *Robotnik Wybrzeze* inside the shipyards. Earlier that year she had been arrested for collecting candle stubs from graveyards in order to make commemorative candles for those who died in 1970. On 17 April 1980, after her trial for stealing candles had been resolved, she was informed that the Regional Commission on Labour had decided to reinstate her to the shipyards.

Even though she had fought her case in court and had won on appeal, the management of the shipyard were determined to use her 'criminal activity' to get rid of the trouble maker. On 30 July she was stopped at the gate of the yard and detained, then after being held for one-and-a-half hours, released. From then until 5 August every time she went to work she was confined – sometimes detained – in the cloakrooms and was not allowed to proceed to her workplace. When she was finally allowed to start work her crane was switched off by one of the foremen, her locker was pried open and given to another worker. She demanded that the decision of the Regional Commission be put into effect. She spoke with the general manager who suggested that she transfer to another department. At this point the Regional Commission reversed its decision, saying it had made a mistake and that in fact she was not to be allowed back into the shipyard.

At home and ill from the prolonged tension, she was served on 7 August 1980 – only five months before her official retirement date – with an official dismissal notice. On 14 August the Free Trades Union of the Coast organised a demonstration with the aim of getting Walentynowicz reinstated. The demonstration – joined by Lech Wałęsa who climbed over the shipyard wall to avoid the guards – grew into a strike and an occupation; strike demands mushroomed from the reinstatement of a victimised fellow worker, to question the fundamental assumptions of the Party, its right and fitness to govern. Within a few hours the strike at the Lenin shipyard had spread to the Gdańsk repairs shipyard, to the Northern shipyard, to the Elmor works in Elbląg, to the Paris Commune shipyards in Gdynia; next day the Adolf Warski works in Szczecin came out in support, and within hours a series of MKS – inter-factory strike liaison teams – had been set up. By the end of the week over 400 works and factories had affiliated to the struggles of Solidarność. The Baltic coast as an industrial region was paralysed.

It was at precisely the time that Poland was least under threat from West Germany that those Germans still resident in Poland came under most pressure. Of the 1 million Germans, over 300,000 were thought to have expressed a wish to emigrate to West Germany. In spite of the 1970 treaty, Poland had restricted all such emigration because these people were still economically useful. Also in terms of Poland's external relations, these people were a bargaining chip. Poland tied the question of their emigration to persuading the West Germans to part with an additional 3 billion marks. When the West Germans showed signs of reluctance, the Poles closed down German-speaking village schools, shut down German-language newspapers and set up a discriminatory employment scheme that effectively barred all Germans who wished to emigrate from obtaining or retaining employment. In a move that was particularly distressing to the older generation the authorities in Gdańsk, Wrocław and Opole began to close down, bulldoze and redevelop German cemeteries and graveyards as housing land. By March 1976 the situation for many Germans was so dire that the Federal German government, inundated with letters of protest from the West German relatives of the 'Polish' Germans, agreed to buy out 120,000 Germans at the rate of 15,000 per year for the sum of 2.3 billion marks.

By 1980 Poland, ranking eleventh in the league of industrialised nations, found itself the world's second largest debtor, and the first of all its creditors was West Germany. By 1981, when Poland's international debt had risen to over US$27,000,000, the West German banks were owed some $4,500,000 – less than half of this secured by government guarantee. The Deutsches Bank, the Dresdner Bank, the Für Gemeinwirtschaft Bank and the Commerzbank were owed a total of over DM 3,040,000. The West German government, while honouring what it called 'a deep seated historical obligation to Poland' refused to lend a further DM 100,200,000 because of the risk of unbalancing its own budget, but nevertheless set aside over DM 1,000,000 to cover the anticipated failure of Poland to pay back some of its state-guaranteed credits. It is worth pointing out that between 1976 and 1980, the West German government continued to buy out Polish Germans even though the West German banks bore the bulk of Poland's international debt.[12]

Of the 180,000 Germans who remained in Poland after 1980 very little was heard until June 1988, when Chancellor Kohl announced that under the new Soviet regime that advocated *glasnost* and *perestroika*, General Secretary Gorbachev had agreed that by the end of that year 160,000 ethnic Germans from the Soviet Union's Baltic republics, and from Romania and Poland, would be resettled in West Germany. This was said to be the largest bulk population transfer since 1958. Of these immigrants 75 per cent were between 20 and 45 years old; more than half did not speak German. The estimated cost of rehousing them and teaching them

German totalled over DM 10 million – and even then a further half million 'ethnic Germans' were thought to be still resident in the East bloc.[13]

The arrival of the Polish Germans in the West through the late 1970s aggravated a number of tensions already present in West German politics – particularly on the subject of guest-workers. Turkish guest-workers – some of whom had children who were born in Germany – were still living in temporary accommodation after 20 or 30 years, while the new German arrivals were immediately provided with their own flats. Many of the older Polish Germans spoke dialect rather than standard German, while the younger ones spoke only Polish. For the most part the Polish Germans were ageing country dwellers who had no experience of an advanced capitalist society; many of the younger people had been brought up on a diet of myths about life in the West and some very odd stories about the defeat of Hitler. They all had an intense dislike of Poles and Communism. But if they did not fit in with the Polish state they were leaving, they hardly felt better about their new state either. The fact that a large number of West Germans regarded them in more or less the same light as guest workers from Turkey and Yugoslavia, and referred to them contemptuously as *'Wasser Polacken'* (water poles) cannot have helped. The tensions they generated, the problems their plight as immigrants and anti-Communists highlighted, and their eventual discontent and confusion about the nature of capitalist society fed indirectly into the rise of extreme right-wing anti-Communist opinion in West German politics during the 1980s.

The rise of the Right in West Germany was part of a move towards a more reactionary style of politics throughout the West in the late 1970s and early 1980s. For the Poles the election and then re-election of Helmut Kohl as West German Chancellor was particularly worrying, since he seemed determined to return to the confrontational propaganda of the Adenauer years and to reverse the achievements of SPD Chancellor Willy Brandt. The Chancellor's party, the CDU, and its sister party the CSU had both campaigned that the 1970 Treaty with Poland should not be ratified when it came up for renewal in 1975.

It is tempting to dismiss the exiles' unions as gatherings of oldsters in moth-eaten regional costumes who guzzle sausages, beer and potato-pancakes and who search for some lost Heimat of dubious memory; in themselves they are are quite harmless, even if they are led by windbags with barely disguised Nazi tendencies. However, the growth of the right wing in Germany meant that the various exiles' unions began to enlist political support from politicians anxious to exploit their grievances and win votes. Through the 1950s these unions had not been able to exert much influence on West German foreign policy because that policy was monitored so closely by the Allied Army of Occupation, but by the 1970s West Germany's nominal independence had been turned into real sovereignty.

In January 1985 Helmut Kohl was returned for a second term as Chancellor, and within a month had agreed to address the Association of Silesian Exiles, the largest and most vociferous of the exiles' unions. As late as 1980 it was still possible to see roadside hoardings paid for by the various exiles' unions showing a map of Germany with its 1939 boundaries. Although the Bonn government had been quietly subsidising these unions since the war Kohl was the first West German Chancellor to take public notice of these people in over 20 years.

From within a NATO dominated by Thatcher, Kohl and Reagan the rise of anything that discomforted the Communists was seen to be fair and legitimate. In this spirit it was possible for both Thatcher and Reagan to support Solidarność while attempting to neuter their own unions at home. In spite of this, Kohl's decision to address the exiles was greeted with a storm of protest since the motto of the rally, which was to be written on a banner above Kohl's head, read: 'Forty Years of Expulsion – Silesia Remains Ours.' Kohl, anxious not to lose his support on the Right, refused to order that the motto be changed, and it was only the tone of foreign (mainly NATO and EEC) reaction that persuaded the Association to alter its motto. Kohl eventually appeared under a banner which read: 'Forty Years of Expulsion – Silesia Remains Our Future in a Europe of Free Peoples.' The Polish authorities could take the idea of a Free People any way they wished, but the message as a whole was only slightly muted.

Lest there should be any doubt as to Kohl's position with regard to Poland, communism, the Lost Lands and German history in general, the Chancellor stated that neither he nor West Germany had any territorial claim on Poland, but he went on to say: 'the [1970] treaty with Warsaw does not prejudice a peace treaty for the whole of Germany, and thus provides no legal basis for existing borders today.'[14]

In other words, without a peace treaty signed by a united Germany, a treaty made by one part of Germany could not be binding should Germany become united at some future date. The echo of Hitler's comments on the Versailles Treaty did not pass unnoticed. While Kohl urged reconciliation between Germany and Poland he never once attempted to discourage the extremists or the exiles from their belief that one day Germany might re-unite, might reclaim its old, pre-1945 borders – the borders of the Greater German Reich. As Herbert Hupka, CDU member of the Bonn government and Chairman of the Association of Silesian Exiles, said at the same meeting: 'Germany is bigger than the Federal Republic and if we speak of the German Reich, we refer only to our national history and the democratic will of our people.'[15] The assembly of 100,000 expellees greeted this statement with 'wild applause'.

Kohl fuelled Polish fears in other ways too. On 5 May 1985 – just a few weeks after the Silesian rally – he visited the cemetery at Bitburg and held hands with President Reagan. This was by no means a simple act of reconciliation between the US and West Germany. That particular cemetery contained the bodies of SS-men – the instruments of German genocide and racial policy in the murderous drive to colonise Poland and the east. In visiting the cemetery in this way Kohl showed that the CDU/CSU sanctioned a whole range of reactionary ideas and opinions that had come to be associated with Germany's discredited Nazi past. If he did not actually attempt to reclaim Nazi aims and policies as the acceptable concerns of a legitimate and shameless German history, then he came uncomfortably close.

The survivors of Hitler's camps were quick to spot what was at stake:

What has become increasingly strong in the past few years has been a desire expressed in different ways across the political spectrum for a return to 'normalcy'. This desire is in part an expression of the changed constellation of power in the world. For the Social Democrats for example, it expressed itself in the increasing desire that West Germany act politically and economically in a sovereign manner vis-a-vis Eastern Europe and the Soviet Union. Under the Kohl government the desire that the postwar period be finally ended is expressed in a different manner, as a desire for reconciliation with the German past. An example of this change is the new law passed by the Bundestag, making it a criminal offence to deny or speak lightly of the Holocaust and of the expulsion of the Germans from the East in 1944–5, a law in other words that equates the suffering of the Germans with that of the Jews and thereby seeks to wipe the historical ledger clean ... Finally, and most seriously, was of course, Kohl's equation of the First and Second World Wars expressed in his insistence that Reagan should hold his hand in a gesture of reconciliation at Bitburg, just as Mitterand had done at Verdun. The equation of the two was meant to imply, of course, that with marginal exceptions (i.e. the Holocaust) the Second World War was a war like any other. It implied that Germans had neither to confront nor welcome their past – nor that they had to continue hiding it. It meant, within limits, that they could now affirm their own past.[16]

Kohl's government was to claim that it had been necessary for them to move to the right and make these particular gestures in order to contain and control the growing power of the extreme right wing – particularly the NPD and the FDAP. The NPD had won 8 per cent of the poll at the 1984 European Parliament elections and had therefore qualified for EEC funding. However, the reasoning behind the pro-phylactic move to the right proved to be spurious: at the 1987 Bundestag elections the CDU/CSU found that its share of the poll had dropped by over 5 per cent, while the vote of the NPD had tripled. Chancellor Kohl's government was leading its public in the direction it wanted to go. Without doubt the election of Kurt Waldheim to the post of Austrian Chancellor in spite of (or perhaps because of) his implication in the murder by the SS of partisans and commandos in Yugoslavia and Greece during the war meant there was further justifi-cation for the growing feeling on the right that perhaps, after all these years, the Western Allies had finally come to understand Hitler's poli-cies with regard to the East, that the Nazis were not so wrong after all.[17]

It would be quite unfair to locate Poland's anxieties about con-tinued possession of the Recovered Territories solely within the ambiguous context of a rise in right-wing ambition in the West. Poland's fears apply even to the behaviour of fraternal neigh-bouring states. In the spring of 1981, while Solidarność was still a force to be reckoned with, the East German media fostered a thor-oughly anti-Polish mood by blaming East German economic difficulties on the chaos of the Polish economy and on the failure of the Poles to deliver contracted coal, materials and manufac-tured products. The East German government sanctioned the broadcast of a number of TV and radio programmes and the release of a series of articles in various magazines which attempted to rehabilitate the anti-Polish history of the Prussian state and show the *Drang nach Osten* in a more favourable light.[18]

There was a powerful suggestion that perhaps the *polnische Wirtschaft* (Polish economy) could only be improved by yet another partition – a thought which brought protest from the East German Evangelical Church, notice from the CIA-backed 'Voice of America' radio station, and sharply critical attention in the Polish media too. At the same time the Soviet Union launched a vigorous campaign to show that West German willingness to lend millions of Deutschmarks – with the apparent approval of President Reagan and Prime Minister Thatcher – to promote and support Solidarność was in fact a neo-Nazi bid to drive a wedge between Moscow and its allies, to disrupt Soviet communications and military supply routes to East Germany prior to a West German bid for reunification. The Russians were keen to show the Poles that by supporting Solidarność they were playing into West German hands and that Poland's western lands would be the first victim of a unified Germany's territorial claims. Chancellor Kohl's speech to the Silesian expellees was to show that perhaps the Russians had not been so far wide of the mark after all.

Such politicking understandably makes the Poles very jittery, and may have given an edge of urgency to General Jaruzelski's military coup of December 1981. Had Jaruzelski failed to implement the coup, it is quite possible that the Soviet Union, the East Germans and perhaps the Czechs had a plan for another partition of Poland: the East German and Soviet media campaigns, and the flotation of the idea of partition, were certainly sanctioned from the very top of the Soviet hierarchy and may well have been intended to pave the way for this eventuality. General Jaruzelski was better placed than most to know the extent of any such threat.

It comes as a surprise to West Europeans to find that Poles fear their western borders are still under threat, and worry that the state's internal political life might be subverted to the territorial advantage of the Germans. But these things are part of the fabric of Polish political consideration. The report 'Experience and Future', commissioned by Gierek in the mid-1970s but never published in Poland, has several anonymous contributions on the theme:

Respondent No 17 writes: 'The German question weighs on the minds of the Poles and must affect the nature of Polish politics. It cannot be left out of any deliberations on the future of our country. This does not mean that we should abandon our attempts to arrange our relations with our western neighbours so that they will be better than in the past and shape them in the spirit of peace and mutual respect and understanding. In the future such a process should lead to the healing of the wounds of the past and to a situation in which no one will exploit the Polish–German problem as a useful tool for political manipulation, intimidation, and the pursuit of their own aims. A precondition for such a relationship, however, must be universal acceptance of Poland's western frontier as a fundamental and inviolable prop of European peace.' Respondent No 37 adds: 'The hope of some FRG circles for a return to solving the problems of Central Europe by Bismarckian methods runs counter to the aims of European peace and stability. It is true that the main guarantor of Poland's western frontier is the Soviet Union, but the permanence of this frontier does not depend entirely on the USSR. A nation of 35 million people cannot be a 'displaced people'; everyone in Europe must understand that questioning

Poland's western frontiers threatens peace and prompts violence and dangerous reactions on the part of the Poles. On this question the Polish nation is completely unified.[19]

Within a few days of the birth of Solidarność the Polish Communist Party voiced the opinion that the disturbances in Gdańsk 'have already encouraged West German revisionists, who openly admit that recent events in Gdańsk and on the coast are very welcome to them'.[20]

We will probably never know exactly what part threats to Poland's territorial integrity played in the declaration of martial law in 1981, but the idea of partition may have forced General Jaruzelski's hand. In his TV address to the nation on the first morning of martial law, General Jaruzelski said: 'A national catastrophe is no longer days but only hours away.' He also said that the nation stood on the 'abyss of fratricidal warfare'. Even allowing for the chaos of Poland in the previous few months, this is dramatic language. And even if the General is a convinced and loyal Communist, he is also a patriotic Pole. In this context it is worth noting that General Jaruzelski spoke of the threat to the 'nation' rather then the threat to the 'state'. It seems unlikely that he would risk the odium of history and the contempt of virtually the entire nation for anything less serious than either biological threat to the life of the nation or the threat that the state that sheltered the nation would be dismantled by external forces.

It is worth emphasising General Jaruzelski's particularly intimate relationship with the Western Lands. By 1981 Jaruzelski had fought for the western Polish border, and been wounded there, had defended the new border as garrison commander at Szczecin, had married there, and had been a parliamentary deputy for two of its most important cities.[21] Like many other Poles Jaruzelski came to believe that the man Hitler and the country Germany had been defeated, but the ideas which had led Germany into its drive to conquer the east had never been confronted and remained untouched. Germany was still tied to eastern ambitions, to the phantom limb of its marcher lands. The continuing German threat to Poland over the matter of its western lands is one to which Jaruzelski has returned again and again.

Jaruzelski has stressed repeatedly that Poland's place in Europe is far from assured, that enmity from Germany has not been overcome and – much in the manner of Gomułka – that internal dissent and economic chaos are an invitation to disaster on a scale that most European nations cannot imagine:

Observance of the Yalta and Potsdam decisions, as well as the international agreements of 1970 sealed by the Final Act of the Conference on Security and Cooperation in Europe is a pre-condition for peace on our continent and, by the same token for Poland's security. Today anyone who speaks out against these principles is playing with fire and aligning himself with the enemies of our country.

The West is not short of politicians pursuing hopeless attempts to revise history, also at the expense of our country. Our response is brief: apart from Poland, and beside Poland, no one shall settle our affairs. Neither by trick nor by force shall Poland let herself be forced away from the borders along the Oder and the Baltic.

The return to the ancient land of the Piast dynasty and its full integration with the Motherland is a historic victory for the Polish nation ... People on the other side of the Elbe who have suddenly discovered over a million-strong 'German minority' in Poland could equally well have discovered inhabitants on the Moon.

A crucial premise for peace in Europe is to render impossible any re-emergence of Pan-German expansionism, revived under the pretext of 'unification'. This is a common duty of all nations which suffered directly or indirectly from the wars unleashed by German imperialism.

With the September 1939 tragedy and the genesis of the Nazi attack still vivid in memory, we have to view the present policy of West Germany in its full historical context and consider, above all, the facts.

The facts are that the Federal Republic, year by year departs further from the military limitations set by the victorious war-time coalition. It tramples even its own obligations by aspiring to the right to manufacture and possess strategic bombers as well as medium and long-range missiles. It has become involved in the confrontational, imperialist policy of the United States. At present, this constitutes the essence and the gravity of the danger.

The recent numerous revisionist acts and statements lead to the conclusion that the conflict between revanchist and co-existence tendencies has not yet been resolved in the Federal Republic. The current of anti-Polish revisionism includes not only 'compatriot organisations' but also Catholic Church circles which still support the fiction of pre-war diocesan divisions.[22]

Solidarność, albeit unwittingly, revealed that the threat to the Polish borders still exists – though perhaps not only from West German claims. Solidarność's industrial strength (located hugely but not exclusively in the western lands) meant that the unresolved question of who is to govern Poland and how it is to be achieved were raised again. Whether the bogeyman of West German threat is real or not is another matter, but the Polish leaders feel that it is real and Moscow, for convenience, for communism, for military security, for conservatism, has supported them in this belief. Where West Germany was not a threat, then

East Germany and Russia may well have been. The question of Poland's border security and its inability to reconcile Polish social, political and economic aspirations to the realities of life within the socialist camp will almost certainly mark out very precisely the limits of *perestroika* and *glasnost* in Poland. As far as Jaruzelski and the other post-war Polish leaders are concerned, they have little doubt that Poland must exist in its present form and location or it will not exist at all.

Ironically, the prospect of the withdrawal of American nuclear missiles and US troops from Europe has done little to make the Poles feel more comfortable. While the official Warsaw Pact line is that Europe would be a much safer place if these things were to take place, the concomitant withdrawal of Soviet forces would hardly help Poland. The Poles are aware that one of the main effects of the Second World War was to shift the real centres of world power out of Central and Western Europe altogether, and to reduce the European nations' ability to wage war by cementing them within much larger schemes of military and political power. The Poles know that the West Germans cannot make war from within NATO and the EEC, but they are also aware that, according to the latest estimates, the West German economy will overtake the Soviet economy by the year 1999, and by that time they will also dominate the EEC. The Poles feel that American and Soviet withdrawal from Europe will restore the sovereign states' ability to make war on each other, make the reunification of Germany inevitable, and leaves the whole of Eastern Europe open to German economic dominance.

Lamentably, after 45 years Poland's borders – its possession of the old east German provinces, towns and ports – is still an issue. Poland's possession of Gdańsk, Szczecin, Wrocław, Opole and the rest, the threat – real, potential or imaginary – to its territorial integrity, the undeniably volatile nature of its abused and discontented workforce, the importance of the Recovered Territories to the ailing Polish economy, the long-standing problem of political legitimacy, the massive failure and corruption of the centralised planning system, the suspicion that all economic aid is a West German plot to regain its old lands – all these things are intricately and intimately linked in ways that have hardly changed since Gomułka started work as Minister for Recovered Territories in 1945. To touch one is to threaten all.

13
History and the Censor

In the growth and development of Central European archaeology we can see reflected the tensions, demands and claims of the rival German and Slav national identities. In his *Pomeranian Chronicle* (c.1530), one of the earliest attempts to describe the area from a historical point of view, T. Kantzow described the structure of tombs, barrows and megaliths with great accuracy. A short while later C. Schütz, in his *Historia Rerum Prussicarum* (1592), identified pottery vessels found near Danzig as Slav burial urns. Because there was some continuity of pagan practice into historical times in Pomerania there was very little doubt that the various barrows of the area were burial mounds. The Slav population called them *mogela* (modern Polish mogiła). The fact that the Slav population knew what the mounds were and had names for them was one indicator of Slav rather than Germanic cultural continuity in the area. Yet until the middle of the seventeenth century German archaeologists, rather than credit them to earlier Slav peoples, preferred to describe the mounds as giants' graves. Where the Slavs were given credit for archaeological remains a certain fanciful quality entered the debate. J. Bugenhagen in his *Pomerania* (c.1525), described the ancient Slav settlement of Vineta at the mouth of the Oder in considerable detail and seems to have identified the remains for what they were, but it was generally the habit to regard early hill forts and earthworks as sites of ancient pagan sacrifice rather than as Slav fortresses or sites of Slav settlement.

As the political and ethnic composition of Pomerania changed, the question of what to attribute to the Slavs and what to the Germans became even more problematic. By the end of the seventeenth century the attribution of archaeological finds to definite peoples was rapidly becoming a matter of political principle rather than developing scientific method. Consistently throughout the Enlightenment the area where archaeological effort was at its greatest was in the north-eastern corner of Germany – Prussia. It was there that ethnic, linguistic and commercial tensions made the subject a more sensitive issue than elsewhere.

The last king, Stanisław II Augustus (1764–95), was a great enthusiast of archaeology and in 1786 he and his nobles drew up a plan of systematic research which included the creation of a special museum. The spirit of the Enlightenment also allowed J.C.C. Oelrich to publish a bibliography of Pomeranian materials in 1771, but nothing came of Stanisław's plans or of Oelrich's bibliography because the spirit of disinterested research fostered by the Enlightenment was soon overtaken by the rising tide of nationalist feeling. The spirit that allowed Stanisław's archaeological plans to grow was crushed and humiliated by the Russians, Prussians and Austrians and by the facts of daily life in partitioned Poland.

Archaeology was to have a much more important place in Polish society than elsewhere in Europe precisely because of Poland's partitioned status. But given the political, national, social and educational situation in the partitioned lands, nothing much could be expected from Polish archaeology at this time: there was no material or financial basis for extended work and no facilities for detailed analysis. Learned historical and antiquarian societies were not founded on any large scale in Poland until after the partition – the Royal Society of the Friends of Science (Warsaw 1800), and the Association of the Friends of the Sciences (Warsaw 1800), disbanded after the 1830 rebellion, was reformed again in Poznań in 1857. In spite of the difficulties it was at precisely this period that interest in Polish antiquities began to grow.

In Poland, however, state sponsorship of Polish history was impossible and any collection of historical artefacts was almost certainly the property of an individual nobleman. It is from this period that the major Polish collections date and these private collections were eventually to form the basis of present-day Polish museums – the S.K. Potocki collection at Wilanów was started in 1804; the J. Ossolinski collection was initiated in Warsaw in 1814; the Lubomirski collection began in Lwów in 1823, and the Czartoryski Collection was started at Puławy 1800–9.

Polish reaction to Prussian anti-Polish feeling and later to the Germanisation policies were to foster and support cultural institutions by raising their own funds. The first Polish archaeological society was formed in Szamotuły in Prussian Poland in 1840, but its activities offended the Prussians, who did not wish to see any growth of consciousness and identity in their non-German subject peoples, and they abolished it by special decree in 1846. Undaunted, the Prussian Poles founded the Poznań Society of the Friends of Science (1857), and at the same time Poznań received its first museum of Polish and Slav antiquities. Polish interest in archaeology was steady in all the areas of partition: in Austrian Poland the Scientific Association of Kraków established an archaeological section in 1850; and in Russian Poland the Museum of Fine Arts in Warsaw was founded in 1862 and was eventually to metamorphose into the Polish National Museum. By this time, though, the spirit of Enlightenment in Poland was rapidly hardening into the Romantic spirit of resistance to alien rule, to the creation of sustaining national myths and heroes. Pomerania suffered from neglect during the Romantic period simply because archaeologists were looking for picturesque sites with imposing ancient monuments whereas Pomerania had little more than burial mounds to offer.

In Germany, as the patchwork of principalities melded into a unified state, the private collections of objects that had begun to develop in the seventeenth century were gradually taken over by the local and state authorities. They flourished under the patronage of the growing and increasingly wealthy Prussian bourgeoisie, and by and large they confirmed that class's growing sense of identity and self-satisfaction. In the nineteenth century Germany created a number of new professorships of non-Classical archaeology, and there was a massive increase in research activity. In Stettin the Baltic Society published a journal devoted to Pomeranian and Baltic finds.

While German archaeology was already beginning to exhibit disturbing signs of chauvinism, among a minority of scholars it was acknowledged that Slav pottery – decorated with parallel wavy lines – could be distinguished over a very wide area of the German east ranging from Pomerania and the sacked Slav fortress of Arkona, south through eastern Germany to Bohemia. The attribution of pottery sherds to ancient Slavs (G.C.F. Lisch, 1847; M. Lüssner, 1853; L. Šnajdr, 1858; R. Virchow, 1874) was finally accepted at the Stockholm archaeological congress of 1878. The full extent of Slav settlement was nevertheless still minimised. Scientists had long decided that hair rings of a particular design were Slav, yet the occurrence of these rings together with shards of Slav pottery in ancient graves, and the survival of some of the early written records of the region, were not publicly acknowledged as evidence that the eastern borderlands had been populated by Slavs before the arrival of the Germans until 1878, when R. Virchow addressed the Kiel German Anthropological Society.

German archaeology also inspired the artists of nationalism too. In 1828 there was an exhibition of K. von Blechen's paintings of ancient German tribesmen in Berlin. In Regensburg there was a whole series of 'Walhalla' carvings on a similar theme by L. von Schwanthaler of Munich. The 'finds' of these years inspired other areas of endeavour too. On the Polish side there were a number of forged Slavonic epic poems of a Romantic cast. In the 1760s a Neübrandenberg goldsmith called Sponholz faked a series of carvings: known as the Prilwitz idols. They pretended to show various Slav gods and had fake Slav runes carved into them. The carvings caused quite a stir and controversy raged from the time of their discovery until the mid-nineteenth century. In 1855–6 several stones were discovered at Mikorzyń in Prussian Poland. These too were said to bear Slav runes and they generated a great deal of interest and controversy before they were declared fakes by the Kraków Society of the Sciences in 1872. The epic poems and archaeological forgeries were all attempts to strengthen Slav national consciousness and to provide material to counter the claim that Slav culture was inferior to German – a constant problem for Poles living in Prussia.

After 1870 scientific objectivity became increasingly dominated by nationalist concerns. As nationalist opinion throughout Europe rose, so it became the duty of every archaeologist to prove that the peoples buried in the various grave sites were of one 'nation' (usually the author's). The powerful bond between state power and nationalist opinion made all archaeological finds a weapon in the armoury of national consciousness. It allowed contesting nationalisms to claim primacy over particular stretches of disputed territory. Claiming that the bones of some long-dead inhabitant were Slav or German meant a claim of right to the territory in which the bones were found. Archaeology became, not only a part of the growth of national feeling, but a significant part of contemporary politics, the justification of both the status quo and of territorial ambition.

After Poland regained its independence in 1918, archaeology was high on the list of subjects for promotion at university level – particularly in the old Prussian territories. In 1920 a chair of prehistory was established in Warsaw, the Polish Prehistoric Society was set up, and a State Committee of Conservers of Prehistoric Monuments came into being; in 1921 a professorship and department of Prehistory were established in Warsaw; that same year a new professorship was created in Lwów; in 1928 a State Archaeological Museum was set up and various archaeological journals began publication – in particular *Przegląd Archeologiczny* (Poznań, 1919) and *Wiadomości Archeologiczne* (Warsaw, 1920). In 1928 Poland passed a law protecting all ancient monuments, but lacked finance to follow this up with research. It was not until the late 1930s that large-scale excavation was undertaken at some of the major prehistorical sites in Poland: the timber fortress at Biskupin – the product of the Lusatian urn field culture – was excavated from 1934 onwards, and the old Slav fortress at Gniezno was examined only in 1936. Understandably the Poles did very poorly in such a situation, and the Polish archaeologists came under increasing pressure from German opponents.

The Germans themselves were under a different kind of pressure. As scholars slowly pieced together the evidence of the Indo-European population movements and the growth and separation of the various languages, many German scholars found the new theories unacceptable. They rejected the notion that the 'Germani' were part of the inferior cultures of the east and reacted with hostility to the notion that they might have their origins anywhere outside of a Germanic northern Europe. They put forward the theory that Germany was the cradle of European civilisation, that the Germans were the founders of European culture, that the history of the Indo-German peoples was of more importance than that of any Indo-European race, and that they, the first settlers, had been in evidence on German territory even during neolithic times. They argued that the Germans were the original inhabitants of Europe and had at some stage in the past spread from their Scandinavian heartlands to occupy the whole of Europe. At the edges of their territory however, they had met, married into and been debased by inferior invading peoples of the east who had gradually come to dominate them in certain areas and had reduced the area of pure German settlement to what was visible in modern times. Alfred Rosenberg, editor of the Nazi *Völkischer Beobachter*, declared publicly that the first German state had its origins, not with Charlemagne as was widely supposed, but with the ancient Megalith builders. More sensitive and sensible Germans voices were raised in opposition – C. von Schuchhardt, in particular – but in general opinions favoured by the Nazis prospered and eventually came to dominate.[1]

These nationalist theories were promoted by Nazi ideologues of the Third Reich and served up to the German bourgeoisie in such a way as to soothe their fears and identity problems by providing them with a fake racial solution to all their problems. The primitive simplicity of racist thinking that sustained these theories was just what the Nazis and the German people needed to revive their damaged egos after the shame of defeat and the imposition of the Versailles Treaty. As the Nazis gained ground a number of archaeologists disappeared and others lost their jobs. Many took the hint and fled the country. R. Virchow's German Anthropological

Society, which had acknowledged Slav settlement in the German east from the very first – was disbanded for failing to toe the Nazi line, while Gustaf Kossina's Society for German Prehistory grew under Nazi sponsorship to become the Reich Union for German Prehistory. Between 1933 – the year that the Nazis came to power – and 1935 no less than eight new chairs of archaeology were created: all were filled by Nazi appointees. Under the Nazis H. Reinerth became Professor of Archaeology at Berlin and at the same time Rosenberg's deputy in the Ministry for the Eastern Territories.[2] 'German Heritage' and 'Aryan archaeology' were taught in the army and at schools through teachers supplied by the *Ahnenerbe*, which was controlled by the SS.

Gustaf Kossina was the main proponent of the German theories. He spoke as Professor of Berlin University and had a long string of impressive publications to his credit. Kossina claimed to be able to trace a continuous line of Germanic culture to the very earliest times, proving that the Germans were an autochthonous people who had once settled vast areas of Europe and who held the difficult historical role of Kulturträger – bringers of civilisation – to the wanderers from the east. Right up to the end of his life Kossina refused to admit that any evidence of settlement could be evidence of Slav settlement. In his desperation, rather than acknowledge that the Bronze Age urnfields of Lusatia might not be German but Slav – in fact they probably predate both German and Slav settlement – Kossina decided that if they were not German then the urnfields were Thracian or Illyrian! In 1927 Kossina attempted to prove that Pomeranian prehistory had been substantially German long before it had experienced any Slav influence.[3]

Kossina's theories provoked criticism from various quarters, but it was in Prussian Poland that they were greeted with particular resistance. The Poles felt that some sort of united front should be presented against the increasingly chauvinist attitude of the German school, and the work of coordinating such a front fell very largely to the energetic Józef Kostrzewski, who is now regarded as the founding father of Polish archaeology. He had been appointed Professor of Archaeology at Poznań in 1919, was chairman of the Polish Archaeological Society, chairman of the Polish Prehistorical Society, and author of numerous books.[4] Kostrzewski had studied under Kossina in Berlin and knew his style of thinking very well. However, instead of avoiding Kossina's methods, Kostrzewski and his allies adopted them and soon proved that they could be as chauvinist as the Germans. Among other things they sought to demonstrate that the Slav nations had their birthplace in the Odra-Vistula basin. In 1899, for example, E.

Majewski had tried to show that the Slavs had grown up in this area as an entirely autochthonous people. Now this claim was taken up and amplified in a dozen different ways. W. Surowiecki tried to identify the Slavs with the shadowy and possibly seagoing tribe of the Venedi or Veneti mentioned by Tacitus, and to link them with the Slav Wends of East Germany and with the Polabians and Pomeranians along the Baltic shores.[5] But German scholars replied by linking the Venedi with the Germanic Vandals. In response to Kossina's claim that the Lusatian urnfields were Thracian, Polish scholars took the predictable line that they were Slav – an opinion still held by many Polish scholars – and before long there was a vicious war of pamphlets between German and Polish archaeologists. The idea that the graves might be Celtic was considered by neither side.

Polish archaeologists were among the Nazis' first victims. Although one-sixth of all Poles died in the Second World War, over a quarter of all archaeologists perished – a far higher proportion than the average for other professions. Kostrzewski survived only because he disguised himself as a farm labourer and worked out the war under an assumed name in a remote village. The Nazis created a special unit under Professor E. Petersen of Rostock University – his post was a Nazi creation – systematically to remove or destroy Polish source materials, and to loot libraries and collections. In an attempt to cover over any ancient Slav contribution to European history the Nazis destroyed the state archive at the Archaeological Museum in Warsaw, the important and controversial site at Biskupin, and burned down the Raczyński Library in Poznań.

Although there were a number of Polish writers working to produce a comprehensive prehistory of Poland, the financial difficulties of the inter-war Polish state meant that most of their research had to wait until after the Second World War to reach the public – by which time the Nazis had destroyed much of the material from which the Poles were working. However, by their brutal policy of genocide the Germans had given some of the more exaggerated Polish nationalist claims a considerable boost and this was a development that suited the post-war government of the new People's Republic of Poland very nicely. After the war Kostrzewski and his department in Poznań were again to become the centre of fierce opposition to German argument – this time over Poland's historical claim to the new western borders. After the war, however, the work of the Polish archaeologists was aided by the office of the Censor.

Throughout the post-war period Polish books and publications relating to the Recovered Territories have been subject to considerable and detailed scrutiny by GUKPPiW – the Office of the Censor.

All accounts of Poland's post-war years were heavily censored because any open and honest appreciation of the early years of Communist rule would have to acknowledge in detail that the Moscow-backed Communist Poles had been unwelcome, had been badly organised and poorly led, had established themselves by brutality and mendacity, and that they relied upon Moscow as their guarantee of continuance.

Areas of Polish experience that did not appear in print or were substantially censored were: the Molotov–Ribbentrop pact; the Katyn massacre; the persecution of the AK – the London-based Home Army which unlike Soviet-backed units had fought right through the war; the contribution of Polish units serving outside Communist control at Arnhem, Monte Casino, Falaise; the Russian contribution to the bloody end to the Warsaw Uprising; the civil war of 1945–7. The Polish censors allowed no mention of the lost Polish oil fields in Galicia, the lost fur trade from Lithuania and the Ukraine, the lost industry and lumber, the lost agricultural lands from the south-east. There was to be no open discussion of the conditions under which the Poles were expelled from the east, nor could it be suggested that Poland was not getting enough land in the west since this would imply that Poland had territorial claims against the fraternal socialist state of East Germany. When Gomułka and then Gierek came to negotiate loans from West Germany the ban on all mention of the mistreatment of the Germans in Poland and of the continuing expulsions remained in force lest any revelations should compromise negotiations. Discussion of the economic, political and social implications of the expulsions was also forbidden.[6]

The Polish censors also set out to tidy up Polish history. They were resident in the offices of all newspapers and journals, they reviewed historical research at universities, they supervised the publication of archaeological findings, they censored memoirs and books, they interfered with encyclopaedias and tourist guide books, they even monitored newspaper announcements of weddings, baptisms and deaths, obituaries and gravestone inscriptions to make sure that there was no reference to particular events or dates – the Polish calendar is a political minefield. The censor would allow nothing so vague as 'the German–Polish border', but instead insisted that all publications should specify either the 'Odra–Nysa border', or the 'border between Poland and the Democratic Republic' even though no other German–Polish border existed. In order to drive home East Germany's acceptance of this border, the relevant treaty had to be referred to by its full official title: 'The Treaty Between the Polish People's Republic and the German Democratic Republic of 6 July 1950 Concerning the Established and Existing Polish–German National Border'. In this way the Poles made a very clear distinction between the German state that recognised their borders and the German state that did not.

In writing the history of a place like Gdańsk the mundane problems resolved themselves in ways which were determined not by the attempt to present and understand these events as a complex whole, but as a way of justifying the status quo, of presenting it as both right and inevitable. First it was forbidden to mention the old German name of the city – or any other old German city. The implication of such a move over a period of years was that Poles came to assume that Polish usage had a foundation in history and was also the international designation. In writing about the prewar events in Danzig – which had now become Gdańsk – although it was allowed to quote total population figures, it was forbidden to show language surveys or census returns that would indicate the historical weakness of the Polish presence in these places. The street and place names were all changed into Polish too, and the effect of this over the years has made it difficult for Poles to believe that any language other than Polish was ever spoken there.

Accuracy and truth are not encouraged by censorship, and over a long period of time the effect of censorship is to create a world which is little more than a circle of darkness, and one which while it might be perfectly consistent within itself bears very little resemblance to the world as seen by those who live outside the circle. As George Orwell said, 'Indifference to objective truth is encouraged by sealing off one part of the world from another, which makes it harder and harder to discover what is actually happening.'[7]

Instead of claiming that the new western border was theirs by right of conquest and recompense, the Poles reacted to the long years of partition and the horrors of the German occupation with their own national, defensive psychosis. It was as if the Polish Communists who sat nervously atop the post-war Polish volcano were determined to establish themselves by assisting Poland to pass some kind of national authentication test. In 1947, in order to promote a more deep-seated, satisfying intellectual claim to the western lands the Polish government set up the Poznań *Instytut Zachodni* or Institute of the West whose job it was to create a specifically Polish history for the Recovered Territories and to assist the work of the censor in conducting a campaign to convince the world, massively and finally, of Poland's historic claim to its new western borders and the Recovered Territories – the very use of the word 'Recovered' indicates very clearly the nature of the process they wished to promote. The scholarship of the Institute of the West was based on the work of the inter-war archaeologists – that is, on the reaction to the steady German denigration of Polish identity in the borderlands. After the war it became necessary to find Polish roots in the new lands – roots that were more substantial than the lingering and very weak Polish presence that remained from the highwatermark of the Slav westward migrations in the prehistoric period.

Danzig's connection with the Polish state, though undeniable, had always been less direct and less complete than the Poles had liked: the city had never held more than a questionable allegiance to the ancient Piast state, had never been a corporate part of the more recent Polish states, and for most of its history had been content to be a vassal or client of Poland. Yet the Institute of the West and the Office of the Censor insisted that Danzig had always been Polish, that German occupation had been a mere temporary phenomenon, that through hundreds of years of occupation and 'alien' rule the city had never lost its 'Polish' character. The facts that Danzig had been under the control of an independent-minded and increasingly German population since 1308, and since at least that date the Poles in the city had constituted a minority of the citizenry, were quietly brushed under the carpet.

German Danzig disappeared from Polish history books and a rather vague, strangely inactive, phantom city – Polish Gdańsk – began to appear in its stead. A string of 'research documents', tourist guides, school textbooks and scholarly works began to appear in which the lives of the tiny Polish minority were accentuated, and from which the bulk of the German population were almost entirely absent. Although Johann Hevelius (1611–87), Gabriel Fahrenheit (1696–1736) and Artur Schopenhauer (1788–1860) were all Danzigers it is unlikely that the average tourist would ever find this out from Polish tour guides and history books. The name of Günter Grass, perhaps Danzig's most famous son, has yet to appear in such material either.

Under the leadership of Kostrzewski, the anthropologist J. Czechanowski, the philologist Konrad Jażdżewski, and the linguist and ethnologist T. Lehr-Spławiński developed further the inter-war theory that the people who had become the Polish nation had not migrated to Poland from elsewhere, but had always been there. In a stream of publications for domestic and international consumption the Institute attempted to show that the first ever settlers in those lands, just after the glaciers had retreated, were proto-Poles. They proposed that the Lusatian peoples of the Odra-Elbe basin and the earliest inhabitants of Pomerania and Danzig were all Proto-Slavs, that the Bronze Age peoples who emerged from the Scythian, German, Goth and Celtic invasions were Slavs, that the various tribes mentioned by Tacitus as living along the Roman borders had been Slavs, that the major developments of human society on Polish territory between the retreat of the glaciers around 8,000 BC and the tenth-century court of King Mieszko I had all been in a direct line of Slavonic descent.

The writers of the 'Poznań School' presented the Poles as a unique, persistent and authentically autochthonous population, who had grown up in the place in which nature had first planted them, and who, despite everything that history had subsequently thrown at them, had remained. The theory minimised 'alien' contributions to the cultural development of the area by demoting Gothic, Baltic, Celtic and German incursions to mere 'transient phenomena'. According to this theory, the possibility that Balt and Goth place names had survived to indicate lengthy and early occupation by non-Slav peoples were either mere coincidence, or alien corruptions of the original Slav names. The theory developed Majewski's idea that Poland had been the cradle, the very matrix, of all Slav culture and that the Slav peoples had grown up on Polish soil to disperse and develop the various Slav languages and nations at a later date. Evidence of early inhabitants in the lands which became Poland in 1945 was taken to be evidence of Slav settlement. Anyone who said differently was guilty of a monstrous slur against Poland and the Poles. It was chauvinism of a persistent, insidious but thoroughly understandable kind.[8]

The creation of the Poznań Institute brought Polish historians as a whole into international disrepute. The claims made by the Institute and the questionable nature of its 'proofs' went against a substantial body of historical evidence that indicated a Slavonic presence in the German east from very early times – from at least the seventh century AD – but an increasing and finally overwhelming German presence since about the thirteenth century.[9]

The Danziger Günter Grass has given a picture of prehistoric Danzig and Pomerania that is far from dogmatic, and probably quite accurate. Indeed, part of his irony stems precisely from his weary, wary understanding of the typically Pomeranian ethnic mix in his own background:

... the region of the Vistula estuary was inhabited, apart from us old established Pomorshians on the left bank and the Prussians who had settled on the right bank of the river, only by vestiges of the peoples that had passed through: Gepidic Goths, who had been pretty well stirred together with us Pomorshians, and Saxons who had fled from the missionary zeal of the Franks. Slavic Poles trickled in from the south. And the Norse Varangians raided us whenever they felt like it ... [10]

It was this image of an ethnically impure Pomeranian 'Pole', of Poles migrating into Pomerania, this independent ironical detachment about the identity of the Pomeranians that made Grass's work so suspect to the Polish censor and which contributed to the long delay in the issue of his novel *The Tin Drum* in Polish translation. Quite simply the novel did not sit well with post-war Polish politics, nor with the history that the *Instytut Zachodni* had constructed.

The undertaking of the *Instytut Zachodni* had little validity in academic terms, yet it answered a deeply felt need in the battered Polish public. The basic problem lay in the question of where the 'real' Poland was located, of what lands constituted the authentic Poland: the much abused Polish state – through little fault of its own, a shifting sandbank in the river of history – had been configured differently in each of its appearances, and never more so than in 1945. Danzig, Breslau, Oppeln and Stettin had always had sizeable Polish minorities living in them, and some of these people may have been the descendants of the earliest Slavs to settle the area. However, that did not make a place 'Polish' in any meaningful sense.

Poland's claim to the Recovered Territories had little to do with establishing an accurate picture of ancient history, but had a great deal more to do with the Communist Party's efforts to ensure the co-operation of a suspicious and surly populace and to shape and control post-war Polish perceptions of identity. Their experience of German ambition had given the Poles good cause for alarm in the past, and in the post-war period they strove to project their fears backwards on to distant and primitive peoples who had no concept of the nation-state, and whose refusal – in Pomerania at least – to identify with any power beyond their immediate tribal and family horizon had been a continual source of frustration to the Polanie state. The image of an embattled proto-Polish population fending off all comers in its ancestral homeland, the long struggle to 'recover' that homeland against massive opposition and continued threat, had more to do with modern history than it had to do with the lives of the ancients.

So strongly entrenched are these ideas in the popular imagination that even for the powerful Polish underground press –

arguably the largest and best organised in the whole of the East bloc – traditional anti-government attitudes have rarely moved to question the 'official history' of the Recovered Territories. Even during the Solidarność period, when scholars and pamphleteers were far freer than at any other time in the last 40 years and might have put forward an alternative vision of Polish history or the history of Gdańsk on a speculative basis, there was no such move. Not only is there still very little official history of Poland before the Poles, of Gdańsk before 1945, there is very little unofficial history either.

After the declaration of Martial Law in 1981 there were signs that the Polish authorities were prepared to develop a more realistic and sensitive version of the prehistory of Poland. Scholarly and popular works allowed by the censor began to demonstrate a plurality of opinion that was previously unthinkable: Łowmiański and Moszyński, for example, proposed that Poland, including Gdańsk-Pomerania, was once occupied by peoples who were not Slavs, and that the Slavs migrated to Poland from the Dniepr basin between the third century BC and the fifth century AD – a theory that hardly differs from that of Gimbutas.[11] However, the 'truth' of the received chauvinist opinions propagated by the *Instytut Zachodni* lingers on in common public lore, in nationalist mythology, in school textbooks, archaeological reports, philology texts, historical research, tourist guides, atlases, and books about Poland designed for foreign consumption.

Clearly difficult questions about the nature of a national identity and its roots in the past do not admit of easy or simple answers. The prehistory and early history of Polish territory are very complex and still the subject of surprisingly bitter dispute. Given the nature of Poland's experience, continuing and underlying unease about its present territory, questions of legitimacy and national identity, its possession of towns that many Germans still regard as German, opinions such as those shaped and fostered by the censor and the *Instytut Zachodni* – even in well educated and informed official circles – may take a long time to fade out entirely.

14
Günter Grass and Disappearing Danzig

Günter Grass was born in Langfuhr, a lower-middle-class suburb of Danzig, in 1927 – the year that the Nazi Party first fought an election in the city. His mother was part Kaszubian and his father was a German shopkeeper on Labesweg. The Grass apartment house was sandwiched between the walls of the Aktien brewery and a large concrete basin set in a traffic island, dignified with the title: 'Langfuhr and District Auxiliary Fire Fighting Pond'. Further down the street was a Catholic Church, and round the corner and under the railway bridge was a second. The district had the usual complement of shops: nearby there was a butcher and a baker, a beer house and garden, a synagogue, a children's park, a goods depot, a passenger station. To the north the district was fringed by the bathing beaches of Gletkau, the old City Cemetery and the open expanse of the Zaspe airfield. To the west the villas of the wealthy lined the shady Jäschkentalerweg, and beyond them lay the low, gloomy sand hills of the Jäschkentalerwald. To the east was a series of uniform workers' housing developments. Beyond that lay the cranes and wharves of the shipyards. To the south – at the end of a long tram ride – lay the city centre and the port. Langfuhr, along with the suburb of Emmaus, was consistently less Nazi than the rest of Danzig and always returned the lowest Nazi vote.[1]

The young Grass followed the usual path for Germans of those times: he joined the *Jungvolk* or Hitler Cubs when he was 11, and graduated to the *Hitlerjugend* in 1941. The following year he was conscripted into the airforce and was later transferred to the armoured infantry on the Eastern Front. As the German armies reeled back from the charnel house of the east Grass was injured in the fighting around Cottbus.

After a spell in a hospital Grass ended the war in an American PoW camp in Bavaria. In 1959, Grass's first novel, *The Tin Drum*, was published to instant critical acclaim. By 1984 the book was clearly a bestseller of massive proportions: it had sold over 2 million copies in West Germany, and a further half million in the US; it had been translated into 20 languages and the Penguin paperback alone had been through 18 reprints.

Grass is an obsessional writer. Again and again he has written out of, and explored through an experience of nationality and marginality, of compromised identity. Readers and critics in the West have been slow to acknowledge the specific culture and history of the German–Polish borderlands that underlie his work – perhaps with good reason. For the most part it is a very complicated and unpleasant history but it is one which nevertheless reverberates in the present.

Danzig, the world of Grass's childhood, has been lost to him in several senses. Through the passage of time he has grown to adulthood, but also, through exile from the place of his birth, by its physical destruction in the final days of the war, and by the loss of the city's territory to Poland, Grass is separated from the subject of his writings. Since the lifetime of Danzig lay before the defeat of Hitler, and before Grass's 'education' in the American PoW camps, since the ending of his childhood was almost simultaneous with the death of Danzig and the Third Reich, the city is also an ambiguous symbol of loss, of weakness, of the failure of democracy, of the folly of the Nazi solution that lurked within that Weimar failure and within German history as a whole. For Grass Danzig is lost, lamented, longed for and feared.

In *The Tin Drum* Grass recognised that in order for a work of epic stature to succeed it had to be determinedly local. The tension between these two apparently opposite ideas allowed Grass to explore a whole set of cultural and political values in a highly original and individual manner. All history, to paraphrase Croce, is contemporary history. Our past shapes our present, and our future depends on how we see our past. The past shapes us, and we, in our turn, shape our past; but our past determines how we will shape our past. The past determines exactly how we will ransack our personal and collective experience to solve current and future problems. No entity – neither a person nor a people – can ever become something utterly different from the entity they were. Grass's 'crime', for that is how many on the West German Right characterised his work, was that he looked to the past and pointed up continuities with the present.

When Grass looked to the past it was not to discover martyrs, but to uncover complexities; it was not to glory in past revolutions, but to parody and ridicule the simplifications foisted on him as a child by the Nazi revolution. Grass was intent on undermining any stubborn, secret glory, any false national consciousness that lingered on in the German Right, to uncover the ambitions that he felt still lurked in bourgeois German life. Grass undercut any cosy nostalgia about Danzig by refusing to divorce it from the unsavoury context of the German eastern marches. For Grass Danzig had been a corrupt, sprawling, brawling, ugly, fascinating, decadent city that had fallen on hard times. It was a city whose foolish citizenry had put their trust in the dream of a man who had read their basest desires most accurately. Grass was dealing with the details of the dream, the nuts and bolts of empire, glory, conquest, the middle-class values contained within the middle-class scheme of identity. Grass was determined to reject the drug of Nazi supremacy, and equally determined to reject the amnesiac glitter of the West German economic miracle. Instead he plunged with gusto into the maelstrom of history in one place and the meaning of that history for all places.

For Grass it was not possible to claim that Hitler and the Nazis were some kind of aberration. They had grown out of a long and sinister German border history and claimed a long ancestry that included Bismarck and Frederick the Great, that stretched back to the Teutonic Knights, the Margraves of Brandenburg and Charlemagne's *Limes Sorabicus*. *Lebensraum* and the *Drang nach Osten* were an intimate part of his own family background. Grass was to analyse the inner logic of a culture and a nation; by examining the Germany that the Nazis had created Grass also examined the Nazis that Germany had created

In terms of age, geography and ethnic background Grass stood on the very edge of Nazi society. His was a series of marginalities that worked not to make him a fervent Nazi, but to convince him that all Germans were the victims of the Nazis. 'From Labesweg to Max-Halbe Platz, thence to Neuschotland, Marienstraße, Kleinhammer Park, the Aktien Brewery, Aktien Pond, Fröbel Green, Pestalozzi School, the Neue Markt and back again to Labesweg.'[2] This passage could have come from any of Grass's novels. It is typical. Pilenz makes similar lists in *Cat and Mouse*; Ott's escape route is detailed in *From the Diary of a Snail*; Harry Liebenau rattles off street names with practised skill in *Dog Years*; Oskar drums his way round Langfuhr with all the precision of a Baedeker. The obsessive listing of place names, of locations, personal names, phrases, Oskar's drumming itself, are all part of a specific technique by which Grass makes words mean what he wants them to mean. It is a way of building a trustworthy vocabulary, a technique for making words and phrases the Nazis had rendered untrustworthy, gather and accumulate new precise meanings. It is also a kind of magic incantation, a way of summoning up Danzig, the lost city, the lost childhood, the innocence perverted by the Nazis. It is an imaginative act of conjuration by sheer willpower. The satire, the fantasy, the deployment of Grass's massive verbal skills were all part of the much larger pattern of the national epic, rooted in the absolutely real world of contemporary Germany and in the remembered-real world of Danzig.

Grass uses the epic technique to puncture some of the mysteries of the Nazi era – and through them the inheritance of the Prussian East. The epic technique allows him to illuminate conflicts peculiar to the German–Polish borderlands, particularly the struggle for national identity. Grass works to expose the simplifications of the nation-state, to question the labels 'German' and 'Polish'. Herbert Truczynski, for example, is a Pole in a German-speaking Free City, but he is clearly a loyal citizen of Danzig rather than a disaffected nationalist. The scars on Herbert's back chart his experiences in Neufahrwasser's rowdy Sweden Bar. Oskar learns that every scar has a story, indeed Herbert's back bears ample testimony to the conflicts of competing nationalisms in the inter-war years, the legacy of grievances enshrined and exacerbated by the Versailles Treaty.

From the insecure vantage point of his own ethnic background Grass asks awkward questions about the more local loyalties that go to make up the larger loyalty of the nation-state. He asks what it is to be Kaszubian, or even part-Kaszubian, when at various times in their history both Germany and Poland have expanded their territory and definition of themselves to include peoples who did not regard themselves as either Polish or German. For the most part Grass speaks only of the Kaszubians, but there are other peoples involved in a similar fashion: Kosznavians, Mazurians, Silesians, Pomeranians, Wends and Sorbs. Grass reminds us that each large nation is made up of a series of smaller nations – some of whom have a historical memory of their own – who disappear inconveniently slowly, who for the most part are invisible to 'official' history, and yet whose history (such as it might be) is still not identical with the larger, visible and legitimate entity of the nation-state that contains them.

Grass's Kaszubian origins give him a uniquely ironical, worm's eye view of what his more confident and powerful neighbours are up to. This irony is a constant thread of sanity: the blue-eyed, blond-haired Oskar is a German-speaking German. But perhaps not. He is also a German-speaking, blue-eyed, blond-haired part-Kaszubian. And given that his presumptive father is a Pole rather than a German, he might also be a German-speaking, blue-eyed, blond-haired Kaszubian Pole. In fact Oskar could be German or Polish or Kaszubian or any combination of these three. Oskar's grandmother is Kaszubian, but as Oskar tells us, the Kaszubians 'got themselves Germanised':

The old folks had been turned into Germans. They were Poles no longer and spoke Kashubian only in their dreams. German Nationals, Group 3, they were called. Moreover, Hedwig Bronski, Jan's widow, had married a Baltic German who was a local peasant leader in Ramkau. Petitions were already under way, which when approved, would entitle Marga and Stephen Bronski to take the name of their stepfather Ehlers.[3]

Under the Nazis the Volksliste categorised everybody in terms of racial origin and standing within the Reich. There were four main categories. First were the *Reichsdeutsch* – Germans born within the Reich; second were the *Volksdeutsch* – Germans born outside the Reich or those who could claim German ancestors for the preceding three generations; third were the *Nichtdeutsch* – non-Jewish non-Germans who might be suitable for Germanisation. In this last category the Nazis usually thought of the Kaszubians and Poles from Pomerania, Mazuria and Silesia as possible future Germans, if not in this generation then in the next, and accordingly they allowed Kaszubians to become Germanised on paper, or they simply stole 'racially promising material' – children – from schools, nurseries and homes for education in special Germanisation camps. In practical terms the idea that a Kaszubian adult could become Germanised was yet another Nazi legalism. In reality it made no real difference at all since they merely shifted about a little in the sub-section to which they had been assigned. Neither they nor their children, nor their grandchildren would have become 'proper' Germans under Nazi law. The fourth category on the list was *Juden:* Jews.

Grass mocks the whole mentality whereby the identity, worth, social standing, and security of individuals and whole ethnic groups can be altered and reversed by the stroke of a pen. Stomma, in *From the Diary of a Snail*, says that he is unsure which is safer: 'For a Kashubian to remain Polish or For a Kaszubian to get himself Germanised'. They all share in a change of status. Oskar's maternal grandmother takes the whole thing a step further and defends her gift of a goose with the words: 'Don't make such a fuss, Alfred. She's no Kashubian goose, she's a German National bird and tastes just like before the war.'[4]

It is a linguistic mix too. In *From the Diary of a Snail* Stomma and his family spoke Kaszubian at home, German at school and Polish to visitors. After 1918 their village was ceded to Poland, so Lisbeth Stomma spoke Kaszubian at home, Polish at school and German to visitors. Uncertainty extends to family names too, and the variety and history of the various surnames in Grass's novels is another indication that the nation-state is a far more varied creature than its surface uniformity would at first allow. 'Putty', one of the leading members of Oskar's gang of Dusters is in fact the son of von Puttkamer, of mixed Polish, Pomeranian and Prussian descent. Tulla Pokriefke is ostensibly German, but her family are in fact Kosznavian – another of the almost invisible tribal survivals from the Slav–German borderlands – and in Polish her surname means 'saucepan-lid'. In Grass's novels people change their names with the ebb and flow of power: just what a family name might be at any point depends on who is in power at the time and precisely where the national borders are placed:

> ... the fashion for Germanising Polish-sounding names ending in ki or ke or a – like Formella – was taken up by lots of people in those days: Lewandowski became Lengnisch; Mr Olczewski, our butcher had himself metamorphosed into Mr Ohlwein; Jurgen Kupka's parents wanted to take the East Prussian name of Kupkat, but their petition, heaven knows why, was rejected ...[5]

By daring to show the process by which Slavonic names become Germanised, Grass is mocking the basis of Nazi ideology and practice in the eastern borderlands. He is also questioning the possibility of an ethnically pure German Reich, a pure German race and ultimately questioning the German identity itself. It is no accident that the Nazi Sawatzki in *Dog Years* should have a Germanised version of a Polish name (in Polish Sawacki), since that in itself is a way of exploring the insecurities that the Nazis managed to turn into a national phobia, and also a way of insisting on the rich ethnic mix that made up the borderlands before 1945.

Uncertainty, plurality, variety extends especially to geography and to place names:

> I really ought to go into the statistics of history at this point and say something about the changing linguistic mixture in the villages of the Karthaus district. When was Klobschin called Klobocin, and why was Klobocin called Klobschin? When and how often was the hamlet of Neuendorf, west of Turmberg, called Nowawies in Polish? Why does Seereson, which lies between Karthaus and Zuckau, appear as Derisno when first mentioned in 1241, as Sehereson beginning in 1570, and alternately as Seroson and Serosen in the period after 1789. Why in the nineteenth century did it become Seeresen, though concomitantly it appears time and time again in Polish and Kashubian as Dzierzazno? Such is history as its fallout affects the countryside.[6]

Grass has good reason to mock. The straightjacket of identity imposed on eastern and central Europe after Yalta and Potsdam was but a variation of the uniformity that the Nazis had sought to impose. Ironies abound: arguably the sense of Polish nationality, intense Polish nationalism and national identity that cut across regional, class and dialect differences were the result of German efforts to prevent or eradicate these very things. Poland only became a monocultural, monolingual society as a result of the defeat of Hitler; both Polish and German national identities were simplified by Hitler's defeat. It is a lunatic world, yet it is a world which Grass delights in disassembling for us. It is not something he does with bitterness or rancour, but rather with resigned patience:

> That's how it is with the Kashubes. They always get hit on the head ... the Kashubes are no good at moving. Their business is to stay where they are and hold out their heads for everybody else to hit, because we're not real Poles and we're not real Germans, and if you're a Kashube, you're not good enough for the Germans or the Polacks. They want everything full measure.[7]

National identity is some endless conundrum, some labyrinthine joke. And nowhere is this more apparent than in Grass' treatment of the relationship between Germans and Jews in *Dog Years*. There the seemingly irreconcilable opposites are posed: the Master Race meets the Chosen People. Except that the Germans are not real Germans and the Jews are not real Jews. The cry 'Sheeny, Sheeny, Sheeny' is echoed and answered by the cry 'Nazi, Nazi, Nazi'. It is an ugly equation. There is a weird symmetry at work in the relationship between Matern, the sometime maybe Nazi, and Amsel, the sometime maybe Jew. Matern and Amsel are literally blood brothers. They are linked in ways they do not understand, in much the same way that the history of Israel is linked to the history of nationalism in Germany and Poland. The growth of Zionist opinion as it manifested itself in Germany, Poland and Russia at the end of the nineteenth century, was arguably the product of traditional intolerance exacerbated by the increasing pressure of industrialisation and the homogenisation of the labour and product markets of the various national blocks working through uncertainty about national identity and loyalties. The pressure of industrialisation increased pressure on all the 'marginal' identities to move to extreme positions; to conform to the national norms – as the Kaszubians seem to have done – or to resist that conformity – as the Zionists did.

Grass is interested in a relationship that works through the insecurities of both parties, in their zig-zag opposition, competition and outright adoration of each other. Grass is interested in the idea of the Jew, the idea of the Nazi. Neither of Grass's two main Jewish characters – Amsel in *Dog Years*, and Herman Ott in *From the Diary of a Snail* – is really Jewish at all. Ott, simply, is not a Jew: Amsel's ethnic Jewish origins are so distant that they have no meaning for him. Yet they are seen to be Jews by those around them. Their Jewishness consists of their opposition to the dominant political and social trends of their society; it has more to do with available social roles than with ethnicity – the enemy within, scapegoat, outcast, foreigner, competitor, traitor, conscience. Like other forms of national identity in the borderlands, 'Jewishness' is a threat when it is not a convenience; it is a threat that, unlike a Polish or a German identity, has no army or navy to back it up. The Jews had almost by tradition been inserted into the slow growing economies of Eastern Europe to the advantage and disgust of those higher up the social hierarchy, and to the disadvantage and frustration of those lower down the social scale. As such Jews were vulnerable to attack from all sides. It is an interesting paradox that while the Nazis were supposed to be supermen, their appeal was to Germans who felt themselves to be far from super; Nazi support came from ordinary Germans who looked to the Nazis and to their refined spearhead, the SS, as their models. While Nazi propaganda stressed the superman image Germany was said to be under threat from the *Untermenschen*, from the lesser and inferior races. How could that be? Clearly the relationship between these ideas is exceedingly complex.

Grass is profoundly committed to his own time and his own place. The characters he creates are all hopelessly entwined in the events of a history that their ambition and uncertainty have helped to create. Their habits of thought have delivered them into a chaos of their own making, into an uncertainty of a different order from anything they have ever known. There is a powerful pedagogical streak in Grass too, and the fact that by the time he had begun work as a novelist his own children were beginning to ask him questions about his past, and his activities under the Nazis helped to give his work a very clear style, direction and purpose. By insisting on the continuities between the Third Reich and the post-war West German state, Grass produced a series of merciless portraits of a society brought face to face with its own inner doubts and uncertainties, with the results of its attempts to force a bloody resolution on its neighbours, and with its overpowering wish to both forget and rewrite its history. He stressed that although the whole of Germany shared in the moral surrender of Hitler's legitimate rise to power, not all those who gave passive assent to the the NSDAP were Nazis. In Danzig ordinary people who walked their dogs, conducted illicit affairs, ran scout troops, went fishing, cut holes in the ice to bathe in the sea, ran grocery shops, played the trumpet, voted for the Nazis.

In many ways Grass's novels conform to the basic patterns of 'exile literature'. The sense of loss is overwhelming, the ability to

recall is total. What is missing is self-pity. In German art and literature self-pity and exile are very closely linked to the cloying
emotions of very German notions of home, fatherland and
comfort, *gemütlichkeit*, a sense of order and fitness of things, a
sense of rightness – and through that to a sense of identity, of
place and function within an ordered and secure community.
Given the dangers of these emotions Grass's balancing act
becomes all the more dangerous. It is no accident that the decline
of Romantic art forms into the growth of Kitsch art coincided with
the growth of *Völkisch* opinion. The easy sentiment and the surrender of both taste and responsibility in art go hand in hand with
the same things in the political sphere. Kitsch is an art and politics
of the dead. That is, it revels in the collapse of standards. Kitsch is
an art form for the surrender of taste and sensitive discrimination;
it is an art form of easy forms, easy sentiments, swim-with-the-
tide-conformity. Grass has to combat this powerful undercurrent
lest his own works become appropriated by some simplistic exile-
sentiment, an easy prey to those who would set back the clock and
make a bid to recover the lost lands of the German east.

Grass's narrators are always the wounded, the weary and the
wary speaking out for those still to come in order to avoid a repeti-
tion. Grass laments the loss of the city, but he also laments the
stupidity that led to that loss. While he castigates the decadence
and moral bankruptcy of the Danzigers who supported Hitler, and
lashes the West Germans for accepting unrepentant Nazis in government, the police force, in industry, in the media and in the
law-courts, never once does Grass allow himself to lapse into
emotive pleas that Danzig and all the other German lands lost to
Poland in 1945 should be returned: never once does Grass give in
to the calls of the German exiles' unions, or acquiesce in
Chancellor Kohl's barely veiled promise that one day the Polish
city of Gdańsk will be reclaimed for Germany as the ancient city
of Danzig.

A Kaszubian – and even more a German-speaking part-Kaszubian
– is on the margin of both German and Polish society. It is a
worm's eye view that does not attract critical attention simply
because it is an angle on national life that does not accord with
'mainstream' cultural and linguistic experience. Where Grass's
unique viewpoint is noticed at all it is dismissed as exotic but basi-
cally marginal to the interests of both German and Polish readers
– and of course through them marginal to the official interests of
both states. And yet it is clear from the popularity of *The Tin Drum*
alone that Grass works on his readers in ways that they don't
quite understand.

Grass, in his own way is a determined provincial – the division of Germany, the disappearance of his home, the Berlin Wall, all left him with little choice in the matter. But Grass examines the central core experience of his nation from a very particular point of view. He reverses the normal order of totalitarian power by turning the provincial scepticism against the mainstream identity to which the provincial identity usually aspires. On the margins there is never any doubt that literature is political: even the basic choice of language – and hence the choice of audience – is a political act of the gravest consequence.

* * *

When Grass wrote of his work for the Polish Communist Party journal *Polityka* he said:

> I began this book *The Tin Drum* when I was 26 years old. When, five years later, I finished the manuscript I was certain that this theme – Danzig/Gdańsk, Germans and Poles – would never leave me: more, that I would be compelled in a continually changing quest to struggle with this theme anew ...[8]

Günter Grass has continually sought good relations with the Polish authorities – he has conducted research for his novels there without problem, visits his relatives without hindrance, and has even helped make a documentary TV film about the reconstruction of the Danzig/Gdańsk city centre.

No matter how well intentioned, Grass's personal obsession with a city that had ceased to be German Danzig and was now Polish Gdańsk was bound to stir fears on the part of the Polish authorities who clung to their old German territories as a way of helping to maintain their legitimacy and power. The more reactionary and less forgiving among the Polish bureaucracy think they discern the outlines of traditional German hostility towards Poland, or at least a certain ambivalence about the issue of Poland's current territorial configuration in virtually everything that does not emanate from within their own national borders or, more specifically, from within their own Party machinery. It was also inevitable that his work should worry many individual Poles for whom the horrors of the German Occupation – in which one fifth of the Polish nation had perished – were still vivid.

Intellectuals know of Grass by reputation, travellers have purchased copies of one or other of his novels, but the general reader and students in Gdańsk – even those who live in Wrzeszcz, Grass's old district of Langfuhr – know almost nothing of his work. A few of his letters have been published, several well informed but circuitous articles and a monograph about his work have appeared, some short extracts translated from *The Flounder* and *From The Diary of a Snail*, and a limited edition of *Cat and Mouse* have also been allowed, but the bulk of Grass's work – and that part of it most relevant to Polish–German relations – has remained unavailable to Polish readers. Only in 1983 – 24 years after its appearance in Germany and 20 years after its translation into most other European languages – did *The Tin Drum* appear in Polish.[9]

By 1983 the official Polish translation of *The Tin Drum* had been ready and waiting for publication for over 15 years – a fact that was often rumoured, but not officially admitted until that time. There had in fact been two previous translations – both underground, unofficial and strictly illegal. These had been remarkable in themselves, but were printed on paper of varying sizes, with a wide variety of print styles and had been produced in such small numbers that they passed from hand to hand as *Samizdat* or Padlock literature. The decision to release an official translation of the book must have been very difficult, since any effective translation would puncture the myths so carefully nurtured by the postwar regime.

Just before the release of the translation an article in the Communist Party journal *Polityka* said frankly that although the book was about to be published, it would never actually 'appear' because the edition had sold out long before copies ever reached the shops. The article went on to say that there had been a number of practical problems which had beset the work. It mentioned the paper shortages that had plagued the print and publishing industries in Poland for nearly 20 years, the expense of acquiring the translation rights, the chaos of the Polish economy in the late 1970s, the collapse of 1980–1, and the restrictions of Martial Law.[10]

Yet for all this, the real factors that held up publication were not economic, but cultural and political. On the one hand the government was worried that publication of the book would cause an increase in anti-German feeling just at the moment when Poland was looking (yet again) for financial help from the West German bankers. On the other hand they worried that the book would outrage the intensely inward-looking Polish nationalist literary culture by revealing to it a glimpse of a Polish history that was free from the manipulations of the Party and the pressure of 'geopolitical realities'. It was rightly feared that the book challenged the accepted orthodoxies of official history in the Polish People's Republic, and accordingly the print-run of this edition was minimal: 20,000 copies, with an additional 250 review copies for the critics and the literary establishment. If the aim had been to restrict the influence of the book by making it difficult to obtain, then the policy backfired hopelessly. Scarcity turned the book into a highly sought after cult object, if not exactly a banned book, then certainly some variety of political pornography. When it first appeared the official price was 300 złoties: three years later the price of a second-hand copy on the open market had risen to 3,200 złoties.[11]

But what exactly were Polish readers getting in this official translation?

There were a number of major problems. The first was that of deciding whether or not to translate place names into Polish. Since 1947 it has been official policy never to refer to any place or city in the Recovered Territories by its old German name lest this should somehow emphasise German rather than Polish history in the area. Grass's use of German names was thorough and gave a very clear indication of the marginality of the Polish community in Danzig. Just how many Poles were there in the Free City of Danzig in the inter-war period? In 1910, according to the census, there had been 315,281 Germans, 9,491 Poles, 2,124 Kaszubians and 3,021 others living in the area that was to become the Free City. The precise number of Poles resident in the city just after the Versailles Treaty, when the city was obliged to allow Poles to live there if they so wished, is very difficult to calculate since some of the Poles in Danzig were Jewish citizens of Poland trying to emigrate, some were Danzig Poles, some were Kaszubians, some were Polish Poles and others were Germanised Poles whose connection with Poland over several generations had become rather tenuous. Much statistical information about the population in the inter-war period is lacking, but by 1937, as a result of migration from rural Kaszubia, an influx of unemployed from nearby towns and because of the large number of Jews in transit through the city who became trapped there after a change in US immigration policy, there were certainly no more than an estimated 17,000 Poles of all kinds - that is about 4 per cent of the total population of nearly 400,000. (H.S. Levine calculates: 375,972 recorded residents plus 17,000 working in the Reich and another 2,000 working at sea.) The very small Polish minority is confirmed by the fact that from 1927 to 1935 the Poles had only three and then two of the 72 seats on the Danzig Volkstag, and that the recorded vote cast for these seats was consistently low as most of the Polish community were not citizens of Danzig but migrant workers or immigrants and therefore ineligible to vote. These figures – which emphasise that the Polish element in the community was very small and that the city was far from being 'Polish' – are not widely known or published in Poland.[12]

Though the Polish community in the city had its own names for a number of places and streets in the city, those names did not appear on any street map or guide since all place names were in German. When the Polish administration took over the city in 1945 they set up a special Commission to change all the German street names into their Polish equivalents. The translators of *The Tin Drum* were in a difficult situation. To leave the German names unchanged would undermine Polish claims that the place had always been strongly Polish, yet to translate the German names into their post-war versions would be historically inaccurate, would substantially alter the nature of Grass's use of place names, and in some cases would make absolute nonsense of the text. It would also leave the Poles open to charges of national chauvinism and the substantial mistreatment of a book that was already established as a modern European masterpiece.

The translator, Sławomir Błaut, explained his decision to translate the place names into their post-war Polish equivalents by saying that the German names had been too remote for Polish readers.[13] He argued that contemporary Polish names were more vivid and immediate because they were in everyday use and that this somehow reinforced the naturalistic aspects of the book. This may sound reasonable, but Grass used the German names for a specific purpose. He was writing about Danzig, not Gdańsk. His book was a magic incantation for a dead, lost city. To alter that facet of his epic was to alter the use to which he put the city in his fable.

To take but one example: the road now called Aleja Zwyczęstwa. In the early days of the nineteenth century the road started out from Danzig under the name Allee nach Langfuhr. In the reverse direction it started out from Langfuhr under the name of Allee nach Danzig. Later, when it had been widened to become a major highway, it was renamed Grosse-Allee. In Langfuhr the road, which was a main shopping area as well as thoroughfare, was called Hindenburgallee. By 1933, as the 'Gleichschaltung' or Nazification of the Free City progressed, the section of the highway that ran through Langfuhr became Adolf Hitlerstraße. As far as it is possible to tell the Danzig Poles always referred to the road as 'Ulica Główna' – Main Street, but their name for it appears on no official maps. After the war the new Polish administration renamed that part of the street which had been Adolf-Hitlerstraße as Aleja Grunwaldzka after the victory over the Teutonic Knights, and renamed the part that had been Hindenburg-Allee as Aleja

Zwyczęstwa – the Alley of Victory.[14] Victory over who? Technically the full title of the street – 'Aleja Zwyczęstwa nad Faszyzmem' – indicates the victory over fascism, but in simple parlance this translates into victory over the Germans. What's in a name? Everything. In that series of name changes lies a whole history of struggle.

In this translation the name 'Danzig' – with one particular exception – is not used; nor does Oskar's home district of Langfuhr make an appearance. Instead the city is called Gdańsk, and Oskar lives in Wrzeszcz. The city of Gdańsk, however, has only been in existence since 1945, and it is not the subject of Grass's work. Knowingly to present a name which is anachronistic and misleading is not only to shirk the real history of the place, to present the history of Danzig as being somehow Polish, to present the history of Gdańsk as that of Danzig and to present the Polish reading public not with a solution to a purely literary problem, but with a propagandist fabrication of considerable proportion in which Grass has no place.

But having started along this path it was necessary to continue. Telling two lies to make one lie come true, there are a number of small but very interesting alterations to Grass's text. Błaut's translation effectively rides roughshod over some of Grass' finer ironical points. To take one verbal crux: Herbert Truczynski's back. Herbert's back charts his experiences on the Sweden Bar in Neufahrwasser. Oskar learns that every scar has a story. Oskar presses a scar and Herbert talks:

> First they were sitting at the same table like brothers. And then the character from Gdingen says: Russki. The Ukrainian wasn't going to take that lying down; if there was one thing he didn't want to be it was Russki ... and I had to separate the two of them, soft and gentle the way I always do. Well, Herbert has his hands full. At this point the Ukrainian calls me a Water Polack, and the Polack, who spends his time hauling up muck on a dredger, calls me something that sounds like Nazi. Well, my boy, you know Herbert Truczynski: a minute later the guy from the dredger, a pasty-faced guy, looks like a stoker, is lying doubled-up by the coatroom. I'm just beginning to tell the Ukrainian what the difference is between a Water Polack and a citizen of Danzig when he gives it me from behind – and that's the scar.[15]

The whole legacy of nineteenth-century nationalism and national struggle underlies this passage. In Grass's original text the phrase 'citizen of Danzig' is 'Danziger Bowke', which is Danzig slang for a Danziger. The nearest equivalent in British English would be something like a Scouser, a Brummie, a Cockney, a Swansea Jack. Danzig exiles in Hamburg, Ahrensburg, Lübeck and

Kiel still use the phrase 'Danziger Bowke'.[16] In Polish the phrase is translated as 'gdańskim swojakiem', the meaning of which is literally, 'one of Gdansk's own'. This is not a fine point of translation, it is a total change of meaning. Herbert Truczynski was not a citizen of Gdańsk, but of the Free City of Danzig: he says so in German, but not in Polish. Grass shows a Danzig Pole as a loyal citizen of Danzig, indeed it is his loyalty to the city that causes the contempt of the the customers and gets Herbert knifed in the back. The Polish translation implies that somehow the city was Polish, attempts to hide Herbert's poor sense of himself as a Pole, and makes nonsense of the Gdingen sailor's violence. In this context the mistranslation of Grass is a subtle form of censorship since it is designed to hide both the weak Polish presence in the city, and the very poorly developed Polish identity of that community.

There are other examples where Grass's irony and his subtle balancing of historical events and processes are not just missed, but are actually perverted, where revealed historical uncertainty is buried with a deft twitch of the translator's pen. When Oskar visits the Polish Post Office he lies in a laundry basket full of letters. He says: 'I slept in a basket full of letters mailed in Lodz, Lublin, Lemberg, Thorn, Krakau, Tschenstochau or addressed to people in Lodz, Lublin, Lwow, Torun, Krakow and Czestochowa.'[17]

The joke is that these are the places which to different people have different names. There are a large number of towns in Eastern Europe that have carried German, Polish, Russian and other names at various times in their history, but Lwów is not the same historical entity as Lemberg, nor is Thorn the same thing as Toruń. Names of places, whether they are German or Polish, conjure and indicate precisely delineated borders, patterns of government and the administration of power. As Professor Norman Davies has said:

... the key to East European place-names lies in fixing each name in its relevant context of time, space, and usage. Much of the reigning confusion dissolves if the student can reflect why, where, when, and by whom any particular name might have been used.[18]

If the German and British printers had been able to handle the Polish diacritical marks the difference between Polish and German names would have been visually even more apparent: Łódz, Toruń, Kraków, Częstochowa. Grass's point – that one man's Danzig is another man's Gdańsk – is made with superb economy. In Polish, however, because of the policy of using only the Polish names for places, it is a point which is more than lost. The reader does not need to understand Polish to see that the translator, instead of setting the German town-names against the Polish, names has simply used the Polish names twice over. The same passage in Polish reads: 'Spałem w koszu od bielizny pełnym listów, które chciały dotrzeć do Łodzi, Lublina, Lwowa, Torunia, Krakowa i Częstochowy, które przybyły z Łodzi, Lublina, Lwowa, Torunia, Krakowa i Częstochowy ...'[19]

There was also a problem in Grass's treatment of the Defence of the Polish Post Office. This incident has been presented to post-war Poland as one of the very pinnacles of Polish bravery. The Post Office building is located on the site of the old castle of the Teutonic Knights, and as such was seen as a key site in the thousand year history of confrontation between Teuton and Slav. Polish historians often forget (or at least rarely mention) that it was not only the Polish and Lithuanian army that fought the Teutonic Knights at the battle of Tannenberg/Grunwald in 1410. A wide range of peoples had reason to want the defeat of the Teutonic Order, and the army opposed to the Knights included substantial numbers of Czechs, Hungarians, Ruthenians and Tartars. It is also worth pointing out that the Danzigers themselves were in revolt against the Knights and in the ensuing Thirteen Years War bore the brunt of the economic, if not the military struggle to break the power of the Teutonic Order – facts which go a long way to undermining any simplistic later notions of Polish–German conflict. That many of the Knights had not been German, that the Knights had been primarily an independent organisation out for its own profit rather than the extension of specifically German territory, that the encounters with the Knights took place before the formation of modern nation-states in Poland and Germany, and that the eventual defeat of the Knights had been brought about by armies which included Danzigers and thousands of other non-Poles – all these things were largely ignored in school textbooks, or were suppressed by the censor. The postal workers who died in the defence of the Post Office in September 1939, and those who survived the battle only to be shot at the Zaspe cemetery the following month, were likened to the Polish Knights who beat the Teutonic Knights in 1410.[20]

Long before Grass's novel appeared in Polish, the Post Office had become a place of peculiar significance to the post-war regime. The Post Office gave the post-war regime an emotive subject on which to focus the threat of a German return and allowed them to promote the role of the Poles in Danzig, while claiming the Polish 'martyrs' as its own. Also, constant reference to German revanchism allowed the government to divert attention away from a highly unsatisfactory connection with the Soviet government, away from the far more explosive subjects of recent Polish history. Yet in their hasty drive to claim the Polish postmen as heroes of the People's Republic of Poland and to commemorate their deaths with plaques and headstones and an eternal flame, the Communist Party apparatus overlooked the fact that several postmen had escaped from the Post Office in the chaos of the closing minutes of the siege. Two of these had been located by Grass on his research trip to Poland in 1958. Grass mentioned these survivors in his novel.

It was clear that Grass had exposed a bureaucratic blunder – at best a simple mistake and at worst an attempt at emotional manipulation: it is far more effective to claim even by omission that all the defenders perished. Survivors detract from that effectiveness. Grass's treatment of the subject threatened to show that the events at the Polish Post Office had become a propaganda victory, but little more. In this respect it is interesting to note that the survivors received no official recognition and were not mentioned in print until after Grass's novel had been published in Poland.[21]

Another major problem for the translator lay in Grass's treatment of the 'liberation' of Danzig and the expulsion of the German population. Very few Poles had actually witnessed the brutality of the expulsions, and these had either been bought with the bribe of ex-German property and promotion, or had been censored into silence: all reference to the cruelty of the expulsions had been removed from official publications, books and films. The shock of Grass's text lay in the simple fact that although he did not dwell on the horrors – while he hints at more, Grass shows only one rape, one beating and some aggravated looting – it was nevertheless clear that the Poles had behaved in a way that they had come to associate not with themselves, but with the Nazis. There may have been some justification for this behaviour, but its revelation in a German text of international standing would deal a blow to the simplifications wrought on the nationalist psyche by the post-war regime, and would undercut many of the assumptions young Poles made about the conduct of their country's foreign policy and their attitudes toward West Germany.

There was one further major objection to the publication of *The Tin Drum*. The historians of the Poznań *Instytut Zachodni* had laboured long and hard to create and publicise a Polish historical and ethnographic claim to the Recovered Territories. The Poznań Institute had attempted to legitimise a fundamental revision of the Polish boundaries brought about by a military victory, by claiming prehistoric peoples as its citizens. The claims had more to do with the need to explain and justify the enforced abandonment of Jagiellonian Poland, the resumption of old Piast Poland, the westward shift of the Polish state than it had to do with history or archaeology, and while they were not acceptable to many serious scholars both inside and outside Poland, they had entered into popular mythology as correct and legitimate Polish history.

Grass's novel did not confront these issues directly, but it did touch on them at several points. Oskar's comments on the ancient history of Pomerania and his lineal descent indicate a knowledge of the past that is significantly at odds with the history authorised in Warsaw:

> First came the Rugii, then the Goths and the Gepidae, then the Kashubes from whom Oskar is descended in a straight line. A little later the Poles sent in Adalbert of Prague, who came with the Cross and was slain with an axe by the Kashubes or Borussians. This happened in a fishing village called Gyddanyzc. Gyddanyzc became Danzig, which was later turned into Dantzig, later written without the t, and today the city is called Gdansk.[22]

A passage like this was bound to cause problems because it suggested that the Rugii, Goths and Gepidae – all Germanic or Scandinavian peoples – had settled in Pomerania before the Kaszubes. It also suggested that there was a difference between Poles and Kaszubes and that the changing orthography of the city's name did not bear out the idea of an overwhelmingly Slavonic past.

The passage was translated into Polish with the orthographic development of the Germanic name for the city intact and unchanged because it was thought that the word 'Gyddanyzc' with its characteristic Slavonic 'sk' ending, was close to the modern Polish form, Gdansk. 'Gyddanyzc' dates from the tenth-century *Life of Saint Adalbert of Prague*, now kept in the Vatican Library, a document which constitutes the first historical record of the city/settlement's existence. It was thought that if the earliest recorded form of the name suggested the modern Polish name then it would also suggest that the people who inhabited the place were Polish.[23]

While the translation preserved the orthographic history unscathed, the passage still did not escape entirely undamaged. In German Grass refers to the tribe of the Rugii. These were a Germanic people who migrated across the Baltic from Scandinavia and who settled along the coast of Pomerania as far west as the Danish border, and as far east as the modern town of Darłowo

(Rügenwaldermunde). Tacitus referred to them in this location around the year 98 AD, and it seems they gave their name to the Island of Rügen. Their location predates the first sighting of Slav peoples in the area by some 600–900 years. In the Polish version of *The Tin Drum* the name Rugii does not appear. Instead the word 'Ranowie' is used. It might at first be surmised that Ranowie is merely the Polish word for Rugii, but this is not the case. The Ranowie were one of the Slav tribes who lived east of the Elbe in the seventh and eighth centuries AD. They supplanted the Rugii and turned the Germanic island of Rügen into the Slavonic island of Rana. Their main settlement at Arkona remained a centre of pagan and tribal worship until it was sacked by marauding Christian Danes in the twelfth century. The last trace of the Ranowie before they succumbed to absorption into a German identity was the Slav language used on Rügen until the seventeenth century. Thus the Germanic Rugii were supplanted by the Slav Ranowie, only to find themselves supplanted by the Danes. To change the Rugii into the Ranowie is not just to confuse time scales, but to substitute one people about whom we know little, for another about whom we know precious little more. It is to ignore the few recorded facts and purposely to confuse and conflate evidence in the most blatant manner for reasons of national chauvinism.[24]

The culture of a nation-state differs from that of a national culture only in the extent to which the former has managed to impose state control over cultural life. That is, national culture becomes nation-state culture when state censorship and self-censorship coincide and agree. In time, given the degree of control that the state exercises over cultural life in the nation-states of the East bloc, it is inevitable that national culture should become nation-state culture. The culture of the nation-state is narrow, self-observing and self-supporting: the less sincere and trustworthy the political and public life of that nation then the more nation-state culture becomes exclusive of outside influences and less tolerant of challenges to its authority and centrality.

With these points in mind, it is probably better to refer to *Blaszany Bębenek* as a Polish version of *The Tin Drum* rather than a translation.

It is not possible to say exactly what part the censors took in controlling this version of The Tin Drum: all such debate is hidden from the Polish public. It is only possible to say that the book has been substantially neutralised and that this has been done consistently and from a very particular nationalist rather than ideological point of view. Whatever desire the authorities may have had to make available to the Polish people a classic work of modern European fiction, it has been carried through in such a way as to make the book conform to well established patterns of post-war propaganda. It is a translation that reflects Poland's continuing unease about German ambition in the east, understandable concern about its location on the map of Europe, justified fear over its claim to current borders: in their long joint histories, the German peoples have rarely given the Poles reason not to fear their intentions.

The tragedy is that this version of *The Tin Drum* has more to do with Polish fears than it has to do with Grass's intentions. And yet this tiny, gagged, official version must be welcomed. Taken together with the release of information about the survivors from the Polish Post Office and with the tentative development of a less chauvinist version of Polish prehistory, it may just be that we are witnessing some tiny part of the reforms presaged by Solidarność and by the recent talks between the union and the government about how to restructure the economic and political life of the country.

That such material has become available under the military regime of General Jaruzelski should not mean that it is dismissed as meaningless or hopelessly compromised – no matter how ambiguous the gesture. In time the reform of the economy will allow further relaxation of Polish life – including intellectual and academic freedoms to discuss the material history of Poland's present situation. General Jaruzelski knows better than most the unpleasant spectres that lurk in the interface between history and contemporary politics in Poland. Although matters of editorial policy cannot in themselves improve Poland's economic or political situation, the General and the more sensitive members of his government are aware that Poland can only help itself if it is allowed access to vast quantities of information about the workings and history of its society – information which up to now has been manipulated, censored out of recognition or merely denied.

Modern Polish history contains a number of items which the censor has not allowed – the Molotov–Ribbentrop pact of 1939, the loss of the eastern Polish territories and the expulsions of 1945, the rigging of the 1947 referendum, the fate of the Home Army, the imposition of Communist rule and the persecution of pre-war leaders, and the Katyn massacre. To a very great extent the legitimacy of the present regime is compromised by this past. In order to claim legitimacy any new government in Poland faces the unenviable task of owning up to that past – acknowledging the many skeletons in the closet.

The release of the Polish version of *The Tin Drum* may have been some kind of an optional cultural extra within the general process of reform, but given the extent and influence of censorship over the last 40 years, and the still vivid and complex issues that the book touches on – not the least of which is the question of the legitimacy of the Communist regime – it must also be seen as a gesture of good faith. If this version of Grass's novel is not the 'full, merciless, honest confrontation' with its own history that Poland so desperately wants and needs, then it is at least a step in that direction. [25]

15
Passing Time in Gdańsk

To be peripheral in another's empire is to be held in underdevelopment, to be held in stasis, to stagnate, to die slowly.

Just because the Second World War is finished and the partitions of Poland are over, it does not mean that the patterns of thought and feeling established at that time have disappeared. On the contrary the limits set on what Polish and German national thought might be or become have been very largely set for generations to come by those experiences. (Some might say that Germany, dismembered by the victorious Allies in 1945, has now experienced something of the anguish it once imposed on Poland.) In both Poland and Germany the patterns of social and political behaviour survive, often in subconscious forms, to provide seemingly modern nations with a political culture that is deeply dependent for its emotional content on the echoes of events long in the past.

Of reductive and simplistic nationalist thought it is possible to say that if the individual is aware of a social or political current, something bigger and stronger than them, which exerts power over their volition, they tend to think of it as somehow universal, impersonal, as if to say 'Well, that's life.' To think this is to think of the political process, of history itself, as somehow inexplicable and undifferentiated, and within this it is to propose a special personal endurance and courage, perhaps even national destiny, for the sheer fact of survival.

This is not to say that the individual will never think outside this closed system, never resist, that they will accept every evidence of injustice that the system allows. It means merely that the sense of historical tragedy within which they have their own being, origin and identity is somehow larger than the needs of the individual and their desire for substantial explanations.

It is to say that the tragedy still looms over the individual to the point where the desire for substantial answers that lie outside the nationalist ghetto must remain in suspension. Yet for all that, the history which both the German and the Polish nationalists neither know nor seek is still there: and that tragedy is part of the situation. It belongs to the experience. The substantial truths in any story lie somewhere between different versions.

The disputes between Germany and Poland were never purely concerned with languages, people, territory and nationality. They were clashes over a border that marked two stages in economic development, two stages in the growth of capitalist organisation. The Polish–German border was racked and stretched across ten centuries of expansionism, and in the late nineteenth century came to mark the divide between a country frustrated in its efforts fully to join the twentieth century, and another country desperate to drag itself out of the eighteenth century. The border around Danzig and right down into Silesia was, in modern parlance, an interface between two time zones. It still is.

In the borderlands, however, in true Einsteinian fashion, the idea that time moved at another pace elsewhere – to east and to west – was difficult to grasp. In the Polish–German borderlands Eastern state capitalism was to meet Western National Socialism, where both were melded into national disputes over territorial and economic requirements. There the eighteenth century became the twentieth century, peasants became factory workers, Germans became Poles, Poles became Germans, human beings became animals, and everything was reduced to ash and bone. The borderlands were the place where Central Europe was stretched on the rack of its slowest and its fastest rates of change, and where the mechanisms that underlay the nation-state were revealed for what they are.

National identity is not in itself the cause of violence, but it is a thing which other forces – the military, industry, politicians – manipulate. Sometimes they manipulate identity for their own ends, sometimes because they feel that national destiny is working through them personally. Identity is a thing that can be manipulated precisely because it is such an uncertain commodity. National identity is often formed under pressure of a wide-ranging and thorough penetration of every aspect of life – in response to the raw facts of exploitation. Without an ideology to contain it, rather than be contained by it, a nationalist response becomes a suspect moral arbiter, a dangerous armour of complacency: the nationalist identity alone is as useless as a skull cap in a hurricane, as any surviving Danziger can testify.

There are personal, psychological pressures at work within the broader political questions. The world that is the nation – our nation – presses and clamours everywhere about us. We live in it, work in and for it, eat of its fruits, sleep within its protection.[1] It is an undeniable part of the fabric of our lives, and beyond 'our nation' the world that is not our nation presses with apparently limitless and unpredictable power. If we have little ability to alter the course of events within our nation, then we have even less chance of altering them outside our nation. The nation, however, building from this basic insecurity in the individual, recognises no limits to its desire to alter everything – that from which it is made and that which is not itself – for its own purposes. This is the logic of the capitalist world. To ask someone to consider or examine their national identity is often to ask them to question all aspects of their existence and identity – their sexual preferences, shopping habits, taste in foods, racial origins, language, the way they vote ... It is in fact to call into question the one thing about which people become more aggressive and assertive in direct proportion to their uncertainties and fears.

Love of place, way of life, a landscape, the investment of blood, tears and sweat, the burial of family – all these can be deceptive. They are not in themselves achievements, though they may feel like it. They are the flavour of the daily round, the screen behind which the endless pressures flow. They can become the focal point for a crusade, a campaign, a war, but in themselves the personal and poetic aspects of these things will remain insufficient to generate nationalist feeling; they can only focus national feeling into nationalist feeling when they are put under pressure to become something else, when their continuity is threatened. It is then that they become the media of national identity and achieve a significance far beyond the mundane.

The world of the nationalist is a world under pressure. It is peopled by those who make the pressure and by their victims, though there are allies on both sides. It is a real world with real people responding to real problems. They may not understand their problems in their entirety – who does? – and the solutions on offer may be utterly inappropriate to them personally. As Czesław Miłosz has written: 'The chain of historical causes from which any collectivity is forged stretches far back into the past, and the individuals who conform to its pressures do not stop to consider what has marked them with this or that stamp'.[2]

But as people protest at the conditions of their life, as the nation beckons, it would appear that the answer must lie either within or without the security of the nation-state. It is frightening to remain outside, tempting to get inside. The Irish poet W.B. Yeats described his nationalism and sense of identity as a coat covered with embroideries out of old mythologies, but went on to say that the fine thing he had wrought was taken up, worn and abused by fools; he concluded that there was 'more enterprise in walking naked'.[3] But not many can step outside their situation far enough to see such a perspective and few can realistically choose to walk naked in a world where the nation-state goes armoured.

Old Danzigers, Poles and German, still live in Gdańsk. Not for them the political and historical calculation involved in the renaming of roads: the main road that runs north to south is named after neither Hindenburg nor Hitler, nor Grunwald nor Victory neither: for them it is simply 'Ulica Główna" or 'Hauptstrasse' – Main Street in both main languages. Danzig Poles preserve other oddities of speech. When visiting relatives in Kaszubia they say in the idiom of 50 years ago: *Jadę do Polski.* 'I'm going to Poland ...'

Slowly the Danzigers have returned to view their old homes in Gdańsk. They do it with a mixture of morbid curiosity, hideous sentimentality, and genuine interest. Some do it with discretion. A letter to the current occupier of the old home: 'Would you mind if ... I'm in my eighty-fourth year ... a last look ... some photographs for my children ... it would mean so much ... I intend no harm.' Others drive up in their Mercedes, barge into their old home, inspect the property without permission as if they were still the owner, make barely veiled threats to return in strength. In Gdańsk it is not unusual for unwary German tourists to be beaten up; but it is not unusual for German tourists to be offered traditional Polish hospitality – bread and salt, a guest in the house is a god in the house, as the Polish proverb has it.

As the tourists saunter down Ulica Długa, past the souvenir shops with their displays of postcards, carved wood, necklaces of amber, the clock on the Town Hall tower staggers out the melody of Maria Konopnicka's 'Rota', the Oath, a staunch and bristling nationalist anthem. Time has passed by most of Konopnicka's other works, but this particular lyric is different. Ignacy Paderewski, the pianist who was later to become Premier of Poland, introduced this specially composed anthem to the Polish public when on 15 July 1910 he unveiled a statue on Plac Jana Matejki opposite the Barbikan in Kraków, to commemorate the five hundredth anniversary of the Polish victory over the Teutonic Knights at the battle of Grunwald. The statue, which had been paid for by public subscription, was destroyed by the Germans in 1939 but rebuilt and restored by the Poles in 1976.[4]

It is no accident that this song was chosen to mark the passage of every hour in Gdańsk. The lyrics, which almost every Pole knows by heart, are:

We will not surrender our father's lands
Nor bear our tongue suppressed.
Poles our nation, Poles our people,
Established since the Piasts.
The cruel invader frights us not
So help us God, so help us God.
We won't be spat on by the Teutons,
Nor let our children become Germans!
We follow the blast of the Golden Bugle,
Under our leader, the Holy Ghost.
Our armed might shall lead the march,
So help us God, so help us God.[5]

West German tourists, bedecked with Leicas and mostly in their sixties and seventies, some even older – a few in leather shorts, in old student or regional association costumes, others with feathers in their alpine hats – stride, stroll or sit around on Ulica Długa. If they can find Danzig in Gdańsk they will take a picture of it. Several perhaps. Meanwhile Konopnicka's hymn wafts over their heads.

What says the Baltic? Blubb, pfff, pshsh ... In German, Polish: Blubb, pfff, pshsh ...[6]

Notes

Unless otherwise indicated, place of publication is London.

Introduction

1. T. Kur, *Prózna Fatyga Kata w Gdańsku*, Warsaw, 1981. pp. 136–7.
2. J. Kuroń, 'Is there a Threat of Intervention?' *Labour Focus on Eastern Europe*, vol. 4, nos. 4–6, 1981, p. 56. This article first appeared in *Robotnik*, no. 68–9, 1980.

Chapter 1: Early History - Gyddanyzc to Danczik

1. M. Gimbutas, *The Balts*, 1963, p. 64. It is important to emphasise that the early history of the area has been subject to intense nationalist bias and that much of the prehistory of Pomerania must remain conjectural. In contrast to the theories of Gimbutas, the 1988 edition of the *Encyclopaedia Britannica* states categorically that the earliest inhabitants of Pomerania were Celts – see vols 9 and 20. It is also important to emphasise at this point that Polish and German scholars have produced quite different versions of the prehistory of Pomerania – see Chapter 13 for further details.
2. W. Czapliński & T. Ładogórski, eds. *Atlas Historyczny Polski*, Wrocław, 1973.
3. Ibid., p. 30. Gimbutas, 1963, p. 56.
4. N. Davies, *God's Playground*, vol. I, 1981, p. 45.
5. Herodotus, *History*, Book IV, Chapter 18.
6. The identification of common Slav plant and animal names was first carried out by K. Moszyński, J. Rostafiński and J. Rozwadowski: M. Gimbutas, *The Slavs*, New York, 1971, p. 23. See also: C.L. Barber, *The Story of Language*, 1972, pp. 93–4; N. Davies, *God's Playground*, vol. I, 1981, p. 43; R.G.A. De Bray, *Guide to Slavonic Languages*, 1951; W. J. Entwistle & W.A. Morison, *Russian and Slavonic Languages*, mcmxlix.
7. Gimbutas, 1971, p. 99. N. Davies, *God's Playground*, vol. I, p. 46.
8. Gimbutas, 1971, pp. 106-8.
9. A Victor Weluhn is one of the defenders of the Polish Post Office in Günter Grass's novel *The Tin Drum*.
10. In March 1986 thieves broke into Gniezno Cathedral and stole the seventeenth-century silver sarcophagus made to hold Saint Adalbert's remains. The Polish government and the Episcopate co-operated to offer a reward to recover the sarcophagus and identify

the thieves. Their swift response indicates that both regard Adalbert as important to their image of Poland – the Church because he is one of its founding fathers, the state because he is a symbol of Polish unity and influence in the western borderlands. 'Crime in the Cathedral', *Polish Perspectives*, Warsaw, vol.XXIX, no. 3, p. 56.

11. Hagelsberg may be of early Baltic derivation: *Hagel could be a version of the name Jagel, known mainly through the Lithuanian Jagiełło dynasty.

12. Relentlessly the Slav province of Branibor was Germanised to become the province of Brandenburg. The work of absorption may be charted from the foundation dates of the various bishoprics: Halberstadt 827, Havelberg 934–46, Brandenberg 946–8, Oldenberg 946, Kołobrzeg 1000. In 1168 the Danish King Waldemar took the island of Rana by storm. Saxo Grammaticus, *The History of The Danes*, trans., P. Fisher, 1979, section XIV. Rana maintained a Slav Polabian language until the seventeenth century, and metamorphosed into Rügen between 1630 and 1780.

13. Prussian derives from Borrussian, the name of one of the Baltic peoples who lived in the area but who were killed off by the Germanic invaders who took over their name. M. Gimbutas, *The Balts*, 1963, pp. 22 and 176.

14. 'The General Prologue', II. 52–4. *Geoffrey Chaucer: The Complete Works*, ed. F.N. Robinson, 1957.

15. Thomas Walsingham, *Historia Anglicana*, Book II, ed. H.T. Riley, 1863–4, p. 198. K. Górski, 'The Teutonic Order', *Mediaevalia et Humanistica*, no. 17, Colorado, 1966; M. Biskup, 'Rola Zakonu Krzyzackiego w XIII-XVIw', in *Stosunki Polsko-Niemieckie w Historografi*, Poznań, 1974; T. Jones, *Chaucer's Knight: The Portrait of a Medieval Mercenary*, 1980.

16. W. Czapliński & T. Ładogórski, eds, *Atlas Historyczny Polski*, Wrocław, 1973, p. 10.

17. Both paintings are in the Muzeum Narodowy in Gdańsk. P. Abramowski, *Danzig als Kunststadt, Danziger Heimatdienst*, Verlag Dr. F. Osmer, Berlin SW61; nd.

18. S. Arnold & M. Żychowski, *Outline History of Poland*, Warsaw, 1965, p. 39.

Chapter 2: Danczik to Dantzig

1. OED: Horde – from Polish *horda*; earliest recorded use 1555. Sable: from Polish *soból*; earliest recorded use 1432, common after 1508. Spruce: from Polish *z prus*, literally 'from Prussia'; earliest recorded use 1308, common after 1487.

2. N. Davies, *God's Playground*, vol. I, 1981, p. 257. H. Barty-King, *The Baltic Exchange*, 1977, pp. 14–15.

3. James Sanderson, 'A Short Account of the Present Estate of Dantzig: 1675'. Public Records Office SP/88/14.

4. Topolski, p. 79.

5. M. Neumann, *Geschichte des Wuchers in Deutschland*, Berlin, 1865, pp. 618–19.

6.   See also: I. Rhode, *Das Nationalitätverhaltnis in Westpreussen und Posen*, Poznań, 1926, p. 17.

Chapter 3: Prussian Danzig

1.   W.W. Hagen, *Germans, Poles and Jews*, Chicago, 1980, pp. 15 and 17.
2.   Ibid., p. 17. Hagen says the population fell to 55,000; Szermer offers the figure of 36,000. B. Szermer, *Gdańsk: Past and Present*, Warsaw, 1971, p. 63.
3.   J. Topolski, *An Outline History of Poland*, Warsaw, 1986, p. 120; W.W. Hagen, p. 42.
4.   B. Szermer, p. 66.
5.   W.O. Henderson, *The Industrialisation of Europe 1780–1914*, 1969, pp. 44, 74–6.
6.   J. Topolski, p. 163.
7.   F. Engels, 'Po und Rhein', (1859) in *Marx-Engels Werke*, vol. XIII, p. 267.
8.   C. Hadfield, *World Canals*, 1986, p. 157.
9.   A.J.P. Taylor, *Bismarck*, 1965, pp. 7 and 130. Also: W. Jakóbczyk, *Bismarck*, Warsaw, 1971.
10.   W.W. Hagen, pp. 323–6. Also: W. Tuchmann, *Die Nordlichen Deutschen Rheinlande*, Leipzig, 1935, p. 215.
11.   Topolski, p. 185.
12.   Ibid., pp. 182–3; G.R. Gayre, *Teuton and Slav on the Polish Frontier*, 1944, pp. 20–1, 60.
13.   J. Łukaszewski, 'The Government and National Organisation', *Bendlikon*, Posen, 1864: A. Michnik, *Letters from Prison*, California, 1987, p. 227.
14.   H. Arendt, *The Origins of Totalitarianism: Imperialism*, New York, 1968, p. 103. M.S. Wertheimer, *The Pan German League: 1890–1914*, New York, 1924.
15.   *Posener Tageblatt*, 14 January 1914.
16.   J.J. Kulczycki, *School Strikes in Prussian Poland, 1901–1907: The Struggle over Bilingual Education*, Columbia NY, 1981.
17.   W.W. Hagen, p. 177.
18.   *Statistik des Deutschen Reichs*, vol. 451, no. 1, Berlin, 1935.
19.   W.W. Hagen, pp. 177 and 321; R. Donald, p. 152.
20.   W.W. Hagen, pp. 184–5.
21.   R. Donald, p. 276.
22.   N. Davies, *God's Playground*, vol. I, p. 48; Professor E.H. Minns in the 1911 edition of *Encyclopaedia Britannica* estimated their numbers at 200,000. Ralph Manheim in his notes to Günter Grass's *The Tin Drum* estimates that in 1945 they numbered about 150,000. The figure of 110,000 is from R. Donald, *The Polish Corridor*, p. 32. It is difficult to say how many Kaszubes there are now. Certainly they are not thriving under the Polish regime and many feel that they are given only grudging cultural assistance and recognition. The 1988 edition of *Encyclopaedia Britannica* gives their number as 210,000, but this is improbably high; it is likely that today there are no more than 75,000 people speaking

Kaszubian as their normal daily language. The Lebans are in an even worse situation as their language is given no recognition at all and at less than 5,000 speakers, all clustered around the town of Łeba and the Lake Łebsko, the language is unlikely to survive into the next century.

23. R. Donald, *The Polish Corridor*, nd., p. 34.
24. B. Szermer, p. 68. W. Witt, *Atlas Von Pommern*, Berlin, 1934.
25. G.R. Gayre, *Teuton and Slav on the Polish Frontier*, 1944, map no. 40.
26. Donald, p. 23; R. Machray, The *Polish German Problem*, 1941.

Chapter 4: Polenpolitik und Kulturkampf

1. L. Davidowicz, *The War Against The Jews 1933–1945*, 1979, p. 50.
2. F. Engels, *The Peasant War in Germany*, Moscow, 1965, p. 163.
3. A. Gramsci, *Selections From Prison Notebooks*, 1986, p. 83.
4. D. Blackbourn, *Populists and Patricians: Essays in Modern German History*, 1988.
5. P. Mathias, *The First Industrial Nation*, 1969, p. 318.
6. A.L. Morton, *A People's History of England*, 1974, p. 496.
7. C. Harman, *The Lost Revolution*, 1982, pp. 21–2.
8. P. Hayes, *Industry and Ideology: IG Farben in the Nazi Era*, 1988.
9. F.V. Grunfeld, *The Hitler File: A Social History of Germany and the Nazis, 1918–1945*, New York, 1979, pp. 9–10. Paul de Lagarde's major work was *Deutsche Schriften*, 1878. See: F. Stern, *The Politics of Despair*, Berkeley and Los Angeles, 1961. Norman Cohn has traced this impulse in German politics back past De Lagarde. 'He identifies a long and very definite strand of German folk belief: uncannily similar to the phantasies which were the core of National-Socialist "ideology" ... There is the same belief in a primitive German culture in which the divine will was once realised and which throughout history has been the source of all good – which was later undermined by a conspiracy of capitalists, inferior, non-Germanic peoples and the Church of Rome – and which must now be restored by a new aristocracy, of humble birth but truly German in soul, under a God-sent saviour who is at once a political leader and a new Christ. It is all there – and so were the offensives in West and East – the terror wielded both as an instrument of policy and for its own sake – the biggest massacres in history - in fact everything except the final consummation of the world-empire which, in Hitler's words, was to last a thousand years.' Norman Cohn, *The Pursuit of the Millenium*, 1970, p. 125.
10. R. Luxemburg, *The Accumulation of Capital*, Berlin, 1923, pp. 273 and 361.
11. J.R. Fiszman, *Revolution and Tradition in People's Poland*, Princeton, 1972.
12. Hermann Broch, 'Notes on the Problem of Kitsch', a lecture given to the German Faculty at Yale University, winter 1950–1, *S. Lem Microworlds*, 1985, pp. 67–71; M. Kundera, Interview in *Granta*, no. 11, 1984, p. 29.
13. S. Wyspiański, *Wesele* (The Wedding), Kraków, 1901, III 16.

14. R. Luxemburg, *The National Question*, ed. H.B. Davies, New York, 1967.

Chapter 5: Danzig and Versailles

1. A. Hitler, *Mein Kampf*, Boston, 1943, pp. 205–6.
2. R. Donald, *The Polish Corridor*, n.d., p. 23.
3. G.R. Gayre, p. 21; O. Górka, *An Outline History of Poland*, 1942, p. 90.
4. Polish 22.1 million (69%); Russian 80,000 (0.25%); Lithuanian 80,000 (0.25%); Ukrainian 4.8 million (15%); Byelorussian 1.5 million (4.7%); Jewish 2.7 million (8.5%); German 700,000 (2.2%); Czech 30,000 (0.09%). N. Davies, *God's Playground*, vol. II, p. 406; D. Lane & G. Kolankiewicz, *Social Groups in Polish Society*, New York, 1973, p. 3.
5. H.N. Brailsford, *After the Peace*, 1920, p. 82.
6. F.E. Ian Hamilton, *Poland's Western and Northern Territories*, 1975, p. 16.
7. O. Górka, p. 103.
8. J. Topolski, pp. 183–7, 208–21; N. Davies vol. II, Chapter 5 passim; S. Arnold and M. Żychowski, *Outline History of Poland*, Warsaw, 1964, pp. 187–8.
9. R. Donald, p. 80.
10. H.S. Levine, *Hitler's Free City*, Chicago, 1973, p. 37. Ian F.D. Morrow, *The Peace Settlement in the German–Polish Borderlands*, 1936, pp. 499, 507–8.
11. H.S. Levine, p. 37; R. Donald, p. 135.
12. O. Górka, pp. 99–100.
13. E. Kwiatkowski, *Dysproporcje: Rzecz o Polsce Przeszeja i Obecnej*, Kraków, 1933, p. 183. Levine, p. 93. Eugeniusz Kwiatkowski (1888–1974) was Deputy Premier and Minister of Finance and Commerce - that is, the man responsible for the detailed development of Gdynia. Kwiatkowski's book was reprinted and praised by General Jaruzelski in 1983.
14. The 1937 census figures are from the NSDAP's survey of 'their' city, *Statistik des Gaues Danzig der NSDAP*, Danzig, 1937.
15. Ilse Kohl interview, May/June 1982. Ilse Kohl was a teacher at the Viktoria School in Danzig. Her husband was a science teacher who worked at the Conradinum in Langfuhr.
16. A. Drzycimski and S. Górnikiewicz, *Wojna Zaczęa sie na Westerplatte*, Warsaw, 1979.
17. *Projekt Progamu KPP*, Warsaw, 1932, p. 284. Because of the position of the Polish *szlachta* as the leaders of Polish national movements, the potential for action by any socialist party in Poland has always been very limited. The Proletariat Party, for example, said that Kosciuszko's uprising was a conspiracy of magnates to abuse the proletariat by restoring political power to the nobility. Understandably, such an attitude was not popular with the intelligentsia and the new Polish middle classes, who under foreign rule had begun to see their future as Poles in the protection and nourishment of the old *szlachta* cultural values and ideals. See: T.

Deutscher, 'In Memoriam: Proletariat Party, 1882–1886', *New Left Review*, no. 143, Jan–Feb 1984, pp. 109–19.

Chapter 6: The Danzig NSDAP

1. O. Dietrich, *With Hitler on the Road to Power*, 1934, p. 29.
2. J. Pool & S. Pool, *Who Financed Hitler?*, 1980, p. 414. See also: D. Orlow, *The History of the Nazi Party 1919–1933*, Pittsburgh, 1969.
3. H.S. Levine, *Hitler's Free City*, Chicago, 1973, p. 20. H.L. Leonhardt, *Nazi Conquest in Danzig*, Chicago, 1942; C.M. Kimmich, *The Free City: Danzig and German Foreign Policy, 1919–1934*, New Haven, 1968; S. Mikos, *Wolne Miasto Gdańsk a Liga Narodów 1920–1939*, Gdańsk, 1979.
4. H.S. Levine, pp. 20–1 and 35.
5. A. Forster & W. Löbsack, eds, *Das Nationalsocialistische Gewissen in Danzig*, Danzig, 1936, p. 279.
6. H.S. Levine, pp. 70–2.
7. *Danziger Vorposten*, 10 June 1932.
8. Wojewódzkie Archiwum Państwowe w Gdańsku, document, KGRP/592, 'Raport o wpłynięciu ORP 'Wicher' do portu gdańskiego, 15 VI 1932', pp. 2–4.
9. S. Mikos, pp. 273–4.
10. H. Rauschning, *Gespräche mit Hitler*, New York, 1940, p. 168.
11. Rauschning's best known work is *Revolution of Nihilism*, New York, 1937; Zürich, 1938; Warsaw, 1939.
12. W. Jędrzejewicz, pp. 225–31.
13. Ibid., p. 200.
14. Ibid., p. 211.
15. *Documents Concerning German Foreign Policy*, Series C, vol. IV, nos 65–258.
16. Royal Institute of International Affairs, *Agrarian Problems from the Baltic to the Aegean*, 1944, p. 81. A. Zauberman, *Industrial Progress in Poland, Czechoslovakia and East Germany, 1937–62*, 1964, p. 1; N. Davies, *God's Playground*, vol. II, 1981, pp. 393–434; Z. Landau, 'The Influence of Foreign Capital on the Polish Economy, 1918–1939', in *La Pologne au XII Congres des Sciences Historiques a Vienne*, Warsaw, 1965, pp. 133–45; J. Topolski, *An Outline History of Poland*, Warsaw, 1986, pp. 213–21.
17. H.S. Levine, pp. 116–17; Jósef Lipski, *Diplomat in Berlin: The Papers and Memoirs of Jósef Lipski Ambassador of Poland, 1933–1939*, ed. W. Jędrzejewicz, New York, 1968, pp. 257–65; S. Mikos, p. 320.
18. *Documents Concerning German Foreign Policy*, Series D, vol. I, no. 19.
19. W. Jędrzejewicz, p. 267. *Documents Concerning German–Polish Relations*, no. 117. Later, at Nuremberg, Burckhardt was to write in defence of Wiesäker. The file of Burckhardt's correspondence to the League of Nations, at the UN Library in Geneva, is still closed to the public. Burckhardt's reluctance to speak out about German policies of genocide when he was Vice Chairman of the International Committee of the Red Cross, and was particularly well informed about such matters, has since become a matter of

scrutiny and deep embarrassment to the Swiss-based Red Cross organisation: Iain Guest, 'Skeletons in the Red Cross cupboard', *Guardian*, August 27, 1988, p. 7.
20. Ibid., p. 464.
21. *Statistik des Gaues Danzig der NSDAP*, Danzig, 1937, pp. 1–20.
22. A. Forster & W. Löbsack, p. 279.
23. S. Mikos, p. 347.
24. H.S. Levine, p. 38.

Chapter 7: NSDAP and the Danzig Jews

1. See also: S. Schwartz, ed., *Danzig 1939: Treasures of a Destroyed Community*, New York, 1981; E. Lichtenstein, *Die Juden der Freien Stadt Danzig*, Tübingen, 1973; and S. Echt, *Die Geschichte der Juden in Danzig*, Leer and Ostfriesland, 1972.
2. H.S. Levine, *Hitler's Free City*, Chicago, 1970, p. 129.
3. H.S. Levine, p. 104 and p. 122.
4. C. Burckhardt, *Meine Danziger Mission*, Munich 1960, p. 205.
5. H.S. Levine, p. 132.
6. W. Jędrzejewicz, ed., *Diplomat in Berlin*, Columbia, 1968, p. 412.
7. R. Vishniac, *A Vanished World*, 1986, p. 176.
8. W. Pobóg-Malinowski, *Najnowsza Historia Polityczna Polski 1864–1945*, vol. II, London, 1956–61, pp. 614–29. L. Davidowicz, *The War Against the Jews, 1933-1945*, 1977, p. 288.
9. S.L. Bethell, *The Palestinian Triangle*, 1980, p. 92; B. Wasserstein, *Britain and the Jews of Europe 1939–45*, 1979, pp. 60–77.
10. Public Records Office: PMO 4/52/5. PRO: PREM 4/51/2/116.
11. Public Records Office: FO 371:29161. PRO: CO 733/445/76021/31.

Chapter 8: The NSDAP and Danzig: 1939

1. W. Jędrzejewicz, ed., *Diplomat in Berlin: 1933–9: Papers and Memoirs of Józef Lipski, Ambassador of Poland*, New York, 1968, p. 512.
2. T. Kur, *Prózna Fatyga Kata w Gdańsku*, Warsaw, 1981, p. 161.
3. E. Raczyński, *In Allied London*, 1962, p. 10.
4. *Documents Concerning German Foreign Policy*, Series D, vol. 5, no. 90, 1949.
5. *Documents Concerning German–Polish Relations*, Misc. no. 9, doc. 28, 1939.
6. Ibid., no. 29.
7. Ibid., nos. 31–2; H.S. Levine, pp. 70 and 213; S. Mikos, *Wolne Miasto Gdańsk a Liga Narodów 1920-39*, Gdańsk 1979, pp. 340–9. R. Hoess, *Commandant at Auschwitz*, 1974, pp. 270–1. *Pravda*, 2 July 1939.
8. W. Jędrzejewicz, pp. 544–5.
9. W. Shirer, *Berlin Diary*, 1941, pp. 141–3.
10. DGPR, no. 57.
11. W. Jędrzejewicz, p. 571.
12. *Documents Concerning British Foreign Policy*, Series 3, vol. 3, no. 767, 1950.
13. DCGPR, no. 117.
14. Interview with Ilse Kohl, June 1982.

15. Fr. Bogacki and J. Romanowski, *Obrona Poczty Polskiej w Gdańsku*, Warsaw, 1966.
16. The countries that fought Hitler were not exactly free from the things the Nazis stood for. For example, the army of the United States was segregated into units for blacks and whites until after the war and South Africa's contribution to the war was particularly ambiguous (see Doris Lessing, *The Golden Notebook*, 1962, p. 83).

Chapter 9: Germanisation

1. A. Koestler, *The Case of the Midwife Toad*, 1976.
2. Evert, Zeitschrift des Kgl. *Preussen: Statist. Landesamts*, Munich, 1908, p. 155.
3. H.F.K. Günther, *Rassenkunde des deutschen Volkes*, Munich & Berlin, 1938; *Adel und Rasse*, Munich, 1927; *Rassenkunde Europas*, Munich, 1929. Norman Cohn has said that Günther was the 'official theorist of racism in the Third Reich' (*Warrant for Genocide*, 1967, p. 198) but Professor Gayre visited Günther in his Berlin workshops in 1938 without noticing, or at least without commenting on, Günther's Nazism. B. Möller-Hill, in *Murderous Science*, New York, 1988, argues that Günther disliked the use the Nazis made of his work.
4. W. Kruse, *Die Deutschen und ihre Nachbarvölker*, Leipzig, 1929.
5. H.F.K. Günther, *Rassenkunde des deutschen Volkes*, Munich, 1938, pp. 489–90.
6. R. Julien, *Petermann's Geographische Mitteilungen*, Berlin, 1920.
7. M. Gimbutas, *The Slavs*, 1971, p. 142. The OED traces the word 'Viking' and suggests that this derives from the Old Frisian forms: *witsing* and *wising*, from which the Anglo-Saxon forms *wícing* and *wícingas* are derived. The word is probably formed from *wíc* meaning a temporary encampment.
8. R. Dixon, *The Racial History of Man*, New York, 1923, p. 109.
9. In 1942 Gruppenführer Odilio Globocnik, a passionate amateur archaeologist, believed he had discovered an ancient Germanic settlement at Zamość and obtained permission from Himmler to let him restore the place to its true 'Nordic' character. To do this he expelled 110,000 Poles.
10. W. Frischauer, *Himmler: The Evil Genius of the Third Reich*, 1953, pp. 135–6.
11. C. Henry and M. Hillel, *Children of the SS*, 1976, p. 145.
12. Schallmayer (1857-1919) would probably have disagreed with Nazi application of his theories. See: S.F. Weiss, *Race Hygiene and National Efficiency: The Eugenics of Wilhelm Schallmayer*, California, 1988.
13. Pilichowski, *No Time Limit for these Crimes!*, Warsaw, 1980, p. 23.
14. *Testimony of Zygmunt Krajewski*, born 17 April 1933, Poznań, sent to a Germanisation camp at Gmunden in Austria. Henry and Hillel, p. 160.
15. *Zycie Warszawy*, 11 June 1948. In 1988 Jerzy Kaszubowski made *The Road Home*, a film about one of the children kidnapped by the

Nazis under the Lebensborn programme and his eventual return to Poland after the war.

16.   Z. Jaroszewski, 'Compte rendu du XXe Congres des Psychiatres Polonais', *Cahiers Pologne-Allemagne*, nu. 3, Warsaw, 1959, pp. 34–45.
17.   C. Pilichowski, pp. 25–8.
18.   Ibid., pp. 47–8.
19.   Ibid., p. 30.
20.   *Obozy Hitlerowskie na Ziemiach Polskich 1939–45*, Warsaw, 1979, pp. 492–506. T. Szkutnik, *Stutthof*, Gdańsk, 1980.
21.   C. Pilichowski, Appendix X.
22.   Ibid., p. 67. A. Męclewski, *Neugarten 27: z Dziejów Gdańskiego Gestapo*, Warsaw, 1974.
23.   *Trial Records of Albert Forster*, Polish State Archive, Warsaw, Dok. nu.609 z/III, pp. 1–80.
24.   H.S. Levine, *Hitler's Free City*, Chicago, 1973; H.S. Levine 'Local Authority and the SS State: The Conflict over Population Policy in Danzig-West Prussia 1939-45', *Central European History*, vol. II, 1969. D. Orlow, *The History of the Nazi Party, 1919–1933*, Pittsburgh, 1969.
25.   Ibid., p. 136.

Chapter 10: The Last Days of Danzig

1.   J. Costello and T. Hughes, *The Battle of the Atlantic*, 1980. N. Frankland and C. Webster, *The Strategic Air Offensive Against Germany*, 1961.
2.   Interview with Ilse Kohl, 1982.
3.   T. Skutnik, *Stutthof*, Gdańsk, 1980, p. 26.
4.   Balis Sruoga, in T. Skutnik, p. 27.
5.   For maps of the Danzig-Pomeranian campaign see *The Times*, 22 February, 2, 6, 9, 12, 13, 14 March 1945.
6.   J. Thorwald, *Flight in the Winter*, 1953, pp. 120–2.
7.   A.M. De Zayas, *Nemesis at Potsdam*, 1979, pp. 62–4. *Ost-Dokumente* 2, 8–21, Bundesarchiv Koblenz.
8.   J. Thorwald, p. 141.
9.   Ibid., p. 141.
10.   Interview with Ilse Kohl.
11.   The sinking of the *Wilhelm Gustloff* is the world's largest maritime disaster with a greater loss of life than either the *Lusitania* or the *Titanic*.
12.   C. Foley, *Commando Extraordinary*, 1954, p. 155. G. Boldt, *Hitler's Last Days*, 1973, pp. 50–3.
13.   Letter to Ilse Kohl, dated 26 March 1946.
14.   Letter to Ilse Kohl, April 1946.
15.   J. Tolland, *The Last 100 Days*, 1966, pp. 330–4.
16.   F.A. Voigt, 'Orderly and Humane', *Nineteenth Century and After*, DCCCXXV, November 1945, pp. 195–6.
17.   J. Thorwald, p. 149.
18.   F.A. Voigt, p. 196. See also: D. Mackenzie, *Daily Times*, New York, 7 October 1945.

19. Ibid., p. 196.
20. Interview with Ilse Kohl.
21. A. Solzhenitsyn, *Gulag Archipelago*, vol. 1, 1974, p. 21. Solzhenitsyn's impressions upon crossing the border into East Prussia are recorded in *August 1914*, 1974, p. 140.
22. A. Werth, *Russia at War*, 1964, p. 964.
23. C. Ryan, *The Last Battle*, 1980, pp. 366–7.
24. K. Dönitz, *Memoirs*, Cleveland, 1958, p. 179.

Chapter 11: Winning the West

1. A.B. Lane, *I Saw Freedom Betrayed*, 1949.
2. S. Mikołajczyk, *The Rape of Poland: The Pattern of Soviet Domination*, Connecticut, 1948, p. 213.
3. T. Toranska, *Oni: Stalin's Polish Puppets*, 1987, pp. 250–1.
4. J.Y. Potel, *The Summer Before the Frost*, 1982, p. 2.
5. Count H. von Lehndorf, *East Prussian Diary*, 1963, pp. 228–9.
6. J. Andrzejewski, *Ashes and Diamonds* (Warsaw 1948), London, 1980, p. 143.
7. F.E. Ian Hamilton, *Poland's Western and Northern Territories*, 1975, p. 21.
8. F.A. Voigt, 1945, p. 198.
9. F.A. Voigt, 'Orderly and Humane', *Nineteenth Century and After*, DCCCXXV, November 1945, p. 197. C. Miłosz, *Native Realm*, 1988, p. 225.
10. A.M. Voigt, 1946, pp. 99–100. T. Schieder, ed., *Dokumentation der Vertreibung*, Koblenz, 1969. S. Schimitzek, *Truth or Conjecture? German Civilian War Losses in the East*, Poznań Instytut Zachodny, 1966. M.J. Ziomek, *Przemiany Demograficzne w Polsce Ludowej na Obszarze Województwa Gdańskiego*, Gdańsk, 1965.
11. J. Topolski, *An Outline History of Poland*, Warsaw, 1986, pp. 260–76.
12. F.A. Voigt, 1945, p. 197.
13. *The Times*, 16 December 1944, p. 7.
14. F.E. Ian Hamilton, p. 12.
15. A.M. De Zayas, *Nemesis at Potsdam*, 1979, p. 103.
16. 'As I Please', 2 February 1945, in George Orwell, *Collected Essays, Journalism and Letters*, vol. III, 1971, p. 373.
17. A.M. De Zayas, p. 69. F.A. Voigt, 'Eastern Germany', *Nineteenth Century and After*, DCCCXXIX, March 1946, p. 101.
18. *Report of the Joint Relief Commission of the International Red Cross, 1941–6*, Geneva, 1948, pp. 203–4.
19. F.A. Voigt, 1945, p. 200.
20. *The Times*, 10 September 1945.
21. *Time*, 12 November 1945.
22. N. Clarke, *News Chronicle*, 24 August 1945.
23. A.B. Lane, *I Saw Freedom Betrayed*, 1949, pp. 153–4; also, *The Foreign Relations of the United States*, vol. II, Washington, 1945, pp. 1290–1325.
24. W. Gomułka, *Artikuły i Przemówienia*, vol. II, 1946–8, Warsaw, 1962, p. 435.

Chapter 12: Saddling the Cow

1. S. Mikołajczyk, *The Rape of Poland: The Pattern of Soviet Domination*, Connecticut, 1948, pp. 140–1.
2. T. Toranska, *Oni: Stalin's Polish Puppets*, 1987, p. 274.
3. D. Lane and J. Kolankiewicz, *Social Groups in Polish Society*, Columbia, 1973, pp. 7–15. J. Topolski, *An Outline History of Poland*, Warsaw, 1986, pp. 264–5. F.E. Ian Hamilton, *Poland's Western and Northern Territories*, 1975, p. 26 and p.40.
4. A. Szczypiorski, *The Polish Ordeal*, 1982, pp. 41–2.
5. N. Bethell, *Gomułka: His Poland, His Communism*, 1972, p. 93.
6. T. Toranska, *Oni: Stalin's Polish Puppets*, 1987, pp. 268–9.
7. Ibid., p. 299.
8. D.M. Nuti, 'The Polish Crisis: Economic Factors and Constraints', in R. Milliband and J. Saville, eds, Socialist Register 1981; *Fakty i Komentarze: Stan Gospodarki Kraju Po i Kwartale*, nu. 14, April, Warsaw, 1981. N. Davies, *God's Playground*, vol. II, pp. 566–7.
9. *Labour Focus on Eastern Europe*, vol. 4, nos. 4–6, 1981, p. 15. Alina Pieńkowska, *Solidarność*, no. 8, 28 August 1980.
10. A. Kemp-Welch, *The Birth of Solidarity*, 1983, pp. 64–5.
11. Ibid., p. 184.
12. A.M. De Zayas, *Nemisis at Potsdam*, 1979, pp. 180–1. In 1977 British Prime Minister James Callaghan announced a deal in which British shipbuilders would construct 22 cargo ships and two crane barges for Poland. Britain made a net loss on the deal of £72,500,000. In effect British taxpayers subsidised Polish foreign trade. The size of the loss is an indicator of the level of cuts and savings that the Polish yards were forced to make in order to compete internationally. 'Polish ship deal fears', *Guardian*, 27 September 1977; 'Losses on Polish ship deal', *The Times*, 3 December 1981.
    Anna Chmielewska has written:

    The making of the external enemy is a good example of applying a symbol arousing negative emotions to an area that is neutral, or even positively charged. In the newspaper version, the Western world usually admires our accomplishments and acknowledges our international standing, but when it is time for a campaign, it suddenly turns out that the West is full of hostile and inimical forces. Among them pride of place belongs to West Germany. In fact, playing on the anti-German animus is a phenomenon occurring with monotonous regularity. Thus among the currencies not spurned by the supporters of 'hostile forces in Poland', only the Deutschmarks are mentioned, and among the Western papers slandering our society, it is chiefly German titles that are singled out.

    'The Enemy Within', in A. Brumberg, ed., *Poland: Genesis of a Revolution*, New York, 1983, p. 233.
13. T. Garton Ash, *The Polish Revolution*, 1985, p. 318. Anna Tomforde, 'East Bloc Germans prove embarrassment to Bonn', *Guardian*, 15

June 1988; Anna Tomforde, 'East European refugees pose problem for Bonn', *Guardian*, 8 August 1988.

14.   A. Tomforde, 'Neo-Nazis heckle Kohl at Silesian Rally', *Guardian*, 17 June 1985. Also: 'Kohl Denies any Claims on Poland', *Guardian*, 28 February 1985; 'Silesians Change their Tune', *Guardian*, 23 January 1985; C. Husbands, 'The German New Right', *New Society*, 23 January, 1987; S. Winchester, 'Filling the Cracks', *Sunday Times*, 23 January 1983; J. House, 'Trying our History', *Fuse*, Spring, 1985; P. Toynbee, 'Nazi! Nazi!', *Guardian*, 16 June 1986. S. Sullivan, 'Ghosts of the Nazis', *Newsweek*, 20 April 1987.

15.   A. Tomforde, *Guardian*, 17 June 1985.

16.   M. Postone, 'Theses on Fassbinder, Anti-Semitism and Germany: A Frankfurt Autumn, 1985', *Radical America*, Spring 1986, p. 29.

17.   BfV, the West German State Security Service, estimates there are 22,000 neo-Nazis from 70 different organisations calling for a Fourth Reich, plus 22,000 'extreme' right-wingers. Tony Catterall, 'Just a shade to the Right – for now', *New Statesman*, 2 October 1987. The dramatic rise of the nationalist Republican Party of both East and West Germany in the winter of 1989–90 and its impact on the drive to reunify Germany and reclaim lost lands in the east took many European liberals by surprise. The import of the Republicans on Chancellor Kohl and the politics of the right-centre has yet to be seen.

18.   G. Schöpflin, 'Poland and Eastern Europe' in A. Brumberg, ed., *Poland: Genesis of a Revolution*, New York, 1983, pp. 133, 314. On the recent rise of interest in the old Prussian state in both East and West Germany see: R. von Thadden, *Prussia: The History of a Lost State*, 1988.

19.   M. Vale, ed., *Poland: The State of the Republic*, 1981, pp. 271–2.

20.   *Solidarność*, no. 2, 24 August 1980.

21.   Among those who stormed the 'Pomeranian Wall' in January 1945 was a young Lieutenant Wojciech Jaruzelski, in charge of a regimental reconaissance team in the 5th Regiment, 2nd Infantry Division, of Berling's 1st Polish Army. He was commended for his wounds and bravery in actions around the Pomeranian towns of Złotów, Jastrów, Rederitz, and Frydląd Pomorski. He was twice awarded the Cross of Valour, three times the Merited in Battle, and was also decorated with the Virtuti Militari – the highest Polish award for bravery. Between 1957 and 1960 he was the commander of a mechanised division in Szczecin. In 1961 he became a *Sejm* deputy for the Szczecin constituency, and in 1970 took part in the negotiations with the strikers in the Szczecin shipyards. In 1972 he was elected as *Sejm* deputy for Wrocław.

22.   Address to the *Sejm*, 21 July 1984, in *Jaruzelski: Selected Speeches*, ed., Robert Maxwell, 1985, pp. 96–7. The threat of German claims to the Recovered Territories was used throughout Martial Law to stir up fears for the safety of the nation: when *milicja* arrested Józef Pinior – Wrocław Solidarność member and later founder member and vice-premier of the independent PPS (Polish Socialist Party) – TV news claimed that he 'wanted the Germans here, that he

wanted Wrocław to be Breslau'. 'Interview with Maria Pinior', *International Socialism*, no. 41, Winter 1988, p. 53.

Chapter 13: History and the Censor

1. C. von Schuchhardt, *Vorgeschichte von Deutscheland*, Berlin, 1928; *Alteuropa*, Berlin, 1919.
2. H. Reinerth, *Vorgeschichte von deutschen Stämme*, Berlin, 1940.
3. G. Kossina, *Die Herkunft der Germanen. Zur Methode der Siedlungsarchäologie*, Würzburg, 1911; *Die Deutsche Vorgeschicht, eine hervorragend nationale Wissenschaft*, Würzburg, 1912; 'Die indogermanische Frage archaologische beantwortet', *Zeitshrift für Ethnologie*, 1902, Berlin. G. Kossina, *Altgermanische Kulturhohe*, Leipzig, 1927.
4. J. Kostrzewski, *Wielkopolska w czasach Przedhistorycznych*, Poznań, 1914; *Prasłowiansczyzna*, Poznań, 1946; *Dzieje polskich badań prehistorycznych*, Poznań, 1949; *Z dziejów badań archeologycznych w Wielkopolsce*, Wrocław, 1958.
5. E. Majewski, *Starozytni Słowianie w ziemiach dzisiejszej Germanii*, Warsaw, 1899. W. Surowiecki, *Śledzenie Początku Narodów Sławiańskich*, Warsaw, 1924.
6. J. Leftwich Curry, *The Black Book of Polish Censorship*, New York, 1984, p. 362.
7. G. Orwell, 'Notes on Nationalism', *Collected Essays 1943–5*, vol. 3, 1971, p. 421.
8. N. Davies, 'Poland's Dreams of Past Glory', *History Today*, November, 1982, p. 24: K. Sklenář, *Archaeology in Central Europe; The First 500 Years*, New York, 1983.
9. S. Arnold and M. Żychowski, *Outline History of Poland*, Warsaw, 1965, p. 7. M. Siuchiński, *An Illustrated History of Poland*, Warsaw, 1979, p. 6.
10. G. Grass, *The Flounder*, 1978, p. 107.
11. L. Moszyński, *Wstęp do Filologii Słowianski*, Warsaw, 1984; K. Mosyński, *Pierwotny Zasięg Języka Prasłowianskiego*, Warsaw, 1957; H. Łowmiański, *Początki Polski*, Warsaw, 1963. H. Cierlińska, ed., *A Panorama of Polish History*, Warsaw, 1982; J. Topolski, *An Outline History of Poland*, Warsaw, 1986; B. Klimaszewski, ed., *An Outline History of Polish Culture*, Warsaw, 1983.

Chapter 14: Günter Grass and Dissappearing Danzig

1. H.S. Levine, *Hitler's Free City*, Chicago, 1973, p. 125.
2. Günter Grass, *The Tin Drum*, 1974, p. 64.
3. Ibid., p. 301
4. Ibid., p. 302.
5. Günter Grass, *Cat and Mouse*, London, 1963, p. 124.
6. Günter Grass, *From the Diary of a Snail*, London, 1974, p. 137.
7. *The Tin Drum*, p. 416.
8. 'A Letter from Günter Grass', *Polityka*, 8/1/1329, Warsaw, January 1984.

9. Günter Grass, *Blaszany Bębenek,* trans. S. Błaut, Warsaw, 1983. The monograph referred to is Z. Światłowski, *Günter Grass,* Warsaw, 1987.

10. A. Krzemiński, 'Krzyk Gówniarza z bębenem na Brzuch', *Polityka,* Warsaw, 1/1392, 1984.

11. *Blaszany Bębenek,* p. 636. I give the bargain price I paid for a second-hand copy in fair condition in December 1986 at the Kraków Sunday book-market.

12. Sir Robert MacDonald, *The Polish Corridor,* London, nd., p. 23. Also R. Machray, *The Polish German Problem,* 1941, shows 1910 census returns and 1911 schools census in map form. The 1937 figures are from the NSDAP's survey published in *Statistik des Gaues Danzig der NSDAP,* Danzig, December 1937. Readers may feel that a Nazi document is untrustworthy, but H.S. Levine has written that the survey 'was intended to give party officials an accurate picture of the Gau Danzig as of 31 December 1937 and was not for general publication. The information contained in the survey has a greater claim to accuracy than most Nazi published statistical material': H.S. Levine, *Hitler's Free City,* Chicago, 1973, p. 121. See also: C. Burckhardt, *Meine Danziger Mission,* Munich, 1960, pp. 205–6; J.B. Mason, *The Danzig Dilemma,* Stanford, Calif., 1946. p. 103.

13. *Blaszany Bębenek,* 'Od tłumacza', p. 631.

14. *Pharus Plan Danzig,* 1924; *Neuester Situations Plan von Danzig,* 1887; *Danzig Stadtplan,* Reichsbüro Danzig, 1938; *Gelandeplan Freie Stadt Danzig,* 1927–40, sections E9, D9, D10; *Plan Gdańska,* Warsaw, 1975.

15. *The Tin Drum,* pp. 179–80; Günter Grass, *Die Blechtrommel,* Darmstadt, 1974, p. 145.

16. *Danziger Houskalender,* Danziger Verlagsgesellschaft Paul Rosenberg, Hamburg, 1981; letter from the editor 'Meine lieben Danziger Landsleute!', *Blaszany Bębenek,* pp. 182–3.

17. *The Tin Drum,* p. 221.

18. N. Davies, *The Heart of Europe,* 1986, p. 486.

19. *Blaszany Bębenek,* p. 227.

20. Fr. Bogacki and J. Romanowski, *Obrona Poczty Polskiej w Gdańsku,* Warsaw, 1966.

21. Günter Grass, *On Writing and Politics 1967–83,* London, 1985, pp. 28–9. Grass was given the names and addresses of the survivors by an official of the Polish Ministry of the Interior. Augustyn Młyński was one of the survivors. For his account see: B. Zwarra, ed., *Gdańsk 1939,* Gdańsk, 1984, pp. 350–4.

22. *The Tin Drum,* p. 395; *Die Blechtrommel,* p. 327. *Blaszany Bębenek,* p. 417.

23. There are a very large number of variant names and spellings for the city that is currently called Gdańsk: Danczik, Dantzik, Dantzike, Gdanie, Gydanie, Dantzk, Dansk, Dansig, Dantzigk, Dancyg. Before standardised spelling, Danzigers themselves used a wide variety of forms, sometimes two or three within the same document.
    The first record of the city, in the *Life of Saint Adalbert of Prague*

(AD 999), uses the name Gyddanyzc, from which the later Polish forms, Gydanie and Gdanie and their Latinised versions Gydanum, Gdanum and Gedanum, are probably descended. The other Latin version of the name is Dantiscum. One of the earliest forms of the name is Dantzike, given on the oldest town seal, written in Latin and dating from about 1299.

In the years 1573–1653 the Dutch, Germans and British all referred to the city as Dantzigk and Dantzik, though it was quite normal to find Dansk, Dantzk and Dansig among English six-teenth- and seventeenth-century variants. The French used Dantzik until 1815.

The Dutch used Dantzic in the early eighteenth century and the British used this form as late as 1863. Dantzick came into fashion between 1690 and 1725, and from the 1730s to the mid-1780s was used by the British, French and Germans. It could still be found in use in the 1850s. Dantzig (British, German, Dutch) came in around 1610. It remained in German use until about 1783, and was in use in France until about 1919. Danzig was used intermit-tently from about 1625 in Danzig, Berlin and Paris, but only became the standard accepted spelling from around 1810–30.

The word Gyddanyzc is close to the modern Polish form, Gdańsk. It has been suggested that the modern form of the name derives from the earliest name and that – reading the evidence backwards – this indicates early Slav settlement in the city. However, it is possible that the early Slav name for the place was derived from Goth settlers who lived in the area before the arrival of the Slavs, and that the name of the city, in all its various forms, commemorates Germanic settlement at a time before the Slav tribes had arrived in Poland. In the years 600 BC to AD 230 the Goths settled the Baltic coast around Gdańsk, Gdynia, the Vistula delta and the lower Vistula valley.

The *Oxford English Dictionary* gives several plural forms for the word 'Goth': Gota, Gotte, Gotten, Gothi, Gotthi, and the conjec-tural forms *Gutes and *Gutans. This last is remarkably close to 'Gdańsk', 'Gyddanyzc' – the name for the city recorded in the tenth century – and to Gdanie and Gydanie the early Polish vari-ants. The initial consonant cluster of 'Gd' is rather rare in Polish and here represents a contraction of the tenth Century 'Gydd' element, which, combined with 'an' to form *Gyddan, may be one of the many variant plural forms for the word 'Goth'.

The *Wielki Słownik* (1970) lists only about 17 words beginning with a 'Gd' cluster, and the *Atlas Historyczny Polski* (which acknowledges Gothic settlement on Polish territory without problem) lists only three place names beginning with 'Gd' – Gdańsk, Gdynia and Gdów. Gdańsk and Gdynia are well within known areas of Gothic habitation. It is possible that Gdów (lying south east of modern Kraków) was also a Gothic site, perhaps a far flung outpost of the coastal settlement and penetration inland along the great Vistula river that began around 400 BC. Alternatively perhaps, when the Goths migrated out of Poland along the Vistula and Bug rivers to Crimea (150 BC – AD 230), some of the migrating Goths might have traced the Vistula westwards, to settle in the Carpathian foothills. The name Gdów quite clearly has a Polish genitive plural ending, so possibly the meaning of the place name that has come down to us is literally 'of the Goths'.

If the 'Gd' + 'an' is a form of a word for 'Goths' then the medieval Latin name for the city of Gdańsk – Gedanum (third declension genitive plural, literally 'of the *Gedans') – would lead us to suppose that *Gedan was another plural form for the word Goths and suggests very strongly a derivation of the name that acknowledges the Goths in early Gdańsk. The 'sk' ending is common in Slav place names and may represent a Slavonicising of a Germanic place name. In other areas of known Gothic settlement place names have survived which appear to commemorate the fact: Göteborg, Gothem, Gedsted, Gedser, Gotland, Gedesby. It would be most unlikely that Polish places of known Gothic habitation over a 600-year period would not preserve some similar reminder. The same argument about the possible development of the name of Gdańsk also applies to Gdynia, where *Gdyn is probably another plural variant of the word 'Goth'.

In 1939, after his victory over the Poles, Hitler changed the name of Gdynia – German Gdingen – to Gottenhaven in order to emphasise its Gothic – and therefore German – past. To set this action in a specifically Nazi context, just before the German invasion of Soviet Russia Hitler had his troops issued with maps that showed the whole of European Russia as having once 'belonged' to Germany. Gothic tribal settlement was claimed for Germany on behalf of the nation in much the same way that the Poles claimed early peoples on Polish territory as 'Proto-Poles'.

24. Tacitus, *Agricola and the Germania*, London, 1970; Saxo Grammaticus, *History of the Danes*, trans. P. Fisher, London, 1979; W. Shakespeare, *Hamlet*, ed. H. Jenkins, 1981. W. Czapliński and T. Ładogorski, eds, *Atlas Historyczny Polski*, Wrocław, 1973.

25. 'Full, merciless, honest confrontation.' The phrase is from Neal Ascherson, 'The Polish Ghosts' in *Games with Shadows*, 1988, p. 233.

Chapter 15: Passing Time in Gdańsk

1. 'After primal man had discovered that it lay in his own hands literally, to improve his lot on earth by working, it cannot have been a matter of indifference to him whether another man worked with him or against him.' S. Freud, 'Civilisation and its Discontents' (1929–30), *Pelican Freud Library*, vol. 12: *Civilisation, Society and Religion*, 1985, p. 288.

2. Czesław Miłosz, *Native Realm*, 1988, p. 143.

3. W.B. Yeats, 'A Coat', *Selected Poetry*, ed., A.N. Jeffares, 1962, p. 63.

4. J. Adamczewski, *Kraków od A do Z*, Kraków, 1986, p. 133.

5. Maria Konopnicka, *Wybór Poezji*, ed. J. Karłowicza, Chicago, 1945.

6. Günter Grass, 'Kleckerburg', *In the Egg and Other Poems*, 1978, p. 123.

Index